Multi-period credit portfolio selection

by

Christian Schmieder

Tectum Verlag
Marburg 2006

Schmieder, Christian:
Multi-period credit portfolio selection
/ von Christian Schmieder
- Marburg : Tectum Verlag, 2006
Zugl.: Ulm, Univ. Diss. 2005
Umschlagabbildung: www.pixelquelle.de
ISBN 978-3-8288-8984-2

Tectum Verlag
Marburg 2006

Acknowledgements

My gratefulness is principally addressed to Professor Dr. Klaus Hellwig, who has been my PhD supervisor. His theoretical guidance and constant friendly encouragement, patience and freedom to conduct my research have been an excellent support. I am also grateful to Professor Dr. Gunter Löffler for his critical comments that lead to a permanent improvement of this work and my experience. Especially, I would like to thank Professor Dr. Svetlozar Rachev from the University of Karlsruhe for acting as a third referee.

Especially I want to thank Professor Dr. Gholamreza Nakhaeizadeh, who has enabled my dissertation at the DaimlerChrysler Research and Technology Center in Ulm, giving me the opportunity to base my research on a practical background and the opportunity to visit the London School of Economics and to my colleagues of the Finance group and the project team "Accord" at DaimlerChrysler Services in Berlin. The experiences gained within various projects have substantially widened the scope of my knowledge and will be a reliable asset for my future career. The financial support of DaimlerChrysler AG Research and Technology is gratefully acknowledged.

I am grateful and indebted to, Dr. Rafael Schmidt, Timo Tonn, Jürgen Bohrmann, Dr. Stefan Trück, Dr. Miriam Selinka, Andreas Ott, Dr. Steffen Hinss, Professor Dr. Paul Wentges, Dr. Walter Gruber and Mrs. Vera Haseloff for the collaboration and the support offered to me.

Personally, my entire gratefulness belongs to my wife Mariana, to my parents Elle and Rolf, and to my brother Philipp for their selfless support, optimism and love, and for constantly accompanying me.

Bad Vilbel, December 2005 Dr. rer. pol. Christian Schmieder

To
Maja,
Elle & Rolf,
and Philipp

Preface

While single obligor's credit analysis have been performed since the origin of lending and have been pulverized with the initiation of empirical (computer-based) discrimination models in 1968, credit risk portfolio models were emerging tools, used only by innovative manager's in the world's first tier financial institutions still a decade ago. Recently, regulators and risk managers perceive these models with increasing interest. Meanwhile, credit risk portfolio models are on the threshold of common recognition and application all over the banking industry. The last burden of credit risk portfolio models is to be accepted by the regulatory frame, what probably only happens in the "Basel III" Accord.[1]

With the establishment of models to *passively* manage credit portfolio risk in practice during the last ten years, the credit risk modeling focus is more and more directed towards *active* credit portfolio management, tackling Markowitz' ideas of portfolio optimization.[2]

And this for good reason: Deutsche Bank, for example, allocated in 2004 most of its economic capital for credit risk (42 %), while market risk, business and oprational contributed only a portion of 38%, 3% and 17%, resepectively.[3]

As a consequence of the increasing number of bankruptcies of financial institutions in the 1970's and 1980's after the collapse of the Bretton Woods agreement, a regulatory framework has been established in 1988 known as the Basel Accord (Basel I). This regulatory framework did, however, not foresee risk-adjusted capital charges for credit risk. By consequence, there might be a substantial discrepancy between regulatory and economic capital, what lead to the consideration and application of active credit portfolio management

[1] See Hirtle et al. (2001), for example, for a discussion of the usag of credit risk models for regulatory purposes.

[2] See Saunders (1999), p. 3, for example.

[3] See Deutsche Bank (2004), p.238. This result stresses the importance of credit risk for banks as Deutsche Bank tends to focus more and more on market risk activities.

techniques within the last decade to circumvent the regulatory framework.[4] More specifically, innovative credit risk products (derivatives, securitization) were used to eliminate from the banking book particularly those assets with a favorable risk-return structure from the internal economic capital perspective on the one hand, and a relatively high regulatory capital contribution on the other hand, e.g. investment-grade corporate obligors.[5] In the course of the application of active credit management techniques, non-investment grade credits tend to remain in the banking books, as their regulatory capital requirement is lower than from the bank-internal perspective. Such a tendency increases credit risk in banks' credit portfolios, which is certainly not in line with the regulatory incentives underlying the establishing the Basel framework in 1988.

Selling credit risk is, however, related to transaction costs. Moreover, once risk has been bought into the banking books, its selling may be related to considerable costs as the buyer wants to be compensated for his/her risk bearing activity. It is therefore desirable to *initially manage credit portfolios actively.*

A major purpose of this work has been to discuss the following question: Are the existing models for credit risk adequate for the task of measuring and managing risk in typical credit loan portfolios, which mainly consist of non-traded obligations that are usually held to maturity?

The traditional focus on volume that has dominated banking for decades[6] is history. Markowitz-type credit portfolio optimization enables to select risk-return balanced, efficient credit portfolios.

However, credit loan portfolios of financial institutions comprise a substantial number of relatively homogenous exposures and may therefore often already per se be regarded as (relatively) well-diversified. In order to manage well-diversified credit loan portfolios, multi-period models are desirable.

---

4 See Carey (2002), for example.

5 See Carey (2002), for example. This effect is known as *capital arbitrage*.

6 See Manz (1998), for example.

Since Markowitz-type models do, however, offer only single-period solutions. Furthermore, multi-period portfolio selection based on utility theory faces several shortages for practical purposes, an alternative methodology has been searched for.

Within this work, a multi-period portfolio model proposed by Hellwig (1987) has been applied to credit portfolios in order to both account for present value considerations and to circumvent utility theory. Thereby, a promising methodology has been added into the field of sophisticated models for active credit portfolio management.

Table of Contents

List of Figures

List of Tables

List of Abbreviations

ABS	Asset Backed Securities
APT	Arbitrage Pricing Theory
BIS	Bank of International Settlement, Basel
BCBS	Basel Committee on Banking Regulation and Supervision
Bps	Basis points
CAPM	Capital Asset Pricing Model
CF	Cash Flow
CIR	Cost-to-income ratio
CVaR	Conditional Value-at-Risk
DM	Default Model
EAD	Exposure at Default
EC	Economic Capital
ECB	European Central Bank
EDF™	Expected Default Frequency (conform to PD, trademark by KMV)
EL	Expected Loss
EVA™	Economic Value Added
EVT	Extreme Value Theory
Fed	Federal Reserve Bank
FI	Financial Institution
FC	Fixed Costs (Overhead and administrative costs)
GOPS	Growth-oriented portfolio selection
IBOR	Interbank Offered Rate (also LIBOR, EURIBOR)
IRB	Internal Rating Based approach (Basel)
LEE	Loan Equivalent Exposure
LGD	Loss Given Default
LPM	Lower Partial Moments
M	Maturity
MCM	Money and Capital Markets
MDA	Multivariate discriminant analysis
MIM	Market Interest Rate Method
MPT	Modern Portfolio Theory
MTM	Mark-to-Market approach or Marked-to-Market approach
NPV	Net Present Value
OCC	Office of the Comptroller of the Currency
OPT	Option Pricing Theory
PD	Probability of Default
P/L	Profit/Loss- distribution
PMPT	Post-modern Portfolio Theory
PV	Present Value (methodology)
QIS	Quantitative Impact Study of the Basel Committee
RAPM	Risk-adjusted Performance Measurement

RAROC	Risk-adjusted Return on Capital
RCB	Risk Contribution
RC	Risk Capital
RFC	Refinancing costs
ROC/ROE	Return on Capital /Equity
RORAC	Return on Risk-adjusted capital
RR	Recovery Rate
RWA	Risk-Weighted Assets (Determinant for regulatory capital)
SBF	Strategic Business Field
SD	Stochastic Dominance
SME	Small and Medium Enterprises
S&P	Standard & Poor's
SV	Shareholder Value
SVA	Shareholder Value Analysis
SWOT	Strengths, Weaknesses, Opportunities, and Threats analysis
UDA	Univariate discriminant analysis
UL	Unexpected Loss
VaR	Value-at-Risk
VMP	Value Management Problem (*see GOPS*)

1 Introduction and summary

In order to answer the question whether credit risk management is an important issue in the practical environment of banking, we will deal with a striking example, representing the daily business of a credit analyst according to Bluhm et al. (2003, p.15):

"Let us assume a major building company is asking its house bank for a loan in the size of 500 million Euros. Somewhere in the bank's credit department a senior analyst has the difficult job to decide whether the loan will be given to the customer or the credit request will be denied. Let us further assume that the analyst knows that the bank's chief credit officer has known the chief executive officer of the building company for many years, and, to make the things even worse, the credit analyst knows from default studies that the building industry is under hard pressure and that the bank-internal rating of this particular building company is just on the way down to a low subinvestment grade."[7]

Bluhm et al. (2003) provide a conclusive answer. The most convincing action in this situation would be that the analyst should refuse the deal as the financial outlook for the specific building company is pessimistic and, additionally, the expected market situation for the firm's industry sector is negative as well. Alternatively, the analyst could propose to grant the loan under certain constraints, for example, if the loss potentially arising from the engagement is insured by means of a credit derivative, in terms of securitization, or, at a minimum by an adequate risk-adjusted credit pricing.

It lies, however, in the nature of lending that similar situations will happen occasionally and impose difficulties to the credit officer to come to a decision under such complicated conditions as in typical credit loan portfolios the bankruptcy of obligors "belongs to the daily business of banking the same way as credit applicants do" (Bluhm et al. 2003, p.15).

[7] Borrowers are generally divided into the investment grade and the speculative grade, indicating low and high risk for the bank, respectively.

Nevertheless, credit risk analysis and management techniques seek to base decision-making on a (more or less) sophisticated theoretical ground in order to manage credit risk more thoroughly, what will be the subject of this work. The focus is, however, not on single credit entities, but on the management of the overall portfolio and subportolios, respectively.

Currently, credit risk departments within financial institutions are facing crucial challenges. As in every recession period, banks are first confronted with the dilemma to accomplish a twofold mission in both supporting sales on a macroeconomic level and in creating shareholder value.[8] Second, margins are constantly becoming thinner due to a more intense worldwide competition and require taking competitive advantage by making use of existing market inefficiencies.[9] Online lending improves market transparency, as potential borrowers are given improved access to information. As a result, the opportunity of borrowers to evaluate the available range of credit spreads increases, particularly for the retail credit business.[10] Third, the growing acceptance for risk-adjusted pricing[11] in the overall credit market is supported by regulatory tendencies and is supposed to lead to converging prices for traded and non-traded credit risk in the near future. Forth, credit risk portfolio models allow risk managers to visualize the inherent credit risk of a portfolio by means of credit loss (and profit) distributions. Thereby, the marginal contribution of single exposures to credit portfolio risk and return can be determined and active portfolio management is enabled.

---

[8] See Manz (1998), Gabler (1988) and Mueller (1995), for example. From the perspective of a captive leasing and financing company, for example, the situation is similar even within the company itself: supporting sales enables growth of turnover, but causes credit risk on the other hand and may be negative from the overall perspective in the end.

[9] Conditions for efficient markets have been provided by Kendall (1953) or Grossman and Stiglitz (1980), for example.

[10] Further information about crucial changes for banks can be found in Caouette et al. (1998) or Saunders (1999), for example.

[11] To grant credit according to the underlying credit risk.

Given these revolutionary changes and challenges for credit risk measurement and credit portfolio management, active credit portfolio management gains an increasing importance.

In this manner, the whole attitude towards credit risk has completely changed as noted by Caouette et al. (1998, Preface). Traditionally, credit risk was viewed as "a cost of doing business" and thus "a hazard to defend against". Nowadays, credit risk is seen "as something of value that can be packaged and traded".

Taking an active role in the whole lending carry-out process (application – decision – outpayment – repayment) has become a prerequisite for successful FIs. Caouette et al.'s (1998, Preface) description of this situation is striking: "When a loan was made in the past, the associated credit risk remained on the lender's balance sheet until the debt was repaid or written-off." Meanwhile, the loan (and/or risk) have become "just as likely to be resold and/or reconfigured for the incorporation into a structured financing", what is, however, related to transaction costs. Consequently, a major portion of credit loans are (still) supposed to be held to maturity.

The focus on capital in terms of shareholder value plays an increasing role both as a consequence of company-wide controlling concepts known as *risk-adjusted performance measurement* and given the regulatory framework to finance credit partly with a bank's own capital. To fulfill shareholder's demands, an active credit portfolio management technique is a prerequisite to handle credit portfolio risks actively.

A potential answer to solve the portfolio problem imposed by bringing together adequate techniques to manage credit risk (credit pricing, capital management and portfolio theory) within a **multi-period credit portfolio management framework** will be given in this work.

Section 2 to 4 set out a general overview on credit risk measurement and management presenting especially the eligible credit risk portfolio measurement and management techniques, starting from the classical approaches that have been applied to the domain of credit risk.

In section 5, a framework for the application of a multi-period model for credit portfolio selection that has been designed for well-diversified credit loan portfolios is presented. Finally, the model is evaluated and further areas of research are suggested followed by a conclusion in section 6.

2 Strategic aspects of credit risk modeling and management

The words of one of the most famous scientists born in Ulm will guide us through this work.

"The grand aim of all sciences is to cover the greatest number of empirical facts by logical deduction from the smallest number of hypotheses or axioms." Albert Einstein[12]

2.1 Introduction: The purpose of this work

While the field of portfolio management has been blessed with numerous scientific methods and attempts, only a small portion qualifies for the management of credit loan portfolios. as the majority of the methodologies for credit portfolios have been designed for single periods and thereby neglect time-related aspects of portfolio management.

The aim of this work is to fill this methodological gap by providing a framework for multi-period credit portfolio management, enabling an investor to base his/her portfolio decision on (net) present value considerations for arbitrary PV growth targets. Rather than modeling the forecasted output of a credit decision based on exposure-related cash flows, the ex ante expected cash flows are standardized with the (regulatory or economic) capital that is necessary to perform lending activities. Thereby, the performance of a credit portfolio is directly comparable with other business lines of a financial institution and portfolio management may be termed capital management.

2.1.1 The general problem to be solved

The overall framework for credit portfolio decisions within banks is summarized in Figure 2-1 according to Blache and Bluhm (2001). The credit portfolio strategy to be chosen has to be embedded into the overlapping interests of shareholders and regulators (Basel) besides external factors like the

[12] This quotation has been taken from Caouette et al. (1998), p.102.

technological revolution within banks (E-Commerce) and the increasing worldwide competition (Globalization).

Clearly, the banking strategy and - more specifically - the credit strategy has to be determined by means of state-of-the-art methods and products if a bank intends to be a successful worldwide player. The building blocks for credit portfolio management to support decision making in banks will be presented and extended step by step in section 4f.

Figure 2-1: The overall decision frame of a bank (Blache and Bluhm 2001, p. 297)

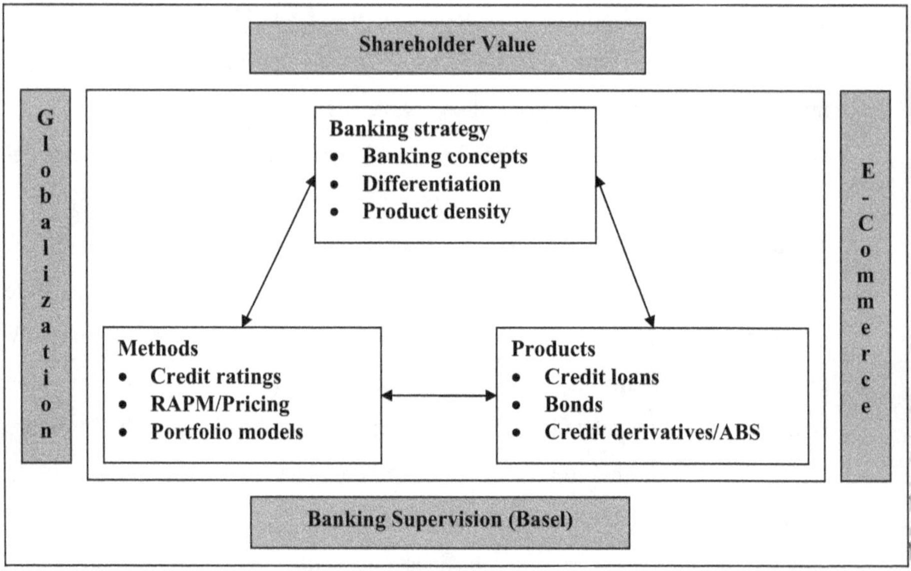

2.1.2 The specific objective to be solved

In the non-traded domain of credit portfolio management of a universal or automotive bank (particularly retail and SME), portfolios might be regarded as relatively homogeneous with respect to the pairwise (default) correlations between the credit exposures as well as the amount financed and the maturity of each exposure. Additionally, it can be assumed that these portfolios comprise a substantial number of credit entities[13] and may therefore be regarded as well-

[13] For example 100,000 or more.

diversified. Credit loan portfolios are usually divided into homogeneous risk segments (rating classes), which might be regarded as investment alternatives, as pricing usually depends on the creditworthiness of a borrower.

Accordingly, the portfolio problem may be faced from a two-fold perspective:

- From a *managerial viewpoint,* the target is to maximize the (net) present value of the returns generated by the portfolio. It will be enabled to set arbitrary growth targets for the desired development of the portfolio's present value and to decide about withdrawals accordingly. Annual withdrawals in form of dividends are demanded by a corporation's shareholders, for example. Based on the specific growth targets set by an investor, it can be decided which portion of the portfolio's growth is reinvested in the portfolio or withdrawn.
- Given a corporation with a variety of interest groups setting common intertemporal growth targets is substantially easier than finding an appropriate utility function that reflects the preferences of all interest groups (*technical viewpoint*). This is the technical advantage of the framework provided.

While passive credit risk portfolio models focus on credit risk measurement both on the single and the portfolio level, active methods provide solutions for credit decisions on a single borrower's level and on the subportfolio and portfolio level.

Common portfolio models are usually directed at risk-return optimization for single periods. Given well-diversified illiquid credit loan portfolios with a pre defined risk-return structure, the aim within a multi-period horizon may alternatively be to manage the withdrawal sequence[14] in terms of present value maximization conditional on portfolio growth targets. A potential solution to this purpose is called growth-oriented credit portfolio management (Growth-oriented portfolio selection, GOPS). The intention of this work is to provide a

[14] Comprising withdrawals over time and the final portfolio value as potential withdrawals.

concept for the practical application of growth-oriented portfolio selection within the domain of credit.

2.1.3 Overview on the work

Portfolio management as a strategic decision support tool has to be embedded into the process of strategic planning within a financial institution. Only then it can fulfill its foreseen role imposed by a financial institution's management. We will therefore present aspects of strategic planning first (section 2) before skipping to credit risk measurement and management (section 3 and 4).

In order to solve the specific objective as defined above a framework for credit portfolio management and selection will be built vertically like a house (see Figure 2-2). Initially, the major credit risk parameters on a single credit exposure's level are defined and best-practice methods for their estimation are presented (section 3.3) followed by a brief presentation of management techniques for single credit exposures (section 3.4). Subsequently, portfolio effects, technical concepts for credit risk portfolio modeling and the corresponding best practice models are discussed (section 3.5). Active credit portfolio management techniques, especially capital management, credit risk pricing and controlling and economic capital allocation are addressed in section 4.1 and 4.2. An overview on credit portfolio optimization techniques will be given in section 4.3f. In section 5, a model for multi-period credit portfolio selection is presented and a framework for its use in practice is designed.

Figure 2-2: Development of a framework for credit risk measurement and optimization: House concept

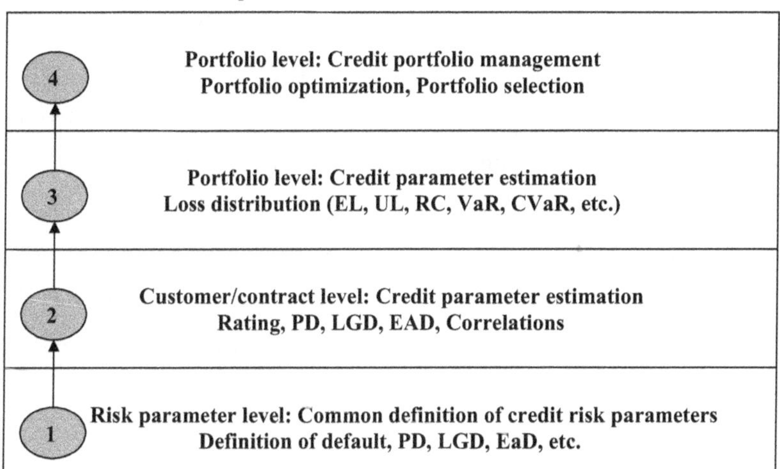

From the illustrative graphic above it becomes clear that a decision based on several (dependent) layers can only be regarded as reliable if all of the layers are stable, similar to the fundament of a house.[15] A sound and solid credit risk measurement and modeling framework tailored according to the internal needs of FIs has therefore to be in place (up to level 3 in Figure 2-2) and is a fundamental prerequisite for the application of credit portfolio management as intended within this work.[16]

In the following, past and present trends in the banking field will be presented followed by strategic aspects of bank management (risk controlling and performance measurement) and major aspects of risk management. In order to fully understand the decision framework for portfolio management, the situation of a credit portfolio manager is gradually approached.

[15] Hence, the thresholds for the applicability of each framework developed in section 5 have to be thoroughly chosen.

[16] A critical assessment of the designed framework can be found in section 5.4.4f.

2.2 Banking: History and current trends

2.2.1 Historical traces of banking and banking regulation: Four phases

In this section, we will review the history of banking and banking regulation following a summary by Matten (2000). **Generally, three phases in regulation of the banking industry can be distinguished** which resulted in pressure on capital. In the **first stage** until the late 1970s, "banks were in general **highly regulated and highly protected** entities" (Matten, p. 11). The rigorous regulation of banks after the 1930s has been a consequence of the worldwide depression and the political impact of the economic crises (hyperinflation) in Europe. While banks have been strictly regulated on the one hand, they have - in turn - been protected from competition.

This protection has been supported by the system of Bretton Woods[17], established in 1944, which ensured interest rate stability (through stable exchange rate) and led - in conjunction with a severe control of banking licences - to "government-dictated interest rates on consumer deposits" (Matten 2000, p.12).

In the 1970s, the Bretton Woods agreements[18] broke down and resulted in a remarkable increase of the volatility of exchange rates and interest rates. With the rising uncertainty, the exchange-control regulation became sequentially less stringent. Hence, only interest rates remained for central banks as a monetary policy tool. Matten (2000, p.12) concludes that the "only solution" to banks' "increasingly volatile environment", accompanied by a "very inelastic pricing control over their assets and liabilities, which were still subject to both government regulation and protective cartel arrangements" was a **deregulated banking supervision**, referred to as **stage two**. With the end of the '*3-6-3*

[17] The International Monetary Fund (IMF) was founded in December 1945 during a United Nations Monetary and Financial conference held at Bretton Woods, New Hampshire, in 1944. In addition to the IMF, the World Bank was subsequently created as part of the Bretton Woods institutions.

[18] Particularly the principle of *'snake in the tunnel'* for currencies.

banking'[19], "the cold wind of competition arose" (Matten 2000, p.12). This progress was inspired by the aims of policymakers "to break up what was seen as a cozy cartel" (Matten 2000, p.4). At the same time, a technological revolution started and lead to a globalization of at least commercial banking, which has been a closed market in former times. An intensifying competition drove banks to set market share as their primary objective, and the consequence was that "an industry unaccustomed to competitive pressures became suddenly prone to excess", resulting to over-lending to Latin American governments, over-paying for stock broking firms in London, etc. (Matten 2000, p.12).

In the following period, the capital hold by banks decreased permanently, and caused large banking collapses, especially in Japan. A consequent step of international policy was to establish an inofficial international banking supervision, the *Basel Committee on Banking Regulation and Supervisory (BCBS)*.[20] With this **third stage** in banking regulation more rigorous, worldwide consistent standards have been established to guarantee both the security of the system and a "fair level-playing field" (Matten 2000, p. 5) although also this stage has suffered from up- and downturns. The reaction of banking supervision to downturns has been an assessment of the reasons, followed by an adjustment (i.e. more stringent rules) of the regulatory framework to stay away from re-occurrence as described below.

Matten (2000, p.5) claims that it would be possible that the **forth phase** has started now, "in which the cycle of crises/examination/regulation is slowly becoming to be seen as fruitless - each time a new refinement to the rules is added, banks find increasingly clever ways around them, and if there is one phrase which strikes a chill in the heart of banking regulators it is *regulatory arbitrage*"[21]. **In each of the past three phases, the aim of banking regulation has been to protect the banking systems from insolvencies.** A comparison of

---

[19] Borrow at 3%, lend at 6% and be on the golf course by 3 p.m; Some authors refer to *"3-8-5 banking"*, e.g. Caouette et al. (1998, p.35) and Matten (2000, p.2).

[20] Originally, the committee was called *Cooke committee* after its chairman.

[21] See section 2.3.2

the distinct stages shows, that new capital requirements have just replaced the former regulatory measures of regulated deposit rates, cartel agreements etc. In the following, we will give a brief overview on the current competitive environment of banks.

2.2.2 From traditional banking to modern value management[22]

While in the 1970s volume and market share thinking had been the favored lending strategy of banks, the premise of a consequent concentration on return (return-oriented bank management) and simultaneously not neglecting risk and growth (market share) substituted this strategy in the 1980s (see Schierenbeck 1983, for example). In the 1990s, however, an additional strategic technique emerged: **Value based management**. An overview of the trend in banking management is given below.

Value based management does imply a consequent orientation on the concept of *Shareholder Value*[23] and is a consequence of the **increasing competition on capital** within the capital markets. A major step towards a value-based risk-return management of a FI is to explicitly take into account and quantify capital[24] costs in terms of demanded returns of shareholders, i.e. the long-term sustainable growth of the firm value.[25]

The development of the state-of-the-art management techniques in banks is shown below.

[22] A comprehensive illustration of the FI' developments from the 1960s on can be found in Paul (2001), p.7f.

[23] The SVA concept has been established by Rappaport (1986).

[24] Equity will consecutively be termed as capital.

[25] The shareholder value concept will be presented in section 2.4.4.

Figure 2-3: Trends in banking: From 3-6-3 banking to value based management (KPMG 2001, p.6)

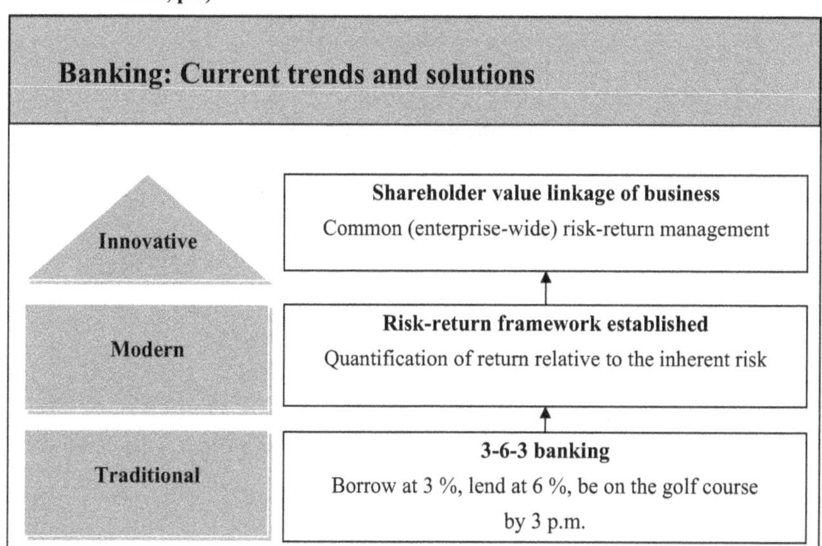

2.2.2.1 Development of credit spreads

The credit spreads in German banks are constantly decreasing (see Paul et al. 2004), the most impressively within German private banks, which were faced to spreads of roughly 1% in 2002 (a decrease of 50% since 1994), while the savings banks ("Sparkassen") and the cooperative banks ("Kreditgenossenschaften") still do have significantly higher cread spreads of 2.5% (equaling a decrease of 28% and 20% since 1994).

Similar developments can be perceived in Switzerland, where the margins are on a similar level as for the German private banks, while in the US the spreads are according to the German cooperative banks or even slightly better (see Manz 1998).

Figure 2-4: Decrease of credit spreads in German banks 1994-2002 by banking tiers (according to Paul et al. 2004, p.8)

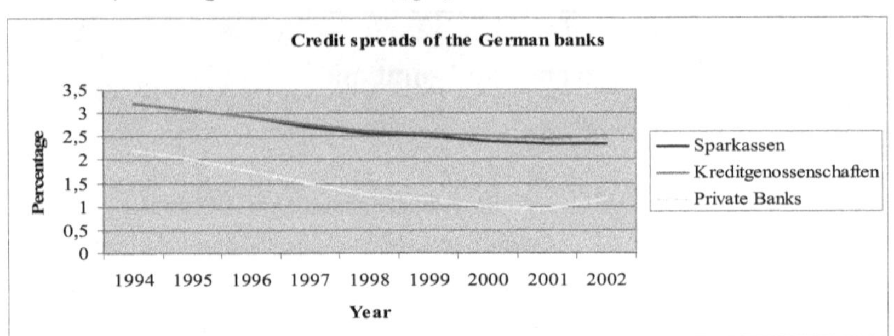

2.2.2.2 Development of borrower insolvencies[26]

Within the last decade, the number of insolvencies in Germany increased substantially. In 2002, the total number of insolvencies jumped from 49,510 to 82,400 (see Appendix). The development of the number of business insolvencies in Germany over the last 25 years is shown in Figure 2-5 below. The number of business insolvencies increased continuously within the last ten years and their number doubled since 1995. However, similar developments can be perceived in other countries as well. For example, both Japan and the USA were faced to business insolvency records in 2002. The business insolvency rate in Japan increased almost five percent in one year, resulting to 19,750 defaulted companies in 2002. The total number of insolvencies (both private and commercial) in the USA was more than 1.5 million in 2002. However, this remarkable number is driven mainly by private insolvencies, as “only” 38,537 business insolvencies occurred (which is comparable to the German figure). An overview of the development of the insolvencies in the European Union can be found in the Appendix.[27]

---

[26] See www.creditreform.de/eng/services/economic_research/Insolvencies_in_Europe_2002_2003/07.php. Rev. March 2005.

[27] See https://www.uc.se/ucswe/d_aktuellt/030303_konkursstatistik_europa.pdf, for example. Rev. June 2004.

Figure 2-5: Development of the number of insolvencies in Germany[28]

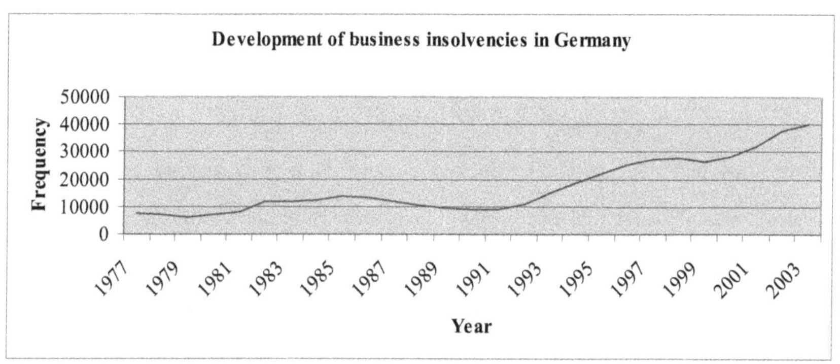

Based on the description of the historical and current trends in banks and the situation of banks from a competitive viewpoint, strategic aspects of bank management will be addressed subsequently.

2.3 Banking regulation and Basel II[29]

As a result of the consultative process among the *Group of Ten countries* (G10)[30] the BCBS[31] circulated a final version of a document entitled the '*International Convergence of Capital Measurement and Capital Standards'* (**Basel I**) in July 1988.[32]

---

[28] See www.wfg-rhein-erft.de/download/rating_19_11_2003.pdf (Rev. June 2004) and Bröker (2000), p.6.

[29] Basel II is an abbreviation for "Basel Accord II", a regulatory standard focused on internal banks in order to guarantee a stable banking system worldwide as a core basis for a stable economic development, which will become valid in 2006. For further information see www.bis.org.

[30] The Basel Committee on Banking Regulation and Supervision comprises representatives of the central banks and supervisory authorities of the Group of Ten countries (Belgium, Canada, France, Germany, Italy, Japan, Netherlands, Sweden, the UK and the US) as well as Switzerland and Luxembourg.

[31] The Bank for International Settlement, located in Basel, Switzerland, was founded in 1930 and is a global round-table for banking supervisors and central banks of the major industrialized nations to discuss and coordinate risk policies. The Basel Committee (originally known as Cooke Committee after its chairman) is, however, not a part of the BIS organisation. As the committee meets every quarter year in the Bank for Internal Settlement (BIS) in Basel, Switzerland, it is called the "*Basel Committee*".

[32] The capital framework was subsequently approved by the G10 central bank governors. Although the agreements submitted in the capital accord are not legally binding, member countries of the G10 are honorably bound to implement the framework in their respective

The 1988 agreement may be understood as the first international minimum capital guidelines that are linked to bank's capital requirements, even though only to the credit exposures in their portfolios.[33] Until now, the Basel Capital Accord (Basel I) remained the global benchmark for solvency requirements among the world's largest banks. Meanwhile, the prospective *New Capital Accord* (Basel II, see Basel 2004) has been published and is supposed to introduce the Basel II regulatory framework from 2007 on. We will indicate what regulatory capital means, and give a crude overview of the evolving process of regulatory capital definitions.

2.3.1 Concept and targets of the Basel I framework

The capital adequacy framework of 1988, Basel I (Basel I Accord) has two fundamental objectives (Basel 1988):

1. The framework required to "strengthen the soundness and stability of the international banking system" by defining common minimum capital adequacy requirements for globally operating banks.[34]
2. "The framework should be fair and have a high degree of consistency in its application to banks in different countries with a view to diminishing an existing source of competitive inequality among international banks."

2.3.1.1 The 8%-rule

The best known rule of the Basel I accord is the *'8-percent-rule'*.[35] According to this rule, banks have to confirm that their overall capital level exceeds 8% of their so-called *risk-weighted assets (RWA)*, which are determined for all balance

---

supervisory functions and to turn it into national law by December 1992. Prior to the full implementation of the Basel Accord in 1992, capital regulations consisted primarily of minimum capital standards uniformly applied to banks, regardless of their risk profiles and ignoring off-balance-sheet activities.

33 And has subsequently been transformed into national law, e.g. KonTraG (Kontrolle und Transparenz im Unternehmensbereich) and MaK (Mindestanforderungen an das Kreditgeschäft) in Germany.

34 …"that are commensurate with the amount of credit risk each bank takes into the portfolio" (Ong 1999, p.2).

35 See Bluhm et al. (2003), for example.

sheet positions.[36] The RWA were computed by a straightforward weighting method as shown below.[37]

The assignment of risk weights is summarized below.

Risk weight (%)[38]	Type of counterparty
0	Government exposures to OECD countries
20	OECD banks and non-OECD governments
50	Mortgages
100	Other banks, corporate and private loans, other remaining exposures

The 8%-rule is considered as a minimum requirement, i.e. banks may naturally hold more capital.

2.3.2 Response to criticism of Basel I: Basel II

Apart from the criticism that has been addressed to Basel I[39] banks have tried to compute their market[40], credit and operational risk according to their internal viewpoint (Ong 1999). In terms of credit risk, for example, the sum of the required **regulatory capital** is internally allocated to the different credit

---

36 The total RWAs of a bank were subsequently calculated as the sum of all of the bank's exposures' RWAs, resulting in a regulatory capital of 8% of the the RWAs.

37 See Ong (1999), p.36, for example.

38 For loans to any other government institution the risk weight was set to 0%, reflecting the opinion that the governments of the world's industry nations are unlikely to fail their financial obligations. The risk weight for lending to OECD banks was fixed at 20%. In terms of corporate loans, the committee agreed to a risk weight of 100%, independent of the riskiness of a borrowing firm.

39 Three fundamental criticisms were held against the 1988 Basel Accord from the viewpoint of their impact on the largest and most complex international banks (Ong 1999, p.19):

1. First, as the capital requirements are not related to the default probabilities, they are more or less arbitrary.
2. Second, apart from the 1996 amendment of the Accord to include capital requirements for market risk, there is no additional capital requirement other risk types.
3. Third, the current Accord does not account not foresee capital adjustments for diversification (e.g. by means of hedging or other advanced risk management techniques) in credit portfolios except the recognition of internal market risk models.

Further limitations can be found in Ong (1999), p. 49f.; On the other hand, the Basel Accord had delivered advances (see Ong 1999). First, the current intense debate on capital adequacy has forced the convergence of two words: risk and capital. Second, the 1988 Basel Accord has reversed the decades-long decline in bank capital cushions.

40 Beginning with the 1996 amendment (and its full implementation in 1998) to incorporate market risk into the regulatory frame, banks have been allowed to develop and use their own internal value-at-risk models for risk management purposes and, more importantly, for market risk capital adequacy purposes.

business lines (and single exposures) according to the bank's own estimate of the required risk capital, the so-called **economic capital**.[41]

The main weakness of the Basel I capital accord was that it makes no distinction between obligors of different creditworthiness.[42] This may cause *capital arbitrage*.

Capital arbitrage has been identified according to three major types (Matten 2000, p.125f.):

- Cherry picking,
- Re-engineering on-balance sheet exposures into off-balance sheet exposures (securitization[43] and credit derivatives[44]),
- Switching between trading and banking book (credit derivatives).

2.3.2.1 The Basel II Accord

The new Basel Capital Accord (Basel II) has been published on June 26, 2004 (see Basel 2004). The core innovation proposed by Basel II is a progress from "rule-based to process-oriented regulatory practices and methods".[45] The consequence for regulatory practices is a shift of stress from the currently strict

---

41 See Ong (1999), for example, and section 3.5.1.5.6.3.1 for a broader disctinction.

42 Other weaknesses according to Ong (1999, p.49ff.) were static measures of default risk, no recognition of term structures of credit risk, simplified calculation of potential future counterparty risk, constraints on an integrated view on credit risk, lack of recognition of portfolio diversification effects.

43 *Securitization of assets* stands for illiquid 'hold-to-maturity' assets (as loans, receivables and other illiquid assets with similar characteristics) sold from the balance sheet as portfolios via secondary markets (Ong 1999). Thus, "securitisation transforms non-traded bank assets into marketable securities" (Ong (1999, p.23). This process can be considered as "*arbitrage between regulatory and economic capital* in its purest form", because "the risk-based capital adequacy guidelines required of financial institutions generally place a higher risk weight on loans than on securities" Ong (1999, p. 23).

44 *Credit Derivatives* principally "separate and isolate credit risk, thereby facilitating the trading of credit risk with the purpose of replicating credit risk, transferring credit risk and hedging credit risk" (Ong 1999, p. 27 according to Das 1998). In so far, "taking on or off-loading credit risk with pre-defined risk and reward parameters adds value to a portfolio without the acquisition of the credit-risky asset itself" (Ong 1999, p.27). The key to the usage of credit derivatives lies in the '*credit paradoxon*'. Wong and Song (1997) illustrated, using a simple example, that two banks using a credit derivative (e.g. a credit swap) end up in a "win-win" situation, with decreased regulatory capital requirements for one of the banks and higher RoC's for both of them.

45 Derviz et al. (2001), p. 9 according to Karacadag and Taylor (2000).

rules towards a more distinguished and flexible framework.[46] Accordingly, corporate or retail obligors which receive a risk weight of 100% under the Basel I approach may be assigned a considerably lower or higher risk weight depending on their specific credit risk as shown in Figure 2-6.

Figure 2-6: Regulatory Capital according to Basel I and Basel II (according to Basel 2002[47])

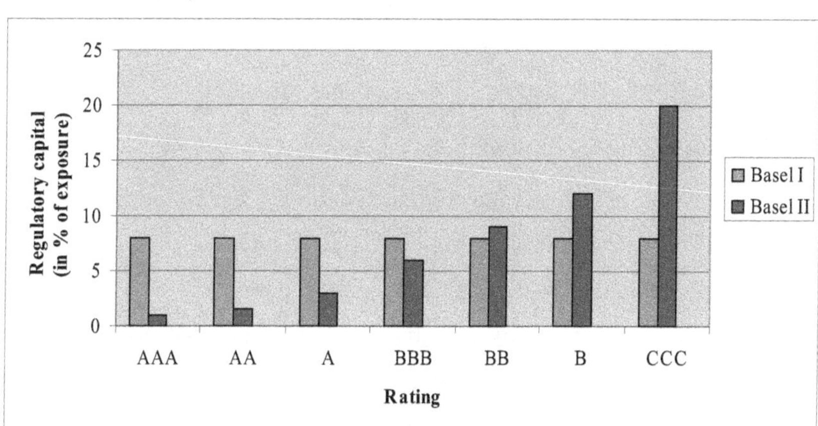

Within this work, we will refer to the Quantitative Impact Study 3 (*QIS 3*, Basel 2002) as the actual depiction of Basel II in quantitative terms. In January 2004, the QIS 4 has been initialized and their results have been published by mid 2005. The major difference to QIS 3 is that regulatory capital will not comprise cushion against expected losses, which are supposed to be covered instead by adequate pricing and provisioning, respectively (see section 4.2.1).

The Basel II framework for credit risk is based on three so-called pillars (Carling et al. 2002, p.3):

- The **first pillar** describes the quantitative rules for the computation of a bank's required regulatory capital, intended as a buffer against credit losses.

[46] See Derviz et al. (2001), for example.

[47] At the stage of QIS 3, the Basel capital framework still included capital charges for expected losses, which are meanwhile subtracted from the required capital portion required according to the framework (see Basel 2004).

- The **second pillar** is directed towards the supervisory review process of banks' internal procedures and processes. It is thereby assessed whether the bank-internal framework is conservative enough to capture the potential credit risk.
- The purpose of the **third pillar** is to raise the transparency of banks' risk profiles for the public through disclosure requirements in order to ensure market discipline.

The three pillar system is graphically shown in the Appendix.

2.3.2.2 Basel II: Eligible approaches for credit risk

As opposed to the 1988 Basel Accord, the new Basel Capital Accord explicitly distinguishes between *market*[48], *operational*[49] and *credit risk.*

For credit risk, the new Basel Capital Accord proposes two main exclusive[50] methodologies to be chosen by each bank to determine regulatory capital: a **standardized approach** and two approaches based on banks' **internal rating systems** (IRB). In case of the *standardized approach* the risk weight of each exposure is derived according to standard credit rating systems of external rating agencies. Under the *internal ratings based approach* (IRB), the capital requirement for each exposure is determined based on the output of each bank's internal rating systems. The rating system of each bank has to be in line with certain regulatory rules.[51] Banks are thereby allowed to develope their own rating methodologies subject to supervisory approval and control as shown below.

[48] Regulatory capital for market risks covers unexpected changes in the portfolio's value due to underlying changes in the market conditions (changes in interest rates, exchange rates, etc.).

[49] Operational risk originates in unexpected adverse effects due to flaws in the internal operation of the bank.

[50] For a limited period, a parallel running is allowed.

[51] Further information can be found in Basel (2004).

The main elements that enter the calculation of the risk weights will extensively be explained in section 3.3.[52]

As shown below, the IRB approach differentiates furthermore between:

- **The foundation approach**[53] and
- **The advanced approach**[54].

Figure 2-7: Basel II: Different approaches eligible for the future (according to Hartmann 2002, p.28)

Basel II: Future approaches for credit risk

➢ **Standardised approach**	Standard method based on external ratings (e.g. Moody's, S&P, Fitch IBCA)
➢ **IRB Foundation approach**	Basic version with internal ratings (3 Y. history) Bank-internal determination of ratings and PDs, external inputs for LGD and EaD. Initially „Cap" of max. 5% (later 10-20 %) reduction of equity compared to Standardised approach.
➢ **IRB Advanced approach**	Advanced approach based on internal ratings (7 Y. history) All relevant variables for the determination of the risk are estimated independently by the bank Initially „Cap" of max. 10 (later 20 %) reduction of equity compared to Standardised approach.

IRB: Internal Rating Based

Under the IRB approaches, each exposure has to be assigned to one of the following categories: corporate, retail, sovereign, inter-bank, project finance and equity (see Basel 2004). Dependent on the exposure's category, the input data (i.e. the PD, the LGD and the EAD) to determine the risk weights are estimated according to the regulatory guidelines, dependent on the IRB approach.

[52] The Probability of Default (PD), Exposure at Default (EAD), Loss Given Default (LGD), Maturity and Granularity. Granularity aspects will be subject to Pillar II as opposed to the original draft of Basel II.

[53] In case of the foundation approach, the banks may only calculate the PD based on their internal rating system, while the other estimates are predefined by the Basel II framework (Basel 2004).

[54] In case of choosing the advanced approach, banks are allowed to estimate all credit risk parameters bank-internally, which are subsequently used as inputs for the Basel II formula. However, the advanced IRB banks have to fulfill more stringent regulatory rules with respect to their internal rating systems.

2.3.2.3 Timetable for Basel II

On June 26, 2004, the final Basel II guidelines were published (Basel 2004). The implementation of the New Basel Capital Accord is supposed to start by 2006 and 2007, respectively (see below).

Figure 2-8: Timetable for the Basel II Accord (see www.bis.org)

Basel II timetable

June 26, 2004	Publication of the **New Basel Capital Accord (Basel II)**
From 2006 on	Parallel application of Basel II and Principle I (Basel I) (while principle I remains relevant)
From 2007 on	Implementation of the New Basel Capital Accord (Basel II)

2.3.2.4 Illustrative example: Regulatory capital ratios of Deutsche Bank

As an illustrative example, we consider the capital structure of Deutsche Bank in 2003/04 (see Deutsche Bank 2003 and 2004). Obviously, the 8% minimum is not definitely seen as a lower threshold for the bank's capital, as the total capital ratio exceeds the 8% minimum by more than 50%.

Table 2-1: Regulatory capital ratios of Deutsche Bank 2003 to 2004[55]

Capital	**2003**	**2004**
Tier 1	10.0%	8.6%
Total capital ratio (Tier 1+2+3)	13.9%	13.2%
Regulatory capital (absolute)	29.9 Bill Euro	28.6 Bill Euro

A discussion of the capital ratios held by banks can be found in Matten (2000), for example, oriented on two questions, namely how much capital a bank really needs and why banks hold more than the minimum capital required.

2.4 Strategic planning within financial institutions

The process of strategic planning in banks has graphically been illustrated by Schierenbeck (2003a) and will serve as a guideline for the development of the

[55] Tier 1 capital roughly refers to the liquid core capital, while tier 2 and tier 3 capital is more illiquid. There are rules about the portion of tier 1, 2 and 3 capital for regulatory purposes.

credit risk framework within this work. Market analysis have to be carried out both internally (financial institution) and externally (environment) in order to base business decisions on an integrated strategic framework as shown below. The organizational structure thereby plays a crucial role and decentralized targets have to be in line with the bank-wide strategy vice versa.

Figure 2-9: The strategic planning process in banks (according to Schierenbeck 2003a, p.532)

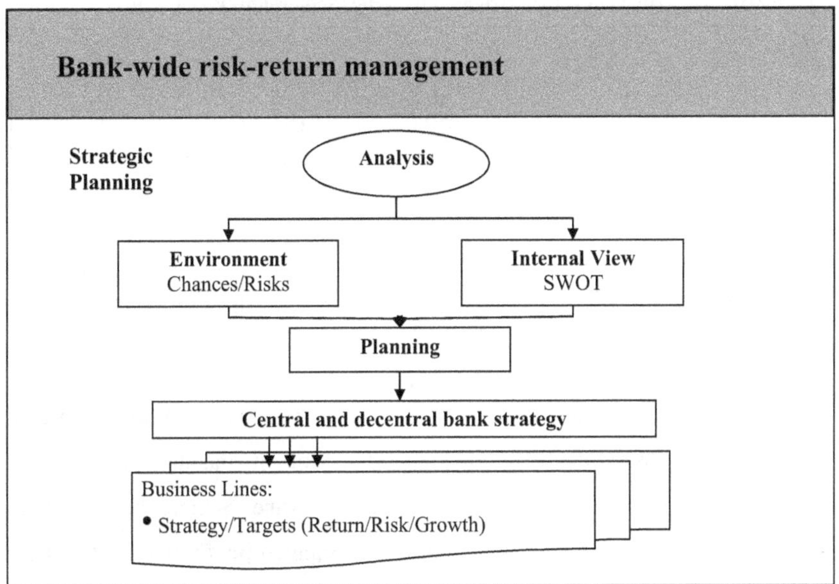

2.4.1 Company-/bank - wide management strategy

The overall management strategy within a bank may be oriented[56]

- *Top-down* or
- *Bottom-up.*

Strategic planning and management (as generally explained in section 2.4) have closely been linked to the term *dual steering model* (Schierenbeck 2003a). The concept is based on Schmalenbach's (1947) idea of *pretial business steering*, i.e. to enable decisions on a decentralized level, which are in line with the global

[56] See Theiler (2002b), for example.

banking strategy and to supervise decentralized decisions by an adequate controlling.

Schierenbeck (2003a) therefore suggests an integrated concept for the management of a bank. He concludes that a strategy focused on return[57] must include two other primary targets, referred to as the **'trilogy' of return-oriented banking** (see Figure 2-10).

Figure 2-10: The trilogy of return-oriented banking (Schierenbeck 2003a, p.1)

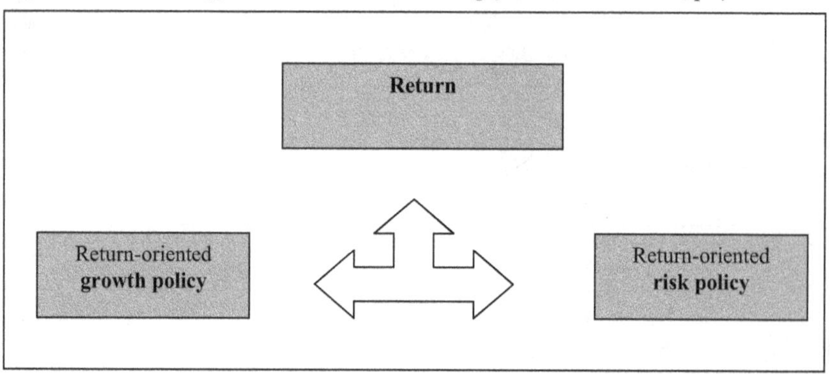

A return-oriented management of a FI has to be based on an integrated controlling. A prerequisite for the measurement of business risk is the establishment of an **adequate organization structure**. Schierenbeck (2003a) favors a **matrix organization** with a customer-oriented **profit center structure** as explained below.

2.4.2 The organization of a bank and bank-wide management strategies

Schierenbeck (2003a) distinguishes between three different organizational structures of a bank, namely referring to

- Business lines (*Product viewpoint*),
- Customers groups (*Customer viewpoint*) or
- Geography (*Local viewpoint*).

[57] A definition of return can be found defined in Loistl (1992), for example.

Strategic business fields (SBF)[58] represent the organizational entities of a bank, be it with a product, customer or geographical focus.

The characteristics of SBFs (or profit centers[59]) within a matrix organization of a firm are the following:[60]

- Decentralized structures, personal responsibility,
- Return and risk responsibility according to profit center scope,
- Concept of leading by target- setting: '*Management by Objective*',
- Regular evaluation of the actual performance: '*Management by Exception*',

to be illustrated subsequently.

An illustrative example of the organization of a bank in terms of Strategic Business Fields (SBF) in terms of a product viewpoint is shown below according to Theiler (2002b).[61]

58 The term strategic business field (SBF) has been favored by Hinterhuber (1996). A SBF is a product-market- combination with a unique, delimitable strategy.

59 We will use SBF and profit centers synonymically.

60 See Theiler (2002b), p.13.

61 However, the product-oriented organization form has the limitation of an effect that plays a crucial role within modern banking for banks faced to decreasing margins: *cross-selling*. Cross-selling defines an overall customer view with a bank's intention to offer various products to "profitable" clients, and to earn from the overall relationship (with the possibility of losses in some transactions). In fact, incorporating cross-selling into strategic planning is related to a trade-off between long-term relationships (traditional bank target) and short- term targets (profit maximization). Cross-selling orientation of banks favors SBFs according to a bi-dimensional view on customers (i.e. retail, corporate, and wholesale) and regions.

Figure 2-11: Organization of a bank (Theiler 2002b)

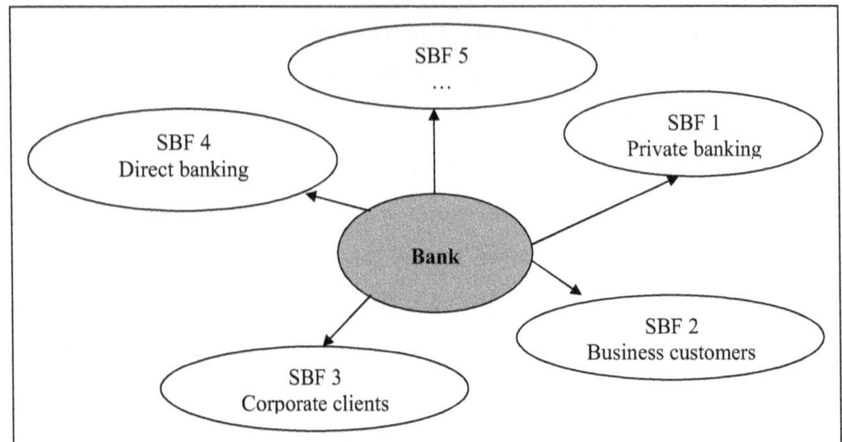

It is best-practice to manage profit centers both *top-down and bottom-up.* Bank-wide targets thereby serve as benchmarks from a top-down view, while information will be aggregated from a decentralized level (bottom-up).[62]

Two management concepts are used for this purpose:[63]

- Management by objectives and
- Management by exception.

The principle *management by objectives* will play a major role throughout this work. On a decentralized level the profit center objectives comprise return, capital and volume. *Management by exception* is a technique applied on a personal level and more a question of organization and will thus be neglected by the author. The architecture of profit center management is shown below.

[62] Pros and contras of this method can be found in Theiler (2002b), for example.

[63] See Theiler (2002b), for example.

Figure 2-12: The 'Top-Down' controlling process (Theiler 2002b)

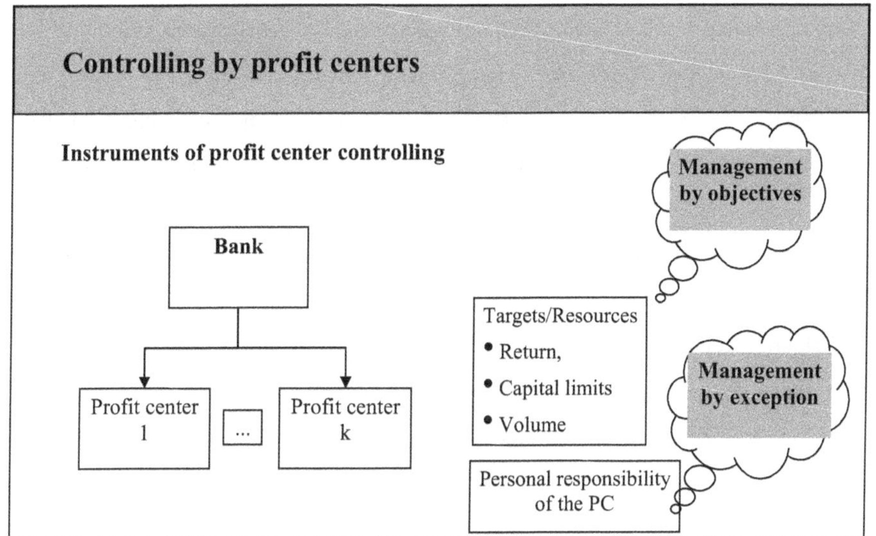

2.4.3 Methods and concepts for strategic planning

In the 1980s, strategic planning techniques for banks have been propagated by Porter (1998a/b)[64] addressed on providing **relative competitive advantages**. According to Porter, three '*norm strategies*' can be deduced:

- Cost leadership,
- Differentiation and
- Focusing on partial markets.

Within the banking field, seeking for cost-leadership is a bank-wide process that can be captured by a bank's external rating (credit policy, credit culture influencing refinancing costs), administrative costs (organization), the finance structure of a FI (Shareholder's demanded return, 'target-ROC' or 'hurdle rate'), and the credit portfolio itself (diversification, correlation structure). Traditional banking was focused on long-term relationships (relationship banking), but the consequences of risk concentration effects led to the establishment of portfolio management to support diversification concepts. The contrary viewpoints of

[64] An from a marketing viewpoint by Tanew-Illitschev (1982).

sales to built up relationships with customers on the one hand and portfolio management (risk) on the other hand is know as the credit paradoxon, what can only be solved by the isolation of credit decision and long-term risk bearing (see Saunders 1999, for example). Product differentiation and focusing on partial markets are opportunities for big and small players, respectively, to gain competitive advantages.

Similar concepts proposed later were *customer benefit banking*[65] (proposed by Schierenbeck 1999) and *lean banking*[66].

Schierenbeck (2003a) suggests pooling the two methodologies in order to follow a policy that is in line both with customer's demands and productivity targets.

In general, all three basic management concepts focus on the identification of the three major cost drivers in banks: processes, products and staff. Processes can be optimized by means of standardization, simplification, animation and outsourcing, for example.[67]

A comprehensive discussion of these areas of conflict and the implementation on a company-wide level can be found in Manz (1998) and Schierenbeck (2003a). Manz (1998) performed a SWOT analysis in the Swiss banking market,

---

[65] The concept of customer benefit banking is related to a marketing strategy of providing mainly three comparative competitive advantages to the customers:

- Better (customized, convenience, competence),
- Faster (reaction, processing, decision),
- Cheaper (Price policy/formation/adoption).

Schierenbeck (2003a) suggests SWOT analysis of strategic success factors, i.e. market potential, market share, competitive situation, customer habits/needs, condition sensitiveness of customers, Shift ability of overhead costs, risk quality of the business, image of the bank, sales net, acquisition performance, regulatory policy frame.

[66] The lean banking concept is derived from Total Quality Management (see Schierenbeck 2003a, for example). The target is to focus on three comparative productivity advantages:

- Processes (standardization, simplification, outsourcing, etc.),
- Products (Reduction of complexity, standardization etc.) and
- Human resources (Flexible work hours, decentralization of responsibilities etc.).

[67] See Paul (2001), p.16. The process of risk measurement and management within a financial institution has to be accompanied by a reengineering of credit risk processes, ensuring a risk-adequate organization structure. Process innovation will not be the focus of our interest. Solutions have been proposed by Manz (1998), Merz (2001) and Dresel (2002), for example.

while Schierenbeck (2003a) gives a strategic overview on eligible competitive strategies of FIs.

Figure 2-13: Business political concepts and effects (Schierenbeck 2003a, p.555)

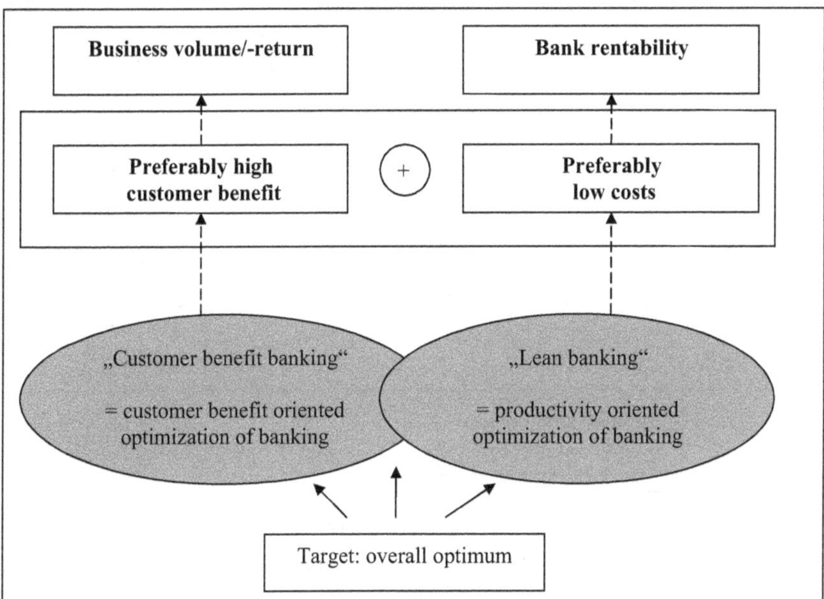

Bringing the return, growth and profitability targets together is the query for a successful credit business. Schierenbeck (2003a, p. 531f.) suggests weighing up the business from a return perspective in order to find an equilibrium between profitability and growth represented by:

- Profitability need,
- Profitability potential and
- Growth rate of the business volume,

in order to fulfill the target imposed by a company's shareholders. Figure 2-14 illustrates their qualitative relationship.

Figure 2-14: Interrelation between profitability need/potential and growth rate of the business (according to Schierenbeck 2003a, p. 537)

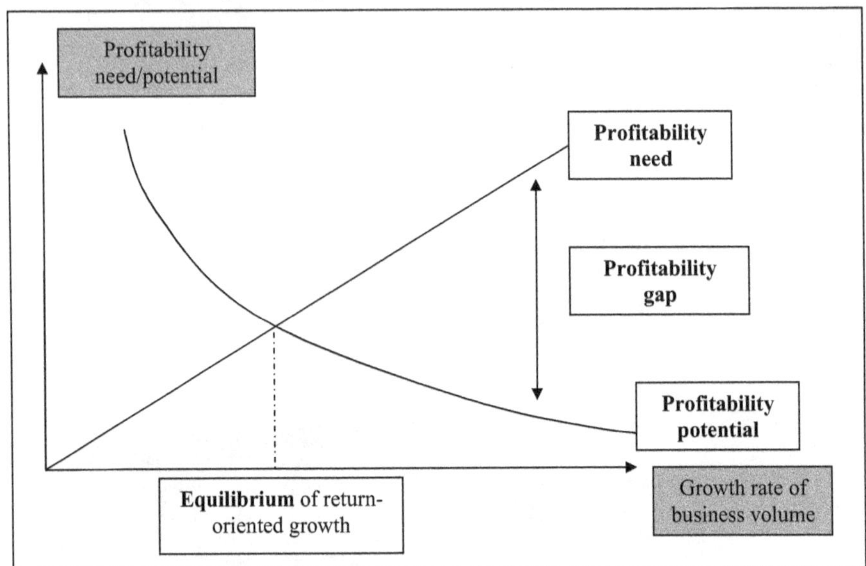

The main message of the graphic is that an extension of the market share is mostly related to lower profitability, and that the business strategy of a firm therefore has to be carefully balanced.[68]

2.4.4 Dimensions of bank-wide performance measurement: Shareholder value focus and annual performance measurement

2.4.4.1 Performance measurement on a bank-wide level

Schierenbeck (2003a) defines the **operating profit of a bank** according to the following scheme. The oprating profit of a bank decomposes into the central result, the customer business and the overhead costs. The central result can be furthermore subdivided into the **trading result**, the **treasury result** and the **investment result**. Customer business (including credit risk) refers to the decentralized profit center results.[69] Overhead costs do influence the operating profit negatively.

68 Further information can be found in Schierenbeck (2003a).

69 And may be measured based on the MIM technique, for example (see 4.2.1.4).

Further information can be found in standard text books of finance and controlling.

Figure 2-15: A bank's operating profit (according to Schierenbeck 2003a, p.411[70])

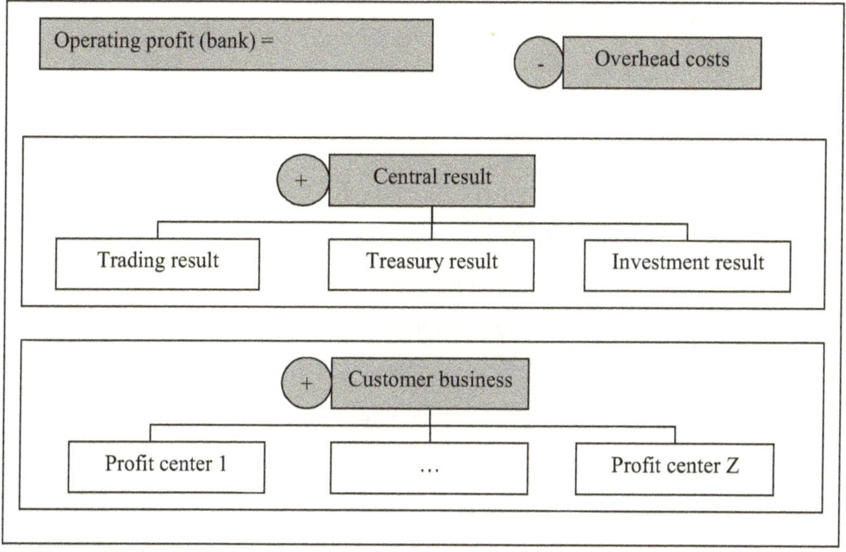

2.4.4.2 Performance measurement on a decentralized level: The result of a profit center

Schierenbeck (2003a, p.386f.) distinguishes between three different profit components:

- **Market result,**
- **Risk result** and
- **Productivity result**.

Section 4 provides the information necessary for a better understanding of risk controlling. Based on **the Market Interest Rate Method** (MIM, see section 4.2.1.4), the result of a profit center can conveniently be divided into three return components as shown in Table 2-2 below from a bird's eye's perspective. We will refer to the risk result of a bank.

---

70 Schierenbeck (2003a) further accounts for the productivity result from the different business lines.

Table 2-2: Evaluating the result of a profit center (Schierenbeck 2003a, p.411)

Profit center result		
Market result	**Risk result**	**Productivity result**
= Interest condition contribution + provisions - risk costs - Standard risk costs - Capital costs	= Standard risk costs - Actual risk costs	= Standard operating costs - Actual operating costs

2.4.4.3 Shareholder value

Volkart (1995) defines shareholder value as the net firm value or the market value of a firm's capital, which equals the market capitalization of a company.[71] The market capitalization, furthermore, is the net present value (NPV) of all expected future cash flows to the shareholder (dividends, stock price increase). Volkart (1995, p. 1064) claims that the terms "shareholder value" and "free cash flow" are principally "nothing substantial new", albeit the fashion of using them as buzzwords.[72]

It is convenient to derive the shareholder value from the free cash flow of a firm (Manz 1998). A firm's free cash flow per period is the residual amount of financial assets derived from operative earnings minus the required investments as graphically shown in the Appendix.

2.4.4.4 Performance measurement of a bank: Best-practice banks

Schierenbeck (2003a) recommends that the target return of banks has to be oriented on *best-practice* banks with the highest empirical *Return on Capital* (*ROC*) ratios as a representation of a bank's ability to generate return both to satisfy shareholder demands and, preferably, to generate additional profit. The

71 See Volkart (1995), p. 1064 or Manz (1998), p.72.

72 Shareholder value (SV) is the residual value that remains for the shareholders after subtracting the demands of all other interest groups. Maximizing SV has consequently to be an integrative part of a FI's risk-return strategy (as a decision criterion) that has become fashionable in the 1990ies under the term value based management as outlined in section 2.2.2. A comprehensive discussion about the business policy of a firm related to the shareholder value concept can be found in Spremann (1996). An illustrative overwiev on cash flow, free cash flow and growth has been provided by Spremann (2000), p.248.

following table shows the ROC (in %) of selected international banks from 1999 till 2001 (pre-tax result).

Table 2-3: ROC ratios for selected top tier FI from 1999 to 2001 (in %)[73]

Name of the Bank	1999	2000	2001
British Banks			
Lloyds TSB Group plc	30.9	27.8	22.8
Barclays	21	21	16.4
National Westminster Bank plc-NatWest	18.3	25.4	23.6
Standard Chartered plc	11.2	17	9.8
HSBC Holdings plc	17.6	16.8	12.2
U.S. Banks			
Citicorp	19.3	21.4	17.7
Chase Manhattan Corporation	20.5	15.6	3.7
Wells Fargo & Company	16.8	16	12
German Banks			
Deutsche Bank AG (US GAAP)	10.4	66.8	0.4[74]
Dresdner Bank AG (IAS)	8.5	12.4	1.2
Commerzbank AG (IAS)	8.3	11.1	1.2
Hypovereinsbank (IAS)	2.8	5.9	3.8
Swiss Banks			
UBS AG (IAS)	18.8	19.8	11
Credit Suisse Group	15.4	19.5	5.1

Lloyds has always been among the outperformers, while the poor performance of German banks is clearly visible[75], what becomes more obvious from the table below showing both the ROC and the *Cost-to-Income Ratio* (*CIR*) for German banks in 2002 according to Roland Berger (2004).

Table 2-4: ROC and CIR ratios of German banks 2002 by SBF (according to Roland Berger 2004)

	Retail Banking		Private Banking		Corp. & Investm.		Asset Man.	
	CIR	ROC	CIR	ROC	CIR	ROC	CIR	ROC
Deutsche Bank	57.5	38.6	91.3	7.3	77.1	0.6	87.1	4.4
HVB	84.4	-9.6	85.4	9.8	53.7	1.6	NA	NA
Dresdner Bank	86.7	-1.9	NA	NA	102.6	-38.6	75.3	NA
Commerzbank	87.3	2.5	NA	NA	42.7	17.1	145.4	-40.2
Best Practice	40	40	70	>25	40	>25	70	25

[73] See Schierenbeck (2003a), p.503.

[74] In 2003, Deutsche Bank reached 13 % and Ackermann announced 25 % as a strategic target. www.tagesschau.de – Rev. February 5, 2004.

[75] Except Deutsche Bank in 2000 due to extraordinary effects.

After relatively broad discussion of strategic aspects of FIs, we will now turn to risk management as a tool to support strategic considerations.

2.5 Risk management in financial institutions

2.5.1 Risk management in financial institutions: Why is it needed?

There are several reasons for the increasing interest for (credit) risk management and the intention of many financial institutions to develop new approaches (Saunders 1999, p.1-3):

- Capital markets became accessible for smaller firms with weaker credit ratings.
- The dissatisfaction with BIS' 1988 imposition of capital requirements on loans which require banks to underlie all loans of the private sector with the same 8 percent capital ratio.
- Advances in computer systems and IT have enabled banks and financial institutions to investigate high-powered modeling techiques.
- Recent economic crisis (e.g. the Asian crisis) have shown that asset and property values are very hard to predict and their liquidation may be hard to realize.
- The growth of credit exposure because of the phenomenal expansion of of-balance-sheet derivative markets has extended the requirement for credit analysis further than the loan book.
- Despite a decline in the average quality of loans, interest margins have become very thin. By consequence, the risk-return trade-off from lending has become worse.
- A structural increase in bankruptcies can be perceived worldwide.

As a consequence to the cumulative number of aims with respect to risk management, senior managers within FIs more and more often need dependable risk measures to allocate capital to business segments, approximates of the amount of potential losses to keep liquidity limits, and mechanisms to supervise positions and to provide incentives for prudent risk-taking by profit centers and risk managers (Pyle 1997).

2.5.1.1 Risk management from a theoretical and empirical viewpoint[76]

Risk management allows diminishing the volatility of the annual cash flows via diversification (hedging). Thus, the target of risk management within a company is primarily not the diminution or elimination of risk, but, in contrast, the foundation and conservation of the creation of value (MacMinn 2002).

From a neoclassical viewpoint, Hu (1996) claims for a complete market that risk management on a company level is dispensable when investors can remove the systematic risk by the use of diversification. As soon as shareholders have a significant influence on the strategy, such a diversification is not possible. Hence, Smith (1995) concludes that in the case of shareholder value orientation, risk management has its place within a company. A discussion of the advantages of risk management in complete capital markets can be found in Bartram (2000), for example.

Empirical results show[77] that risk management plays a role both in non-financial and financial institutions and therefore imperfect capital markets would have to be assumed (Stiglitz 1974).

Capital market imperfections in practice comprise among others:[78]

- Transaction costs,
- The existence of taxes,
- Information asymmetry[79].

---

[76] The discussion of risk management from a theoretical viewpoint (section 2.5.1.1 and section 2.5.1.2 follows Dresel (2002), p.7f. Risk management is embedded into the theory of finance. The following authors have provided milestones within the field of finance (see Zimmermann 1996, for example): Markowitz (1952, 1959), Sharpe (1964), Lintner (1965, 1972), Mossin (1966), Ross (1976), Modigliani/Miller (1958), Black/Scholes (1973) and Merton (1974).

[77] Bartram (2000) gives an overview on the application of risk management in non-financial institutions.

[78] See Dresel (2002), for example.

[79] Information asymmetry leads to agency conflicts and subsequently to agency costs (due to moral hazard). See section 3.1.1.

In an *incomplete market*, the danger of insolvency exists due to uncertain expectations about the future cash flows. This is an additional important reason for the existence of risk management (Dumas 1978). An increasing leverage leads to an ascending number of risk management activities.[80]

Within non-financial firms, another function of risk management is the balance of interests between debt capital donators and shareholders. The financiers of debt prefer a low-risk policy as opposed to the shareholders, who seek for high returns and subsequently for high (or at least higher) risks. As shareholders do have voice within a company as opposed to financiers, they influence the risk policy of a firm (Jensen and Meckling 1976). Financiers are thus anticipating this influence leading to increased financing spreads and credit rationing (Dresel 2002). Risk management counterbalances these interest conflicts and ensures sustainable growth. As an overall assumption within this work, a complete capital market is consequently denied.

2.5.1.2 Risk management as a process

Risk management is „the process by which managers satisfy the counterbalancing task of identifying key risks, obtaining consistent, understandable, operational risk measures, choosing, which risks to reduce and which to increase and by what means, and establishing procedures to monitor the resulting risk position“ (Pyle 1997, p.2). In this context, risk may be defined as a reduction of the firm value due to changes in the business environment (Öhler and Unser 2001).

Prudential risk management (i.e. a defensive attitude twowards risk management) is directed at defending risks which are threatening a bank's solvency (Ong 1999). According to Ong (1999, p.63) following a proactive strategy which goes further than loss avoidance and risk measurement, however, would have become "vital to the continued well-being and prosperity of a bank" in the enforced worldwide competition.

---

80 See Gay and Nam (1998) or Graham and Rogers (2002).

The overall process of risk management can be divided into four phases according to Schierenbeck (2003b, p.194) as shown below:

- **Risk identification**: Basic risk parameters, analysis of single borrower risks.
- **Risk measurement**: Portfolio measures on a bank level.
- **Risk evaluation/steering**: Risk limiting, risks as a potential for returns.
- **Risk controlling/management**: Ex ante vs. ex post evaluation.

Figure 2-16: The process of risk management (Dresel 2002, p.5)[81]

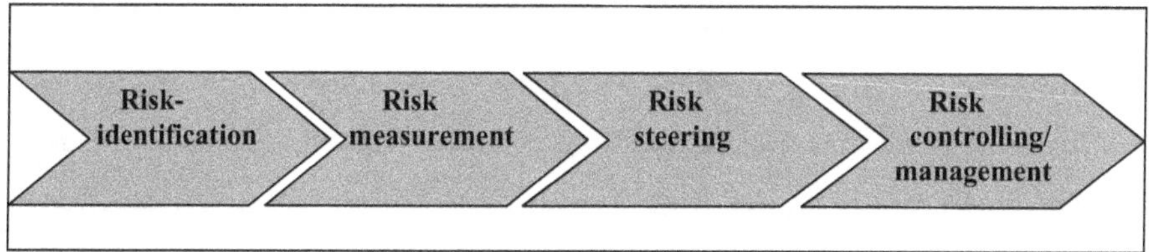

This process of (credit) risk management will accompany the reader throughout this work and is oriented on Schierenbeck (2003b, p.194f.).[82] Risk management should not only be understood as risk controlling, but furthermore as the basis for an active portfolio management of the overall company (and/or profit centers) (see Rudolph 1993).

2.5.1.3 Major types of risks in finance

Four key types of financial risks can be distinguished (Pyle 1997, p.3):[83]

- **Market risk,**
- **Credit risk,**
- **Operational risk,**
- **Performance risk.**

---

[81] According to Schierenbeck (2003b). A similar view on risk management has been proposed by Öhler and Unser (2001).

[82] Credit risk identification, credit risk measurement and passive credit risk management will be subject to section 3.2f. and credit risk controlling and active credit risk management (portfolio management) is presented in section 4ff.

[83] General risks for non-financial companies are according to Bühler (1998): liquidity risks, legal risks, operational risks subject to processes, fraud, production, etc.;

"The change in net asset value due to changes in underlying economic factors, as interest rate, exchange rates and equity or commodity prices" is called **Market risk.**[84] **Operational risk** arises "from costs incurred through mistakes made in carrying out transactions such as settlement failures, failures to meet regulatory requirements and untimely collections."[85] "Losses resulting from the failure to properly monitor employees or to use appropriate methods" are called **performance risk**.[86] "The possibility that a bond issuer" (or, more generally, a counterparty) "default by failing to repay principal and interest in a timely manner" is called **credit risk** (or default risk).[87]

Büschgen (1998)[88] has classified the inherent risks within a financial institution from a systematic viewpoint resulting in credit, market and operational risk, what is shown in the following Figure 2-17. Performance risk is subject to strategic risk in this context.

84 Pyle (1997), p.3.
85 Pyle (1997), p.3.
86 Pyle (1997), p.3.
87 See www.investorwords.com; Rev. Dec. 2004;
88 See Büschgen (1998), p. 870.

Figure 2-17: Distinctive risks in banks (Büschgen 1998, p. 870)

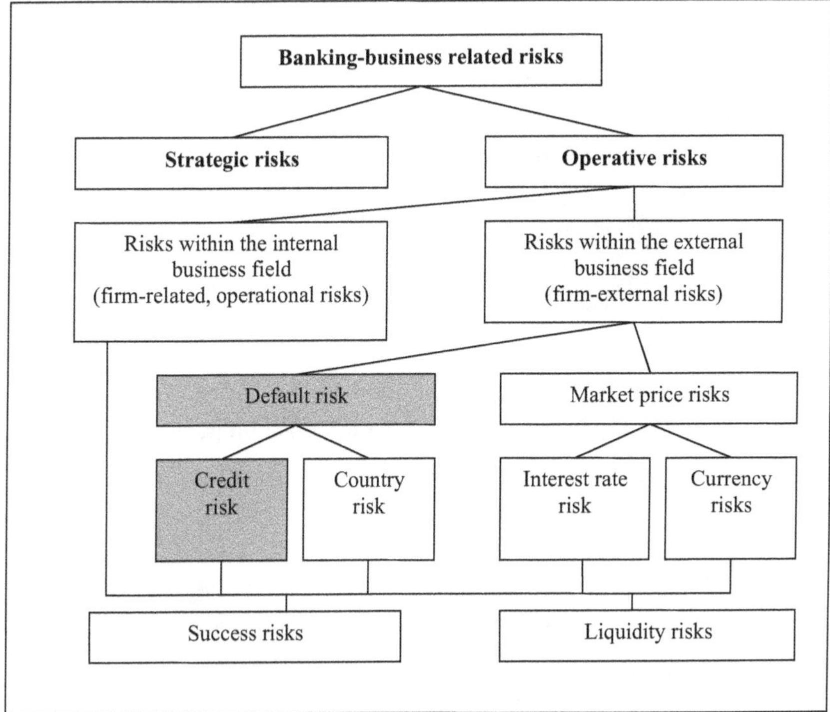

As both performance risk and operational risk is not likely to be measured effectively[89], a bank-risk management system would mostly integrate sophisticated methods to measure credit and market risk and rather rudimentary methods for other financial risk types.

Nevertheless, it has to be noticed that of the financial risk types large international banks are faced to and which were the specific focus of banking regulation (particularly Basel II), "credit risk is still fundamentally the most important and most pressingly urgent issue" (Ong 1999, p.16). Ong's claim is clearly shown below at the example of Deutsche Bank (2004) although the capital portion assigned to the credit sphere has decreased as a consequence of the reduced size of the credit portfolio during the last five years.

89 See Pyle (1997), for example. Nevertheless, minimum regulatory capital requirements for operational risk are covered e.g. by Basel II (see Basel 2004).

Figure 2-18: Economic capital allocation[90] (Deutsche Bank 2004)

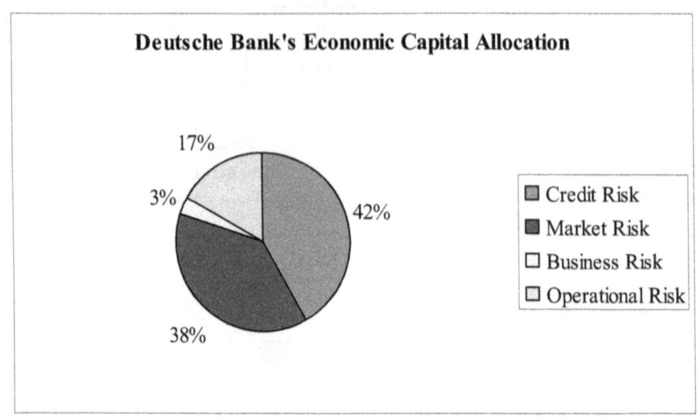

In the following sections, we will introduce the basic properties of credit risk before dealing with techniques for credit risk measurement and credit portfolio management.

2.5.1.4 Risk management methodologies for credit risk

Credit risk measures and instruments allow limiting credit risk on a portfolio level, but credit risk aspects play a role on single obligors' level as well. Schierenbeck (2003b, p.194) suggests a two layer concept to deal with credit risk, namely by means of

- **A causal viewpoint** influencing credit risk in a positive way and
- **An effect-related perspective** for risk shifting and credit risk transfer in case of occurred losses

as displayed in Figure 2-19.

[90] For credit risk and market risk, Deutsche Bank accounts for portfolio diversification, while the other risk positions are standalone measures. The nominal amount of diversification yields to 0.87 billion Euros, which decreases the sum of the economic capital for credit and market risk by 7.6%.

Figure 2-19: Causal/effect - related view on the occurrence of losses (Schierenbeck 2003b, p.194)

Causale limitation of credit risk = Influence on the probability function and amount of potential losses			**Effect-related limitation of credit risk** = Measures to cushion and shift the consequences of occurred losses	
Risk avoidance (1)	**Risk reduction (2)**	**Risk diversification (3)**	**Risk transfer (4)**	**Risk provision (5)**

The following discussion of appropriate methodologies for credit risk management is closely oriented on Schierenbeck (2003b, p.194), who claims that credit risk management has to go beyond pure risk avoidance and risk mitigation. In particular, risk compensation is a superior task that may be supported by *risk-based pricing* (see section 4.2.1). Consequently, credit decision making must not be a binary process resulting in either approval or rejection, but, to an assessment of credit risk linkage of risk and return. In the following, five measures to handle credit risk as shown above are further specified.

2.5.1.4.1 Risk avoidance

Within the field of credit risk, risk avoidance is synonymy to excluding business because unexpected losses can never be fully eliminated (Schierenbeck 2003b).[91] Only an extremely conservative borrowing strategy with securities prohibiting losses even in case of bankruptcy events allows following a risk avoidance strategy.

2.5.1.4.2 Risk reduction

If lending is considered which is not fully based on collateral, then risk reduction strategies have to be taken into account.

The basic functions of risk reduction comprise (Schierenbeck 2003b, p.194f.):

[91] Credit risk measurement on the portfolio level is explained in section 3.5.

- Analysis of creditworthiness (section 3.2f.) as a prerequisite for risk-adjusted pricing (section 4.2),
- Setting of exposure limits as well as concentration risk limits (section 3.4.4.1),
- Organizational and personal improvement of the credit risk policy (business process reengineering[92]) and
- Credit revision.[93]

2.5.1.4.3 Risk diversification

Strategies focusing on risk distribution and risk spreading are directed at diversification, which comprises:[94]

- Granularity avoidance and prevention of name concentrations (Exposure size limits),
- Diversification according to industry sectors and/or regions (Avoidance of sector and regional concentration).

Diversification does not only reduce the amount of potential (unexpected) losses, but reduces the consequences of the occurred losses.[95] In order to account for diversification, companys' senior management may set strategic, volume - and gap - limits for a portfolio oriented on a pre-defined *"norm-portfolio"*.[96] Portfolio management, however, allows an extension of rather naïve diversification via limit systems to diversification methodologies in formal terms (see section 4f.).

---

[92] For a comprehensive treatment of business process engineering in FI see Manz (1998), for example.

[93] An independent credit monitoring entity has to be in place.

[94] The two diversification dimensions may be graphically illustrated by a Lorenz-curve, for example (e.g. Klose 1996).

[95] See Bröker (2000), p. 312f.

[96] See Schierenbeck (2003b).

2.5.1.4.4 Risk transfer

Measures that are linked to the transfer of credit risk outside of the banking book by means of credit derivatives or securitization will be subject to section 4.3.10. Risk transfer may additionally be associated with risk-based pricing.

2.5.1.4.5 Risk provision

Recalling Figure 2-19, risk provision strategies are a classical instrument to deal with the remaining credit risk if the four mentioned risk measures may not be successful. Capital allocation has to be sufficient, general and specific provisions have to be accounted for, and a bank's overall capital reserves are crucial.

3 Credit risk modeling and measurement

3.1 The basics of credit risk

3.1.1 Lending: A principal-agent relation

As defined in section 2.5.1.3, credit risk is the possibility that a counterparty will default by failing to repay exposure and interest in a timely manner.[97]

The creditor-obligor-relationship can generally be classified as a **principal-agent relation** as it is known from newer financial theory (see Öhler and Unser 1999). A principal-agent-relation has the feature that a subject (the creditor) puts another subject (the obligor) in charge (by means of an interest rate) for an activity (lending). The immediate power ofor the decision and action has therefore temporarily the agent, what causes risk for the creditor.[98] Additional risks arising from the contract as information risk, delegation risks (i.e. moral hazard) and concernment risks are explained in Öhler and Unser (2001, p.197).

[97] See www.investorwords.com; Rev. January 2005.

[98] See Öhler and Unser (2001).

Figure 3-1: Principal-agent-relation according to Öhler and Unser (2001)

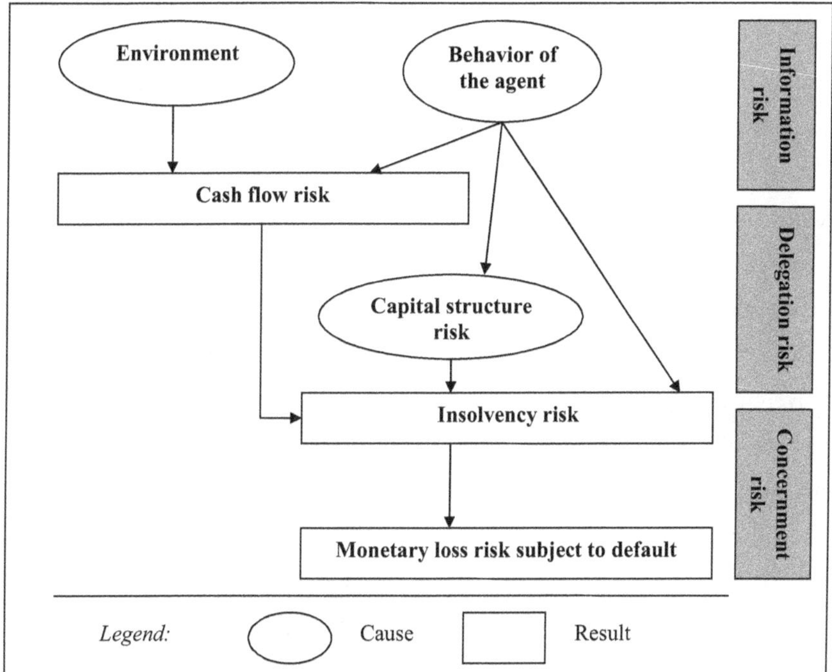

3.1.2 Classic credit analysis and the history of lending

Credit risk is the oldest risk type in the financial markets.[99] Sumer circa 3000 B.C. indicates through written records that interest rates were between 15 and 33%, implying that commercial lending competes with other businesses as the world's oldest profession.[100]

We will review the history of lending by closely following Caouette et al. (1998). Homer and Sylla (1996) report that lending (and therefore credit risk) has been already regulated in Babylon, what is indicated in Hammurabi's code circa 1800 B.C.; Lending is, in fact, unchanged from the ancient Egyptian times: "Now, as then, there is always an element of uncertainty as to whether a given borrower will repay a particular loan" (Caouette et al. 1998, p.1).

99 See Caouette et al. (1998), p.1, for example.

100 See Moody's (2000b) according to Durant (1917).

The banking system as it is known today has been founded in Florence roughly seven hundred years ago.[101] The traditional way of lending and thereby credit evaluation has been "much the same way than a tailor's approach for the creation of a custom-made suit - by carefully measuring the customer's needs and capacities to make sure that the financing is a good fit"[102]. It is interesting to remark that the current approaches cannot be fundamentally distinguished from those used by the ancient banks in Florence.

In recent decades, however, credit risk has become globally omnipresent as "the appetite for borrowing is truly global in scope"[103]. Borrowing is exerciced by souvereigns, regional and local communities, corporations and an extensive number of individuals to fulfill their specific investment (and consumption) targets. Caouette et al. (1998, p.9) calls the rapid increase of the credit volume a *"credit explosion"*. This claim is supported by investigations made by Perold (1995), who reports that America's GDP nearly equalled the payment volume in 1854, when the turnover rate was 1.5, while the turnover rate has meanwhile augmented to 78 in 1992.

Besides the credit explosion, a "dramatic shift in public attitudes"[104] can be perceived, what is stressed by Caouette et al. (1998, p.10), when he recalls a quotation by Shakespeare's Polonius: "Neither a borrower nor a lender be". The advice of Polonius was supposed to reflect the wisdom of an old, respected man. It thereby becomes obvious that the attitude of Polonius is history.

Nonetheless, Caouette et al. (1998, p. 10) state that "the word *debtor* still carries connotations of misery and shame" (…), as the word debtor "may still call to

---

101 See Caouette et al. (1998). Siena and Piacenza are supposed to have been Europe's major banking centers already 75 years before Florence. Between 1300 and 1345 the Bardi, the Peruzzi, and the Acciaiulli dictated the banking scene. However, they became all insolvent as a consequence of overlending, and are probably the first victims of cross-border lending. Their dominance as financiers was sooner or later passed to the Medici, the Pazzi, and others. Among them, the Medici of Florence is the most known group (De Roover 1963).

102 Caouette et al. (1998), p.1.

103 Caouette et al. (1998), p. 9 and p.11.

104 Caouette et al. (1998), p. 10.

mind a pathetic figure going hand in hand to a powerful and possibly scornful banker" although recently even the commercial sphere would slowly be touched by a shift in attitude.

Moreover, it can be noticed that even economic failure "has lost much of its sting", what can be perceived when one remarks that even bankruptcy may well be "accepted as a reasonable strategic option", while it had been "once avoided as a shameful and potentially career-ending debacle" (Caouette et al. 1998, p. 11). In the commercial world, bankruptcy may even be seen as an opportunity to receive funds for growth financing, to remove obligations or to avoid making payments[105]. Individual borrowers may "choose personal bankruptcy" as they know that they can resurrect from insolvency in a reasonable period of time.[106]

It is the aim of this work to give an answer and provide a solution to this development for FIs, by capturing the variety of credit risk parameters (see Figure 3-7) in order to select an appropriate multi-period credit loan portfolio.

3.1.3 Introduction: Historical traces of credit analysis and lending decisions

Commercial lending is nothing new, and neither the econometric models to explore the inherent risks, particularly default risk (Moody's 2000b). Lenders have analyzed accounting ratios at least since the 19th-century in order to investigate the underlying risks (Dev 1974). Nevertheless, the contemporary commercial default prediction has been initiated only by Beaver (1966) and Altman (1968) in the late 1960s.

Traditional credit analysis is a cautiously fostered system and arose from methods called *'expert systems'*.[107] With the emergence of Altman's quantitative multivariate approach (1968), rating and credit scoring systems enriched the classical credit analysis as a common standard. Thereby, a systematic quantification of a borrower's creditworthiness in terms of a PD has been

---

105 Caouette et al. (1998), p. 11.

106 Caouette et al. (1998), p. 11.

107 See Caouette et al. (1998), p.82f. Further information about expert system and especially the "five C's" model can be found in Saunders (1999), p.7, for example.

enabled and lead to a distinction of interest rates to be paid by creditors, known as risk-based pricing (see section 4.2.1).[108] Further aspects about the estimation of a borrower's creditworthiness and credit risk management techniques for single obligations are subject to section 3.3.4.1 and 3.4, respectively.

3.1.4 Classification of borrowing instruments[109]

The margin of a credit product depends on the specific shape of the corresponding borrowing instrument, which can be classified according to *four major modalities* (Bitz 2000, p.43):

- *Outpayment and repayment,*
- *Interest,*
- *Cancellation* and
- *Collateral.*

From an outpayment perspective, the initial amount paid to the customer can be less (or higher) than the nominal value. This gap is called disagio (agio). An example for a disagio is a federal bond that may have a disagio of 2%. The repayment amount usually equals the nominal value and may be spread over multiple periods. Repayment modalities may allow repaying whenever desired (e.g. overdraft) or by a time that has been fixed by a contract. In the latter case, three distinct repayment modalities may be distinguished (Bitz 2000, p.44):

- **Full repayment at maturity** (e.g. zero bonds).
- **Amortization by installments** (equal period installments during maturity).
- **Annuity repayment** (equal amounts to be paid every period).

[108] Principally, credit decisions are always a "reflection of personal judgement about a borrower's ability to repay" and credit decisions are therefore "personal" (Hale 1983). Hale (1983) concludes that credit decisions "can not be made solely on the basis of guidelines or analytic techniques." Indeed, "each lending officer must exercise common sense and good judgement."

[109] The summary of the classification of borrowing instruments follows Bitz (2000) and can be found in various standard financial textbooks.

In case of installment amortization or annuities it has to be defined, whether the annual repayments are due once per year or in under-year intervals and whether repayment is due *in advance or in arrears.*

Interest modalities are related to the reference measure of the nominal interest rate (e.g. exposure) as well as to the date of interest charging and interest payments. Together with payout and repayment modalities, the interest modalities determine the effective credit costs, the so-called **effective interest rate** (see below).

The interest rate level can be adapted in four ways during the lifetime of a credit (Bitz 2000, p.45):

1. The interest rate is fixed.
2. After a predefined period of fixed interest rate, the interest may be changed or the contract cancelled.
3. The interest rate is oriented on other measures, e.g. 3% above the market interest rate (EURIBOR).
4. The creditor can adapt the interest rate to the environment within certain thresholds ("variable interest rate").

The annual interest is derived as a percentage of the reference measure (exposure). There are basically three different eligible reference measures (Bitz 2000, p.46):

a) The original exposure,
b) The remaining exposure (outstanding) and
c) The remaining exposure without taking under-year repayment fully (or at all) into consideration.

After the brief discussion of the underlying interest methodologies for credit pricing in qualitative terms, it is obvious that the nominal interest rate cannot fulfill the task of being a benchmark for the average interest paid to maturity (Bitz 2000). Another interest measure is used, instead, referred to as *'effective interest rate'*, which reflects the average annual interest rate including all interest and repayment amounts to maturity including compound interest effects. In practice, it is common to use approximation formulas to calculate the effective interest rate.

Accordingly, the effective interest rate for a credit of nominal 100.000 Euro, outpayment (C_E) 95%, nominal interest rate (i) 10%, term (T[110]) 4 years and installment amortization in arrears yields to:[111]

$$r = \frac{i + \frac{100 - C_E}{T}}{C_E} \cdot 100 = 12.63\%$$

The exact value would be 12.51%. The effective interest rate allows comparisons between different offers of banks and has been transferred into law, e.g. in the German law “Preisangabenverordnungen” (law about price announcement) it is obliged since 1985 for banks to refer to the effective interest rate when they offer credit.

Information about cancellation and collateral can be found in Bitz (2000), for example.

3.2 Credit risk modeling and measurement for single obligors

3.2.1 Overview

In the following, an overview on credit risk modeling for single obligors is given.

3.2.1.1 Counterparty (borrower) risk vs. issuer risk[112]

It is important to notice that credit risk usually refers to two different risk types: **counterparty risk** and **issuer risk.** While counterparty risk is related to loans (and derivative transactions), issuer risk is usually linked to bonds (Arvanitis and Gregory 2001). Another distinction is the respective time horizon.

---

110 T refers to the average term of the credit payments: the overall term divided by the period before the first repayment is done.

111 See Bitz (2000), p.48.

112 See Arvanitis and Gregory (2001), for example.

Counterparty risk is analyzed over a long time horizon, as it is usually linked to illiquid positions which are unlikely to be traded. Contrarily, liquid credit positions as bonds, for example, exhibit issuer risk, which may be calculated for a horizon of a few days, as a bond may be sold quickly in case of altering risk. We will generally refer to counterparty risk only.

3.2.1.2 Credit risk types: Number of credit states[113]

3.2.1.2.1 (Credit) default risk

Credit default risk is "the risk that an obligor is unable to meet his/her financial obligations".[114] Every credit portfolio is exposed to default risk, as borrower defaults usually result into losses. Credit default risk is usually associated to traditional credit loan portfolios. held to maturity, particularly credit loans and credit derivatives.[115]

3.2.1.2.2 Credit spread risk

A credit spread is "the excess return[116] demanded by the market for assuming a certain credit exposure" (CSFP 1997, p.7). **Credit spread risk** comes into play only in case of a mark-to-market credit policy (to be explained below), which is common for bond and derivative portfolios.

3.2.1.3 Default Mode models and Mark-to-Market models

The distinction between default risk and credit spread risk leads to two types of credit models:[117]

- **Default-Mode models (DM)** and
- **Mark-to-Market models (MTM).**

While default mode models distinguish uniquely between the absorbing default state and the non-default state, models based on the risk of creditworthiness

---

113 A distinction between credit default risk and credit spread risk can be found in various standard finance text books, for example in Arvanitis and Gregory (2001), p.3f or in CSFP (1997), p.7f.

114 See CSFP (1997), p.7 or Ong (1999), for example.

115 See CSFP (1997), for example.

116 The interest rate for financial products beyond the riskless interest rate.

117 See e.g. Arvanitis and Gregory (2001) or Ong (1999), for example.

(mark-to-market) account for different states of creditworthiness (conditional default rate).

Traditional (non-traded) credit portfolios are usually not mark-to-market. Consequently, the only important factor is whether a loan defaults or not.[118] Liquid credit portfolios (e.g. bonds) are mark-to-market, i.e. a transaction with a counterparty whose credit quality has worsened (even if not defaulted yet) will assigned to a loss. The reason for this is that the future cash flows with that counterparty are now more risky and should therefore be discounted at a higher discount rate.[119]

It has been shown by Carey (2002) that when underlying a credit portfolio simulation, information is lost when a default model is applied, at least for short periods. Nevertheless, DM models play an essential role in the contemporary credit business, last but not least as a consequence of the popularity of structural models (see section 3.5.2ff.). MTM models ask for empirically derived transition matrices which are often not available, especially for credit loan portfolios. Moreover, altering creditworthiness is referred to sluggishness, as rating updates are timely discrete. We will thus refer to DM models only, indicating where the modeling approach could be enriched by a MTM model.

In the following, the basic credit risk parameters and eligible methodologies for their estimation will be presented as highlighted below.

118 It is assumed that an obligor who is not bankrupt will pay all his/her obligations as foreseen by the contract.

119 See Arvanitis and Gregory (2001), for example. Kiesel, Perraudin, and Taylor (1999) offer evidence that an altering in creditworthiness is comparable in importance to default risk and should therefore not be neglected.

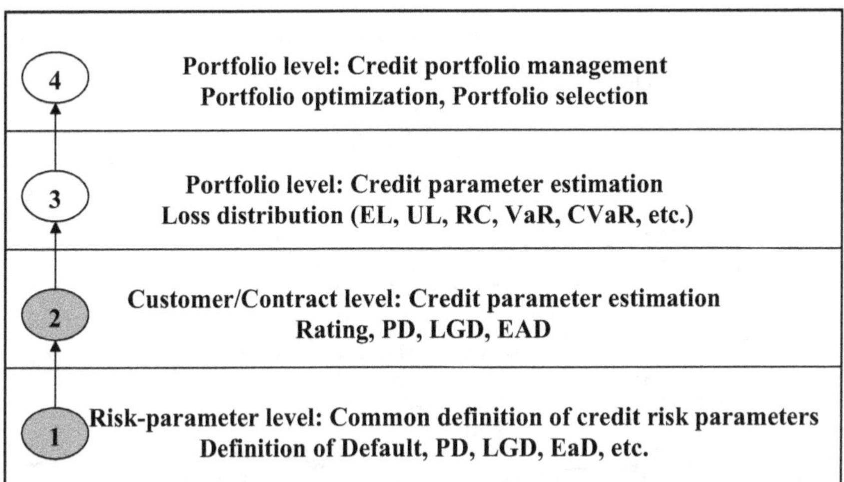

3.2.2 Measuring credit risk for single credit exposures

A selection of major parameters influencing credit risk is shown below. The art to model and measure credit risk for practical application purposes is to do it as simple as possible by still capturing all effects given the diversity of parameters. We will refer to banking book (so-called *"loan portfolios"*[120]) and neglect trading book credit risk.

[120] Ong (1999), p.93.

Figure 3-2: Main parameters influencing credit risk (according to Hartmann 2002, p.11)

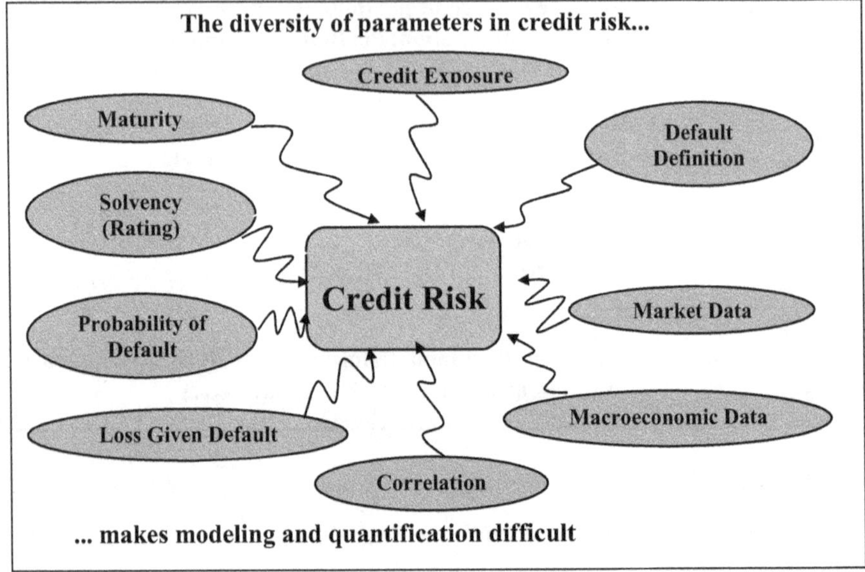

Ong (1999) distinguishes the main components of credit risk according to two groups:

- **Individual risk elements**[121] and
- **Portfolio risk elements.**[122]

Arvanitis and Gregory (2001) extend this classification by a deeper decomposition of individual risk element level:

- **Transaction-level factors** corresponding to single transactions;
- **Borrower-level factors** corresponding to single borrowers; and
- **Portfolio-level factors** corresponding to portfolio of borrowers.

While most credit risk measures and derived measures can conveniently be aggregated from the individual level to the portfolio level, unexpected losses can only be derived top-down, for example (see section 3.5).

[121] The key elements on the individual level are the default probability, the recovery rate and the credit exposure.

[122] On the portfolio level, key elements are default correlations as well as exposure and sector concentration, for example.

3.3 Credit risk parameters on the transaction/borrower level

For simplification purpose, the credit exposures of non-traded credit portfolios are usually clustered into homogenous risk buckets, so-called rating classes. Subsequently, the credit risk parameters are derived for each rating class only, because the estimation of all parameters for each borrower would be too difficult and costly and maybe not more accurate (as there is diversification over the rating segment).

3.3.1 Clustering borrowers into homogeneous subportfolios: Rating

Ratings can be understood as more or less objective estimation of a discrete creditworthiness of borrowers.[123] The final output of a credit rating process is to assign a rating symbol to borrowers (or transactions), which is then usually calibrated to the credit risk parameters. We will refer to Standard & Poor's rating classes and the empirical credit risk parameters that have been related to these ratings. Further information can be found in section 3.3.4.1.1. The meaning of S&P's rating symbols is explained in the Appendix.

3.3.2 Definition of default

The estimation of all credit risk parameters should be based on a coherent definition of default[124] outlined within the guideline of a bank and in line with the regulatory requirements. The default definition of the BIS is as follows.[125]

A default is considered to have occurred with regard to a particular obligor (borrower and/or guarantor(s)) when one or more of the following events has taken place:[126]

---

[123] Similar rating definitions can be found in various textbooks, e.g. Bluhm et al. (2003), p.18.

[124] For simplification purposes, we do not differentiate between default, insolvency and bankruptcy as many authors do. We therefore use the terms synonymously for Basel II default event.

[125] The definition leaves generous room for interpretation.

[126] According to Basel II (e.g. Basel 2004, para. 452/453); See www.bis.org.

- It is determined that the obligor is *unlikely to pay* its debt obligations (principal, interest, or fees) in full;
- A *credit loss event* associated with any obligation of the obligor, such as a charge-off, specific provision, or distressed restructuring involving the forgiveness or postponement of principal, interest, or fees;
- The obligor is *past due more than 90 days* on any credit obligation or
- The *obligor has filed for bankruptcy* or similar protection from creditors.

3.3.3 Credit exposure at default (EaD)

As this study refers to fixed-income credit instruments only, the outstanding exposure conditional on the remaining maturity of the contract is predefined. A crucial role thereby plays the repayment structure of a credit contract, as briefly explained in section 3.1.4. The current outstanding exposure during the term of a loan will be called exposure at default (EAD) for loss estimation and loss anticipation purpose.

From a more general viewpoint, the remaining credit exposure may be referred to the (nominal) outstanding or a commitment[127].

According to Ong *(1999, p.96), outstanding* "is a generic term referring to that portion of the bank asset which has already been extended to the borrowers (in the case of loans and bonds) and to other receivables in form of contractual payments which are due from its customers." In the event of default, borrowers "are unable to repay their contractual obligations and the receivables fail to come in, so the bank is exposed to the entire amount of the (remaining) outstanding." Examples of outstanding are term loans, bonds and receivables.[128]

By contrast, "a *commitment* is an amount that the bank has committed to lend, at the borrower's request, up to the full amount of the commitment", and consists

[127] Bluhm et al. (2003), for example, refers to the EAD consisting of two major parts, outstanding and commitments.

[128] Stochastic exposure (e.g. in case of credit derivatives) is referred to as *'potential exposure'*. Further information can be found in Finger (1999a), Hartmann-Wendels et al. (1999) and Wilson (1999).

of two components, a drawn and an undrawn portion (Ong 1999, p.97). Commitments usually refer to loans (in a broader sense) and are subject to flexible contracts like credit cards, where the borrower is likely to draw of the unused part of the credit up to the credit line if the borrower should come into financial difficulties. Only the drawn amount of the commitments is subject to loss in case of an obligor's default.

The Basel Committee on Banking Supervision (2004, para. 474) defines the EAD for on-balance sheet items "as the expected gross exposure of the facility upon default of the obligor." Within this work, the nominal amount of the exposure[129] will be used as the expected gross exposure at default.

3.3.3.1 The estimation of the EAD

The EAD depends upon the repayment properties of an obligation. It has been explained that exposure may either be outstanding in case of predefined cash flow structures (or a credit derivative) as well as commitments with a maximum line to be drawn. As this work deals with contracts related to fixed cash flow structures, the distribution of the outstanding is predefined to maturity.[130] Further information about the EaD of credit derivatives can be found in Ong (1999) and Arvanitis and Gregory (2001), for example.

3.3.3.2 The handling of the EaD within this work

For the handling of the EaD it will be assumed that repayments occur annually and that the EaD in a period equals the initial nominal amount outstanding of the exposure at the beginning of the corresponding period. Further information can be found in section 5.3.4.1.

---

[129] See Basel (2001b).

[130] Unless a default event occurs.

3.3.4 Probability of Default (PD)

The default probability (PD) or Expected Default Frequency (EDF^{TM})[131] "is the likelihood that a counterparty will be bankrupt or will not honor its obligations at the time when they become due over a given period" (Arvanitis and Gregory 2001, p. 6). It is common and useful to estimated marginal default probabilities over time intervals according to a specific purpose at hand. The marginal default probabilities specify the probability of default for a certain period (e.g. 12 to 18 months). It is usually to refer to a one year period.[132] In this case, the PD is called *annual default probability*. If not indicated otherwise, we will permanently refer to annual default probabilities (and annual default rates in the ex post case). Default probabilities (PD or EDF[133]) are attached to each obligor and/or credit exposures. This may be done either on the basis of historical information[134] (e.g. by rating agencies like Moody's and S&P's), via theoretical methods (e.g. based on the option pricing theory, OPT) or a mixture of both techniques (multivariate statistics, neural networks).[135] The alternative concepts to estimate PDs will be discussed below.

The expected one-year default probability of a creditor according to his/her rating class (and creditworthiness, respectively) based on historical data is shown below. Within this work, we will use similar PDs, adjusted for inconsistencies according to (Caouette et al. 1998).

---

131 This notation was introduced by KMV, and is used by some authors as well.

132 This is also the Basel II definition.

133 EDF stands for '*expected default frequency*' and is a trademark of Moody's KMV.

134 Both qualitative and quantitative information.

135 See Ong (1999), for example.

Table 3-1: One–year default probability based on empirical default rates (Caouette et al. 1998, p. 248)

Rating	PD (%) used vs. empirical PDs	One borrower defaults out of .... borrowers within one year
AAA	0.005 (no default)	20000[136]
AA	0.03 (0.02)	3333
A	0.075 (0.01)	1333
BBB	0.305 (0.15)	328
BB	1.385 (1.22)	72
B	6.245 (6.32)	16
CCC	15	6.7

Annual default rates[137] of a country or banking book are subject to random changes due to cyclical factors and idiosyncratic randomness itself, for example (Carey 1998). A graphical illustration of annual default rates for U.S. bonds for the period from 1978 to 2001 is shown below. It can be clearly observed that the annual default rates fluctuate significantly over time.

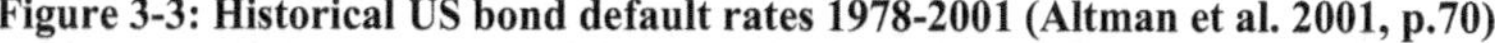

Figure 3-3: Historical US bond default rates 1978-2001 (Altman et al. 2001, p.70)

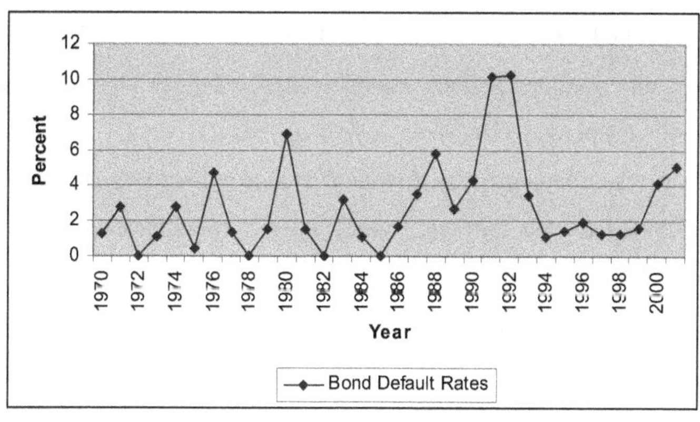

Table 3-2 provides empirical data for the sensitivity of annual default rates for cyclical effects by means of the standard deviation of expected default rates

136 I.e., on average, one of 20000 borrowers defaults.

137 See e.g. www.efalken.com/banking/html's/defaultcurves.htm; Rev. April 2004;

according to Bluhm et al. (2003). The data have been adjusted by Bluhm et al. (2003) in order to overcome inconsistencies resulting from empirical data.

Table 3-2: Credit data (Bluhm et al. 2003, p.116)

Rating	Default rate (%)	StD (%)
AAA	0.0001	0.0023
AA	0.0012	0.0110
A	0.0113	0.0514
BBB	0.1027	0.2406
BB	0.9348	1.1270
B	8.5040	5.2788
Mean	1.59	1.12

A crucial question for every credit risk manager is whether to use point-in-time PDs, through-the-cycle PDs or stress PDs (e.g. worst case PD) to predict default events. In terms of the examples within this work, we will generally refer to through-the-cycle PDs, and leave room for extensions.

Excursus: Multi-period PDs - The mean reversion effect

Besides macro-economic parameters there is another major influence on multi-period PDs, the so-called *mean reversion effect.* The latter effect describes the phenomenom that an investment grade company has a higher chance of a downgrade than of an upgrade vice versa (*effect of mean reversion* in credit ratings), which is a result supported by historical evidence found by means of the application of MTM models (see e.g. Moody's 1997). This means, that the conditional annual PDs of investment grade rated companies increase over time, reflecting the fact that a firm with a high creditworthiness is more likely to be downgraded to a state where the PD is higher than upgraded (see Arvanitis and Gregory 2001, for example). By contrast, non-investment grade rated obligors that do not become insolvent are more likely to improve than deteriorate in credit quality, and therefore their annual PD decreases over time (see e.g. Arvanitis and Gregory 2001). An investor can account for this fact by taking higher conditional annual PDs of investment grade obligors into account when dealing with multi-period decisions and vice versa for speculative grades.

3.3.4.1 Estimation of the creditworthiness and the default probability (PD)[138] of a borrower

As mentioned above, most authors distinguish between two main groups of credit risk models to assess the creditworthiness of single creditors in order to assign a PD to them:[139]

- **Practice-oriented credit risk models** and
- **Theoretical credit risk models.**

Furthermore, a methodological concept for re-calibration and validation of the PDs over time has to be in place. Further information about the validation process can be found in Deutsche Bundesbank (2003).

Practice-oriented credit risk models comprise traditional models (expert systems, credit scoring[140] and rating) and newer (more quantitatively oriented) inductive-empirical models (discriminant analysis, regression analysis, neural networks and genetic algorithms). Theoretical models may be structural (referring to the balance sheet structure of a firm) or intensity-based (oriented on default probabilities).

---

138 We neglect the case that single borrowers may have several contracts.

139 Futher information can be found in Öhler and Unser (2001), p.207, for example.

140 According to Sauders (1999, p.15) "credit scoring systems can be found in virtually all types of credit analysis, from consumer credit to commercial loans." The concept behind credit scoring is to pre-identify certain key factors that determine the solvency of borrowers (and consequently also the PD), and combine or weight them into a quantitative score. This score can be either directly interpreted as a probability of default or used as a classification system (Saunders 1999). It is common to use scoring approaches nowadays for retail customers as opposed to ratings, which are subject to the corporate sphere. A valuable review of the application of credit-scoring models can be found in Altman and Narayanan (1997).

Figure 3-4: Categorization of credit risk models (according to Öhler and Unser 2001)

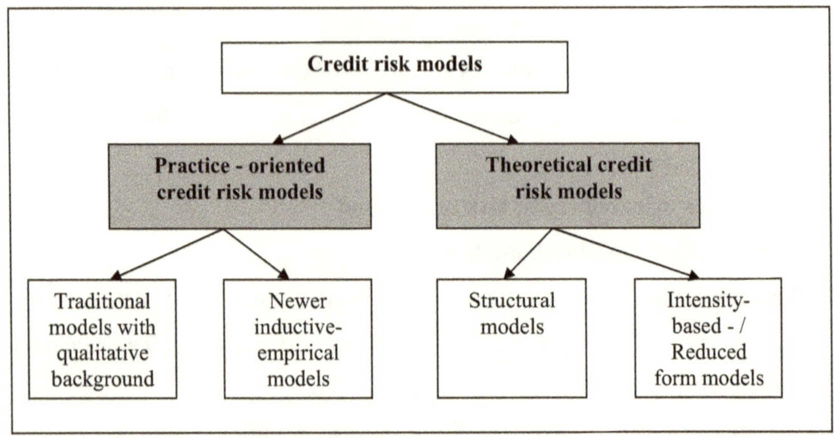

As this work deals with the non-traded domain of credit risk, theoretical models are hardly applicable, as they usually require market data.[141] Rather, newer inductive-empirical models play the major role for the non-traded credit business.

In the following, we will outline the major methodologies and their advantages and disadvantages.

3.3.4.1.1 Traditional credit models: Rating systems[142]

Ratings are supposed „to typically embody an assessment of the risk of loss due to failure by a given borrower to pay as promised, based on the consideration of relevant counterparty and facility characteristics."[143] A rating system thereby includes the "conceptual methodology, management processes, and systems that play a role in the assignment of a rating".

Both quantitative and qualitative information[144] is used to assess the creditworthiness of an obligor, usually with a portion between 70:30 and 50:50. An illustrative overview on a typical rating process can be found in Standard & Poor's (2002), for example.

141 And techniques to map market data to non-traded borrowers are not considered.
142 Scoring systems are used synonymously as "rating systems" for smaller obligors.
143 Basel (2000), p.2.
144 e.g. management's capability, comparative strength in the market (competitors), etc.

Ratings can be subdivided into[145]

- *Internal ratings* and
- *External ratings.*

Internal ratings refer to the internal processes of a financial institution to decide about the creditworthiness of a (potential) borrower. External ratings are assigned and published (mostly for publicly traded firms due to the related costs!) by major rating agencies like Standard & Poor's[146], Moody's[147] and Fitch[148]. External ratings play an important role in today's capital markets and are a major component within the regulatory framework of Basel II.[149]

In the table below, a summary of the long-term rating scales of major rating agencies is provided.

---

[145] Further information about external and internal ratings can be found in various financial textbooks.

[146] Standard & Poor's (S&P's), the leading credit rating organization, traces its history back to 1860 and began to rate debt of corporations already 75 years ago. Since 1966, S&P's is a business unit of the McGraw-Hill Inc., a major publishing company.
S&P's started to rate public debt issues in 1916, seven years later than Moody's. Over the last 30 years, the introduction of new financial products has led to the development of new methodologies and criteria for credit rating. S&P's was the first rating company to rate mortgage-backed bonds (1975), mutual funds (1983) and asset-backed securities (1985).
It now rates more than $11 trillion in bonds and other financial obligations of obligors in more than 50 countries. See www.standardandpoors.com.

[147] Moody's was founded by John Moody's (1868-1958), who laid the foundation for Moody's Investor services in 1900, when he published Moody's Manual of Industrial and Corporation Securities. Moody's traces go back to 1909, when he introduces the first bond ratings as part of Moody's analysis of railroad investments.
Today Moody's Investor Service, a leading global credit rating, research and risk analysis firm, publishes credit options, research and ratings on fixed-income securities, issuers of securities and other credit obligations.
Moody's has become a subsidiary of Dun and Bradstreet, a commercial credit-rating agency and rates $13.7 trillion of debt securities in more than 90 countries. It employs approximately 800 analysts and has more than 1500 associates located around the world. See www.moodys.com.

[148] Apart from S&P's and Moody's, Fitch can be considered as the only major European rating agency, located in Paris, France. See www.fitchratings.com.

[149] As outlined in section 2.3.

Table 3-3: Rating categories of the major rating agencies

	S&P's	Moody's	Fitch
Investment Grade	AAA AA+ AA- A+ A- BBB+ BBB-	Aaa Aa1 Aa2 Aa3 A1 A2 A3 Baa1 Baa2 Baa3	AAA AA+ AA- A+ A- BBB+ BBB-
Speculative Grade	BB+ BB- B+ B- CCC+ CCC- CC C	Ba1 Ba2 Ba3 B1 B2 B3 Caa1 Caa2 Caa3 Ca C	BB+ BB- B+ B- CCC+ CCC- CC C
Default	D/SD	D	DDD DD D

The rating scheme of Standard & Poor's will serve as a benchmark within this work.[150]

[150] The meaning of S&P's rating classes is explained in the Appendix.

3.3.4.1.2 Inductive - empirical models

The fundamental aim of newer methodologies of econometric credit analysis has been to provide more objective forecasts of borrower's creditworthiness by means of standardization and automation in order to be faster and more efficient. The major idea behind inductive-empirical models is to use ex post data to predict future default events. Two major screws have thereby been identified to improve the accuracy of default prediction (see Caouette et al. 1998 or Moody's 2000b, for example): the *identification of adequate financial ratios*[151] on the one hand and the *application of the most appropriate statistical methods* on the other hand.

Quantitative data (partly based on qualitative features) on default and non-defaulted firms are gathered and combined in order to receive a preferably selective value (threshold) for the ex ante classification of credit applicants and borrowers over time. The selective value may be directly related to a PD (*direct methods* for PD estimation) or indirectly by a subsequent calibration (*indirect method*).

In former times of uniform (or at least) interest rates for all borrowers, the purpose of indirect methods has been to enable setting a threshold whether to lend or not. Meanwhile, the additional calibration of the selective score to PDs causes additional uncertainty and therefore indirect methods tend to be inferior to direct methods in terms of their usage for PD estimation.[152]

The main inductive-empirical models commonly used in practice are[153]

---

[151] A list of commonly used financial ratios can be found in the Appendix. Most failure prediction studies done before the 1980's, e.g. Deakin (1972) and Altman et al. (1977) aimed at improved prediction accuracy by appropriate selection of financial ratios for the analysis.

[152] Naturally, ex ante credit decisions based on ex post data are far from being perfect. Thus, if a single credit decision (yes/no) about a loan applicant is made based on an inductive-empirical model, a decision maker will always be confronted with a dilemma (see Öhler and Unser 2001, for example):

- Either there are solvent creditors that are refused because of the inductive-empirical model's output (Alpha failure) or
- More ex post insolvent borrowers are accepted (Beta failure).

[153] See Öhler and Unser (2001), p.214f., for example.

- **Uni- and multivariate discriminant analysis (UDA/MDA)**[154] (indirect method)
- **Regression analysis** (logistic[155] and probabilistic regression) (direct method),
- **Neural Networks**[156] (indirect method), and
- **Genetic algorithms**[157] (indirect method).

Altman and Saunders (1998) provide a detailed survey of today's econometric credit risk measurement approaches.[158] An overview on empirical studies on corporate default has been given by Sobehart et al. (2000).[159]

3.3.4.1.3 Theoretical approaches

There are two major approaches in use to derive default probabilities in an analytical way (Bluhm et al. 2003, p.18):

- **Calibration of default probabilities from market data**

  The concept of Expected Default Frequencies (EDF™) of Moody's KMV corporation[160] is among the most famous frameworks to derive default

---

154 The most famous model for MDA has been provided by Altman (1968): Altman's Z-Score model.

155 Among the first users of logistic analysis in the context of financial distress were Martin (1977) and Ohlson (1980), followed by Wiginton (1980), Zavgren (1985), Watt (1985), Aziz et al. (1988), Aziz and Lawson (1989) and Lennox (1999). General references of the logit model can additionally be found in Greene (1993), Amemiya (1981) and Maddala (1983). Logit analysis can easily be performed with the SAS software package (LOGISTIC), for example, using a procedure that estimates a binary logit model via maximum likelihood.

156 See Tam (1991), Wilson & Sharda (1995), Martin et al. (1993) or Back et al. (1994), for example.

157 See Back et al. (1996).

158 Besides, new analytical techniques have been introduced to this area of research. Well-known examples are recursive partitioning (Frydman et al. 1985), multidimensional scaling (Mar Molinero and Ezzamel 1991), catastrophe theory (Gregory et al. 1991), multinomial logit models (Johnson and Melicher 1994), multicriteria decision aid methodology (Zopounidis and Doumpos 1999) and rough sets (Dimitras et al. 1999).

159 Quantitative bankruptcy prediction started in accounting with the study of Fitzpatrick (1932) in the 1930's. Other pioneers in the field were Ramser and Foster (1931), Winakor and Smith (1935), and Merwin (1942). Since then, numerous empirical studies have been carried out, e.g. Libby (1975), Casey and Bartczak (1985), Mossman et al. (1998) and Shumway (2001).

probabilities from market data and can be classified as a structural model[161]. An alternative concept is to infer default probabilities from credit spreads of traded products bearing credit risk, e.g. corporate bonds and credit derivatives. These models refer to so-called reduced-form models[162].

---

160 KMV Corporation belongs to Moody's since 2003, and has been founded 13 years ago in San Francisco. The firm develops and contributes credit risk management products.

161 The main assumptions of structural models are (Merton 1974):

- All liabilities of a firm become due at the same time,
- Until maturity no further capital is borrowed nor dividend payments or share buybacks are done,
- Default arises if the market value of a firm's assets at maturity is lower than its total debt,
- The asset value of a firm follows a Brownian motion.

The seminal structural model has been provided by Merton (1974). He assumes that the probability of default is determined by the volatility of the assets. A stochastic process driving the dynamics of the assets is assumed. Default occurs if the stochastic process hits a certain lower boundary of the obligations at maturity:

$$dV(t)=\mu V(t)dt+\sigma V(t)dW(t)$$

where μ and σ are the firm's asset value drift rate and volatility, and $dW(t)$ is a Wiener process.

This means that at maturity of the debt, the bondholder is paid the face value of the bond if the market value of the firm exceeds the face value of the bond. If the assets fall below this amount, the payment to the bondholder will be the residual value of the firm. Therefore the bondholder gets back the smaller of two quantities: either the face value of the bond or the firm's assets. This payoff $B(T)$ at maturity T specifically amounts to the face value of the bond B minus the price of a put option $P(V(t),t)$ on the firm's value with a strike price equal to the face value of the bond:

$$B(T)=B-P(V(t),t)$$

$$B(T)=B-\max\{B-V(t),0\}$$

Further information about OPT and Merton can be found in various standard financial textbooks and articles, for example in Leland (1994).

162 The following illustration of reduced-form models is oriented on Ott (2001, p.88f.) and can be found in many other standard financial textbooks. These models, introduced by Bierman and Hass (1975), attach the value of a risky financial asset and its PD no longer causally to the underlying development process of the asset value of a firm. Hence, the original approach is reduced to the derivation of the PDs from historical data. In so far, reduced-form models are built upon exogenously provided PDs.

Following the concept of Markov processes, reduced-form models try to imitate the stochastic process of random variables as realistically as possible, what is usually termed as intensity function (Hazard rate). Non-default states of the creditworthiness are separated from the absorbing default state.

Reduced form models primarily use observable price (credit spreads) differences between risky assets and a maturity conform riskless financial asset to predict default processes and

- **Calibration of default probabilities from ratings**

  According to rating-based (intensity-based) credit models, default probabilities are derived via external ratings or based on bank-internal rating methodologies.[163]

3.3.4.1.4 Evaluation of different credit risk approaches

Moody's (2000b, p.15) argue that theoretical models would be preferred against statistical approaches as "ad hoc data mining is appropriately eyed with skepticism." However, it seems that pure theoretical (i.e. structural) models are perceived with scepticism in economics as well.[164] Accordingly, most approaches comprise the best components of both approaches.[165] In the following, the advantages and disadvantages of the two broad modelling concepts, inductive-empirical models and theoretical models, are discussed.[166]

---

the PDs. Hence, reduced form models are based on market prices for the firm's assets like structural models.

The term intensity based models subsumes all approaches to determine stochastic default based on suitable data. The data can be represented by accounting data and transition probabilities, for example.

Origins of reduced-form models can be found in Jarrow and Turnbull (1995), Jarrow, Lando and Turnbull (1997), Artzner and Delbaen (1992), Flesaker et al. (1994) and Lando (1994). Other contributions were provided by Duffie and Huang (1995), Duffie et al. (1996) and Duffie and Singleton (1997, 1999). Duffee (1999) empirically examined the appropriateness of reduced-form models.

163 Rating-based credit models can be found in many other standard financial textbooks. Another special form for intensity based models are rating-based models.

The simplest way to model a rating process is to assume that it follows a Markov chain (with a finite state space). This implies that the actual rating transition probability is not dependent on the rating history in the past. The "default"-state is one of the probable transition states.

Within the rating-based models there are two distinguishable methods: on the one hand, rating transitions can be derived from historical data and on the other hand from credit spreads. The latter model family could be named "rating based reduced form model".

Initial literature for rating based intensity based models has been provided by Jarrow et al. (1997), Lando (1998), Das et al. (1998), Huge and Lando (1999) and Lando (1999). A famous example for a rating-based model is CreditMetrics.

164 See Moody's (2000b), for example.

165 See Moody's (2000b), for example.

166 The goodness of a credit model in formal terms may be measured using a performance measure as outlined in the Appendix.

The ultimate conclusion for the superiority of any model type or model is (still) unsolved. For banking book credit loans, however, inductive-empirical models seem to be more readily applicable as they do not require market data and are rather easily understandable. In order to explicitely compare two distinct methodologies, specific performance measures are used as explained in the Appendix.

3.3.4.1.4.1 Inductive-empirical models

The advantages and disadvantages of the major inductive-empirical methods are summarized below.

Table 3-4: Pros and cons of the major inductive-empirical models

Model	Pros	Cons
Multivariate discriminant analysis (MDA)	o First model to be used (Altman) o Relatively simple	o Assumption of normality of the distributions of the financial ratios o Indirect method (Output is not a PD) o Backward-looking
Probabilistic regression (Probit)	o Relatively simple o Direct method (Output is a PD) o Output is easy to interpret	o Assumption of normal distribution of ratios o Backward-looking
Logistic regression (Logit)	o Relatively simple o Direct method (Output is a PD) o No assumptions about ratio distributions	o Output is rather difficult to interpret o Backward-looking
Neural Networks/ Genetic algorithms	o Accurate fit of the data	o Method is black box o Indirect method (Output is not a PD) o "Overfitting"- problem o Backward-looking

As a general evaluation of the models, both regression models have proved to be very promising, as their output can directly be interpreted as a PD. As most credit decisions are no longer simply "yes or no", this is an important advantage of the regression models. The choice between logit and probit is unsolved (Greene 1993). Nevertheless, the interpretation of the probit coefficients is rather easier than for logit and is the reason for its usage in practice, e.g. by Moody's. Schmieder (2002), for example, showed that based on a large illiquid

German credit portfolio logit has been marginally superior to probit with respect to its in- and out-of-sample prediction accuracy.

A general shortage of inductive-empirical models is that they are backward-looking and base ex ante probabilities solely on ex post data.

3.3.4.1.4.2 Theoretical models

Moody's (2000b, p.17) claim that "people tend to like" theoretical models as they are "usually presented in a way that is consistent and completely defined so that one knows exactly what's going on." The reason behind that is that there is usually a plausible "*story* behind the model", which helps to make a model "not just statistically compelling, but logically compelling as well".[167] By consequence, users tend to trust in a model without the proof of performance data which make econometric models "that have no explanation" less attractive (Moody's 2000b, p.17).

The advantages and disadvantages of the two types of theoretical models are shown below.

Table 3-5: Pros and cons of theoretical models

Model	Pros	Cons
Structural models	o Theoretical basis o Ex ante oriented design	o Input data problem not yet entirely solved (Asset value of a firm not directly observable) o Only applicable for public firms o Underestimation of PDs for short periods
Intensity-based models	o Theoretical basis o Exogenous PD based on historical data	o Availability of data for rating transitions

The major limitation of structural models is that they have been designed for publicly traded firms, the minority among all firms.

167 Moody's (2000b) p.17. For example Merton's model can conveniently be brought together with the well-developed theory of option pricing.

3.3.4.2 The handling of PD estimation within this framework

In the following, we will briefly denote the PD-estimation methodology that will be used within our credit risk management framework.

In the non-traded credit segment, it is common to assign internal ratings (or scorings[168]) to each borrower (and transaction) (see section 3.3.4.1.1). However, an ordinal order alone will not be regarded as sufficient information for the purpose of risk-adjusted lending, which is linked to quantifiable risk. Ratings are therefore *'calibrated'* to PDs in an additional step.[169]

Calibration can basically be done in two distinct ways. First, the mean default probability can be calculated for each rating class based on empirical data (frequency analysis). In order to receive a continuous rating methodology, the discrete mean PDs of each rating class can be fitted by means of interpolation. Bluhm et al. (2003), for example, favors an exponential function.[170] Alternatively, inductive-empirical methods can be used to derive the PD based on ratings. Logistic regression seems to be an appropriate candidate for this target.

The ultimate output of the calibration of default probabilities to ratings is a mapping[171]

$\text{Rating} \to \text{PD}$, e.g. $\{\text{AAA}, \text{AA}, \text{A}, ..., \text{C}\} \to [0,1]$, $\text{R} \to \text{PD(R)}$,

such that a certain default probability PD(R) is assigned to every rating class R. A calibration of S&P's rating classes to PDs has been shown in Table 3-1. We will refer to through-the-cycle PDs for simplification purposes, but point-in-time PDs may conveniently be used as well.

168 Rating and scoring will generally be used synonymously as their output is calibrated to a risk grade on a master scale and thereby comparable.

169 The process of assigning a default probability to a rating is called calibration.

170 According to Bluhm et al. (2003, p.19), who analyzed historical default data provided by Moody's, there is "strong evidence from various empirical default studies that default frequencies grow exponentially with decreasing creditworthiness."

171 See Bluhm et al. (2003), p.21.

3.3.5 Loss Given Default (LGD)/ Recovery Rates (RR)

Even in the event of bankruptcy some recovery on a credit position will usually remain.[172] This recovery relative to the outstanding exposure defines the recovery rate.[173] There has been a large variability in historical recovery rates (see Arvanitis and Gregory 2001, for example). By contrast, the fraction of the exposure that will be lost in the event of default, or, more appropriately, the fraction of debt the bank cannot be recovered from the obligor once it has defaulted is called loss given default (LGD).

Although the estimation of such loss rates sounds quite simple at a first glance, it is not, because recovery rates depend on many factors, e.g. the quality of collateral (securities, mortgages, guarantees) and the seniority of the bank's claim on the borrower's asset.[174] This is the reason why many authors consider the ex ante LGD "as a random variable describing the severity of loss of a facility type in case of default" (Bluhm et al. 2003, p. 27).

Bank-external sources for recovery data (and and loss rates[175]) come from the rating agencies. Moody's, among others, provides recovery values of defaulted bonds, hereby distinguishing between different seniorities as illustrated in Table 3-7. Empirical data on loss rates for unsecured credit according to S&P's rating classes is shown below (according to Caouette et al. 1998, p. 248) together with the LGD that will be used in our framework. The LGD is considered to be fixed for each risk segment.

---

172 See Arvanitis and Gregory (2001), for example

173 See Arvanitis and Gregory (2001), for example.

174 Bluhm et al. (2003).

175 Ex post LGDs are usually called loss rates in constrast to the ex ante case, where the term LGD is used.

Table 3-6: Empirical loss rates and the LGD used within this work (Caouette et al. 1998, p. 248)

Rating	Loss Given Default (LGD) (%) used vs. empirical loss rates	Recovery Rate (=1-LGD) (%) used vs. empirical RRs
AAA	15 (22)	85 (78)
AA	20 (23)	80 (77)
A	30 (43)	70 (57)
BBB	40 (47)	60 (53)
BB	55 (58)	45 (42)
B	65 (65)	35 (35)
CCC	80 (80)	20 (20)

In the following, distinct methodologies to derive the LGD are outlined.

3.3.5.1 The estimation of the LGD

In general, three distinct methodologies to estimate work-out LGDs can be distinguished:[176]

- **Market LGD**: Derived from market prices of defaulted bonds or marketable loans shortly[177] after a default event,
- **Workout LGD**: Determined from the discounted cash flows occuring during the workout and/or collection process relative to the exposure at default,
- **Implied market LGD**: Derived by means of a theoretical asset pricing model by means of risky (but not defaulted) bond prices.

We will generally refer to workout LGDs, as market prices are usually not available for illiquid credit loans.[178]

The loss of exposure in case of a default event comprises broadly the loss of the outstanding exposure itself (principal), carry-out costs (e.g. interest income foregone) and workout expenses (collections, legal, etc.) (Schuermann 2004, p.9).

The ultimate value of these loss components depends on the[179]

---

[176] See Schuermann (2004), p.9.

[177] In fact, the sources providing market LGDs are sometimes not very precise in describing what "shortly" means. In Moody's case, shortly is supposed to be one month.

[178] Further information about the other two types of LGDs methodologies can be found in Schuermann (2004).

[179] See Jorion (2001), Bluhm et al. (2003), Allen and Saunders (2003), Schuermann (2004) and Franks et al. (2004), for example. It is interesting to notice that loss rates do not seem to depend on the size of the firm (See Schuermann 2004).

- The type of collateral (market value), the specific industry and its pecking order (or seniority see Appendix) and/or
- Type and development pattern of the value of guarantees over time relative to the repayment sequence,
- The state in the business cycle,
- The discount rate used to discount the workout cash flows and
- The length of the workout process itself.[180]

Moreover, the underlying default definition has a crucial impact on loss rate estimates.

Öhler and Unser (2001) point out that the estimation of loss rates and LGDs, respectively, is one of the most difficult tasks in the evaluation of daily business, which is also mainly caused by the lack of empirical data.[181] Dependent on the availability of loss data and the sophistication of the methodology within a bank, Schuermann (2004, p.32) suggests that LGDs may be modeled by means of contingency of look-up tables, basic regression, advanced regression and neural networks (tree methods, machine learning).

Empirical evidence shows that there is supposed to be a positive correlation between default rates and loss rates (see Allen and Saunders 2003, p.20f., for example). However, this issue needs further research as the conclusions drawn from empirical studies vary with the specific case that has been examined.

In the following, basic methodologies for LGD estimation are presented. Further information on major factors with influence on the LGD (collateral value, seniority of the collateral, macroeconomic effects) is given in the Appendix.

---

[180] Which may significantly vary across countries. See Franks et al. (2004).

[181] Ong (1999, p. 105) significantly summarizes this postulate: "Also, individual banks have attempted to estimate LGD from their own historical experience (which can lead to myopia) and there are organizations that attempt to collect statistics (which can lead to mass hysteria). The jury is still out in this regard."

3.3.5.1.1 LGD estimates based on empirical loss rates

Credit rating agencies measure recovery rates (and thereby LGDs) related to the value of debt shortly after default (*Market LGDs*) distinguishing between different seniority and security levels (Jorion 2001). Moody's is supposed to have published the most extensive empirical data on RR (recovery rates), mostly based on US data as shown below.[182] Besides the mean recovery rate, also the percentiles and the volatility of the RR are listed.

Table 3-7: Moody's recovery rates for U.S. corporate debt (%) (1970-1999) (Jorion 2001, p.477)

Seniority/security	Min.	1st quantile	Median	Mean	3rd quantile	Max.	Standard deviation
Senior/secured bank loans	15	60	75	69.91	88	98	23.47
Equipment trust bonds	8	26.25	70.63	59.96	85	103	31.08
Senior/secured bonds	7.5	31	53	52.31	65.25	125	25.15
Senior/unsecured bonds	0.5	30.75	48	48.84	67	122.6	25.01
Senior/subordinated bonds	0.5	21.34	35.5	39.46	53.47	123	24.69
Subordinated bonds	1	19.62	30	33.17	42.94	99.13	20.78
Junior/subordinated bonds	3.63	11.38	16.25	19.69	24	50	13.85
Preferred stocks	0.05	5.03	9.13	11.06	12.91	49.5	9.09
All	0.05	21	38	42.11	61.22	125	26.53

It is difficult to apply these data mainly drawn from a sample of U.S. firms, which fall under the jurisdiction of U.S. bankruptcy laws, outside the US as differences across jurisdictions will create additional uncertainty for the determination of the recovery rate (Jorion 2001). By consequence, these data are merely indicative for non-U.S. recovery rates (Jorion 2001).

[182] Besides Moody's, long-term empirical studies for bond recoveries have been performed by Standard & Poor's (1999).

For European (German, UK and French) recovery rates, Franks et al. (2004) have provided empirical data based on a comprehensive study on Workout-LGDs based on default data from 1993 till 2002. The results of this study indicate, that the length of the workout-period resulting from different legislation may have a significant impact on loss rates.

Moreover, loss rates vary for different portfolios. Credit loans, for example, tend to result in higher recovery rates than bonds, for example, as they are more senior with respect to the pecking order in case of bankruptcy (Schuermann 2004, p. 4).

Nevertheless, it has been found that recovery rates are usually bi-modally distributed besides other common characteristics listed above (see Schuermann 2004, p. 4). Further references on LGD studies can be found in Altman et al. (2005).[183]

3.3.5.1.2 LGD estimates based on simulation or analytical derivation

For a modeling perspective, LGDs may be modeled **stochastically** opposed to the assumption of fixed LGDs. The LGDs estimates may additionally be independent or dependent on the PD.

One may consider, for example, that the recovery rate is defined by a series of further thresholds below the default threshold as illustrated by Arvanitis and Gregory (2001, p. 59f.) to derive PD-dependent LGDs. Underlying an asset value model the intuition is that "the extent by which the (simulated) asset return falls below the default threshold determines the severity of default and consequently the recovery rate" (Arvanitis and Gregory 2001, p. 59). This approach has the following advantages.[184] First, recovery rates can be introduced

[183] Among the well-known studies on loss rates are Asarnow and Edwards (1995), Carty and Lieberman (1996), Altman and Kishore (1996), Carey (1998) and Altman and Saunders (1998) and, more recently, Acharya et al. (2003), Araten et al. (2004) and Grunert and Weber (2005), for example.

[184] See Arvanitis and Gregory (2001).

without drawing an additional set of random numbers, what makes the approach efficient. Second, correlation among recovery rates can be introduced.

Besides, recovery rates may be handled by means of a beta distribution as introduced by JP Morgan and illustrated by Arvanitis and Gregory (2001), for example. Calibrated beta-distributions for recovery rates conditional on their seniority are shown below.

Figure 3-5: Example recovery rates by seniority (J.P. Morgan 1997, p.80)[185]

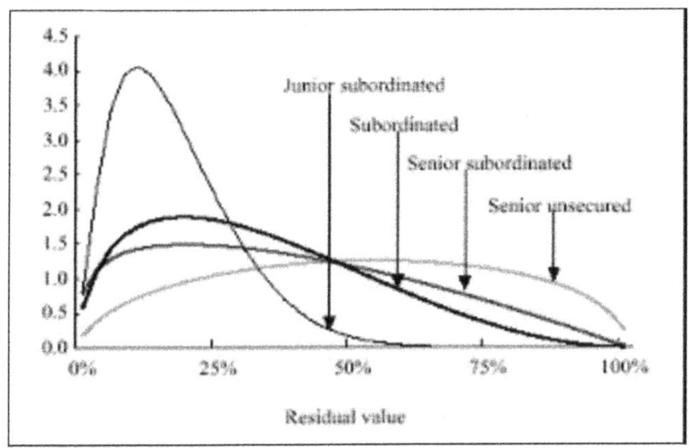

3.3.5.2 The handling of the LGD within the framework

In general, there are basically three assumptions how to treat an empirically derived loss rate that is used for ex ante forecasting of LGDs:[186]

- As a **fixed LGD,**
- As a **stochastic LGD independent of the PD** and
- As a **stochastic LGD dependent on the PD**.

Given the difficulties in dealing with LGDs and recovery rates at the current state, we will refer to empirically derived, fixed[187] LGDs (through-the-cycle

185 The y-axis displays the probability for the occurrence of a specific recovery rate.

186 See Arvanitis and Gregory (2001) and Allen and Saunders (2003), for example.

187 In case of the Foundation IRB approaches, for example, the Basel committee underlies a fixed LGD of 45 %.

LGD) for the S&P's rating classes as shown in Table 3-6.[188] Alternatively, point-in-time LGDs may be used according to a portfolio manager's preferences.

3.3.6 Maturity

The term of a credit is an important component of credit risk especially for illiquid credit loans, as the pre-defined repayment process may not be fulfilled in the foreseen pattern and this risk raises obviously the longer the exposure is held.

Indeed, empirical default rates do not augment linearly over time[189], especially for investment grades. Conceptually, it is common to refer to average (effective) maturities (e.g. the duration).[190]

The Basel IRB formulas have been calibrated so that it accounts for the fact that for longer maturities higher risks for the deterioration of a borrower's creditworthiness have to be foreseen. We will refer to capital ratios oriented on BCBS's proposal which refer to an average (effective) maturity (in the sense of the Basel Committee, Basel 2004, para. 320) of 2.5 years as shown in section 5. Extensions to this modeling approach may conveniently be done.

3.4 Credit risk management for single obligors

3.4.1 Historical trace of credit analysis

The history of credit analysis has been explained at length by Caouette et al. (1998, p.83f.) and will be briefly reviewed accordingly in the following.

---

188 The LGD may be also modelled stochastically (dependent or independent of the PD), but the additional precision gained tends to be rather small (Arvanitis and Gregory 2001). Recent studies may deliver other results dependent on the specific portfolio.

189 Cumulative default rates for 1 to 10 years can be found in the Appendix (A. H).

190 According to Basel (2004, para. 320), the effective maturity M is defined as "the greater of one year and the remaining effective maturity in years as defined below. In all cases, M will be no greater than 5 years.
For an instrument subject to a determined cash flow schedule, the effective maturity M is defined as: $M = \sum_t t \bullet CF_t / \sum_t CF_t$ where CF_t denotes the cash flows (principal, interest payments and fees) contractually payable by the borrower in period t."

Historically, the major activity of a bank was to finance working capital and trade. Thus, they granted usually only credit secured by collateral. This meant that the decision of granting a loan was "largely a matter of deciding whether the proposed collateral was sufficiently valuable."[191] In the last 50 years, however, new lending policies have emerged as banks have shifted from financiers of working capital to fixed assets. From the 1950s on, banks thereby began to account for the need for long-term credit.

It has been a gradual experience of banks to notice that they needed to focus primarily on a borrower's cash flow as debt must be repaid in cash.[192] Secured lending has therefore been replaced by cash flow lending as the principal activity of a commercial bank.

3.4.2 The process of credit analysis

Caouette et al. (1998, p. 85) compare a credit analyst to a detective and concludes that "Sherlock Holmes would have made a good lending officer" by "trying to anticipate problems that might occur in the future". A flow diagram of the process of credit analysis is shown in the Appendix.

3.4.3 Recent developments in credit decisions

Until the last 20 to 30 years there has almost not been made any difference between the interest rates to be paid by different borrowers, so the question of a lending decision was simply whether to lend or not. Indirect inductive-empirical methods (see section 3.3.4.1.2) delivered a single score representing the creditworthiness of a borrower which has been compared to a selective threshold for this purpose.

With the advent of risk-based pricing, the situation changed drastically. In the future (when risk-adjusted pricing will be fully implemented) credit decision could become quite simple[193]: every borrower can receive credit if they pay an

---

[191] Caouette et al. (1998), p.83.

[192] Caouette et al. (1998), p.83, according to Boyadjian and Warren (1987).

[193] If there would not be an intense competition in the markets, of course.

interest rate according to their risk. Unfortunately, there is a dilemma of risk-adjusted credit lending[194]: borrowers with a higher creditworthiness, who could pay high interest rates are supposed to pay only moderate ones, but borrowers who already suffer a shortage of financial resources are obliged to pay much more. Banks react to this situation by credit rationing, what is recently subject to heavy discussions in the context of Basel II. Further conceptual information about creditrationing can be found in Varian (1993), for example.

3.4.4 Traditional approaches to manage credit risk on the individual level

Although sophisticated credit risk management tools exist, traditional approaches to manage credit risk for single obligors such as credit limits, netting agreements, and collateral arrangements are still commonly used.[195]

3.4.4.1 Credit limits

Credit limits are a traditional methodology to control the maximum exposure of a bank with each borrower (Arvanitis and Gregory 2001). Moreover, a cap on the maximum exposure may be defined by senior management, for example dependent on the specific credit rating of the counterparty. Arvanitis and Gregory (2001, p. 8) remark, however, that credit limits would account for the "Banker's Paradox", since a limit implies "that a financial institution should stop transacting with whom it has a very good relationship, but high exposure". As each bank is likely to have a number of large exposures with certain obligors, Arvanitis and Gregory (2001, p. 8) state that pricing credit granted to these counterparties must "be controlled where possible, and the returns must truly reflect the risk taken". Based on portfolio concepts it has become possible to evaluate credit risk from a portfolio perspective allowing to appropriately compute the risk and return contribution of each position. As limit systems simply consider counterparties on an individual basis and not their (risk and

194 See Stiglitz and Weiss (1981).
195 See Bröker (2000), for example.

return) contributions from the portfolio perspective Arvanitis and Gregory (2001, p.8) claim that an integrated portfolio approach would be "safer and more efficient than the somewhat arbitrary approach of credit lines". Illustrative information about risk-based exposure limits can be found in JP Morgan (1997), for example.

3.4.4.2 Netting agreements

Besides exposure limiting systems, there is another legally binding technique[196] to reduce credit risk, netting agreements. However, netting agreements are relevant only when there is more than one transaction with a counterparty.[197] When it comes to a default event, a netting agreement allows exposures to be aggregated. It is thereby possible to net any amount that is to be received and due with a counterparty and solely the net outstanding amount needs to be transfered. This will reduce the overall loss[198] as without a netting agreement, an obligor would have to pay the whole amount due, while only a fraction of the outstanding amount will be received.

3.4.4.3 Collateral agreements

A third (*'traditional'*) credit risk technique to reduce the amount of a credit position is to demand collateral from the counterparty, as it can usually be sold in the event of default and offset against the losses.[199] However, the risk that the exposure at the time of default will be more than the market value of the collateral usually remains (see Appendix). Especially for commitments the collateral value has to be adjusted and monitored during maturity. As it has been discussed in section 2.5.1.4f., full risk avoidance will not be an appropriate business strategy, as it opens the door for opponents.

---

196 Credit-related contracts that are ensured by a signed master agreement.
197 See Arvanitis and Gregory (2001).
198 See Arvanitis and Gregory (2001).
199 See Arvanitis and Gregory (2001). Aspects of collateral have been explained related to the LGD estimation in the Appendix.

3.5 Credit risk measurement on the portfolio level

"Even though many economic and financial variables fall into distributions that approximate a bell curve, the picture is never perfect. Once again, resemblance to truth is not the same as truth. It is in these outliers and imperfections that the wilderness lurks." Peter Bernstein (1996)[200]

In section 3.2f., the basic credit risk parameters and credit risk measurement techniques for single obligors have been introduced. The number of credit portfolio risk modeling techniques has substantially increased within the last decade, although their number is still considerably lower than in the domain of market risk. Recently, there are, however, tendencies towards global standards with respect to definitions and modeling.

In the following, credit risk measurement on the portfolio level will be discussed both from a theoretical background and a practical perspective. In order to classify credit risk portfolio models in the credit management process (step 3 in Figure 3-6), we refer to Saunders (1999, p. 137), who claims, that the models discussed are mostly "not full-fledged from Markowitz' portfolio theory", but their value lies in the linkage between

- Default correlations and loan portfolio risk and
- Portfolio diversification and loan portfolio risk.

[200] This quotation has been taken from Caouette et al. (1998), p.231.

Figure 3-6: Passive credit risk portfolio models within the framework

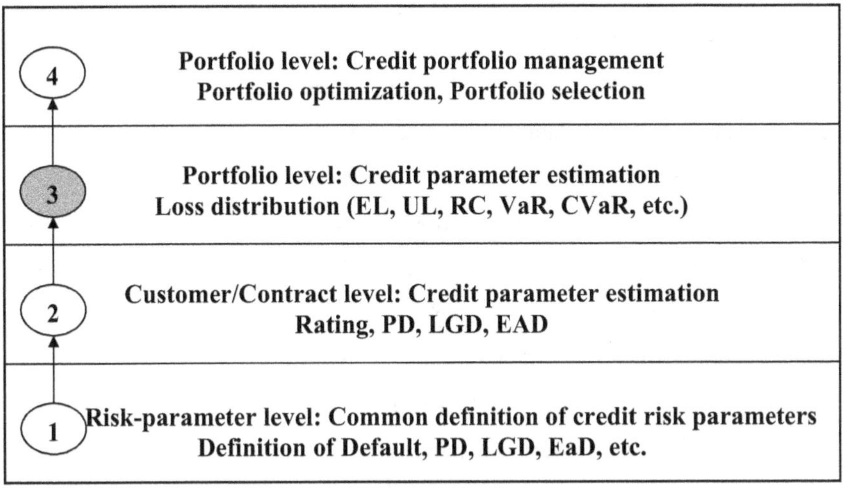

4	**Portfolio level: Credit portfolio management** **Portfolio optimization, Portfolio selection**
3	**Portfolio level: Credit parameter estimation** **Loss distribution (EL, UL, RC, VaR, CVaR, etc.)**
2	**Customer/Contract level: Credit parameter estimation** **Rating, PD, LGD, EAD**
1	**Risk-parameter level: Common definition of credit risk parameters** **Definition of Default, PD, LGD, EaD, etc.**

We will refer to credit risk portfolio models in terms of passive credit risk measurement in contrast to portfolio optimization approaches as presented in section 4.3.

3.5.1 A standardized process to model credit portfolio risk

"In the absence of a *'brilliant'* framework for modeling credit risk"[201] (comprising banking book/trading book/counterparty credit risk), it first has to be decided which elements of credit risk are essential oriented on the fundamental business target, be it to support pricing, capital allocation or portfolio management (Ong 1999, p.62). In the following, we will trace a fairly broad discussion for credit risk modeling and evaluation and indicate how credit portfolio risk is treated within this work.

Figure 3-7 is a simplified graphic to illustrate the relationship between the basic pieces of a *"sound"* internal credit risk portfolio model in order to arrive at the ultimate portfolio outputs according to Ong (1999, p.53).

Naturally, the **initial inputs** (introduced in section 3.2f. as credit risk measures for single borrowers) are vital. The second component of a credit risk

201 An integrated framework would on top incorporate both market and credit risk.

framework is to compute the derived individual credit risk measures[202] (**preliminary output**), comprising expected loss and unexpected loss[203]. Given **supplementary information** and **portfolio effects** (especially macroeconomic effects and default correlations) aggregated portfolio risk measures[204] can be calculated (as a part of the **ultimate outputs**) based on a technical concept[205].

The **ultimate outputs of the internal model** comprise the determination of the risk contribution of single borrowers and portfolio measures related to a credit portfolio's loss distribution, including the portfolio's expected and unexpected loss, the economic capital and other statistical moments (especially the Value-at-Risk (VaR) and conditional VaR). Based on the information available, active credit portfolio management techniques (risk-adjusted pricing, risk-adjusted performance measurement and active portfolio management) are enabled.

202 Denoted with an index i.

203 The ultimate risk contribution of a single asset (the unexpected loss from a top-down perspective) can be derived only from an aggregated portfolio perspective.

204 Denoted with an index p.

205 Ong (1999), p.55: "In order to attach a statistical confidence level to the capital required as a buffer against insolvency, the bank needs to use tools (technical concepts) like Monte Carlo simulation and extreme value theory (EVT) to arrive at a desired loss distribution for the portfolio." Eligible techniques will be introduced below.

Figure 3-7: Essential components of a sound internal[206] credit risk model (according to Ong 1999, p.54)

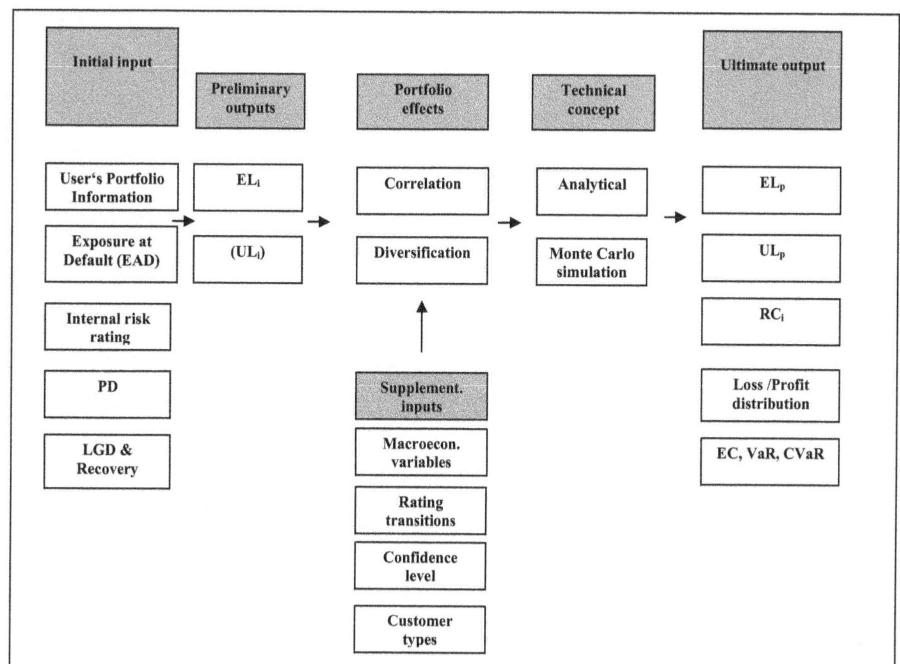

In the following, the major components and methodologies to enable sound credit risk portfolio modeling will be presented.

3.5.1.1 Initial input and preliminary output

In order to give an answer the question "how much credit exposure does a bank have in the event of borrower defaults or credit migrations, and how much of that exposure is the bank likely to lose?"[207] one is obliged to calculate primarily the three basic parameters of credit risk management: the EAD, the PD and the LGD (RR). The latter two are often assigned to each obligor according to their rating. Then one will be able to derive the expected loss (EL) which is just the product of the three basic parameters, and the unexpected loss, which is the volatility of credit loss (UL) or "unanticipated" loss of each obligor.

206 Internal means that the model has been built up internally within a FI.

207 Ong (1999), p.56.

By underlying a simple analytical two-state default process (default or non-default) over a fixed period of time[208] the expected and unexpected loss for a single obligor can be derived according to two equations (see Ong 1999, p.102 and p.113, respectively):

$$EL = EaD \bullet LGD \bullet PD \text{ and}$$

$$UL = EAD \bullet \sqrt{PD \bullet \sigma_{LGD}^2 + LGD \bullet \sigma_{PD}^2},$$

where the variance of the default probability is just $\sigma_{PD}^2 = PD \bullet (1-PD)$, the variance of a binomial distribution.[209]

It can be observed that a single borrower's EL and UL depend on exactly the same variables, except that the expression for UL contains additional second-order standard deviation statistics, where σ_{LGD} and σ_{PD} denote the volatility of the LGD and the PD (Ong 1999). An illustrative example is given in section 3.5.1.5.4.

Moving away from a rather simple analytical two-state default process to more sophisticated default processes, the unexpected loss for single credit entities can only be derived top-down from the portfolio perspective.

3.5.1.2 Portfolio effects

According to Ong (1999, p.135) there are three major effects influencing credit portfolio risk. More precisely, it is crucial to identify a credit portfolio's

- **Correlation structure** (the default/asset correlations),
- **Granularity structure** (the size distribution of single exposures) and
- **Degree of diversification** (the size distribution across industry sectors and countries).

in order to model portfolio effects.

---

[208] See Ong (1999), for example.

[209] Ong (1999, p.114) remarks, however, that in practice it would be "unclear whether or not the assumption of statistical independence [of PD and LGD which underlies this analytical formula for the derivation of the UL] is well justified." Nevertheless, if dependence is assumed, then "only small corrective modification to the expression of the UL" is needed (see Ong 1999, p.114).

The effects are linked through the relationship between a portfolio's unexpected loss and the corresponding individual asset's risk contributions, subject to section 3.5.1.5.2 and 3.5.1.5.3. Major aspects of the three effects will be described below.

3.5.1.2.1 Correlations

In general, it can be stated that the higher the degree of correlation within a credit portfolio, the greater is the volatility of the portfolio value (Ong 1999). It is crucial to consider two levels of correlations for credit portfolios (Ong 1999, p. 136):

- Correlation of default and
- Correlation of credit quality.

Indeed, "the two are related, but not the same" (Ong 1999, p.136). In a binary (i.e. a two-state) default process of either solvency or insolvency (a DM model as explained in section 3.2.1.3) over a pre-specified period of time, it is essential to determine the degree of default correlations, what has been expressed by Ong (1999, p.136) as follows: "How does the default of one obligor affect the well-being (or default status) of other obligors in the portfolio?".

In a multi-stage default process which accounts for credit migration (denoted as MTM model, see section 3.2.1.3), the question alters to (Ong 1999, p.136/137): "How does the credit quality movement of one obligor affect the credit quality of other obligors in the portfolio?".

3.5.1.2.1.1 Default correlations

When one intends to consider a very simple example for correlations, default correlation is caused if one firm is a creditor of another (Lucas 1995). More generally, however, it depicts that the performances of individual companies are linked together via the health of their specific industry or country or via the health of the general economy (sector and market correlation).[210] Lucas (1995,

[210] See Lucas (1995).

p.76) expresses this fact briefly by stating that "to a certain extent, all companies suffer or prospect together."

The division of default and default (or asset) correlation into that

- caused by the general economy and
- that caused by more specific industry and regional factors.

is similar to the concept of systematic and non-systematic risk in equity prices (see Figure 3-8). Default risk caused by the health of the general economy or by the specific industry (firm-external factors) is non-diversifiable, like the systematic risk in the equity market, while default risk caused by the health of a specific company (firm-internal factors), like the idiosyncratic non-systematic equity price risk of individual companies is diversifiable.[211]

Important findings with respect to default correlations can briefly be summarized according to Lucas 1995 based on Moody's research 1970-1993 as follows:

- Default correlations are generally low although they decrease as ratings increase.[212]
- Default correlations generally increase initially with time and then decrease as the horizon extends longer.[213]
- Default among and between specific industries are inconclusive.

Modeling default correlations (and/or asset correlations, see below) is at the same time one of the most crucial things and within the most difficult tasks in credit risk theory.

---

[211] See Figure 3-8.

[212] Ong (2001, p.138) gives a striking comment on that: "Default correlations among highly rated obligors are very small since defaults for these obligors, besides being rare events, are typically the result of obligor-specific problems. Lower-rated obligors on the cusp of default are more susceptible to downturns in the economy and are, therefore, more likely to default en masse in line with shifts in the state of the general economy."

[213] Ong (2001, p.138) elaborates this further: "The explanation may be that the occurrence of defaults over a shorter horizon is necessarily random in nature and the decrease over longer time periods may be caused by the relationship to the average business cycle."

3.5.1.2.1.2 Asset correlations[214]

Besides referring to empirical default correlations (e.g. via the variability of historical default rates) the dependency of equity prices may be used to determine the joint default process of a portfolio and thereby to infer the asset correlations between a portfolio's obligors as asset values are not directly observable in the markets.[215] In the second step, the default correlations can be calculated based on the asset correlations.

The idea behind the concept of asset correlations is to circumvent the lack of default event data (information about default correlations). For non-traded creditors, asset correlations may be estimated via the correlation of comparable firm's stock market returns, for example.

Principally, the concept of asset correlations is very similar to the concept of default correlations. There are, nevertheless, just additional grades of creditworthiness to be taken into account.

The most recent Basel Accord (the QIS 3) foresees predefined asset correlations dependent on a borrower's rating class (and the firm size and portfolio type) and will be presented in section 3.5.2.4.

3.5.1.2.1.3 Default vs. asset correlation

The relationship of default and asset correlation in formal terms is shown below.

3.5.1.2.1.4 The determination of correlations of a credit portfolio

In general, (default) correlations can be estimated in one of the three ways (Ong 1999, p.139):

- Given two obligors' asset volatilities and their variance-covariance structure, their joint probability of default may be calculated analytically and the default correlation may be imputed **(analytical approach)**.

[214] Further information about asset correlations can be found in Ong (1999), for example.

[215] However, Moody's KMV provides asset values, which are determined based on a proprietary model.

- Based on the specific choice of a risky debt model Monte Carlo simulation may be used and the covariance structure may be imputed **(simulation approach)**.
- The third way is to use historical default data by statistically calculating pairwise correlation of default **(empirical approach)**.

For traded obligations, Ong (1999, p.139) evaluates the three approaches as follows: The "brute force" approach based on historical data does not capture any obligor-specific information and therefore "the results can be difficult to interpret." Monte Carlo simulation has the limitation of speed and "enormous number-crunching requirements" and may therefore not be a practical solution. According to Ong (1999, p.139), only the analytical alternative remains as a feasible solution for the estimation of default correlations, which can be derived "from obligor-specific information, namely the asset volatilities and their market-implied asset correlation".

We will present the estimation of correlations based on an analytical and empirical approach in the following.

3.5.1.2.1.4.1 Analytical approach

In case of an analytical representation of a (credit) portfolio's correlation structure, factor models are favored. Besides, multivariate normal distributions offer a convenient way to handle correlations. However, it has to be critically noted that it is not clear whether the joint-default distribution is really normal (Ong 1999, p.139).

Using multivariate normal distributions allows **incorporating multiple correlations**[216] and thereby to go beyond pairwise correlations, as the correlation structure among binary variables is not completely specified by them (Arvanitis and Gregory 2001). More sophisticated approaches like the so-called first passage time model are possible to relax the assumption of normal

[216] The multivariate normal distribution has the attractive property that its entire correlation structure is defined by its covariance matrix, so that all the higher order default probabilities are uniquely determined by the pairwise correlations.

distribution (Ong 1999, p. 150f.). In the following, we will briefly present the normal distribution case for demonstration purposes accompanied by an example.

The default correlation between two obligors i and j can mathematically be derived as follows (see Ong 1999, p.139):

$$\rho_{ij} = \frac{PD_{ij} - PD_i \bullet PD_j}{\sqrt{PD_i \bullet (1 - PD_i)} \bullet \sqrt{PD_j \bullet (1 - PD_j)}}$$

where $PD_{ij} = PD_i + PD_j - PD_{i+j}$ is the joint probability of default and PD_{i+j} is the probability that at least one obligor has defaulted. As there are two unknown elements in the latter equation (the default of both obligors or of the default of at least one of the obligors), there are two ways to proceed (Ong 1999, p. 139):

- Derive the joint probability of default, PD_{ij}, based on a certain assumptions about their joint distribution; or
- Calculate the probability for the occurrence of at least one default (PD_{i+j}).

Given that each default probability is assumed to be standard normal, PD_{ij} is jointly bivariate standard normal (Ong 1999, p. 141):

$$\text{JPD}=\text{PD}_{ij}=\frac{1}{2\pi\sqrt{1-\rho^2}}\int_{-10}^{DD_i}\int_{-10}^{DD_j}\exp\left(-\frac{1}{2(1-\rho^2)}\left[\left(\frac{x}{S_i}\right)^2-2\rho\left(\frac{xy}{S_iS_j}\right)+\left(\frac{y}{S_j}\right)^2\right]\right)dxdy$$

We will proceed with an illustrative example according to Ong (1999, p.140f.) given pairwise asset correlations. The asset correlation between asset i and asset j may be $\rho := 0.19$. Hence, the calculation of the respective default probabilities for asset i and j are given by $PD_i = 0.0062$ and $PD_j = 0.0025$, resulting in asset volatilities of $S_i = 0.3$ and $S_j = 0.6$ for obligor i and j.

Based on the upper limits of integration, which are $DD_i = -0.75$ and $DD_j = -1.404$ respectively for the joint probability of default (JPD)[217], the JDP can be calculated resulting in JDP = $6.5 \bullet 10^{-5}$.

Using the formula for the estimation of the default correlation between A and B leads to

$$\text{Default } \rho_{ab} = \frac{\text{JDP} - \text{PD}_a \bullet \text{PD}_b}{\sqrt{\text{PD}_a \bullet (1-\text{PD}_a)} \bullet \sqrt{\text{PD}_b \bullet (1-\text{PD}_b)}} = 0.0013$$

According to Ong (1999, p. 141) the integration required for the estimation of the JDP "can be simplified to a standardized unit bivariate normal distribution without using the asset volatilities at all".

3.5.1.2.1.4.2 Empirical approach

There is "very strong empirical evidence" that default correlations are lower than asset correlations (Ong 1999, p. 141). Furthermore, correlations of obligors within the same industry tend to be significantly higher as on average over the whole portfolio (Ong 1999), although this result is weakened by more recent studies (e.g. Fu et al. 2004). In the following, empirical data for default and asset correlations will be presented.

Asset correlations

The asset and default correlation structure between customers has empirically been traced by J.P. Morgan (1997) and is shown in Table 3-8 and Table 3-9, respectively, according to Arvanitis and Gregory (2001).

[217] Which is NormInv (PD_a,0,S_a)=ϕ^{-1}(0.0062;0;0.3) and ϕ^{-1}(0.0025;0;0.6) in terms of an MsExcel formula.

Table 3-8: Asset correlations (according to Arvanitis and Gregory 2001, p. 63)

	AAA	AA	A	BBB	BB	B	CCC
AAA	0.28	0.28	0.26	0.24	0.2	0.19	0.19
AA		0.28	0.26	0.24	0.2	0.19	0.19
A			0.24	0.22	0.18	0.17	0.17
BBB				0.2	0.16	0.15	0.15
BB					0.11	0.11	0.11
B						0.1	0.1
CCC							0.1

It can be observed that the asset correlations between better rated customers are higher than between worse rated borrowers. This might be a consequence of the higher influence of systematic risk factors[218] on defaults of investment grades with a healthy firm (idiosyncratic risk) structure. Nevertheless, the paucity of empirical credit risk data has to be taken into account as a caveat and furthermore these data are derived from the very largest firms, which do make up only a very small percentage of obligors.

For traded debt, information about asset correlations is, in fact, available as opposed to default correlations, e.g. by relying on Moody's KMV asset values. Credit risk models based on the option pricing theory and firm-value models do incorporate default correlations via the correlation of the asset returns. In doing so, the empirical database to estimate asset correlations is far more extensive than default correlations based on non-traded debt.[219]

Bluhm et al. (2003) claim that reasonable ranges based on empirical evidence show that for retail portfolios an average asset correlation of [1%;5%] can be expected.[220] For the wholesale business, they same authors assume relatively high asset correlations between 40 and 60%. The revised framework (Basel 2004) underlies average asset correlations of [0.12;0.24] for the corporate and

[218] "*Systematic correlation*" between customers is commonly referred to by means of cyclical effects (GDP growth, market interest rate, unemployment rate, stock index, etc.).

[219] We will therefore refer to asset correlations to perform a simulation for the default process of a portfolio in section 5.

[220] Bluhm et al. (2003).

[0.04; 0.15] for the retail business (see section 3.5.2.4.2).[221]

Moody's estimate the average asset correlations for corporate bonds to be around 25%[222] and Ong (1999, p. 145) claims that the asset correlation across a portfolio would be in the range of 20 to 35%.

Blache and Bluhm (2001) assume that the asset correlation structure of different customer types is as follows:

- ρ= 0.01: A very well - diversified retail portfolio.
- ρ= 0.10: Portfolios of SME customers.
- ρ= 0.30: Wholesale credit portfolio.

Default correlations

Empirical data provided by JP Morgan (1997) for default correlations is shown below.

Table 3-9: Default correlations (according to Arvanitis and Gregory 2001, p. 63)

	ρ (i,i)
AAA	No data
AA	0.0033
A	0.01
BBB	0.0069
BB	0.014
B	0.0327
CCC	No Data

Ong (1999, p.141) documents a "typical range of default correlation" between 1 and 5% on average.

3.5.1.2.1.5 The handling of correlations in this work

According to Ong (1999, p.149), the determination of correlations can be considered as a *'dilemma'* as the main trouble is "the absence of direct empirical

221 These asset correlations, however, do also account for name and sector concentration, as these effects are not covered by BCBS's one-factor-model.

222 Bluhm et al. (2003).

observation of *'simultaneous defaulting events'* from the market over a reasonable period of time" and "not an issue of methodology, of mathematics or of its effects on portfolio concentration and diversification."

However, it would not be prudent (Ong 1999, p.149) to assume independence between the obligors in a portfolio, as there is "very strong evidence" (see Moody's 1997, for example) that insolvencies and the creditworthiness of borrowers are correlated. As the credit portfolio's unexpected loss is the higher, the greater the non-zero credit correlation are, correlation is essential for portfolio managers.[223] By consequence, it would be vital to incorporate credit correlations and to understand their effect (Ong 1999).

Besides the lack of directly observable empirical data it is problematic to consider all possible pairwise default or asset correlations within a large credit portfolio. Obligors are therefore usually grouped by industries and assigned correlations accordingly (see Ong 1999, for example).

Within the credit risk management framework in section 5, given non-traded obligations related to lower correlations and a higher influence of non-systematic risk, a constant pairwise asset correlation structure of 20% has been used, oriented on Arvanitis and Gregory's (2001) correlation matrix (see Table 3-8). The asset correlations have been incorporated into the modeling procedure in terms of the simulation of the stochastic default process of the whole credit portfolio based on a firm value model. For a credit portfolio comprising retail and SME borrowers the asset correlation is assumed to be rather high, but conservative and closely oriented on the regulatory proposal. For the determination of the risk capital, the asset correlation has been chosen according to the revised framework (2004).

3.5.1.2.1.6 Generation of correlated default events by simulation

A methodology to generate correlated default events based on the multivariate normal distribution has been provided by Arvanitis and Gregory (2001, p.55f.),

[223] See Ong (1999).

for example. This section will follow their explanation. The procedure has been used for the simulation of the portfolio's stochastic default process in section 5. In order to simulate correlated (default) events, one can draw from the following correlated multivariate normal distribution[224]:

$$\tilde{Y} = \begin{pmatrix} \tilde{Y}_1 \\ \tilde{Y}_2 \end{pmatrix} \sim N\left(\begin{pmatrix} 0 \\ 0 \end{pmatrix}, \begin{pmatrix} 1 & \dots & \lambda_{ij} \\ \dots & \dots & \dots \\ \lambda_{ij} & \dots & 1 \end{pmatrix} \right) \sim N(0,\Lambda)$$

It is important to notice that the underlying correlation matrix does not represent the default events themselves, but instead the correlation among the multivariate normal variables. It has been shown by Morisson (1976), for example, that if a random vector Y has a multivariate normal distribution N(0,I)[225], then $\tilde{Y} = AY$ has a multivariate normal $N(0, AA')$ distribution. Therefore, it is necessary to factorize the normal correlation matrix according to $\Lambda = AA'$ in order to simulate normal variables according to the latter equation.

A possible solution to this problem is Cholesky decomposition or Eigenvalue decomposition.[226] The procedure is to multiply a vector of uncorrelated normal variables Y by the matrix A. Finally, the correlated default variables $\tilde{Y}_i$ can be transformed into correlated default variables given by $d_i = 1_{\tilde{Y}_i \le k_i}$.

The formal process of the Cholesky decomposition can be found in Meyer (1999, p.442f.), for example, and has been implemented in an Excel add-in macro called *'Corand'*[227] that will be used in section 5.

3.5.1.2.2 Granularity and loss event modeling

Our general assumption with respect to a portfolio's granularity structure is that we deal with a homogeneous credit portfolio comprising loans with credit

224 See Arvanitis and Gregory (2001), p.55.

225 I is the identity matrix, so this is just a vector of uncorrelated normal variables.

226 Further information can be found in Press et al. (1992) or Meyer (1999).

227 For further information see www.kellogg.nwu.edu/faculty/myerson/ftp/addins.htm. Rev. Dec. 2004.

exposures of one currency unit.[228] In case of SME and retail customers, especially for leasing and finance companies, for example, this is a reasonable and realistic approach.[229] In so far, granularity effects will play a subordinated role and will be neglected.

3.5.1.2.3 The effect of diversification for a credit portfolio

A comprehensive model to evaluate diversification aspects of credit portfolio risk must include treatments of two distinct types of risk (according to the classification within the market risk sphere):[230]

- *Systematic default risk* and
- *Non-systematic default risk.*

Systematic and non-systematic default risk refers to portfolio risk linked to systematic and idiosyncratic factors, respectively. As opposed to market risk, default correlations between two obligors are always positive and therefore the diversification potential in credit portfolios is more limited and therefore a higher portion of *systematic credit risk* remains (see Figure 3-8 below).

Non-systematic risk (also called obligor-specific or idiosyncratic risk) denotes the portion of credit risk that may be exploited by means of diversification, as the firm-specific creditworthiness of a high number of firms is unlikely to worsen at the same time. Systematic credit risk, however, is not diversifiable. The relationship between systematic and non-systematic risk is graphically illustrated below.

---

[228] It has been assumed that clump risks must be considered by credit risk management before using a portfolio selection framework.

[229] Captive leasing and finance companies, for example, do mostly have contracts with a homogenous size, e.g. in the automotive industry.

[230] See Hickman and Wollman (2002), for example.

Figure 3-8: Diversification: Systematic and non-systematic risk (Heim and Balica 2001, p. 220)

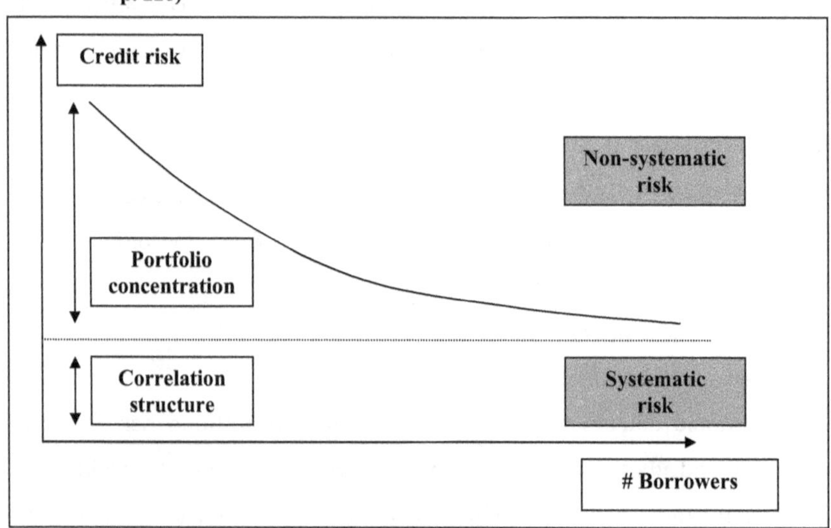

Diversification allows seeking for an average risk result below the expected loss. UBS, for example, established a department called *'risk transformation'* with the target to reduce the occurred losses below the EL based on diversification.[231]

3.5.1.2.3.1 The handling of diversification in this work

The portfolio problem imposed in this work is to manage large, well-diversified portfolios that are homogeneous with respect to exposure, correlation and maturity. In so far, a well-diversified portfolio has been a precondition for modeling purpose. Precondition rules to ensure diversification will be discussed in section 5.4.

3.5.1.3 Supplementary inputs

3.5.1.3.1 Market parameters

Cyclical effects play a crucial role for the determination of credit risk as it has been shown in section 3.3.4, e.g. for the PD. We will therefore refer to credit

[231] See UBS (2000).

risk parameters that are assumed to represent credit risk parameters *'through-the-cycle'*[232]. Future extensions to point-in-time-variables are possible.

3.5.1.3.2 Credit migration probabilities

As opposed to a DM distiguishing solely between default or non-default events, a MTM model allows the distinction of additional states of creditworthiness. In case of a MTM model, losses may already occur as a consequence of a downgrade to a worse rating class. Despite the fact that downgrades cannot be understood as default events, a bank will discount future cash flows at a higher risky rate, or, equivalently, its future expected losses will increase (Arvanitis et al. 2001, p.6). By consequence, a downgrade will cause a decline of the present value of the outstanding payments and therefore a loss if a position is mark-to-market.[233]

Rating transition probabilities are usually depicted by a credit migration matrix, distinguishing between different periods of time. It is common to use historical transition matrices (see e.g. Moody's 1997), which represent average rating transition probabilities based on thousands of firm years and data (Arvanitis et al. 2001, p.13).[234]

A historical one-year-transition matrix provided by Moody's is shown in Table 3-10 which has been determined from a time period of 1920 till 1996. The initial rating at the beginning of the year is shown in the first row, while the first column corresponds to the final rating at the end of the year. The default probabilities are shown in the last column. Given an initial Baa-rated firm, the probability of a downgrade to Ba is 4.76%, for example. The worst outcome of

[232] It is usually assumed that credit risk parameters are oriented on the general state of the economy and economic cycles.

[233] See section 3.2.1.3.

[234] The stability of transition matrixes across time has been traced by Nickell et al. (1998), for example.

the Baa-company would be insolvency, which occurs with a probability of 0.15%.[235]

Table 3-10: Moody's one-year-transition matrix (1920-1996) (in %)

	Aaa	Aa	A	Baa	Ba	B	Caa	Default
Aaa	93.4	5.94	0.64	0.00	0.02	0.00	0.00	0.00
Aa	1.61	90.55	7.46	0.26	0.09	0.01	0.00	0.02
A	0.07	2.28	92.44	4.63	0.45	0.12	0.01	0.00
Baa	0.05	0.26	5.51	88.48	4.76	0.71	0.08	0.15
Ba	0.02	0.05	0.42	5.16	86.91	5.91	0.24	1.29
B	0.00	0.04	0.13	0.54	6.35	84.22	1.91	6.81
Caa	0.00	0.00	0.00	0.62	2.05	4.08	69.2	24.06

In some circumstances, it may not be appropriate or even possible to incorporate credit transitions due to the lack of data to regularly update the creditworthiness of obligors (e.g. for illiquid credit loan portfolios). Additionally, the sample to derive a stable transition matrix has to be of a substantial size, what will often be critical. We therefore do not incorporate rating transition effects within the framework in section 5.

3.5.1.3.3 Confidence level

The confidence level is required by the nature of statistical modeling as it is not possible to cover all possible outcomes, as these could be infinite in theory.

It is therefore usual to define a level of confidence assuring confidently that the potential loss in value over the given time period will not exceed a certain amount (see section 3.5.1.5.5). Each financial institution will define a confidence level for its credit risk policy according to the desire of its external

[235] Further important aspects of the transition matrix have been summarized by Arvanitis and Gregory (2001, p. 13): "There are clearly some inconsistencies in the transition matrix below. For example, the probability of default of an A- rated counterparty is zero; yet, there is a non-zero probability that a supposedly more credit-worthy Aa-rated counterparty will go bankrupt." It is obvious that the inconsistencies are a result of the lack of data for these extremely unlikely events. Additionally, the most likely outcome is that the credit rating remains unchanged, regardless of the category. Transition matrices for longer periods have been published by Moody's (1997), for example. It is important to notice that there is a *mean-reversion effect* in credit ratings, since good ratings (Aaa, Aa, A) are more likely to get worse rather than to get better, whereas poor ratings (Ba, B, Caa) have a greater probability of improving (assuming that they do not default first!). See e.g. Douglas et al. (2004), p.23 in the Appendix.

standing and creditworthiness as illustrated in section 4.2.2.2. Directly related to the confidence level is the amount of risk capital necessary to conduct lending (economic/regulatory capital, section 3.5.1.5.6.3). The higher the confidence level, the higher the level of capital for loss cushion will be. We will refer to a risk capital policy referring to a 99.9% - confidence level.

3.5.1.3.4 Customer types

The Basel II framework (see Basel 2003 or Basel 2004) foresees two general types of customers, retail and corporate (wholesale). Retail customers are usually assumed to have a lower probability of insolvency (e.g. Basel 2004). For the derivation of the "economic" capital in section 5, BCBS's formula for corporate customers[236] (QIS 3, Basel 2002) has been used.

3.5.1.4 Technical concept

In the following, a partial set of scientific concepts for credit risk portfolio modeling will be presented and discussed step by step followed by the state-of-the-art tools based on these theoretical concepts which are used within FIs.

Classification and overview on credit risk portfolio models

So far, **no classification standard** according to specific criteria **for credit risk portfolio models** has been established (e.g. Ott 200, p.81). Schweizer (2001) proposed that credit risk portfolio models may be clustered according to three major dimensions:

- The underlying credit risk definition **(risk term)**,
- The incorporation of default interdependencies between the obligors **(risk interdependencies)** and
- The fundamental technical concept **(technical concept)**.

The first dimension, how credit risk is generally addressed, distinguishes between DM models and MTM models. Default interdependencies

[236] More specifically, we refer to the formula in para. 272 of the revised Framework (Basel 2004).

(correlations) may generally be modeled via a theoretical framework based on (empirical) asset correlations or historical default correlations. For the derivation of the probability distribution (of loss), an analytical or simulation framework may be used. It has to be noted, that all three dimensions are not exclusive, i.e. it is common to combine an analytical approach with a simulation, for example.

Figure 3-9: Classification of credit portfolio models (according to Schweizer 2001)

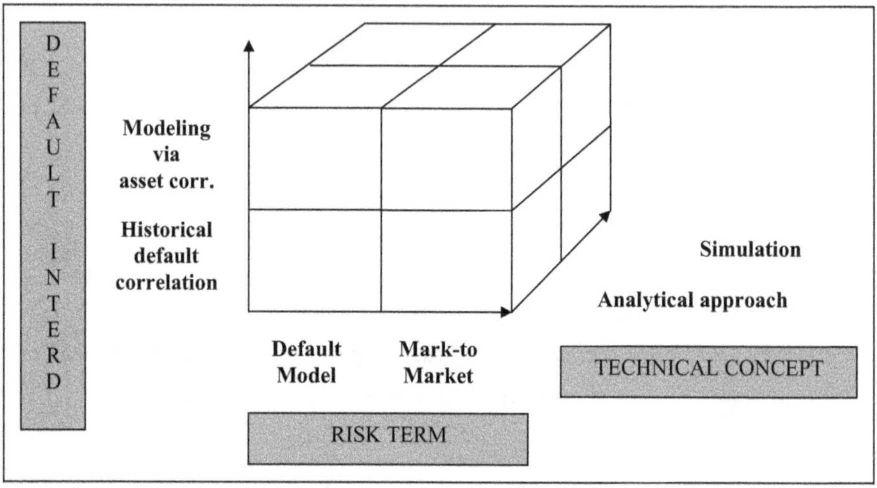

According to Ott (2001), it may alternatively be reasonable to refer to the default event as distinctive characteristic of credit risk models, for example.

3.5.1.4.1 Credit risk models according to the risk term

A standardized classification of credit risk portfolio models according to default models (DM[237]) and mark-to-market models (MTM) has been proposed by the Federal Reserve System Task Force on internal credit risk models (1998) and Basel (1999). The drawback of this attempt is that it includes both the kind of the considered credit event and the chosen evaluation approach and therefore leads to delimitation problems.[238] One of the state-of-the-art industrial credit risk models, CreditPortfolioView (to be explained below), for example, underlies a

[237] The difference between default models and mark-to-market- models has been introduced in section 3.2.1.3.

[238] Ott (2001).

DM for non-traded positions as opposed to a MTM framework for the traded part of the portfolio.

3.5.1.4.2 Credit risk models according to default interdependencies

Distinct methods and basic aspects for the estimation of correlations between obligors in a portfolio have been presented in section 3.5.1.2.1.4.

Modeling asset value correlations is usually done via a factor model. The simplest model has one factor and a uniform asset correlation. The specification of a correlation matrix and drawing of asset values from a multivariate distribution is an attempt that is less common.

Alternatively, correlations may be estimated through the variability of historical default rates.[239] The application of the two available concepts in industry models will be explained in section 3.5.2.

3.5.1.4.3 Credit risk models according to their technical concept

From the perspective of the technical concept of credit risk models, analytical methods and simulation methods have to be distinguished what will subsequently be described at length.

3.5.1.4.3.1 Analytical methods[240]

Analytical credit risk portfolio models aim at approximating a real credit portfolio's loss distribution, which is often unknown by means of a (closed-form) statistical loss distribution. The statistical loss distribution is subsequently used "as a substitute for the *true* loss distribution of the original portfolio" (Bluhm et al. 2003, p. 37).

The common approach in practice is straightforward. Usually, statistical distributions with two (or more) degrees of freedom are selected, which are supposed to adequately represent the characteristic form of credit portfolio's loss or return distributions as shown in the Appendix.[241]

---

239 What is the concept used by CreditRisk+, for example.

240 We will follow Bluhm et al. (2003) to explain how analytical methods are used within credit portfolio risk management.

241 See Bluhm et al. (2003), for example.

Based on the preferably wide set of available information about the true credit portfolio (e.g. credit rating, PD, LGD, EAD) the characterizing moments (usually the first (EL) and second moment (UL)) of the statistical distribution are calibrated. While the determination of the first moment (EL) is relatively simple, the UL can only be computed with a specification of the correlation structure of a credit portfolio. In the simplest case, "one has to make an assumption regarding an *average default correlation* ρ."[242]

Subsequently, it is a reasonable procedure to calibrate several promising statistical distributions in order to arrive at the distribution best matching the true portfolio (Bluhm et al. 2003).

In the following, a selective choice of representative analytical approaches will be presented.

3.5.1.4.3.1.1 Binomial and Poisson distribution

In case of a binary two-state default mode model, the usage of **the binomial distribution** "is most natural" (Bluhm et al. 2003, p.55).[243] A rival alternative is to use the **Possion distribution.**[244] We will follow Bluhm et al. (2003) for a brief discussion of the two alternatives.

The strong law of large numbers implies that for large m and small p $B(m;p) \approx Pois(pm)$.[245] Setting $\lambda = pm$ shows that under the assumption of independent defaults a portfolio's absolute gross loss $L = \sum L_i$ of a Bernoulli loss statistics $(L_1,...,L_m)$ with a uniform default probability p can be approximated by a Poisson variable $L \sim Pois(\lambda)$.

However, the strong law of large numbers does not guarantee that Bernoulli and Poisson approaches are more or less compatible. Nevertheless, several authors (e.g. Gordy (2000b) and Hickman and Koyluoglu (1998)) have made the effort

242 Bluhm et al. (2003), p.37.

243 Bluhm et al. (2003) state that a binomial approach is used by CreditMetrics and the KMV-Model, for example. See section 3.5.2.

244 The Poisson distribution has been applied in CreditRisk+, for example. See section 3.5.2.

245 That is, approximation of binomial distributions by means of Poisson distribution.

to derive a common conceptual frame. Indeed, as Bluhm et al. (2003, p.56) state, there are "to some extent (...) relations and common roots of the two approaches."

Bluhm et al. (2003) have shown, however, that there is a systematic difference between Bernoulli and Poisson (mixture) models and that the models are not really compatible. This would be because a binomial model's mixture model[246] can be expected to deliver fatter tails than the corresponding Poisson mixture model.[247] Besides, this hypothesis would also be reflected by the common credit risk models used in practice, namely CreditMetrics/KMV and CreditRisk+ to be presented in section 3.5.2.

3.5.1.4.3.1.2 The normal distribution

It can be supposed that the normal distribution gives "a reasonable approximation around a mean of the credit loss distribution" what, however, does "clearly" not hold true for the tail region of a credit loss distribution (Arvanitis and Gregory 2001, p.18). It can therefore be concluded that the normal distribution, which can be regarded as "a very powerful and convenient tool" in many field, "must be used with extreme caution when analyzing credit portfolios" as their tails are fat and the distribution is non-symmetric (Arvanitis and Gregory 2001, p. 18).

3.5.1.4.3.1.3 The beta distribution

Similarly to the normal distribution, the beta distribution is a parametric probability distribution with two defining moments delimited to the interval [0;1]. The density function of the beta distribution is given by[248]

$$f(x,\alpha,\beta)=\begin{cases}\dfrac{\Gamma(\alpha+\beta)}{\Gamma(\alpha)\Gamma(\beta)}X^{\alpha-1}(1-X)^{\beta-1}, & 0<X<1\\ 0, & \text{Otherwise}\end{cases}$$

246 In order to introduce correlations into the models Bernoulli respectively Poisson variables have to be mixed. See Bluhm et al. (2003), for example.

247 See Bluhm et al. (2003), p. 66.

248 See Ong (1999), p. 165, for example.

including two fixed constant *shape parameters* $\alpha > 0$ and $\beta > 0$, which define the steepness around the mean and the heaviness of the tail, respectively.

The mean (μ) and variance (σ^2) of the beta distribution are given by[249]

$$\mu = \frac{\alpha}{\alpha+\beta} \text{ and } \sigma^2 = \frac{\alpha\beta}{(\alpha+\beta)^2 \bullet (\alpha+\beta+1)}.$$

The beta distribution becomes a uniform distribution on the interval $0<x<1$ when $\alpha = \beta = 1$ (Ong 1999). An illustrative example about moment matching of a credit portfolio can be found in Ong (1999, p. 170f.). A modification of CreditRisk+ using a beta distribution instead of a gamma distribution has been proposed by Arvanitis and Gregory (2001, p.60f.). Besides, the beta distribution is favored for analytical LGD modeling.

3.5.1.4.3.1.4 Extreme Value Theory (EVT)

Worst-case scenarios may conveniently be caputured by means of a technique from actuarial statistics, called extreme value theory (EVT) (see Ong 1999,p.197f., for example).

In the economical practice of risk management and especially credit risk, EVT is aimed at providing solutions in case of insufficient data in the tail regions of loss distributions (Ong 1999). A large class of suitable EVT distributions is called generalized Pareto distribution, comprising the Gumbel, the Fréchet and the Weibull distribution.[250]

---

249 See Ong (1999), p. 166, for example.

250 Ong (1999, p. 200), for example, provides a formal overview on the generalized Pareto distribution (GPD) family, which has three degrees of freedom and is parameterized by

$$G_{\xi,\mu,\psi}(x) = \exp\left\{ -\left(1+\xi \bullet \frac{x-\mu}{\psi}\right)_+^{-\frac{1}{\xi}} \right\} \text{ for } \xi \neq 0$$

with the scale parameter $\psi > 0$, the location parameter $\mu \in R$ and the shape parameter $\xi \in R$.

Thereby, the generalized Pareto family of distributions consists of three well-known distributions:

$\xi = 0$ Gumbel or double exponential,

$\xi > 0$ Fréchet, which has unbounded support to the right; and

Ong (1999, p. 202f.), for example, has shown that "best-fit" with EVT leads to very powerful results. However, it would be "important to justify the application of EVT and to understand the conditions under which the tail-fit is meaningful", especially convergence requirements Ong (1999, p. 204f.).

The following list subsumes some familiar probability distributions in the maximum domain of attraction of the generalized Pareto family (Ong 1999, p. 207):

- Fréchet class: Ordinary Pareto, Burr, log-gamma, Cauchy, Student's t.
- Gumbel class: Normal, Exponential, Gamma, lognormal.
- Weibull class: Beta, Uniform distributions.

EVT has many bibliographical references, e.g. Embrechts et al. (1997), Embrechts et al. (1998), McNeil (1998) and Coles (2001) and a variety of articles and working papers.

3.5.1.4.3.1.5 Copula

Copula[251] functions are a statistical methodology to construct multivariate distributions, which has been recently been rediscovered as a "valuable technique" in risk management (Bluhm et al. 2003, p. 103). As a consequence of

$\xi < 0$ Weibull, which has unbounded support to the left.

[251] According to Bluhm et al. (2003, p. 103) "a copula (function) is a multivariate distribution (function) such that its marginal distributions are standard uniform. A common notation for copulas is

$C(u_1,...,u_m):[0,1]^m \to [0,1]$ if considered in R^m.

The most commonly applied copula function (e.g. in CreditMetrics, KMV) is the normal copula, defined as

$C(u_1,...,u_m) = N_m[N^{-1}[u_1],...,N^{-1}[u_m];\Gamma]$."

The main advantage of more sophisticated sophisticated copulas is to underly portfolio loss variable that allow representing a stronger tail dependency compared to normal copulas (Bluhm et al. 2003). Sklar (1959) has shown that every multivariate distribution with continuous marginals enbles an exclusive copula representation. Additionally, copulas are used as core elements to generate new multivariate distributions with prescribed marginal distribution and correlation structure (Bluhm et al. 2003). Bluhm et al. (2003, p.105f.) provides examples how copulas can be applied to build loss distributions with fatter tails compared to normally distributed asset value log-returns by referring to normal and t-copulas. For other copulas, one can consult Nelson (1999).

the enourmous interest shown towards this technique, Bluhm et al. (2003) state that the literature on the application of copulas to credit risk would currenly explode, impeding to trace every development. They suggest a small set of introductory literature indicating how copulas may be used for common credit risk problems, for example, Li (1999, 2000), Frey and McNeil (2001), Frey, McNeil and Nyfeler (2001), Frees and Valdez (1997), and Wang (1998).

Concerning the application of copula in practice Bluhm et al. (2003, p. 112) conclude that, underlying a copula framework, "a decision of how fat the tails really should be is never easy and sometimes purely subjective", what would probably be "the reason why people very often rely on asset-value models based on the Gaussian copula." As already mentioned, even the estimation of linear correlations is a great challenge and far from being obvious. Thus, Bluhm et al. (2003, p. 112) believe that "more research combined with empirical evidence is necessary before other than normal copulas will become *best practice* in credit risk management."

3.5.1.4.3.1.6 Conclusion for analytical approaches

The choice of the loss distribution is a controversial task that constantly leads to "very strong and emotional disagreement" (Ong 1999, p.163) as modeling the loss distribution by some kind of an analytical approach is accompanied by significant model risk. A critical issue for the choice of the underlying analytical distribution is the resulting tail. Best practice choices for distributions are the gamma distribution, the F-distribution and EVT (Ong 1999).

According to Bluhm et al. (2003, p.40), analytical approximation methodologies "can be applied quite successfully to so-called homogeneous portfolios". Homogenous portfolios consist of credit exposures and/or obligors with similar risk properties.[252] Examples for credit portfolios that may be considered as homogenous are many retail portfolios and credit portfolios of smaller banks,

[252] Bluhm et al. (2003). This means, for example, that there is no concentration of exposures to single name concentration, that the range of PDs is relatively low and that there is a rather low number of industry sectors and industries (see Bluhm et al. 2003, for example).

which operate only in certain regions (Bluhm et al. 2003). For these credit portfolios, analytical approximations may be used "with sufficient precision" (Bluhm et al. 2003, p.40).

According to Arvanitis and Gregory (2001), however, the estimation of tail events should be done by means of a combination of both simulation techniques and analytical tail-fitting. Similarly, Ong (1999, p.164) claims that "perhaps the only sensible tail-fitting procedure might be to combine *both* analytical loss distributions with numerically derived Monte Carlo simulations." Simulation approaches will be presented subsequently.

3.5.1.4.3.2 Simulation methods: Ordinary and Monte Carlo

To understand the principle of Monte Carlo simulation in contrast to ordinary simulation, we will have a brief look at an introductory example according to Caouette et al. (1998, p.109): Instead of assuming a fixed short-term interest rate of 6 percent, it is more likely to underlie normally distributed interest rates with a mean of 6 percent and a standard deviation of 3, for example. Accordingly, there is a 68 percent probability that the interest rate will be between 3 and 9%.[253]

In case of an ordinary simulation, the entire computation is done only once, leading to a particular random result given a set of initial assumptions. By contrast, in case of a Monte Carlo simulation a high number of simulations are performed, which may be as high as millions of times (Caouette et al. 1998). For each simulation, a random outcome set results dependent on the specified distribution.[254] The ultimate result of Monte Carlo simulation is a distribution of outcome values (Palisades 1996). In the following, we will summarize this

[253] This is based on the property of normal distribution, indicating that 68 percent of the realized values will fall within +/- 1 standard deviation and 96 percent will fall within +/- 2 standard deviations.

[254] The law of large numbers is a core pillar of Monte Carlo simulation.

popular approach[255] to generate non-parametric distributions in a more formal way and deal with the proceeding process.

3.5.1.4.3.2.1 The technical concept of Monte Carlo simulation

Monte Carlo simulation can be defined as a "numerical method that infers information about a particular random process (characterized by a probability density function) by utilizing randomly drawn real numbers" (Derviz et al. 2001, p.35). It is thereby assumed that the random process converges to the real process with the number of scenarios augementing to infinity.[256]

The simulated losses are tabulated in form of a histogram in order to obtain a representative loss distribution of the underlying portfolio. Many refinements can be made to the simulation technique, but they must be individually chosen according to the situation at hand.

In the following, we will follow Ong (1999, p.180f.) with a potential (rather rudimentary) stepwise procedure to simulate the loss distribution of a credit portfolio by means of Monte Carlo simulation:

1. *Estimate PDs and LGDs for each exposure*

   In order to estimate defaults and losses, PDs are assigned to each credit based on an internal or external rating, for example.[257] The LGD is set to an industry (or segment) average of 50%, for example. The standard deviation of the LGD may also be required in some estimation as well as further granularity in the LGD depending on the type of collateral.[258]

2. *Estimate asset correlation between obligors*

   A fundamental prerequisite to calculate a credit portfolio's loss distribution is to underly the dependency structure of the portfolio's individual names. If it is not possible to determine all dependency relations, an asset

---

[255] Monte Carlo simulation is used in CreditMetrics, for example, the first wide-spread credit risk portfolio model.

[256] See Derviz et al. (2001), for example.

[257] A set of commonly used methods for PD estimation has been presented in section 3.3.4f.

[258] According to Ong (1999, p.180), "it is interesting to note that both JP Morgan and Moody's KMV hinted at the possibility of using the beta distribution to model LGD."

correlation matrix for industry sectors as used in CreditMetrics may be used, for example (Ong 1999).

3. *Generate correlated default events*

   Ong (1999) suggests the following procedure to generate correlated default events:

   a. Initially, the asset values of all credit entities are simulated by means of random numbers drawn from a uniform or standard normal distribution.
   b. In the second step, the independent random numbers are transformed into correlated random numbers by means of a decomposition technique (e.g. Cholesky, singular value or Eigenvalue).[259]
   c. In the third step, the default point for each exposure is determined according to the underlying default probability (see step 1).
   d. In the final step to generate correlated events, the correlated random numbers representing the obligors' asset values are compared with the corresponding default point. A default event occurs, if a simulated asset value falls below the default point.

4. *Generate random LGDs*

   In case of a default event, a stochastic LGD may be determined, for example, by means of a uniform random number with a mean and standard deviation of the pre-defined average LGD.[260] Alternatively, a fixed LGD may be used.

5. *Loss calculation*

   Based on the default information, the occurred loss as a fraction of the exposure can be calculated for each *defaulted* exposures as $\text{Loss} = \text{Exposure} \bullet \text{LGD}$. *Non-defaulted* credit entities are assigned a loss of

---

[259] Ong (1999) emphasizes that the asset correlation matrix does not necessarily need to be positive definite.

[260] In case of the assumption that the PDs and LGDs are correlated, a more sophisticated methodology may be used.

zero. The credit portfolio's loss is then the sum of the losses of each obligor.

6. *Loss distribution*

   Each simulated portfolio loss scenario will reveal the random total loss of the credit portfolio. A density function of the credit portfolio's loss is subsequently constructed by means of performing the overall portfolio loss simulation with a high frequency, e.g. 100,000 times. The credit portfolio's loss density function is non-parametric as opposed to analytical solutions.

Figure 3-10 represents a simple flow diagram to illustrate the components of the simulation just described according to Ong (1999). Mathematical details of the simulation process are hinted in section 3.5.1.2.1. An example for performing a Monte Carlo simulation with a sample simulation using the steps outlined above can be found in Ong (1999, p. 182f.).

Figure 3-10: Flow diagram of portfolio loss simulation according to Ong (1999,p.181)

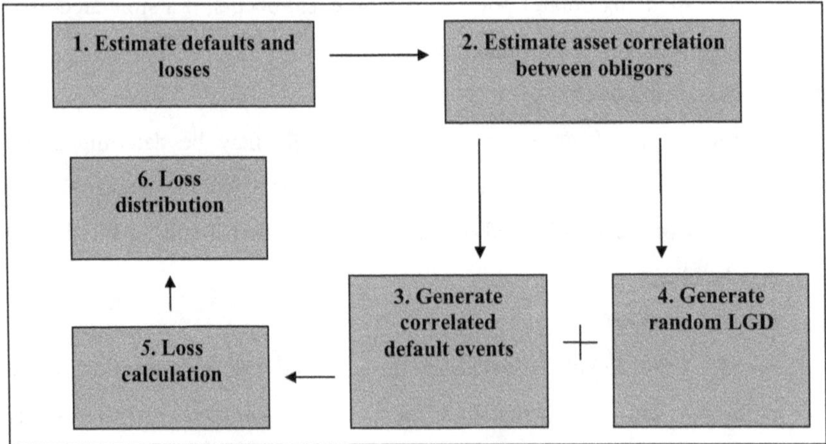

3.5.1.4.3.2.2 Pros and cons of Monte Carlo simulation

The major **advantage** of a Monte Carlo simulation is that it enables to precicely represent a portfolio's correlation structure as opposed to analytical approaches, which are based on a set of assumptions.[261] Additionally, this technique allows incorporating each asset's specific risk characteristics.[262] According to Bluhm et al. (2003), Monte Carlo simulation can be considered as the state-of-the-art technique for credit risk modeling. Particularly, if credit portfolios are heterogenous "one should not trust too much in the in the results of an analytical approximation" (Bluhm et al. 2003, p.41). Monte Carlo simulation tends to be an adequate choice for complex products (Caouette et al. 1998).

A **disadvantage** of Monte Carlo approaches is that they do not enable to capture optionality, which may be present in the financial problem at hand (Caouette et al. 1998). Hence, as simulation is, by definition, forward-looking, a realization in a subsequent period cannot be changed by the algorithms any more. Certainly, another major drawback - in contrast to analytical methods - is that a Monte Carlo simulation for a huge credit portfolio is very time consuming, dependent on the number of assets in the portfolio and the number of required scenarios to ensure that the available tail information is reliable for the chosen confidence interval (Bluhm et al. 2003). With the advent of more advanced IT technologies, this disadvantage becomes less important.

3.5.1.4.4 Handling of the technical concept within this work

In terms of building the credit portfolio framework in section 5, we will refer to a Monte Carlo simulation to generate the input data for portfolio management given its convenient opportunities to handle randomness and to gain a feeling what is done. The risk capital portion will be based on an analytical approach presented in section 3.5.2.4.

3.5.1.5 Ultimate outputs

The ultimate outputs of the credit risk model comprises the determination of the expected and unexpected loss of the credit portfolio, the single asset's risk contributions and the portfolio loss (profit and performance) distribution with its

[261] See Bluhm et al. (2003), for example.
[262] See Bluhm et al. (2003), for example.

characteristical moments and parameters. In the following, the outputs will be presented and discussed.

3.5.1.5.1 The expected loss of a portfolio

In formal terms, the aggregate average loss (EL_p) of two risky assets, A and B, during the analysis horizon is the sum of their expected losses:[263]

$$EL_p = EL_A + EL_B$$

and more generally for N risky assets i

$$EL_p = \sum_{i=1}^{N} EL_i = \sum_{i=1}^{N} (EAD_i \bullet LGD_i \bullet PD_i)$$

where EL_p is the EL of the portfolio.

For homogeneous portfolios with similar exposures i, we assume that the EaD_i are set to a value of one currency unit.[264] The expected loss of the portfolio can then be rewritten as $EL_p = \sum_i EL_i = \sum_i (LGD_i \bullet PD_i)$.

3.5.1.5.2 The unexpected loss of a portfolio

The unexpected loss of a credit portfolio may be referred to as one standard deviation from the mean or to the losses linked to a certain confidence level. We will generally refer to the latter definition, corresponding to the Value-at-Risk concept (see section 3.5.1.5.6.1).

Unfortunately, a portfolio's UL is not just the sum of the single contract's UL as for the EL. An simple analytical representation of a portfolio's UL according to Ong (1999, p.124f.) is as follows:

The UL of a portfolio consisting of N risky assets, denoted by UL_p is given by

$$UL_p = \left[\sum_i \sum_j \rho_{ij} UL_i UL_j \right]^{1/2}$$

with the individual obligor's unexpected losses

263 See Ong (1999), p. 123.

264 This simplification is used by many authors.

$$UL_i = \mathrm{EAD_i} \bullet \sqrt{PD_i \bullet \sigma^2_{LGD(i)} + LGD_i^2 \bullet \sigma^2_{PD(i)}}$$

and the default correlation ρ_{ij} between asset i and asset j,.

The latter equation reveals that (Ong 1999, p.125):

$$\mathrm{UL_p} \neq \sum_i \mathrm{UL_i} .$$

Accordingly, the linear sum of the individual $\mathrm{UL_i}$'s of the portfolio's assets is not identical to the portfolio's UL ($\mathrm{UL_p}$), but usually much smaller (Ong 1999, p.125):

$$\mathrm{UL_p} << \sum_i \mathrm{UL_i}$$

The reason behind this effect is diversification, which entails that there is only a partial contribution of each single exposure's UL to the portfolio's UL. The partial contribution is called *risk contribution* and will be discussed in section 3.5.1.5.3 below. A credit portfolio's expected and unexpected loss are graphically shown in Figure 3-13.

3.5.1.5.3 Risk contributions

The methodological answer to the question "how much incremental risk does a single risky asset contribute to the portfolio as a whole?" is very essential.[265] Ong (1999, p.125) mentions two reasons:

- First, a portfolio's UL ($\mathrm{UL_p}$) is smaller or equal than the sum of individual UL's of the portfolio.[266]
- Second, the frequency of default events augments noticeably in an economic decline.[267] In order to withstand recession periods, a bank must

[265] See Ong (1999), p. 125.

[266] Ong (1999, p.125/126) explains the importance of this reason as follows: "When assigning the risk and return characteristics of a single risky asset in a portfolio context, it becomes necessary to ask how much risk this asset contributes to the whole portfolio and what kind of return can be expected of this asset for the level of risk it contributes to the portfolio."

[267] Ong (1999, p.126) describes the reason for this effect as follows: "Most banks, by virtue of their expertise, are quite specialized in particular industry sectors and therefore, suffer from concentration risk. That is to say, most bank loan portfolios are highly concentrated

therefore be enabled to identify the degree of diversification in their portfolios. The information about the level of diversification may be used for strategic purposes.

The risk contribution is the conceptual measure that provides a solution to the question imposed above. In formal terms, the risk contribution (RCB) of an asset i can be written as[268]

$$RCB_i = UL_i \frac{\partial UL_p}{\partial UL_i}.$$

In this notion, the risk contribution of asset i is measured as a fraction of the asset's UL (UL_i).

In fact, from a portfolio management perspective, the risk contribution is the most important risk measure for assessing credit risk as it denotes the non-systematic (undiversified) risk of each single asset for efficient portfolios (see Figure 3-8) (Ong 1999). It reflects the smallest credit risk entity in a given portfolio that cannot be divided any more (Ong 1999). Hence, the sum of all risk contributions of the single positions equals a portfolio's unexpected loss (Ong 1999, p.127):

$$UL_p = \sum_i RCB_i$$

3.5.1.5.4 A comprehensive example

In order to reflect the formal insights into the credit risk parameters, we will accompany Ong (1999, p.127f.) with an illustrative example, a sample portfolio containing only two risky assets.

Given the data shown in Table 3-11 denoting the credit risk parameters for two single obligations, the desired parameters EL, UL and RCB may be calculated.

in terms of their exposure to specific types of industry and are therefore highly susceptible to correlated default and credit migration events."

[268] Ong (1999), p. 126.

Table 3-11: Derivation of an asset's risk contribution: Individual risk parameters (according to Ong 1999, p.127f.)

Parameter	Description	Value
Obligation 1		
Outstanding (EaD_1)		5 Mio. Euros
PD_1	Rating: BBB	0.0015
σ_{PD_1}	Empirical value of the PDs volatility	0.0387
LGD_1	Fixed to 50%	0.5
σ_{LGD_1}	Random guess of the LGD volatility	0.25
EL_1	$EL = PD \bullet LGD \bullet EAD$	3750 Euros
UL_1	$UL = EAD \bullet \sqrt{PD \bullet \sigma_{LGD}^2 + LGD^2 \bullet \sigma_{PD}^2}$	108186 Euros
Obligation 2		
Outstanding (EaD_2)		1.5 Mio. Euros
PD_2	Rating: B	0.0485
σ_{PD_2}	Empirical value	0.2148
LGD_2	Fixed to 35%	0.35
σ_{LGD_2}	Random guess	0.25
EL_2	$EL = PD \bullet LGD \bullet EAD$	25462.5 Euros
UL_2	$UL = EAD \bullet \sqrt{PD \bullet \sigma_{LGD}^2 + LGD^2 \bullet \sigma_{PD}^2}$	139776 Euros

Table 3-12 shows the derived credit risk parameters for the considered portfolio. The effect of portfolio diversification can be clearly observed in this example: The sum of the ULs of the two obligations exceeds the UL of the portfolio by more than 38%.

Table 3-12: Derivation of an asset's risk contribution: Portfolio risk parameters (according to Ong 1999, p.127f.)

Portfolio EAD = $EAD_1 + EAD_2$		6.5 Mio
ρ_{12}	Default correlation	0.03
EL_p	$EL_p = EL_1 + EL_2$	29212.5 Euros
UL_p	$UL_p = \sqrt{UL_1^2 + UL_2^2 + 2 \cdot \rho_{12} \cdot UL_1 \cdot UL_2}$	179301 Euros
RCB_1	$RCB_1 = UL_1 \cdot (UL_1 + UL_2 \cdot \rho_{12}) / UL_p$	67807 Euros
RCB_2	$RCB_2 = UL_2 \cdot (UL_2 + UL_1 \cdot \rho_{12}) / UL_p$	111494 Euros
Sums of RCB and UL		
$RCB_1 + RCB_2 = UL_p$		179301
$UL_1 + UL_2 >> UL_p$		247963 >> 179301

3.5.1.5.5 Credit risk distribution

The randomness of the total portfolio's losses can be represented in terms of a loss distribution. The methodologies to derive a loss distribution have been discussed above. For the characterization of the loss distribution, especially the first two moments, the mean and the volatility of the losses around the mean (expected loss (EL) and unexpected loss (UL)) are of particular interest. For more sophisticated approaches to credit risk, additional moments may be used or one may refer to a non-parametric representation.

Comprehensive analyses of the output of (internal) credit risk portfolio models has been provided by Ott (2001), distinguishing three types of credit risk related distributions:

- **Loss distribution,**
- **Profit/loss – distribution and**
- **Present value distribution.**

We will closely follow Ott's (2001) findings in the following.

3.5.1.5.5.1 Loss distributions

According to Ott (2001, p.123), a *loss distribution* takes only default events into account and neglects changes of the creditworthiness. The portfolio loss distribution thus equals $L_{pt} = \sum_i L_{it}$

with the individual loss distribution

$$L_{it} = \begin{cases} 0 & \text{with } \Pr = (1\text{-}PD_{it}) \\ (1 - RR_{it}) \bullet EAD_{it} & \text{with } \Pr = PD_{it} \end{cases}$$

where PD_{it} is the default probability of borrower i in period t and RR_{it} is his/her recovery rate in case of insolvency.

There are alternative definitions referred to the term 'loss distribution' in use. Theiler (2002a), for example, measures the portfolio loss as the negative deviation of the portfolio value from the expected portfolio value. However, we will keep with the definition of Ott (2001) and incorporate approaches as the latter one into the profit/loss- distribution.

3.5.1.5.5.2 Profit/loss (PL) distributions

Profit/loss distributions capture possible market value changes of an investment or an investment portfolio, i.e. the difference of possible market values of the actual value at a later stage. In case of credit risk, losses as a consequence of default events do influence the net return of lending negatively.

The profit/loss distribution of a portfolio is thus defined as[269]

$$PL_{pt} = \sum_i PL_{it} \text{ with } \Pr(PL_{1t}, PL_{2t}, \ldots, PL_{Nt})$$

with the single exposure's profit/loss distribution

$$PL_{it} = \begin{cases} i_i \bullet EAD_{it} & \text{with } \Pr = 1\text{-}PD_{it} \\ -(1 - RR_{it}) \bullet EAD_{it} & \text{with } \Pr = PD_{it} \end{cases}.$$

The interest payment portion on the current (average) exposure influences the risk result positively, while losses are counted negatively. Ott (2001) did show

[269] See Ott (2001), p.127.

that the credit loss event probabilities remain the same both for loss and profit/loss distributions, but – in contrast – the impact of a loss event is different. P/L distributions do have a wider range of values and are more skewed to the left as loss distributions.

A profit/loss distribution is shown below related to the risk result of lending (see section 2.4.4.2) in an illustrative way.

Figure 3-11: The credit risk result in terms of profit/loss (Schierenbeck 2003b, p.158)

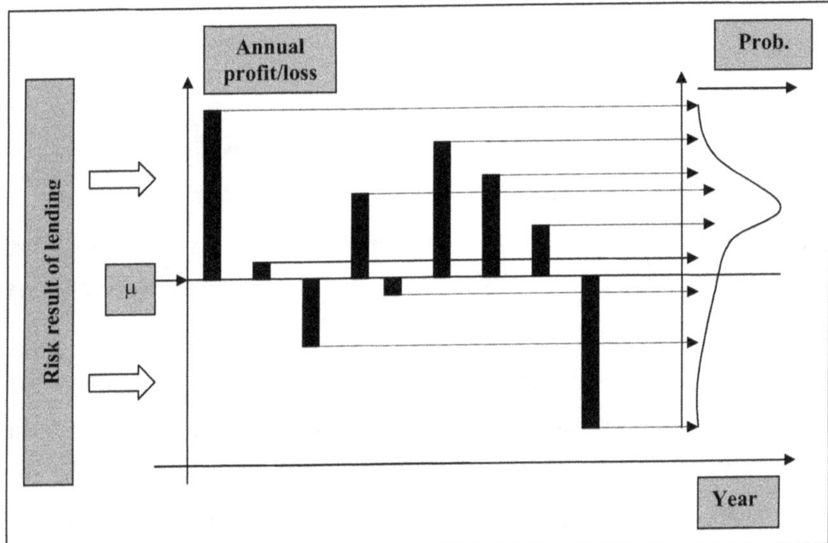

3.5.1.5.5.3 Present value distributions

Present value distributions do not only capture payments within certain periods, but the cash flow of the obligation during maturity. For fixed term obligations, there are three possible loss events in each period with the following cash flow (outcome) sequences:[270]

- In case of default of borrower i at the end of period t: $i_i \bullet EAD_{it} + R_{it}$ [271]
- In case of insolvency during the period t: $RR_{it} \bullet EAD_{it}$
- In case of a default before the actual period t (t′< t): 0

[270] See Ott (2001), p.129.

[271] With the repayment of borrower i in period R_{it}.

The PV of each position can be received by discounting the inherent cash flows approximately. The PV distribution is resolved by linking a probability to each possible PV.[272]

Formal insights on PV distributions can be found in Ott (2001). An example for the application of the PV framework is CreditMetrics, but only for single periods.

3.5.1.5.5.4 Conclusion: Which distribution is the most suitable one?

Ott (2001, p.129f.) investigated the usability of the three different result distributions to reflect the credit risk result and concludes that "the distributions do not differ in the probabilities of the different credit events, but rather in their effect on the size of loss." It could be further observed that "the estimated occurrence probabilities distribute on a wider co-domain for the profit/loss distribution" and that profit/loss distributions "do not seem to be used yet" (Ott 2001, p.129).[273] A famous example for the application of present value distributions is CreditMetrics (and CreditPortfolioView for liquid borrowers). CreditMetrics does refer to one-period horizons and is based on the estimated market value at the end of the period (Ott 2001).[274]

In terms of the derivation of distinct loss parameters, Ott (2001) suggests, that both for the determination of reserves and the economic capital the profit/loss distribution is the most suitable.[275] By contrast, an investor assessing the inherent interest of a credit portfolio should refer to present values, as the

[272] To derive these probabilities, a stationary Markov - process is assumed. This assumption allows underlying that a rating is dependent only on the rating in the previous period and that rating transitions are constant over time. For each rating, a yield curve can be derived.

[273] Meanwhile, it can be expected that the situation has changed, while the focus is "still" on loss distributions.

[274] Oda and Muranga (1997) reduce the present value distribution to illiquid portfolios and model the effect of default on the cash flow of credits. This causes only small modifications to the PV distribution (Ott 2001).

[275] Present value distributions "are not suitable to determine write-offs and the EC-level, because future payments influence the current observation period and cause uncertainty (Ott 2001).

influence of certain risk determinants (repayment structure, term) thereby can be modeled. The suitability of credit risk distributions is summarized below.

Figure 3-12: The suitable definition of loss dependent on the target (Ott 2001, p.120)

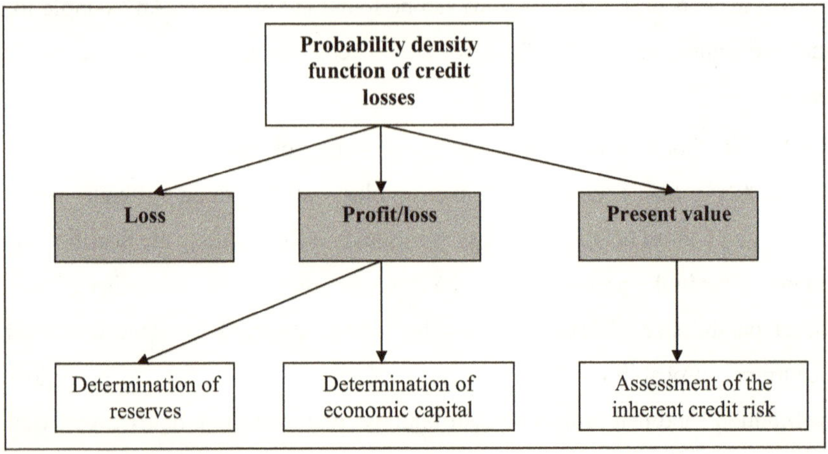

Within the credit risk framework in section 5, we will refer to performance distributions, which are profit/loss distributions that have been standardized with the capital portion used. Present value aspects will be endogenously covered by the portfolio selection model.

3.5.1.5.6 Credit risk distribution related measures

Various credit risk parameters can be derived once frequency distributions for a credit portfolio have been identified. Among the most important parameters are the Value-at-Risk (VaR), the conditional Value-at-Risk (CVaR) and the economic capital (EC), which are explained based on the illustrative Figure 3-13 shown below.

Figure 3-13: The most important parameters related to a credit risk portfolio distribution[276]

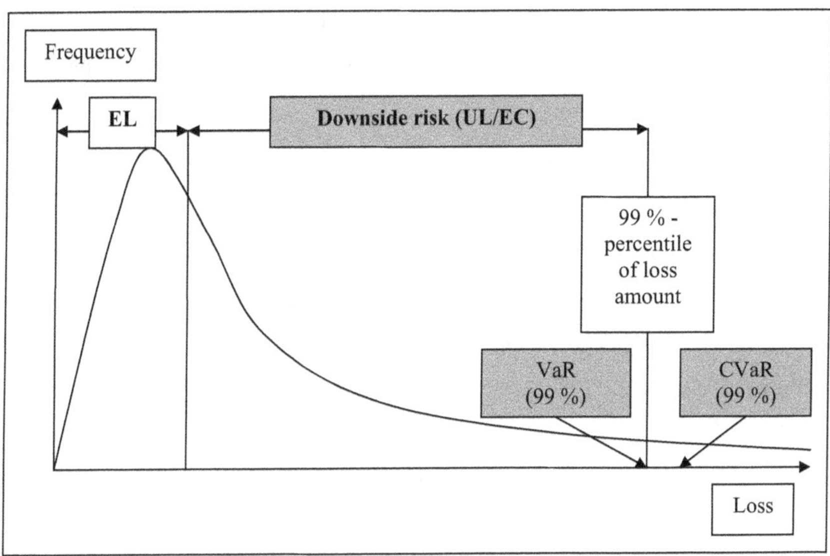

3.5.1.5.6.1 Credit Value-at-Risk (VaR)[277]

The Value-at-Risk (VaR) is defined as a one-side confidence interval on potential portfolio losses over a specific horizon and serves the role of setting the capital requirement for market risks (Ong 1999).[278] As a result of the popularity of the VaR concept within the market risk domain, this measure has been considered (and favored) also for credit risk, last but not least to enable a bank-wide homogenous risk management concept. Compared to the usage of the VaR for market risk, however, the focus of credit VAR is more on solvency than on liquidity, so that the horizon is longer, typically one year (Ong 1999).[279] Moreover, the confidence level is set farily high, typically 99% up to 99.9%.[280]

---

[276] Similar graphics can be found in various textbooks, for example in Theiler (2002a), p.26.

[277] A formal definition of the VaR can be found in Bluhm et al. (2003, p.167f.), for example.

[278] Further information about the usage of the VaR for market risk purposes can be found in Jorion (1997) and Ong (1999, p.45f.), for example.

[279] For market risk the VaR horizon is chosen fairly short, ranging from one to twenty trading days as a consequence of the frequent portfolio revisions. Horizons are e.g. discussed in Kupiec (1997), and Shen (2001).

[280] Ong (1999). Such high confidence level makes model validation by backtesting almost impossible, especially for longer horizons.

As already shown by Harlow (1991), the VaR is an incomplete risk measure for non-symmetric distributions (e.g. in the domain of credit) and has therefore to be treated with prudence. Aspects of risk measures in the context of decision theory will be subject to section 4.3.

3.5.1.5.6.2 Conditional VaR (expected Shortfall)

The expected loss conditional on exceeding VaR (a certain confidence level of potential portfolio losses), or the *conditional VaR* (expected shortfall, mean shortfall risk, tail Value-at-Risk, mean excess loss)[281] is "a logical escape" from the problem of the VaR being an incomplete risk measure (Grootveld and Hallerbach 2001, p.7). The conditional VaR (CVAR) measures the expected loss in case of a loss superior to a certain confidence level and has been suggested by Artzner et al. (1999) as a coherent risk measure.[282]

Formally, the CVAR can be written as[283]

$$CVAR_{\beta}(x) = E[L(x) \mid L(x) \geq VaR_{\beta}(x)]$$

with confidence level β and loss $L(x)$ of the portfolio x.

The CVaR can thus be considered as an upper bound for the VaR (Uryasev and Rockafeller 1999). The relationship between VaR and CVAR can be expressed as follows:[284]

$$CVAR_{\beta}(x) = VaR_{\beta}(x) + \frac{1}{1-\beta} EL .$$

3.5.1.5.6.3 Economic capital (EC)

Portfolio losses exceeding the expected loss (as shown in Figure 3-13 above) are "unexpected" and may threaten the solvency of a FI. In terms of credit risk management, the vital question for a bank is to identify the portion of capital that is necessary to avert insolvency in case of a worst-case loss scenario (Ong

---

281 See Rockafellar et al. (1999).

282 Some references on conditional VaR are Andersson and Uryasev (1999), Palmquist et al. (1999), Testuri and Uryasev (2000), Uryasev (2000) and Uryasev and Rockafellar (1999).

283 See Theiler et al. (2002a) according to Rockafellar et al. (1999). Non-parametric analysis with respect to the CVaR have been carried out by Scaillet (2000), for example.

284 See Theiler et al. (2002a) according to Rockafellar et al. (1999).

1999). The answer to this essential question leads to the economic capital or risk capital.[285] The economic capital thereby corresponds to a portfolio's UL as explained in section 3.5.1.5.2.

For strategic purposes, a bank has to name a confidence level (1-α) being in line with the bank's preferred credit risk rating in order to ensure the appropriate capitalization for any business line (Ong 1999). The linkage between a bank's preferred rating and the equivalent confidence level of its risk policy is shown below. A graphical representation of this relationship is shown in Figure 4-8 in section 4.2.2.2.[286]

Table 3-13: Desired bank rating and confidence level (Ong 1999, p.168)

Desired rating	Confidence level
AAA	99.99%
AA	99.97%
A	99.9%
BBB	99.7%

The confidence levels shown in Table 3-13 should be understood "merely indicative for the average historical default probabilities corresponding to a particular risk rating" as these averages fluctuate over time, e.g. caused by recessions (Ong 1999, p.168).

Mathematically, the economic capital has been defined as follows (Ong 1999, p.168):

Let X_t be a random variable for the occurring loss and α the percentage probability (referred to the confidence level). Then the economic capital is the

285 See Ong (1999), p.57/58. More specifically, the necessary cushion of the economic capital is the amount of capital the bank needs to set aside in anticipation of disastrous market conditions in order to cover the loss at the percentile equal to the chosen confidence level of the bank in the tail region. For example, if the loss rate at the 99th percentile is 5 percent, then a 5 percent capital ratio will be sufficient to prevent insolvency with probability of 0.99.

286 These parameters are at least valid for international US banks (Board of Governors of the Federal Reserve System 1998, p. 33). The rating agencies do not indicate clearly, whether their rating refers to the PD only or if they consider forecasts of future potential losses as well.

minimum quantity v that is needed that a bank remains solvent over a specific period t: $\text{prob}\{X_t \leq v\} = \alpha$

Binding the random variable X_t to the economic background, it represents the UL. Thus, the demanded EC can be expressed such that $\text{prob}\{X_t - EL \leq EC\} = \alpha$.

3.5.1.5.6.3.1 Capital requirements: Economic capital and risk capital

With the establishment of credit risk portfolio models (see section 3.5.2ff.) banks were able to calculate on their own how much individual borrowers or subportfolios (e.g. a rating segment) contribute to their portfolio risk in order to assign to them the corresponding portion of capital, referred to as economic capital[287] (internal calculation) in contrast to the regulatory capital (set by BCBS).[288]

The Basel framework has been explained in section 2.3. According to the Basel I - framework, each credit has to be financed by 8% of a bank's capital as shown in Figure 3-15 below, independent of the borrower's creditworthiness (known as the *"8 % - rule"*). Should a bank issue a credit loan with a nominal exposure of 1 mill. Euros to a company, for example, then at least 80,000 Euro do represent a bank's capital.

[287] The concept of economic capital has been explained in section 3.5.1.5.6.3ff.

[288] Both the economic capital and the regulatory capital will be referred to as generic term "risk capital".

Figure 3-14: Refinancing of the credit exposure: The 8% - rule (Basel I)

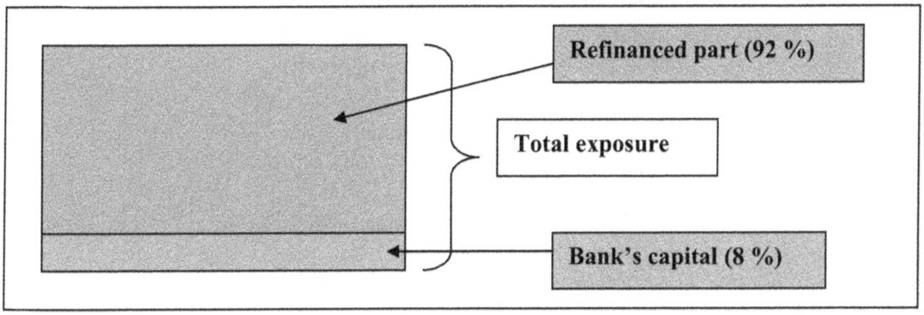

Refinanced part (92 %)

Total exposure

Bank's capital (8 %)

As a CCC borrower with an annual PD of 15% is certainly more risky than an AAA borrower with a PD of 0.005%, a bank may internally assign a lower capital portion than 8% to the AAA borrower and a higher portion to the CCC borrower, for example. The minimum overall capital portion to be set aside by the bank, however, has been fixed at 8% (at least until 2006).

Risk capital according to different methodologies

Table 3-14 shows the risk capital according to four approaches, namely the 'old' Basel Accord (*Basel I*), the standardized approach for the new Basel Accord (Basel II Standard) and the internal ratings-based approach as well as an analytical approach according to Arvanitis and Gregory (2001, p.28) related to a beta distribution within the CreditRisk+ methodology.

Table 3-14: Risk capital according to different approaches

Rating	Basel I	Basel II standardized	Basel IRB (QIS 3)[289]	Analytical approach[290]
AAA	0.08	0.016	0.0008	0.0106
AA	0.08	0.016	0.0036	0.0232
A	0.08	0.04	0.0134	0.0308
BBB	0.08	0.06	0.0372	0.0460
BB	0.08	0.06	0.1001	0.0769
B	0.08	0.12	0.2150	0.1611
CCC	0.08	0.12	0.4229	0.2785

It can clearly be observed that there are huge differences with respect to the treatment of credit risk for the distinct approaches. The IRB approach requires more than five times as much risk capital as the old regulatory framework for a CCC borrower (0.4229 vs. 0.08). For the low risk classes, the differences are even more extensive, but opposite.

3.5.1.5.6.3.2 The effect of diversification on economic capital

The effect of diversification on economic capital is illustrated in Figure 3-15 according to Merz (2001). While the portfolio's mean loss (EL) remains the same, the UL is significantly reduced in portfolio 2 (P2) compared to portfolio 1 (P1). Therefore, the confidence level of P2 is significantly shifted "to the left" and the EC portion can either be significantly reduced (as highlighted below), or, for the purpose of an improvement of the external rating, the confidence level may be increased, for example to a level of 99.97, what would correspond to a rating of AA compared to a BB/B rating before (see section 3.5.1.5.6.3).

289 For the empirical PD and LGD of the rating classes shown in section 3.3. The required capital portion includes the expected loss, which has been excluded meanwhile for the Basel II framework (see Basel 2004, para 272).

290 For a default correlation of 1% and an asset correlation of 20%, respectively.

Figure 3-15: Revenue from diversification (according to Merz 2001)

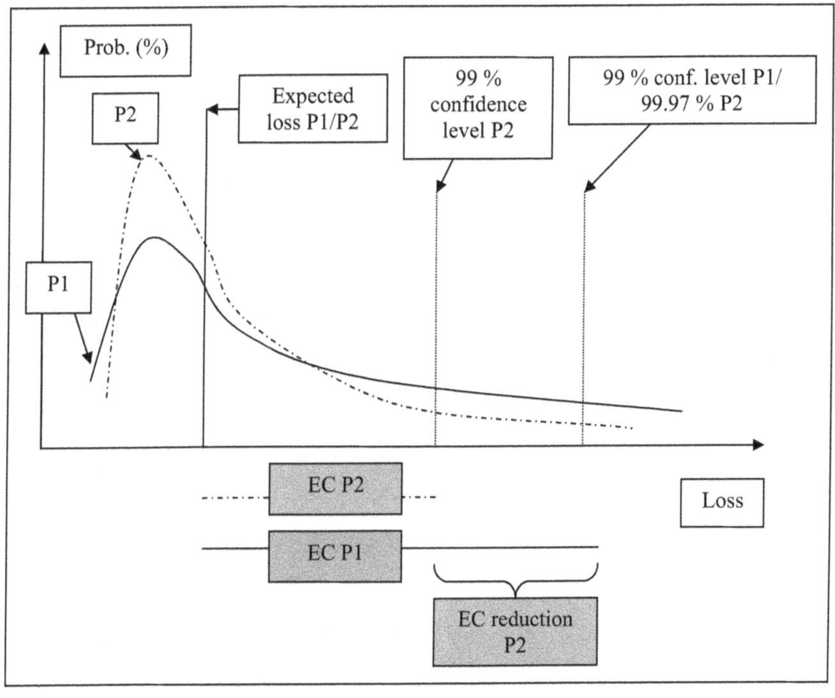

The degree of the diversification of a portfolio may conveniently be captured by the so-called diversification factor (DF, see Manz 1998, for example), especially for homogenous portfolios.[291]

3.5.2 Credit risk portfolio models in practice

There have been a number of different commercial portfolio approaches to measure credit risk over the last five to ten years. Two major challenges have been attempted to be solved by these approaches.

[291] The benchmark is hereby the worst possible position, a homogeneous portfolio with perfect positive correlated elements ($\rho_{ij} = 1$). The DF is calculated as follows (Manz 1998):

$$DF = 1 - \frac{UL_{p[realized]}}{UL_{p[\rho=1]}}$$

The DF can thereby approximately be understood as a measure how diversifiable a portfolio is.

First, the financial industry has placed particular stress on the determination of the default correlation matrix that is a crucial input parameter of credit risk portfolio models (Arvanitis and Gregory 2001, p.29). Second, another major problem in the credit risk business is the lack of sufficient data. It will be indicated how major financial institutions have mastered these two major challenges.

Stimulated by J.P. Morgan's CreditMetrics model in 1997, several portfolio models that have either remained proprietary or become commercially available have been developed by major financial institutions: Credit Suisse Financial Products' CreditRisk+ model, KMV's Portfolio Manager, McKinsey's CreditPortfolioView and RAROC 2020[292] among others.

For almost all credit risk portfolio models used in the industry technical documents are available explaining the underlying methodology, empirical data and the calibration procedure (Bluhm et al. 2003). For KMV's Portfolio Manager, however, major parts of the model properties are kept confidential although even for this model the basic properties are publicly available.[293] Besides the main commercial models various so-called *internal models* can be found in large international banks, which have mostly been inspired by the well-known commercial products (Bluhm et al. 2003).

3.5.2.1 Classification of the major credit risk portfolio models

Figure 3-16 shows four main types of industry models with the default event/risk interdependencies as the distinctive characteristic and specifies the financial institutions and/or authors behind them according to Bluhm et al. (2003, p.66f.). Basically, all industry models are aimed at incorporating default risk and/or the risk arising from credit migration by means of a Value-at-Risk-

---

[292] See Bankers Trust (1995); RAROC 2020 is applicable to all types of publicly traded assets only and not described in further details. It uses correlations based on total returns and is a simulation model that does not explicitly model default probabilities or rating migrations.

[293] See Bluhm et al. (2003), for example.

type framework.[294] However, their conceptual frameworks are different. While CreditMetrics and KMV are based on a Merton-type asset value model, CreditRisk+ is an actuarial model as applied in the insurance industry[295] and CreditPortfolioView is an econometric model incorporating macro-economic effects on credit portfolio risk.[296] From a mathematician's standpoint intensity models provide a "mathematically beautiful" (Bluhm et al. 2003, p.67) approach to credit modeling, but are not applicable for the non-traded credit sphere and thus neglected in this work. Interested readers may refer to Jarrow et al. (1997) and Duffie and Lando (1999).[297]

294 See Derviz et al. (2001), for example.

295 Bluhm et al. (2003, p.67) claim that "CreditRisk+ could alternatively be placed in the group of intensity models, because it is based on a Poisson mixture model incorporated random intensities." Nevertheless, the figure shall "stress the difference between CreditRisk+ and the *dynamic* intensity models based on intensity processes instead of on a *static* intensity."

296 See Derviz et al. (2001), for example.

297 Other sources comprise Duffie and Singleton (1998,1999), Duffie and Gârleanu (1999) and Lando (1997). We let Bluhm et al. (2003, p.81f.) give a striking definition of intensity models: "The basic assumption is that every obligor admits a default time such that default happens in time interval [0,T] if and only if the default time of the considered obligor appears to be smaller than the planning horizon T. The default times are driven by an intensity process, a so-called basic affine process, whose evolution is described by the stochastic differential equation $d\lambda(t) = \kappa(\theta - \lambda(t)) + \sigma\sqrt{\lambda(t)}dB(t) + \Delta J(t)$ where B(t) is a standard Brownian motion and $\Delta J(t)$ denotes the jump that occurs, if it occurs, at time t." Further information can be found in Bluhm et al. (2003, p.82), for example.

Figure 3-16: Today's best-practice credit risk portfolio models (Bluhm et al. 2003, p.67)

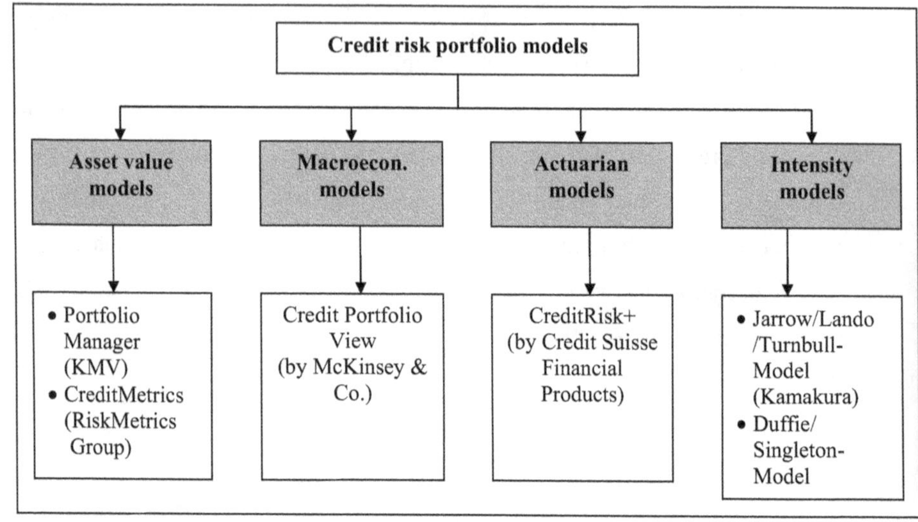

In the following, we briefly review these state-of-the-art credit risk portfolio models and point out both their commonalities and differences.

3.5.2.2 Review of the major credit risk portfolio models

3.5.2.2.1 Moody's (KMV's) Portfolio Manager™[298]

KMV was founded in 1989 by S. Kealhofer, J. McQuown and O. Vasicek and has recently been acquired by Moody's in 2003. KMV's tools are grounded on Merton's asset value model, and comprise a tool for estimating default probabilities (Credit Monitor™) from market information and a tool to manage credit portfolios (PortfolioManager™). The Credit Monitor's core output is the Expected Default Frequency™ (EDF™), which may meanwhile be determined also with a web-based tool called CreditEdge™. The Portfolio Manager's main output is a credit portfolio's loss distribution[299] and an optimal qualitative portfolio strategy for given investment alternatives (buy/sell/hold) based on a portfolio optimization procedure according to a conventional Sharpe (1963,

[298] Basic information about Moody's Portfolio Manager can be found on Moody's webpage.
[299] See Bluhm et al. (2003), including the derivation of the economic capital, for example.

1994) ratio. Additionally, KMV provides various optimized outputs: Optimization at constant risk, optimization at constant return and the visualization of the efficient frontier given the funding constraint.[300] A reference to the basics of the KMV-Model is the survey paper by Crosbie (1999). Most large banks and insurances seem to use at least one of the major KMV products.[301] The Portfolio Manager™ can be classified as a mixture of default-model and mark-to-market (MTM), structural credit risk model.[302]

Advantages and limitations

A major **advantage** of the KMV model is that it explicitly uses a firm's asset/liability structure instead of ratings for the derivation of obligor's default probabilities.[303] It can therefore be assumed that the KMV model is "more sensitive to changes in the quality of obligors" than credit rating approaches (Derviz et al. 2001, p. 45). Based on the Merton-type framework, equity prices are used as a representation of market information.[304] This strengthens the model in so far as it is forward-looking.[305]

However, the usage of the crude Merton-type asset/liability structure has been pointed out as a **limitation** of the KMV model.[306] Moreover, the mapping of the Distance-to-Default (DD) on historical PDs is critical, because the PDs are historical averages and a stationary relationship is underlied, i.e. "the possibility of a cyclical dependent EDF™ for a given DD is not considered" (Jarrow and Turnbull 1998, p.16). Another shortage of the KMV model is that its input data

300 Bessis (2001), p. 719.

301 Bluhm et al. (2003).

302 See Ott (2001), for example.

303 Derviz et al. (2001).

304 Derviz et al. (2001).

305 Changes in the creditworthiness are adapted far more quickly than for external ratings, which may be updated only once a year.

306 See Derviz et al. (2001), for example.

(e.g. the mapping of the DD to EDFs) is based on US data only, which may not be representative when the model is intended to be applied outside the US.[307] Furthermore, the estimation of the non-observable model parameters cannot be traced.[308] Especially the derivation of the default correlation via market data is a weakness of KMV, which is even worse for nontraded firms. Additionally, the general default model framework of KMV can be seen as a disadvantage for the implicit consideration of information referred to market date volatility.[309] With respect to the treatment of credit portfolio risk, the Portfolio Manager is grounded on the assumption that credit portfolios are *'highly diversified'*, what may lead to siginificant misspecifications of the economic capital requirements for concentrated portfolios, for example.[310] Further advantages and disadvantages of the KMV model can be found in Jarrow et al. (1998), Saunders (1999) and Wilson (1999), for example.

3.5.2.2.2 CreditMetrics™

CreditMetrics™ is a trademark of the RiskMetrics™ Group, a spin-off-company of the former JP. Morgan bank, which now belongs to the Chase Group. The CreditMetrics™ framework consists of a tool called CreditManager™, which has a comparable functionality as Moody's (KMV's) Portfolio Manager™.[311] In April 1997, J.P. Morgan brought CreditMetrics into the market, "the first readily available portfolio model for evaluating credit risk" (JP.Morgan, CreditMetrics press release, 1997).

The technical documentation of CreditMetrics (1997) can be regarded as a pioneering record which has guided many banks in developing internal credit risk portfolio models.[312] CreditMetrics™ provides a historical data set that is

---

307 Derviz et al. (2001).

308 See Ott (2001), for example.

309 On the other hand, it seems that KMV has included MTM aspects through the possibility of a transition into other EDF™ categories as explained by Kealhofer et al. (1998).

310 See Derviz et al. (2001), p.45.

311 See Bluhm et al. (2003), for example.

312 See Bluhm et al. (2003), p.42.

freely available from the internet.[313] According to Bluhm et al. (2003, p.42), the great triumph of the CreditMetrics™ framework partly results from the philosophy of its authors Gupton, Finger and Bhatia "to make credit risk methodology available to a broad audience in a fully transparent manner."[314]

JP Morgan (1997) state that the model has been developed to "create a benchmark for credit risk measurement" (…), "promote credit risk transparency and better market tools for managing credit risk" (…), and "encourage a regulatory capital framework that more closely reflects economic risk"[315]

The input data required for CreditMetrics are a rating system, the characteristics of individual assets, equity returns for each obligor and a set of country and industry equity indices.[316] The output of CreditMetrics is to compute two distinct measures for the inherent credit risk of a portfolio, namely the volatility (dispersion) around the average portfolio value and the percentile levels of portfolio loss.[317]

CreditMetrics™ is a mark-to-market (MTM) model and can be categorized as a rating-based model within the intensity based credit risk portfolio models.[318] CreditMetrics is often considered as a structural model. De facto, it is an intensity based approach that models credit risk in form of rating transitions (Ott 2001). CreditMetrics uses only one feature of structural models: the derivation of correlations.

The model does not offer optimization functions.[319] Default risk is explicitly modeled over a horizon of one year ('the credit risk measurement period') and marginal risk contributions are provided (Bessis 2001).

313 See www.creditmetrics.com.
314 What has been the intention of JP Morgan; See JP Morgan (1997), Preface.
315 CreditMetrics – Press release. See www.defaultrisk.com/press_release_creditmetrics.htm. Rev. June 2004.
316 See Ott (2001), for example.
317 See Ott (2001), for example.
318 See Ott (2001), for example.
319 Bessis (2001).

Advantages and limitations

One of the **advantages** of CreditMetrics is that it allows monitoring marginal changes of a credit portfolio's present value (i.e. the expected portfolio value and its variance) by means of a parametric concept.[320] Besides, a non-parametric Monte Carlo framework provides the credit portfolio's Value-at-Risk, which can be regarded as a "reliable estimate of the risk embodied in the portfolio" (Derviz et al. 2001, p. 36). Moreover, CreditMetrics is the first credit portfolio model based on the PV method.[321]

A **weakness** of CreditMetrics is that it uses uniform credit risk parameters (PD and rating transition matrix) for all obligors within the same rating class.[322] CreditMetrics' postulation of uniform credit risk parameters and the usage of long-term average PDs have been doubted by KMV. With respect to the transition matrix, KMV has explored that migration matrices for borrowers within a rating class may differ significantly and moreover, that migration matrices of borrowers from different rating classes may be equal.[323] Furthermore, KMV claims that migration matrices may fluctuate considerably over time and that historical estimates may therefore be inapproporiate. Another limitation of CreditMetrics is the assumption of deterministic default free interest rates, what impedes the incorporation of market risk and cyclical fluctuations.[324] Third, CreditMetrics is vulnerable in terms of its usage of correlations, as equity correlations are used as a substitute for asset correlations. Fourth, CreditMetrics' time horizon for the assessment of credit portfolio risk is usually one year, even if other (longer) interval lengths could be used.

CreditMetrics requires an external rating. This causes substantial problems for the practical applicability, because transition probabilities and yield curves are available only for a minority of firms and most borrowers are assigned an

---

[320] See Derviz et al. (2001).

[321] See Ott (2001), for example.

[322] See Derviz et al. (2001).

[323] See Derviz et al. (2001).

[324] See Derviz et al. (2001).

internal rating by a financial institution only.[325] Moreover, yield curves are only available for publicly traded firms with market values.[326] In so far, the only way out of this weakness of CreditMetrics for loan portfolios is to map the internal ratings to external agency ratings.[327]

3.5.2.2.3 CreditPortfolioView™

CreditPortfolioView™ was developed by McKinsey & Co. and considers macroeconomic variables (e.g. the unemployment rate). It is based on Wilson's ideas (1997) and is used up to now as a tool supporting McKinsey & Co.'s credit risk consulting projects.[328] From a conceptual viewpoint, CreditPortfolioView can be classified as an econometric, ratings-based credit portfolio model that explicitely models cyclical fluctuations and the correlation structure of a credit portfolio via Monte Carlo simulation.[329] CreditPortfolioView is a mark-to-market (MTM) model and another intensity-based credit risk portfolio model besides CreditMetrics.[330]

Advantages and limitations

The big **advantage** of CreditPortfolioView lays on the macro-economic dependent modeling of the default rate and transition probabilities.[331] Unconditional models, i.e. models that do not include macro-economic factors have the disadvantage that they do not model time-dependent defaults.[332]

CreditPortfolioView distinguishes between liquid and illiquid positions, what is positive, but may cause problems as well (see e.g. Ott 2001). Special aspects of

[325] See Ott (2001). Further information for the process of (internal) ratings can be found in section 3.3.4.1.1.

[326] See Ott (2001).

[327] See Ott (2001).

[328] See Bluhm et al. (2003), for example.

[329] See Arvanitis and Gregory (2001).

[330] Based on ratings. See Ott (2001). Further information can be found in Crouhy et al. (2000).

[331] See Ott (2001), for example.

[332] Ott (2001). For Germany this has been shown by Hamerle et al. (1998). A distinction between conditional and unconditional models can be found in Basel (1999).

the model are, for example, the implementation of country risk and the method for discounting cash flows.[333]

Hamerle et al. (1998) did show that the model can be improved with a time-delayed application of the multi-factor-regression model. This would have the benefit that the PDs of the next period can be forecasted with realized macro-factors. It can be assumed that correlation is influenced almost uniquely by macro-economic factors, what strengthens McKinsey's approach additionally and has been shown by Hamerle et al. (1998).

The pros of the model are, however, accompanied with the prerequisite of data availability to calibrate the model. By consequence, a potential lack of the model's required input parameters (e.g. historical average PDs and economic data for different rating, industry and country pairings) may be seen as a practical **complicatedness** for the usage of CreditPortfolioView.[334] Moreover, the regularly sparse input data available for the calibration of the model disaggregated to the specific portfolio segments naturally come along with an increasing inaccurateness of the estimates.[335] This potential shortage of the model makes it difficult "to verify the accuracy of such an economic model other than by observing default probabilities increasing during economic downturns" (Arvanitis and Gregory 2001, p. 26). As a further problem of the model, Arvanitis and Gregory (2001) mention model risk: It would generally be questionable whether the underlying economic factors allow CreditPortfolioView to correctly depict the default process provided that these factors are correctly modeled at all, what has been summarized by Arvanitis and Gregory (2001, p.26) as follows: Criticism leads to the opinion that "few institutions can predict interest rates, let alone the resulting default rates based on these."

333 See Ott (2001), for example.
334 See Arvanitis and Gregory (2001), for example.
335 See Arvanitis and Gregory (2001), for example.

3.5.2.2.4 CreditRisk+™

Credit Suisse First Boston (*'CSFB'*)[336] has been exploring new risk management methods already 15 years ago.[337] As a result of a huge project aimed at developing a sophisticated framework for credit risk portfolio management initiated in 1993, CSFB presented CreditRisk+™ in December 1996.[338] CreditRisk+™ has been designed for various credit risk products, namely for (corporate and retail) loans, traded bonds and credit derivatives.[339] It is publicly available.[340] CreditRisk+™ is a default-model (DM) and, dependent on the methodological design either a reduced form or a non-reduced form intensity-based credit risk portfolio model.[341]

Advantages and limitations

A core **advantage** of CreditRisk+ is the requirement of a relatively small set of input data, which principally consist only of the individual exposures and default probabilities.[342] Based on these input data, the derivation of the portfolio loss distribution using CreditRisk+ is "rather easy" (Derviz et al. 2001 p. 48). Furthermore, the model is freely available.[343]

A potential **drawback** of the rather limited input data is that the model's handling of individual obligor's default rates may be seen critically[344] as it is assumed that the user of CreditRisk+ is able to specify each obligor's default rates and their variation as the model does not provide a methodology for their

---

[336] Credit Suisse First Boston is a leading global investment bank. It operates in over 60 offices across more than 30 countries and six continents and has over 15,000 employees.
[337] See CSFP (1997).
[338] See CSFP (1997).
[339] See CSFP (1997).
[340] And can be downloaded via www.csfb.com/creditrisk/. Rev. Dec. 2004.
[341] See Ott (2001).
[342] See Derviz et al. (2001) or Ott (2001), for example.
[343] See www.csfb.com/creditrisk/. Rev. Dec. 2004.
[344] See Derviz et al. (2001), or Arvanitis and Gregory (2001), for example

determination.[345] Second, the influence of market risk is not incorporated in the model.[346]

3.5.2.3 Comparison of the best practice credit risk portfolio models[347]

A broad evaluation of different credit risk portfolio modeling approaches has been provided by Hickman and Koyluoglu (1998). They conclude that, in spite of their differences, all models would be built on three more or common mechanisms to provide portfolio loss distributions.

Their first common component is a mechanism to generate default rates for each creditor conditional on the random state of nature and a measure of the joint movement of the borrower's creditworthiness in different states of nature. Based on this mechanism, the models allow the determination of conditional default rate distributions for arbitrarily chosen homogeneous sub-portfolios (e.g. rating segments) as if the borrower insolvencies were independent. This convenient property has been enabled by the first step, as the joint default behavior of the portfolio's borrowers has already been captured. In the third step, the conditional loss distributions for the sub-portfolio for each state of nature are determined. Thereby, the average conditional loss distributions (i.e. weighted with the probability of a state of nature) are used.

A similar conclusion has been made by Gordy (2000a), who thoroughly compared CreditMetrics and CreditRisk+. His outcome is that the models have similar mathematical structures and that potential gaps in the prediction of a (sub)portfolio's loss distribution would result from different assumptions with respect to the underlying distribution and diverse functional forms. More generally, Gordy (2000a) tries to receive general insights into the framework of credit risk portfolio models based on his findings. He stresses that the models would be highly sensitive to the choice of the underlying implied distribution of

345 See Derviz et al. (2001).

346 See Derviz et al. (2001).

347 The comparison of best practice credit risk portfolio model is oriented on Derviz et al. (2001) and Carling et al. (2002).

the PDs and the average default correlation (which determine the volatility of the PDs).

Finger (1998) concludes as well, that all the standard credit risk portfolio models reveal similar results for similar inputs. Further information about model comparison can be found in Phelan and Alexander (1999), Crouhy et al. (2000), Frey and McNeil (2001) and Schierenbeck (2003b), among others.

3.5.2.3.1 Conclusion for the usage of credit portfolio models

For the usage of credit portfolio models it can be concluded that

- the **validation of the input parameters plays a key role** and
- the **choice of the model may be oriented on the individual preferences and needs** (data and target portfolio) of the user

as explained in section 3.5.1.4.[348]

3.5.2.4 The simplest case for a CreditMetrics conditional approach: The one-factor-model (Basel II/Gordy 2000b)[349]

Given the methodological pros and cons of the major credit risk portfolio models on the one hand and the calibration and backtesting problem on the other hand (lack of data), the Basel authority decided to refer to a less sophisticated version of CreditMetrics for the Basel II Capital Accord.

The one-factor-model requires as input data only the risk parameters PD, LGD, and EAD for each exposure in the considered portfolio and is based on a pre-calibrated asset correlations close to empirical data provided by Arvanitis and Gregory (2001, see Table 3-8).

Thereby, the model provides rough and conservative estimates of the portfolio's unexpected loss (UL). However, the model is not sufficiently sensitive to the

---

348 See Dunemann (2001), for example.

349 See www.bis.org, Gordy (2000b), Huschens (2001), Rau-Bredow (2002) or Bluhm et al. (2003) among various other references.

specific risk structure of a considered portfolio.[350] It is only valid under the assumption of an infinite granularity of the portfolio without any industrial or geographical risk concentrations, for example.[351]

In the context of CreditMetrics and the KMV model, the one-factor-model implies that the composite factors ω_i (which represents the correlation structure of the portfolio) of all obligors is equal to one single factor, denoted by $Z \sim N(0,1)$.[352] The one-factor model is based on the assumption that a default occurs when the credit quality of an exposure falls below an exposure-specific default barrier and is therefore an asset-value model.

3.5.2.4.1 The design of the one-factor model[353]

The credit quality Y_j of an exposure j is given by[354]

$$Y_j = \sqrt{\omega_j} Z + \sqrt{1-\omega_j} U_j$$

where U_j represents the exposure-specific factor influencing the credit quality, while Z represents a common factor influencing the credit quality of all exposures in order to reflect interdependencies among a portfolio's exposures (*'One-factor'*).

$U_1, \ldots, U_n$ and Z are random variables, which are identically standard normally distributed and pairwise independent.[355] The exposure-specific and the common credit quality are both calibrated by means of the parameters $\omega_i \in [-1,1]$.[356]

[350] See Rau-Bredow (2002), p.15 or Bluhm et al. (2003), p.52, for example. Valuable research in order to develop credit risk models for regulatory purposes has been performed by Tracey et al. (1998), Finger (1999b), Carey (2002) and Hamerle (2002), for example.

[351] See Bluhm et al. (2003), p.52. See also Vasicek (1989) and Schönbucher (2001).

[352] Bluhm et al. (2003), p.83/84.

[353] See www.bis.org, Gordy (2000b), Huschens (2001), Rau-Bredow (2002) or Bluhm et al. (2003) among various other references.

[354] See Bluhm et al. (2003), p.84, for example.

[355] See Bluhm et al. (2003), for example.

[356] See Bluhm et al. (2003), for example.

Then the standard normal distribution function of the asset value changes Y_j can be revealed by the common multi-normal distribution and the correlations $\rho(Y_j, Y_K) = \omega_j \omega_k$, $i \neq j$. The one-factor-model is based on the assumption that loss (default) occurs, when the asset value of an exposure falls under an "exposure-specific" bound (so-called default bound d_j):[357]

$PD_j = p_j = P(A_j = 1) = P(Y_j \leq d_j)$ where $A_j \sim B(p_j)$ is a Bernoulli-distributed default indicator.

Since the Y_j are standard normally distributed random variables, the default bound d_j is given by $d_j = \Phi^{-1}(p_j)$ with the distribution function Φ of a standard normally distributed random variable and the corresponding inverse Φ^{-1}.

For a fixed realization z of the common factor Z, the conditional default probability $p_j(z)$ can be calculated as follows (Bluhm et al. 2003, p.90/91):

$$P(A_j = 1 \mid Z = z) = P(Y_j \leq d_j \mid Z = z) = P(\omega_j z + \sqrt{1-\omega_j^2}U_j \leq d_j)$$

$$= P(\omega_j z + \sqrt{1-\omega_j^2}U_j \leq \Phi^{-1}(p_j)) = P(U_j \leq \frac{\Phi^{-1}(p_j) - \sqrt{p}z}{\sqrt{1-p}})$$

$$= \Phi\left(\frac{\Phi^{-1}(p_j) - \sqrt{p}z}{\sqrt{1-p}}\right) = PD_j(z) = p_j(z).$$

The portfolio loss distribution is then derived by conditioning on quantiles of the latent factor z. Examples illustrating the conditional PDs as a function of the factor realizations Z = z dependent on the state of the economy for the one-factor-model of CreditMetrics/KMV can be found in Bluhm et al. (2003, p.84/85), for example.

357 Bluhm et al. (2003), p.90. The one-factor-model refers to the OPT based on Black and Scholes (1973) and Merton (1974).

3.5.2.4.2 The one-factor-model in the regulatory framework of Basel II

The parameters ω_i should be portfolio-specifically estimated which requires additional data about asset correlations dependent on the estimated PD_j of each exposure j and the corresponding exposure type (retail/corporate/etc.).

However, the Basel Committee proposed to refer to a conservative, pre-calibrated formula within its latest proposals (e.g. Basel 2002 and Basel 2004). The following values have been proposed accordingly dependent on the estimated conditional probability of default PD_j of each exposure j and dependent on the type of exposure (see Basel 2004, para. 270f.):

- *For corporate exposures*

$$\omega_j = \sqrt{0.12 \bullet \frac{1-\exp(-50 \bullet PD_j)}{1-\exp(-50)} + 0.24 \bullet \left(1 - \frac{1-\exp(-50 \bullet PD_j)}{1-\exp(-50)}\right)}$$

with $\omega_j \in [0.12; 0.24]$.

- *For retail exposures*

$$\omega_j = \sqrt{0.04 \bullet \frac{1-\exp(-25 \bullet PD_j)}{1-\exp(-25)} + 0.15 \bullet \left(1 - \frac{1-\exp(-25 \bullet PD_j)}{1-\exp(-25)}\right)}$$

with $\omega_j \in [0.04; 0.15]$.

For a given confidence level $1-\alpha$ (e.g. 99.9%) the UL is estimated as follows. Let $z = \Phi^{-1}(1-\alpha)$, N the number of exposures in the considered portfolio, PD_j the conditional PD of exposure j, LGD_j the LGD and EAD_j the EAD.

Then the quantile $L(1\text{-}\alpha)$ of the loss distribution is estimated as $L(1-\alpha) = \sum_{i=1}^{N} EAD_i \bullet PD_i(z) \bullet LGD_i$ with $PD_j(z)$ as described above.

The required risk capital in the QIS 3 proposal has been defined as $RC = L(1-\alpha)$. In the latest version of the framework (QIS 4), it has been decided that the risk capital will be calculated without the EL of the portfolio, as the FIs will account for the EL in terms of pricing and (general and specific) provisions. Thereby, the RC represents the unexpected loss of the credit portfolio and is derived as follows: $RC = L(1-\alpha) - EL = L(1-\alpha) - \sum_{j=1}^{N} PD_j \cdot LGD_j \cdot EAD_j$.

We will use the "old" proposal of the BCBS for the derivation of the risk capital required for each rating segment in section 5.

The following table shows some combinations of PD and conditional PD (see section 3.5.2.4) dependent on LGD (fixed to 100%), maturity (fixed to 2.5 years) and asset correlation (fixed to 24%):[358]

PD (PD_j)	Conditional PD (P_j)
0.001	0.0393
0.007	0.1496
0.01	0.1872

Comparing the PD with the conditional PD, it becomes clear that the name "conditional PD" may be misleading. The conditional PD represents the total relative amount to the exposure that is supposed to be lost (from a regulatory point of view) by taking (pre-calibrated) portfolio effects into account.

To show the effect of maturity and asset correlations on the conditional PD, we have summarized some additional examples below. The effect is as it would have been expected: With a growing maturity and a growing correlation the conditional PD will rise, while keeping the other components fixed.

Table 3-15: The influence of various parameters on the conditional PD[359]

PD (PD_j)	Conditional PD (P_j)		
	LGD 100%, Maturity 2.5 years, Correlation 24%	Maturity 5 Years, c.p.	Correlation 12%, c.p.
0.001	0.0393	0.0460	0.02047
0.007	0.1496	0.1664	0.08304
0.01	0.1872	0.2064	0.10611

358 Similar sensitivity checks for the one-factor-model have been made by various authors, e.g. Bluhm et al. (2003).

359 Similar sensitivity checks for the one-factor-model have been made by various authors, e.g. Bluhm et al. (2003).

4 Active management of credit risk and capital

"When the only tool you have is a hammer, every problem begins to resemble a nail."
Abraham Maslow[360]

Based on a *sound* credit risk portfolio model, it is possible to focus on active credit portfolio management. Active credit portfolio management is closely linked to capital management, as capital is required for banks by regulators to perform their business. After a review of major aspects of capital management (section 4.1) three major building blocks of active credit portfolio management will be introduced subsequently. They belong to the domain of risk controlling, namely risk-adjusted pricing (section 4.2.1), risk-adjusted performance measurement (4.2.2) and economic capital allocation (4.2.3). We then skip to credit portfolio optimization.

4.1 Capital management[361]

The regulatory framework imposes the banks capital standards as a buffer against unforeseen losses for lending activities. As capital is scarce, the capital providers (shareholders) of a private firm have to be offered an appropriate and fair yield on their capital by a bank to carry out risky businesses as lending.[362] Portfolio management can thus equally be understood as a decision about the capital allocation of a financial institution[363] and capital allocation should therefore not be "ancillary to the business processes, it should be part of them" (Matten 2000, p.1).

With the words of Casserley (1991) in mind, we will start to deal with the nature and importance of efficient capital management[364]:

[360] See www.ag.wasthol.net/aphorism/A-1851, for example. Rev. February 2004.

[361] The presentation of capital management follows Matten (2000).

[362] Indeed, as Matten (2000, p.1) states, "efficient capital management is a fundamental, necessary precondition for the optimization of shareholder value for FIs."

[363] What will be the common nominator in section 5.

[364] This quotation has been taken from Matten (2000), p.1.

"Most businesses shun risk... they try and pass on their financial risk to others so that they can concentrate on making and selling their products. To succeed, however, financial firms must seek out risk. In nearly all their businesses, by being able to separate well priced from underpriced risks, they can prosper. By avoiding all risk, however, they cease to be financial firms at all and will wither away".

4.1.1 Capital in financial institutions: role, perspective, definitions

4.1.1.1 Why is capital important?

The answer to the question why capital is important "lies in the nature of capital" (Matten 2000, p. 29). In the following, we will examine the role of capital in financial institutions and the various existing definitions. In particular, it is very important to distinguish between funding and capital, what is "virtually unique to financial institutions and which is vital to an understanding of the subject of capital management" (Matten 2000, p.11).

We will follow Matten's considerations to understand the interest sphere of capital management of banks to be prepared for a solution to the capital allocation problem in terms of credit portfolio investment in section 5.

4.1.1.2 The role of capital in financial institutions

From the viewpoint of classic corporate finance theory, capital is assigned to two specific roles (Matten 2000, p. 14):

1. *Transference of ownership*: A public company may sell shares to transfer its ownership of assets, cash flow, profits, etc. to the buyers of its shares.
2. *Funding the business*: The transfer of ownership in a non-financial firm is closely linked to its funding, as the firm thereby receives external funding, which has to be invested in a preferably profitable way to earn a yield that is in line with the shareholder's expectations. As a consequence of a distinct treatment of interest payments to bondholders and shareholders with respect to the taxes (interest payments to bondholders are tax-deductible vice versa)

augmenting the debt/equity ratio up to a certain level will be advantagous, at least in theory.[365]

For financial institutions, conversely, the situation is different, as *banks have practically unconstrained funding*. In so far, classic corporate finance theory cannot be directly applied to banks (Matten 2000). The rationale behind this conclusion is that a bank's liabilities are an element of the activities of banks which thereby do not need capital as a key basis of financing, as they can lend by means of their own business at much lower costs than their capital would require.

As opposed to non-financial institutions, there is a third component of capital for banks.

3. *Regulatory capital*: Capital must be set aside to cushion against losses and is thus a key limiting factor for FIs to conduct their business.[366]

4.1.1.3 Five views of capital - five interest groups

Matten (2000) distinguishes between four different interest groups with respect to a bank's capital. Additionally, the view of external rating agencies can be seen as a crucial viewpoint. From the perspective of capital management in a financial institution, Matten (2000, p.35f.) claims that it would be essential to know that the different viewpoints on capital would are too similar to be perceived independently from each other:

- To manage the available capital base and to increase the profitability of the funds invested (**treasurer's perspective**[367]).

---

365 See Matten (2000), p. 14, for example.

366 Apart from our view within this work focussed on the lending business, Matten (2000, p.16f.) states that capital is also meant as a risk buffer for a bank's role as "an intermediary between savers and borrowers, pooling depositor's money and lending it out to those how need credit.(…) If a large number of depositors try to withdraw funds at the same time, the bank may be unable to meet their demands, leading to rumours that the bank is *'bankrupt'* and a subsequent panic what may happen even to perfectly healthy banks." See Matten (2000) for further information.

367 The treasurer has the responsibility for managing the available capital base of the bank.

- To manage the economic capital as the quantity of shareholders' investments which are either used as an insurance of risky business or as future income **(shareholder's perspective).**[368]
- To manage the risk capital which can be understood as a cushion for the occurrence of potential credit losses within a specific period of time and at a desired statistical confidence level by means of a sound risk management framework **(risk manager's perspective)**.
- To manage the regulatory capital according to the supervisory rules and guidelines defining the sum of a bank's qualifying capital in order to meet the regulatory requirements **(regulator's perspective)**.
- To successfully manage a bank's capital ensuring that the taken risks are in line with the expectable profit from a bank-external perspective **(External rating agencies).**

According to (Matten 2000, p. 33) the shareholder's perspective on capital is "arguably the most important one", as it would heavily influence the optimization of shareholder returns, which is supposed to be "the prime objective" of public companies' management. This perspective is, however, closely related to the risk manager's perspective, as the shareholders' opportunity costs as a compensation for the inherent risks of a business have to be considered by a bank's risk management. Further information about capital subject to different interest groups can be found in Matten (2000).

4.1.1.4 Definition of capital

As indicated above, the definition of capital is not always the same when we look at the different perspectives on capital as argued by Matten (2000, p. 30f.):

[368] This perspective should be closely related to the risk manager's perspective. The rational behind that is that the risk degree of the business policy specifies the shareholder's return target return on their invested capital.

- A **treasurer** will focus on all types of a bank's capital (equity, subordinated debt, hybrid instruments, etc.) and on the diminution of the overall capital costs.

  Physical capital may thereby be defined as "all capital instruments issued by the bank, regardless of how and whether they qualify for inclusion in capital by regulatory standards."

- A **shareholder** will center solely on the capital that is related to his/her investment (i.e. the capital of the bank, any retained earnings, share premium accounts, etc.).

  Economic capital may be defined as "the amount of the shareholder's investment which is either at risk in a business or has already been utilized to purchase future earnings."[369]

- From the perspective of a bank's **risk manager**, the risk of loss is crucial, while he/she will not be concerned about the consequences of occurring losses.

  Risk capital may be defined as "the amount needed to cover the potential diminution in the value of the assets and other exposures over a given time period, at a given statistical confidence interval."

- A **supervisor** will focus solely on the regulatory qualifying capital. He/she will thus exclude in part subordinated debt which has to be repaid only a few years before it is due and certain hybrid instruments in full.

  Regulatory capital may be defined as "all qualifying capital instruments issued by the bank, according to official rules and guidelines as to what constitutes qualifying capital."

---

[369] Risk capital + Goodwill = Economic capital. See Matten (2000), p.34.

4.1.1.5 Risk capital within this work

Capital in the sense of this work is related to the regulatory capital foreseen under Basel II (Basel II) including expected losses. As the regulatory capital converges to the economic capital, it is assumed that this capital definition is a compromise between the two risk capital types, leaving room for further extensions.[370]

4.1.2 What is capital management?

Generally, two major sides of capital management have to be distinguished from a bank's internal viewpoint (Matten 2000, p.7):

- To ensure that a bank's overall capital level is in line with the requests of several interest groups, such as
  - The returns expected by the shareholders,
  - The internal assessment of the level of risk being taken (Credit risk management),
  - The requirements of regulators and
  - The expectations of rating agencies.
- To ensure that all potential capital instruments and capital management activities (dividend-policy, share buy-back, etc.) are considered in order to guarantee its efficient usage, which is equal to a treasurers viewpoint.

Good capital management means "that these two aspects are managed as a single, coherent set of processes" (Matten 2000, p. 7), what has been the intention of modeling in section 5.

4.2 Credit risk controlling

Following major financial modeling of risk vs. return (e.g. the CAPM), credit is

370 In so far, regulatory capital is considered to equal economic capital as it is ideally intended to be.

usually granted with a spread on top of the riskless interest rate as a compensation for the inherent risk of a specific contract. The (net) margin (or net profit), which is the potential profit of the creditor dependent on the ex post result of a lending activity is shown in Table 4-2 in section 4.2.1.4.1. It is the task of credit risk controlling to deliver a preferably insightful perspective on the ex ante and ex post result of lending activities.

From a controlling perspective, a margin[371] should serve two purposes according to Schierenbeck (2003a, p.44):

- Give appropriate result information and
- Guide those who manage the business.

In order to serve these two purposes, every appropriate controlling methodology and/or concept designed to calculate the interest margin should follow five principles as described below (Schierenbeck 2003a, p.44):

1. Evaluation of every single transaction with its marginal profit contribution.
2. Delivery of independent and objective result information.
3. Integrated calculation of the ex post (controlling[372]) and the ex ante (pricing) lending result, allowing any desired level of aggregation.
4. Acceptance by senior management as a tool for pricing decisions.
5. Reconciliation with accounting numbers.

The two major techniques of credit risk controlling to fulfill these principles are *risk-adjusted pricing* and *risk-adjusted performance measurement*, to be explained in the following.

4.2.1 Risk-based (adjusted) pricing (RbP)

Traditionally, all creditors with a sufficient creditworthiness to be offered credit are priced at uniform rates. This approach – *'one size fits all'*[373] – leads to cross -

[371] The term margin is used synonymously to spread.
[372] State-of- the-art controlling is related to risk-adjusted performance measurement.
[373] The expression is commonly used by many authors, e.g. Ong (1999), p.20.

subsidies since creditors with a higher credit quality sponsor those of lower credit quality and result to adverse selection as shown in Figure 4-1 below.

It has therefore become a common practice in banks to demand a risk-adjusted premium for each credit and to aggregate these premiums in a bank-internal account (called *expected loss reserve).*[374] Banks thereby generate a cushion to cover average losses arising from insolvent borrowers.[375] Pricing credit according to this principle is a state-of-the-art technique known as risk-based (or risk-adjusted) pricing (e.g. Ong 1999, p.59).

Risk-adjusted pricing methods have only recently become well-discussed among bankers in Europe, although this concept has been applied relatively long in the US for consumer loans, for example (Manz 1998). There exists a common fear that a full realization might reduce the market share of a bank, what causes resistance among the market participants against risk-adjusted pricing. Additionally, it is feared that risk-adjusted pricing drives borrowers with financial problems into further difficulties and even leads to more financial exclusion.[376]

---

[374] Bluhm et al. (2003), p.16.

[375] See Bluhm et al. (2003), for example.

[376] This is commonly subsumed under the term credit rationing. Further information can be found in Stiglitz (1981) and Varian (1993), for example.

Figure 4-1: Modern lending: Adverse selection and profit/loss from a bank's perspective (according to Rolfes and Schierenbeck 2001, p.19)

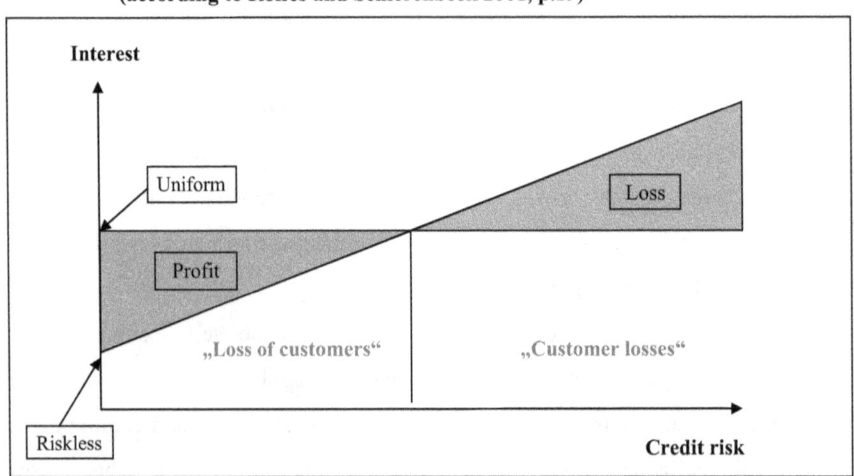

Below, alternative concepts for risk-adjusted pricing will be reviewed followed by a brief discussion of distinct initialization methods for risk-adjusted credit prices. Finally, embedding pricing into risk-adjusted performance measurement will be explained.

4.2.1.1 Eligible risk-adjusted pricing methodologies

Various methodologies exist for pricing credit risk of debt instruments, e.g.:[377]

- The option pricing model,
- The market credit spread model and
- The probabilistic model.

As the first two approaches refer to market driven attempts, the probabilistic model is considered the most suitable one for loan portfolios as the contract's internal risk grade represents the central issue of the probabilistic model.[378]

It is common to refer to a pricing of pools of collectively assessed transactions with common risk characteristics (e.g. rating segments). Therefore, borrowers

[377] See e.g. Jorion (2000), p.489f. Further information about eligible pricing methodologies can be found in various standard financial textbooks.

[378] Hence, one may also refer to this method as the rating/scoring based pricing methodology.

within the same risk bucket are charged the same rate (*pricing grid*). Pricing grids may refer to:[379]

- o Risk grades (rating/scoring),
- o Product types,
- o Collateral types,
- o Loan-to-value.[380]

We will refer to risk grades.

4.2.1.2 The main pricing components[381]

Risk-based pricing is based on various basic credit risk parameters as introduced in section 3. From a formal viewpoint, the two major drivers for setting the interest rate are

- o *Standard risk costs* (Expected losses) and
- o *Risk capital costs* (Interest on the capital portion).

Other important drivers, which are, by contrast, "only" traversing costs, are

- o *Refinance costs and*
- o *Overhead costs.*

A crucial role for credit pricing plays the general interest rate level set by the ECB (the Fed) within the EU (the US). These rates define the refinance rate of financial institutions (IBOR/EURIBOR). Further information and discussion about interest rates can be found in Jorion (2001), for example.

4.2.1.2.1 Standard risk costs (SRC)

Standard risk costs refer to the expected loss which is defined as the average loss anticipated for each single creditor i: $SRC_i = EL_i$.

---

379 Additionally, other segmentation criteria may be considered;

380 The loan-to-value- ratio describes the portion of exposure relative to the value of the collateral.

381 A comprehensive illustration of the pricing contribution components is given in Schierenbeck (2003a), for example, and in various other financial textbooks.

As the standard risk costs of all single contracts are additive, the consideration of the standard risk costs on different portfolio aggregation levels is simplified, in particular

$$\text{Standard risk costs} = \sum_i \text{Standard risk costs of borrower i (or contract i).}$$

4.2.1.2.2 Risk capital costs[382] and profit margin

Risk capital[383] is the amount of capital needed to cover potential losses (unexpected losses) due to fluctuation of the portfolio's credit loss distribution up to a specified upper threshold over a given time period (see section 3.5.1.5.6.3). For the capital portion required for each obligor according to his/her marginal risk contribution within the portfolio, the FI demands a target interest rate (hurdle rate) set on a strategic level.[384] Dependent on the riskiness of a transaction, an additional profit margin may be charged.

4.2.1.2.3 Refinancing costs (RFC)

The residual part of the exposure that has not been financed by capital has to be refinanced by the bank at a rate according to the bank's external rating and the success of treasury.

4.2.1.2.4 Overhead costs (Administrative costs and others)

For the conduction of its lending business, banks charge borrowers overhead costs in form of refinance related costs and other, additional costs (to perform credit risk analysis, for example). We will refer to a general level of 50 bps for the bundle of overhead costs (sometimes also referred to as administrative costs) what is rather high but conservative.

Figure 4-2 below gives an overview over the underlying pricing components.

---

[382] The basics of risk capital can be found in section 3.5.1.5.6.3ff.

[383] As a generic term representing economic capital or regulatory capital. See Matten (2000), p.334, for example.

[384] Each financial institution sets a desired target ROC (RAPM) on a strategic level in order to generate an adequate return on capital for its shareholders. Recently, Deutsche Bank announced a ROC target of 19% (Handelsblatt, October 5, 2003). We will refer to a hurdle rate of 16% for illustrative purposes.

Figure 4-2: Pricing components

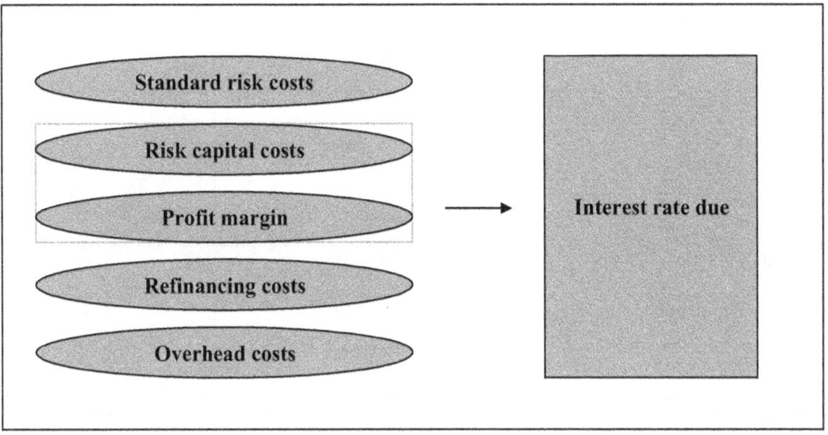

4.2.1.3 Traditional risk-based (or risk-adjusted) pricing (RbP/RaP) approaches

In the following, we will introduce the 'cost + profit' method as a traditional method to price credits.[385] The market interest rate method is a best-practice method and will be explained below.

4.2.1.3.1 A simple credit pricing approach

With the intention of a better understanding of the process of pricing a five-year loan, we will regard an illustrative example, termed as *'cost + profit approach'* according to Caouette et al. (1998, p.253f.). The final minimum annual interest rate to be paid for the considered borrower would be 11.71%, with a spread of 1.71% on the hypothetical refinance rate of 10%.

---

[385] An illustrative example for the pricing of a credit has been provided by Altman (2002), for example.

Table 4-1: Price build-up based on cost plus profit (according to Caouette et al. 1998, p.254)

Item	Calculation	Amount
Borrower's risk rating		BB
Loan maturity		5 years
5-year -PD		6.15%
Capital ratio (Basel I)		8%
Hurdle rate (Interest on capital RoC)		16%
Nominal loan amount		1,000,000
Capital required (8 % of loan exposure)	0.08•1,000,000	80,000
Price buildup		
Annual risk capital costs (16 %)	0.16•80,000	12,800
Annual refinancing costs (10 % fixed)	0.1•920,000	92,000
Annual standard risk costs (SRC)	(0.0615•1,000,000)/5	12,300
Break-even annual interest income	12,800 + 92,000 + 12,300	117,100
Loan interest rate (without funding risk)	117,100/1,000,000	11.71%
Minimum spread	11.71-10.00[386] (%)	171 bps = 1.71%

4.2.1.4 The market interest rate method (MIM)[387] to derive an appropriate margin[388]

The roots of the market interest rate method can be found in a concept for *"pretial"*[389] business steering of Schmalenbach (1947) postulating decentralized management within a bank-wide coordination.

386 The funding rate in the example is fixed at 10%.

387 Or Matched Funds Transfer Pricing Concept (MFTP- Concept).

388 The explanation of the Market Interest Rate method follows Schierenbeck (2003a).

389 In German.

The concept found its first practical appliance in the Money Center Bank (U.S.) for the decision based management of their interest business. McKinsey & Co. brought the concept into the German market (under the term opportunity interest rate method, OIR- method).

Schierenbeck (1985) introduced the term ***market interest rate method*** (MIM). Since then, the concept has been improved and extended and has become an integrated standard of bank-wide controlling.[390]

The MIM's fundamental idea is that a transaction's attainable margin is the calculatory difference between the result of the customer deal and an alternative money or capital market deal.

The MIM is a costing and controlling method that separates interest into three components and assigns responsibility for each separate component (Schierenbeck 2003a, p.71f.):

- Market risk (*Structure contribution*[391]),
- The advantage of the customer contract in comparison to risk-free alternative on the money and capital markets (*Condition contribution from assets*[392]),

[390] In order to initialize a convergence of the practical-oriented application on the MIM-method in the Anglo-American world and the theoretical-oriented, bank-wide focused German concept, Schierenbeck (2003a) has proposed the term "Matched Funds Transfer Pricing Concept" (MFTP-concept). Further information about traditional bank controlling methodologies can be found in Köllhofer (1975), for example.

[391] The structure contribution is a direct consequence of different interest rates on the capital and money markets for distinct terms and interest commitment periods. The structure contribution is the profit/loss due to currency, liquidity, cash flow and fixed interest rate duration mixture mismatches between assets and liabilities. This means, that banks can use different interest commitment periods for profit generation by referring to short-term liabilities and long-term assets for normal interest rate structures and vice versa. The final target of SC yields to interest rate structure risk not considered within this work (Treasury, see section 4.1.1.3). For further reference see Schierenbeck (2003a).

[392] The condition contribution from assets is the yield advantage of a customer transaction with a customer or other bank compared to an alternative transaction in the money and capital markets with the same cash flow, liquidity, currency and fixed interest rate duration structure (often referred to as "matched funding" (Schierenbeck 2003a). The contribution margin is calculated relative to IBOR/Swap rates (i.e. "riskless" transactions to AAA banks). To calculate this advantage, every single transaction is analyzed according to the above criteria.

- The advantage of a specific funding source in comparison to funding on the money and capital markets (*Condition contribution from liabilities*[393]).

4.2.1.4.1 Single transaction pricing based on the MIM- method

For the risk result of a credit risk profit center, the condition contribution from assets is relevant and has to be broken down to the cost components. The following example for a borrower who has been charged an interest rate of 4.6% is taken from Theiler (2002b).

Table 4-2: Profitability measurement for a single credit (according to Theiler 2002b)

Level	Item	Interest (%)
	Lending rate	4.6
	- Refinancing[394](IBOR/Swap)	3.8
Profit contribution level I	**= Condition contribution margin**	**0.8**
	- Standard risk costs	0.05
Profit contribution level II	**= Risk-adjusted margin**	**0.75**
	- Standard operating costs	0.1
Profit contribution level III	**= Net margin/profit**	**0.65**
	- Risk capital costs	0.25
Profit contribution level IV = EVA™	**= Additional profit**	**0.4**

An initial annual lending rate of 4.6% finally yields to an additional profit of 0.4%. Usually, three or four profit contribution levels are distinguished. Level four denotes the final profit over the target ROC demanded by a FI's shareholders. It has been termed as Economic Value Added (EVA™). Further insights into pricing will be given in section 5.3.3.2.

[393] The condition contribution margin from liabilities reflects the yield advantage of using customer deposits as a funding source compared to alternative funding sources in the money and capital markets. These rates are again synonymously called "matched-funding" rates.

[394] $0.95 \cdot 0.04$, referring to an economic capital level of 5%.

4.2.1.5 The pricing process: Initiation of new credit prices[395]

As opposed to other innovations, the price policy ("the right price management"[396]) offers three chances: saving of time, prevention of additional costs and higher increase of return as the price of a product is the "driver unit for profit" par excellence (Öhler and Unser 2001).

The term "value pricing" plays an increasing, strategic role and is embedded into an extensive pricing process.[397]

Wübker (2004) distinguishes between five phases of the pricing process:

- Strategic planning (targets, positioning, competition).
- Inventory control, actual situation/- process.
- Price decision (structure, level, differentiation, bundling).
- Implementation (Organization/responsibility, IT, incentives).
- Controlling/monitoring.

The process is graphically shown below.

Figure 4-3: The five phases of pricing (according to Wübker 2004)

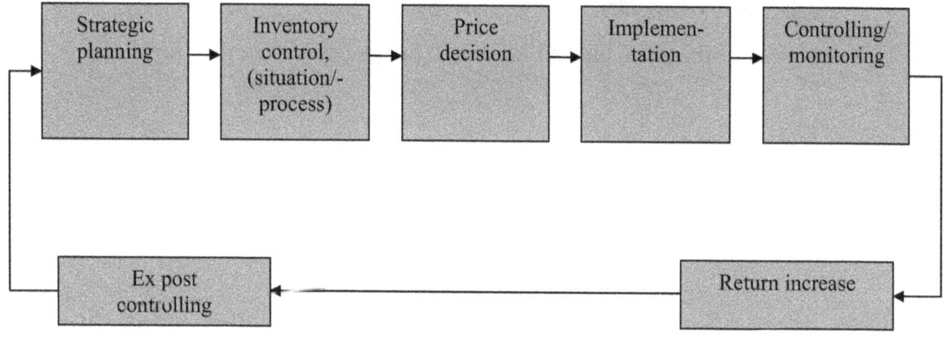

Clearly, offensive pricing is always related to a decrease of market share, and the trade-off has to be analyzed carefully. A strategic illustration of pricing

[395] This section is oriented on Öhler and Unser (2001).
[396] Wübker (2004), p. 7.
[397] See Wübker (2003), p.156f., for example.

aspects is shown below. Strategies for the initiation of pricing strategies can be found in Krall (2000) and will be addressed below.

Pricing strategies for the future ("the time after adverse selection")

Given the shortcoming of the traditional pricing of credit loans last but not least as a consequence of the high influence of the strict regulatory frame, it is crucial for banks to adapt to new pricing strategies (risk-based pricing) as soon as possible dependent on their strategic position within the market. Currently, capital arbitrage is traded via the capital markets, allowing for a compensation of all market participants (see section 4.3.10).

Theory states how to price single credit loans by demanding adequate margins for the inherent risk of a transaction. On the other hand, there are resistances in the market, last but not least because of a bank seeking for an adequate market share has to be compensated with low interest rates. Long-lasting relationships especially with retail customers are an argument that has raising support propagated by conservative credit managers.

Krall (2000) suggests a slow shift of the threshold between the "Me-too" business on the one hand and the rejected engagements on the other hand.

Figure 4-4: Concentration on value-generating contract relationships (Krall 2000, p.26)

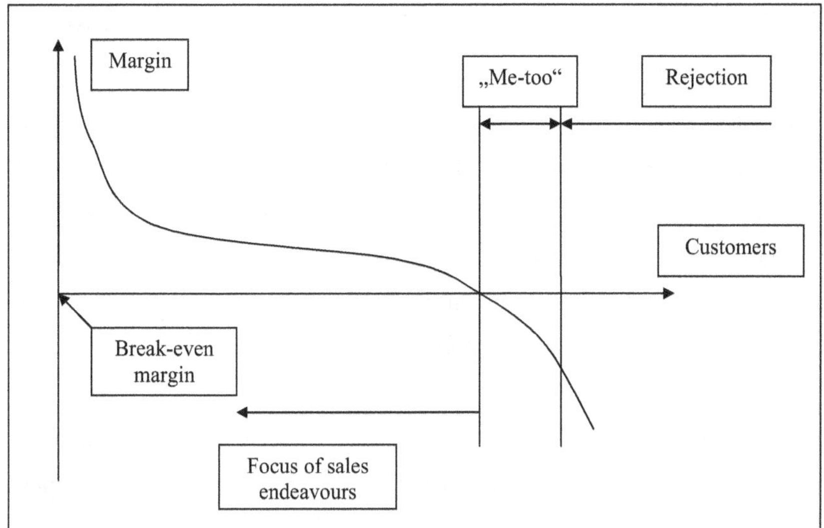

Based on his findings, Krall (2000) suggests and evaluates four possible pricing strategies.

Figure 4-5: Alternative pricing strategies (according to Krall 2000, p.27)

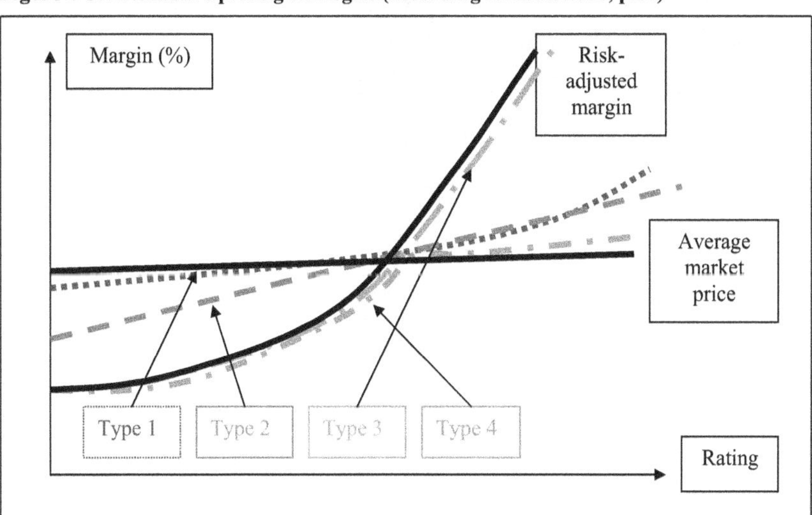

Krall's (2000) evaluation of the pricing strategies reveals the following results:

- The type 1-strategy is concentrated on a slow approach of the realizable process to the break-even margins for lower credit qualities. This strategy enables a performance improvement of ca. 40 bps.
- A reduction of the margin deficit for low-quality loans is a desire of strategy number two besides a modest improvement of the margins for high-quality loans that suffer disintermediation (an evasion into the traded credit market). Krall (2000) expects a potential of 30 bps applying this strategy.
- Following the type 3-strategy, an investor should offer risk-adjusted prices for all risk segments. This strategy would lead to an additional profit of approximately 15 bps.
- Giving away the price pressure on the investment grade sector without a price adoption for low-grade customers would lead to a highly inefficient policy.

According to Krall (2000), the US credit market showed a tendency to follow strategy 2. Öhler and Unser (2001) concludes that the advantage of a sophisticated pricing allows a more accurate forecasting of a bank's performance (via expected, long-term averages).

The knowledge about the impact of pricing strategies should lead to a differentiated pricing strategy and a portfolio restructuring as it has been graphically illustrated by Krall (2000).

Figure 4-6: Differentiated pricing strategy and portfolio restructuring (Krall 2000, p.28)

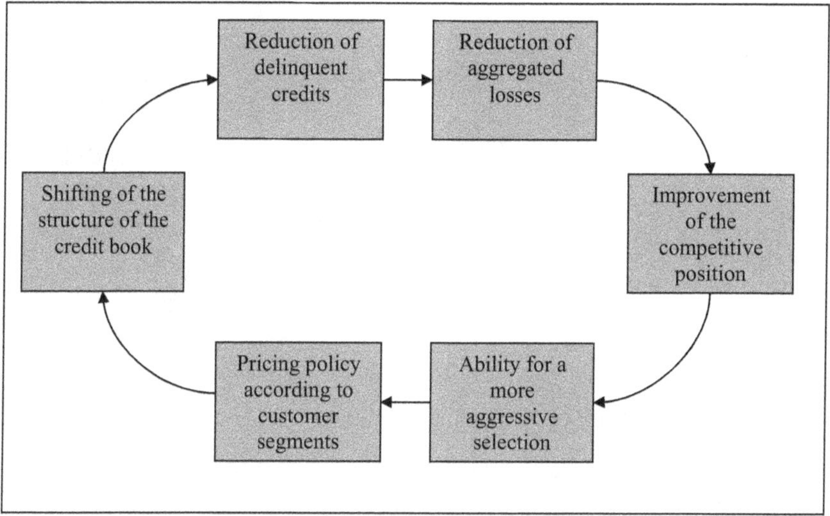

4.2.2 Risk-adjusted performance measurement (RAPM)

Given a preferably risk-adjusted pricing of credits within a bank's portfolio, the stochastic process of defaults (depicted as the risk result) delivers backflow cash flows (from investments) resulting in profit or loss. Given an appropriate segmentation of the portfolio and the ex ante capital portion assigned to borrowers and subportfolio segments according to their risk contribution (in % relative to the nominal exposure), the nominal returns of each segment (or even single obligation) can be compared to each other by comparing risk and return as trade-off measures.

The generic terms used to describe these models is RAPM (risk-adjusted performance measurement), comprising all techniques which adjust returns for the risk incurred in earning those returns both ex ante and ex post. RAPM thereby seems just a "trivial follow-on" of credit pricing (Ong 1999, p.60).

The overall context is illustrated below.

Figure 4-7: Depiction of the outcome of the risk results

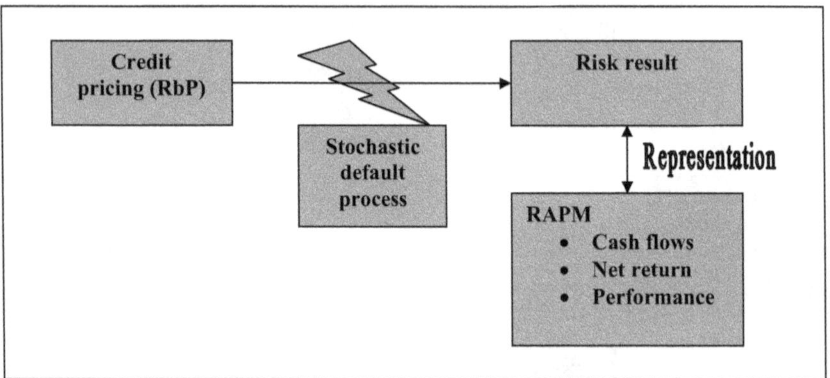

4.2.2.1 What is RAPM? - Distinction of eligible RAPM concepts

Risk-adjusted performance measures have been described by Punjabi (1998) as follows:

"These measures take into account the risk embedded in the returns as well as the returns themselves and provide a common, aggregated framework to access the contributions of various transactions and business units to the firm's value."

Risk-adjusted performance measurement (or RAPM) can be considered as a buzzword in last ten years banking.[398] Indeed, the expression is supposed to embrace "a whole bundle of concepts", as "just about every institution (be it a bank or a firm of consultants) which has introduced or is toying with RAPM will given a different definition of what it means" (Matten 2000, p.146). Apart from the existing RAPM labels, all RAPM can be reduced to a common denominator: "They compare return against the capital invested by adopting some form of risk adjustment, based on internal assessments of how risky something (an asset, a transaction, a business etc.) may be" (Matten 2000, p.146).

Incorporating the risk-adjustment function into the credit modeling process a standard risk-adjusted performance measure may be defined as follows:[399]

[398] See Matten (2000), p.146.

[399] See Ong (1999), p. 218, for example.

$$\text{RAPM} = \frac{\text{Revenues - Costs - Losses}}{\text{(Risk-adjusted) Capital or (Risk-adjusted) Assets}}.$$

The numerator of the RAPM consists of the gross revenues, subtracted by both the costs of doing business, and the potential losses (e.g. the expected mean losses). In making the net profit of a business (the residual of the nominator) comparable, the nominator is standardized by the risk-adjusted capital (or assets) used to generate that net profit - the balancing act between risk and return.

The four most frequently mentioned RAPM measures are RORAA, RAROA, RORAC and RAROC.[400] While the first two ratios are asset-based RAPM measures (derived from the well-known ROA ratio), the latter two ratios are capital-based RAPM measures (derived from the well-known ROE or ROC ratio). The specific distinction of the two ratios within the common definition of assets and capital, respectively, is, whether the risk-adjustment is applied to the nominator (RAROA, RAROC) or the denominator (RORAA, RORAC). We will refer to the capital-based measures only, as capital is the focus of this work:[401]

- **RORAC (return on risk-adjusted capital):** In case of the RORAC, the regulatory capital in the denominator is replaced by an internal measure of capital (e.g. economic capital) compared to the well-known ROC ratio.

- **RAROC[402] (risk-adjusted return on capital):** In case of the RAROC, the nominator is risk-adjusted (e.g. by applying the standard risk costs) compared to the ROC ratio.

Matten (2000, p.147) continues that RAPM definitions may be misleading, as “the same concepts may easily be encountered with a different acronym” vice versa. This could be noticed, for example, as “most RAROC models turn out on closer inspection to use the RORAC equation” (Matten 2000, p.147). The list of RAPM measures has been further extended, for example, by the RARORAC

[400] See Matten (2000), p.147.

[401] See Matten (2000), p.147.

[402] RAROC has been extensively documented in literature, e.g. by James (1996), Zaik et al. (1996) and Stroughton and Zechner (1999a/b).

(risk-adjusted return on risk-adjusted capital).[403] Nonetheless, the potential volatility (of the present value) of a particular transaction or (sub)portfolio remains the common root of all past and future RAPM concepts.

For practical reasons, it is not useful to establish the most sensible, reasonable and practical solutions for implementation, because, "after all, the results of any modeling process that cannot be articulated and explained *in simple terms* to both senior management and regulatory supervisors do not have a chance of being fully accepted."[404] We will refer to the RORAC for exemplified purposes in section 5.

4.2.2.2 Strategic data of a bank: Example

In Table 4-3 below, hypothetic strategic data of a FI according to Theiler (2002b) are listed[405]. The available (overall) risk capital of a FI may be 20 Bill. Euros. A risk-adjusted return target (RORAC) of 17.5% would lead to a nominal return (yield) target of 3.5 Bill. Euros. Opposed to the internal definition of risk capital within a FI, regulators define prerequisites for capital to be used as regulatory capital, intended to prevent a FI from bankruptcy (see section 2.3). Regulatory capital is defined more narrowly according to three tiers.[406] A target ROC would be related to tier 1 capital, leading to 19.4% (= 3.5 Bill/18Bill.). Compared to Lloyds TSB Group (see Table 2-3 above), the prospected performance of this hypothetical bank is, however, rather decent.

Table 4-3: Risk-return data of a bank: Illustrative example (according to Theiler 2002b)

Return target	3.5 Billion Euro
Available risk capital (internal definition)	20 Billion Euro
Target RORAC	17.5%
Tier 1 capital (regulatory definition)	18 Billion Euro
Target ROC	19.4%

403 See Matten (2000), for example.

404 Ong (1999), p.222.

405 Although the data are similar to the actual data of Deutsche Bank.

406 Especially the first tier plays a crucial rule, as this capital portion is the most liquid. See www.bis.org for further details.

Besides performance indicators, risk management and risk controlling provides information about the default risk of a bank. Based on these data, the default probability of the bank itself can be measured (see Figure 4-8 according to Krall 2000).

The default threshold is based on a bank's profit distribution and the external rating of a bank. Major insights of the parameters shown and the related insights have been given in Table 3-13 in section 3.5.1.5.6.3.

Figure 4-8: Confidence level and target of creditworthiness (Krall 2000, p.33)

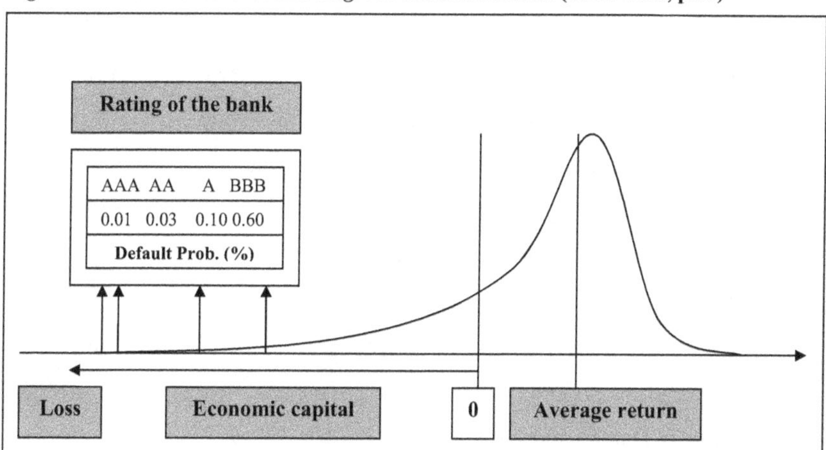

4.2.2.3 Conclusion for the application of the RAPM - concept

The following facets underlie a bank's needs to use some kind of RAPM according to Ong (1999, p.240/241):

- Enterprise-wide risk management
    - Provide an integrated view of market, credit, operational and liquidity risk policies.
    - Establish a common language to communicate risk.
- Business strategy and corporate risk appetite
    - Create a link between strategic, operating and risk management objectives and expected return.
    - Identify, evaluate and measure portfolio risk.

    - Assess the trade-off between risk and reward.
- Performance evaluation
    - Apply risk-adjusted performance measures to refine business strategies.
    - Establish a consistent performance measurement.
    - Establish better reward mechanisms through relative merits.
- Improvement in pricing
    - Price loans and other credit-embedded transactions on a risk-adjusted basis.
    - Define hurdle rates that can be used to evaluate the true profitability of transactions across customers and product lines.
- Arbitrage between economic and regulatory capital
- Future regulatory requirements
    - Prepare the forthcoming regulatory requirements for capital adequacy using risk-adjusted methodologies.
- Better measurement tools for credit derivatives market and asset securitization activities

Ong (1999, p. 241) adequately summarizes the role of RAPM measures from an enterprise-wide viewpoint:

"It is clearly evident that any risk-adjusted performance measure sits at the core of an organization, affecting its internal risk policies and strategic decision function, the execution of these strategies and policies, the measurement of performance, the determination of compensation schemes, and, ultimately, the enhancement of shareholder value."

4.2.3 Economic capital allocation[407]

The task of allocating economic capital within a financial institution and profit centers is a major concern for banks in order to be stable against unforeseen

[407] This sections is closely oriented on Patrick et al. (1999) and Theiler (2002a/b).

losses and competitive. Blache and Bluhm (2001) recognize three hierarchical levels that capital allocation is tangent to:

- *Bank-wide:* As a capital cushion against ULs.
- *Macro level:* Quantification of risk positions on a profit center level.
- *Micro level:* Risk-adjusted pricing of single contracts.

All three levels will be given devoted sufficient attentiveness throughout this work. The new regulatory capital approach by Basel (see Basel 2002 and Basel 2004, for example) tries to unify both portfolio effects and single credit properties (and thereby all three levels) by assigning capital of a well-diversified portfolio to single borrowers. We will generally refer to the Basel approach in section 5.

4.2.3.1 Capital allocation in general

Patrick et al. (1999, p.63/64) have formulated properties that an allocation principle for the measurement of internal risk should meet:

- The allocation method should be risk-adjusted and account for the riskiness of any sub-portfolio, i.e. consider diversification and dependency from the overall portfolio perspective.
- The capital allocation should be additive, i.e. the overall portfolio risk should split into the risk contributions of the sub-portfolios which add up to the total portfolio risk.
- The risk contribution of any sub-portfolio is supposed to be independent from its affiliation to an organizational unit.
- The measurement of the risk contribution must be based on the same underlying risk modeling as used for the overall portfolio (*"a single risk measure"*[408]).
- Furthermore, the allocation should be based on reliable information and be practicable, i.e. obtainable with a reasonable effort.

[408] See Theiler (2002a/b), for example.

4.2.3.2 Capital allocation methodologies[409]

In the following, distinct capital allocation methodologies will be presented. Patrick et al. (1999, p.65-70) assess alternative methods of capital allocation:[410]

- Exposure based (1),
- Stand alone risk based (2) and
- Global risk contribution measures (3).

Exposure based principles relate the capital portion to be allocated according to the exposure of the asset relative to the overall exposure. *Stand alone allocation methods* measure risk contributions by the stand alone risk of the assets. *Global risk measures* define the risk contribution of every sub-portfolio from the overall portfolio perspective and allocate capital to sub-portfolios according to their contribution to the overall portfolio risk.

4.2.3.2.1 Alternative approaches for capital allocation on a bank-wide level

Patrick et al. (1999) come to the conclusion that allocation methods based on global risk measures best meet the demanded properties of capital allocation are discussed acoordingly.[411]

For completeness, we will discuss the first two methods besides three alternative concepts for global risk measures to allocate capital by closely referring to Theiler (2002a/b).

The allocation schemes ranked by their tendency of risk-adjustment are shown below.

[409] A definition of risk capital and its purpose has been given in section 3.5.1.5.6.3 ff. The risk capital is supposed to protect a bank from insolvency as denoted in section 2.4.4.4.

[410] See Theiler (2002a/b). Patrick et al. (1999) used the classification "local", "volume" and "global" risk measure, which is similar to Theiler's classification.

[411] See Patrick et al. (1999), pp. 69-70.

Figure 4-9: Capital allocation methods by increasing risk-adjustment (Theiler 2002b)

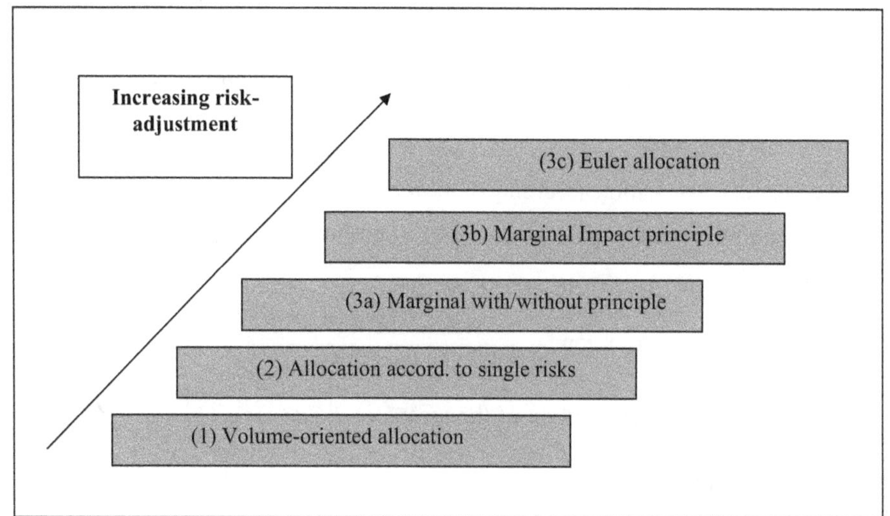

The third global allocation method, also known as *Euler allocation* has been proven to be sound and provides fair risk contributions (Denault 1999).[412] In the following, the alternative capital allocation methods are described more precisely.

4.2.3.2.1.1 Volume oriented allocation

This method lacks the risk-adjustment property as the criterion to allocate capital is derived according to the underlying volume:

$$\text{Relative Risk Contribution}=\frac{\text{Volume Unit}_i}{\text{Total Volume}_{Portfolio}}$$

[412] The Euler allocation is derived from a game theoretical field and is based on the gradient of the overall risk measure. Denault (1999) models a coalitional game, where players, i.e. sub-portfolios of the bank portfolio, are searching for an optimal split of the overall capital costs of the economic capital. While searching an optimal way to allocate the overall capital cost of the full coalition the players try to minimize their own share of costs. Tasche (1999, p.9f.) has shown that under the assumption of a coherent risk measure, the Euler allocation represents the unique solution of the capital allocation problem and thus an efficient allocation principle of the overall portfolio risk. See Theiler (2002a), p.98f.;

and respectively the risk contribution $RCB_j(\mathrm{x})$ of the jth asset is $RCB_{\mathrm{i}}(\mathrm{x})=\frac{\mathrm{X_i}}{\sum_i X_i}$,

leading to a capital allocation for asset i of $C_{\mathrm{i}}(\mathrm{X})=\mathrm{C}\bullet RCB_i(X)$ where C is the total capital of a FI.

4.2.3.2.1.2 Allocation according to local risk measures

Portfolio effects are neglected when risk contributions are measured on a stand alone basis:

$$\text{Relative Risk Contribution}=\frac{\text{Standalone Risk}_{\mathrm{i}}}{\text{Total Standalone Risk}_{Portfolio}}$$

yielding to a risk contribution of the asset i of $RCB_{\mathrm{i}}(\mathrm{x})=\frac{RCB_{\mathrm{E}}(x_i)}{\sum_i RCB_{\mathrm{E}}(x_i)}$ and thus

$C_{\mathrm{i}}(\mathrm{X})=\mathrm{C}\bullet RCB_i(X)$.

4.2.3.2.1.3 Global risk measures: Marginal with/without principle

The pitfall of this global risk measure is the non-fulfilled property of risk additivity when applying the marginal with/without principle:

Relative Risk Contribution = Portfolio Risk with i[th] unit minus Portfolio Risk without i[th] unit, where $RCB_{\mathrm{i}}(\mathrm{x})=\mathrm{RCB}(\mathrm{x})\text{-}\mathrm{RCB}(\mathrm{x}\text{-}\mathrm{x_i}e^{(i)})$ and $C_{\mathrm{i}}(\mathrm{X})=\mathrm{RCB}_i(X)$.

4.2.3.2.1.4 Global risk measures: Marginal impact principle

When measuring the marginal impact of the risk contribution of a single asset, the risk adjustment property is approximately fulfilled:

Relative Risk Contribution=(Partial deviation of i[th]unit)$\bullet$ Volume$_{\mathrm{i}}$

yielding to $RCB_{\mathrm{i}}(\mathrm{x})=\frac{\partial RCB(x)}{\partial x_i}$ and $C_{\mathrm{i}}(\mathrm{X})=\mathrm{RCB}_i(X)$ and $\mathrm{C}(\mathrm{X})=\sum_{J=1}^{n} C_i$.

4.2.3.2.1.5 Global risk measures: Euler allocation

The Euler allocation can be interpreted as a sensitivity measure via partial deviation. All required properties are fulfilled as shown be Denault (1999). The question of the risk contribution of an asset ("How does the overall portfolio risk change with respect to an infinitesimal change of the exposure of a single asset?") can be answered.[413] The general quantitative impact of the measure is shown below:[414]

$$\text{Relative Risk Contribution} = \frac{\text{Marginal change of risk}}{\text{Marginal change of unit}}, \text{ leading to}$$

$$RCB_i(\text{x}) = \frac{\text{RCB}(\text{x}+\text{he}^{(i)})\text{-RCB}(x)}{h} \text{ and } C_i(\text{X}) = \text{RCB}_i(X).^{415}$$

Theiler (2004) formally develops the derivation of risk contribution according to the Euler allocation. We will follow her findings. Let RCB(x) denote a positively homogeneous risk measure.[416] Assuming that the partial derivatives $\frac{\partial RCB(\text{x})}{\partial x_j}, j=1,...,n$ exist at x, we have according to Euler's formula the following representation of the overall portfolio risk RCB(x) for the portfolio x:[417]

$$\text{RCB(x)} = \vartriangle RCB(x)'x = \sum_{i=1}^{n} \frac{\partial RCB(x)}{\partial x_i} \bullet x_i$$

The risk contribution $RCB_j(\text{x})$ of the jth asset is given by the jth term of RCB(x), i.e.

$$RCB_j(\text{x}) = \frac{\partial RCB(x)}{\partial x_j} \bullet x_j, j=1,...,n$$

4.2.3.2.2 Conclusion[418]

The Euler allocation principle generates additive representations of the overall portfolio risk, which is at the same risk-adjusted and takes into account all diversification effects. It allows to sum up the risk contributions on any sub-portfolio level and thus to achieve the economic capital allocation for any organizational unit. It is the allocation principle that leads to minimal economic

---

413 See Theiler (2004).

414 According to Theiler (2002b).

415 'h' represents a marginal number and 'e^{i}' the exposure of the ith unit.

416 The risk measure RCB(x) is positively homogeneous (of degree 1), if $\forall t \in \Re^{+} : r(t \bullet x) = t \bullet r(x)$.

417 See Tasche (1999), for example.

418 The conclusion is oriented on Theiler (2002a).

capital costs of any sub-portfolio and also the efficient risk-adjusted performance measurement ratios.

The capital allocation of economic capital represents the basis for risk-adjusted performance measurement within a banking portfolio. In an analytic approach Tasche (1999) has shown that the Euler allocation is the only allocation principle that is suitable for RAPM. In other words, if we determine the risk contributions by the Euler allocation principle, we achieve reliable management information, as we measure the "right" risk-adjusted performance based on an appropriate risk measure.

Thus, RORAC can be defined as $RORAC_j(x) = \frac{\mu_j(x)}{RCB_j(x)}$, where the risk contribution $RCB_j(x)$ is estimated according to the Euler allocation and the return contribution $\mu_j(x)$ of the jth asset, $j=1,\ldots,n$ is given by the jth term of the return function: $\mu_j(x) = \mu_j \bullet x_j$.

4.3 Credit portfolio management and optimization

"All business proceeds on beliefs, on judgments of probabilities and not on certainties." Charles.W. Eliot (1834-1926)[419]

4.3.1 Active credit portfolio management: An overview

The final stage of the credit risk management process is to actively manage the acquirement and selling of the credit portfolio as shown below.

[419] See www.workingit.com/Work%20articles/Risk%20Management.htm, for example. Rev. May 2004.

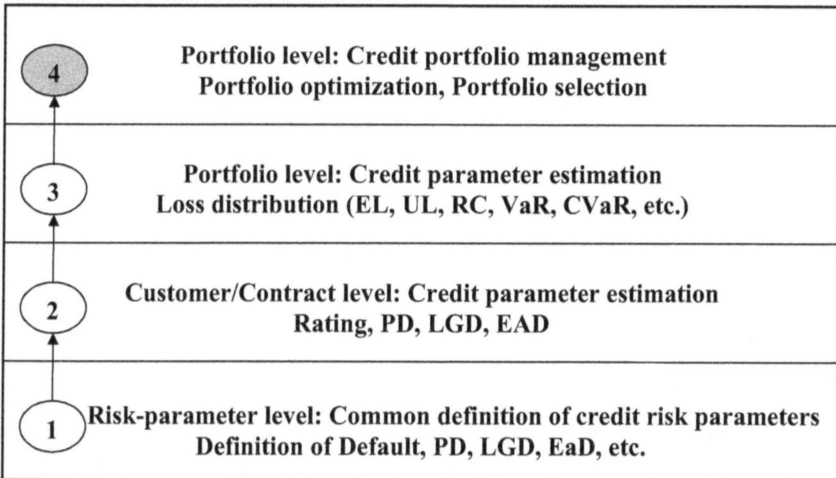

The traditional approach to manage credit portfolio risks is the usage of credit limits, netting agreements and collateral.[420] These techniques have been proven to be inadequate to capture credit portfolio risk effects. For this reason, other approaches have been developed and applied and will be discussed in the following.

The optimal choice of a portfolio has been a longstanding problem for portfolio managers (Grinold and Kahn 1999). It is common to optimize two dimensions: risk and return. However, the direct application of traditional Markowitz (1952) theory to credit portfolios is not feasible as the standard deviation is not a justifiable risk measure given return distributions with heavy tails and a high skeweness.[421] It is therefore possible, for example, to use the unexpected loss at a given confidence level (VaR) or the conditional average of losses exceeding a certain threshold (Lower Partial Moment 1) or a confidence level (Conditional Value-at-Risk) instead of the standard deviation of the portfolio returns.[422]

[420] As explained in section 3.4.4.
[421] See Arvanitis et al. (1998), for example.
[422] See Figure 4-19 in section 4.3.6.1.

Popular risk measuring methods, however, may *not* be *coherent*.[423] The focus on credit loss may be substituted by a focus on return, leading analogously to Earnings-at-Risk (EaR) and Conditional Earnings-at-Risk (CEaR), respectively.[424]

A handicap of two-dimensional Markowitz-type optimization is that investors in a multi-period context might have additional targets.[425] He/she may seek for a constant growth rate of the portfolio's value or a minimum consumption rate, for example (Hallerbach and Spronk 1997). The limitations of Markowitz-type approaches have been picked up in utility function frameworks representing multi-dimensional *preference structures* of investors by Hallerbach and Spronk (1997), for example. Nevertheless, Hallerbach and Spronk (1997, p.278) claim that "it would be utopian to suggest that the investor can list all available alternatives, compare them and choose the best or optimal alternative." Instead, the authors state that the decision process may be described by a stepwise investigation for a portfolio that satisfies an investor's requirements. With respect to the target of the portfolio choice, the *optimizal strategy* is substituted by a *satisfying strategy* (Hallerbach and Spronk 1997).

As comprehensive and all-embracing the multi-attribute utility approach to portfolio management may be, as difficult is the derivation of a utility function that represents the preferences of the distinct interest groups subject to investment decisions. An alternative approach has been proposed by Hellwig (1987), accounting for time preferences of investors within a multi-period context without relying on utility functions.

---

423 In case of the risk measure to be used is not convex there are multiple solutions to an optimization problem and they "are likely to be quite different" (Arvanitis and Gregory 2001, p.102). To be discussed in section 4.3.6.2.

424 See Arvanitis and Gregory (2001), for example.

425 See Hallerbach and Spronk (1997, p.278), for example, who claim that "the *preference structure* of the investor is normally more complicated than the relatively simple utility functions assumed within the mean-variance framework." See also Fama and French (1993) and Lakonishok et al. (1994).

In the following, we will at first briefly review decision and utility theory as the fundamental theory for portfolio optimization. Subsequently, Markowitz' portfolio theory (section 4.3.4f.) will be presented and compared with other eligible approaches. The current state-of-the-art methods for single periods will be presented, compared and evaluated in section 4.3.6 to 4.3.8. Capital allocation can be formulated as a portfolio management problem and will be presented in section 4.3.9. Thereafter, innovative techniques to trade illiquid credit risk are illustrated (section 4.3.10) before focusing on multi-period aspects of credit portfolio management in section 4.3.11.

4.3.2 Decision theory

4.3.2.1 Decision theory: Individual's behavior

Decision theory tries to model the decision environment of a 'Homo oeconomicus'[426] by means of a quantifiable utility. This modeling enables statements about a 'rational' behavior of an investor under risk, underlying certain axioms[427] known as the theory of rational choice (see Arrow 1961, for example).[428]

Naturally, the assumption of individuals being *"Homo oeconomici"* is critical, especially for the field of politics. Simon (1982) has therefore suggested

---

426 It is assumed that a 'Homo oeconomicus' acts in the following way: he/she is self-interested, maximizes his/her utility, is completely informed and acts in a rational way (he/she orders alternatives consistently).

427 See Copeland and Weston (1988), p. 79ff., and Perridon/Steiner (1991), p.112.

428 A striking explanation of rational choice is as follows: "It has been assumed that people are motivated by money and by the possibility of making a profit, and this has allowed it to construct formal, and often predictive, models of human behavior. This apparent success has led many other social scientists to cast envious eyes in its direction. They have thought that if they could only follow the methods of economics they could achieve similar successes in their own studies. These sociologists and political scientists have tried to build theories around the idea that all action is fundamentally 'rational' in character and that people calculate the likely costs and benefits of any action before deciding what to do. This approach to theory is known as *rational choice theory*, and its application to social interaction takes the form of *exchange theory*." See http://privatewww.essex.ac.uk/~scottj/socscot7.htm; Rev. April 2004.
Max Weber (1920), for example, built among the first authors an influential typology of action around purely rational types of action.

"bounded rationality", by relaxing both the assumption of utility maximization and full information. He assumes that individuals are searching for *optimal* rather than for *maximal* solutions and are led by norms. Instead of a 'Homo oeconomicus' he therefore speaks of an individual as a 'Homo sociologicus' as shown below.

Figure 4-10: Homo oeconomicus vs. Homo sociologicus (Simon 1982)

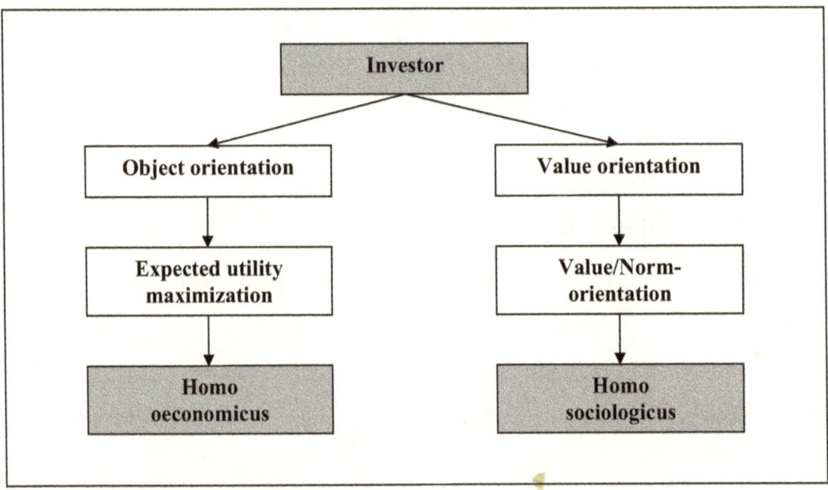

Within an economic world of portfolio optimization, however, it seems to be reasonable to refer to the assumption of 'Homo oeconomicus'.

4.3.2.2 Decision theory: Group preferences and Arrow[429]

It is assumed that the process of choice leads to an equilibrium both for individuals and groups. Arrow (1961), however, has shown that there is no mechanism for a translation of the preferences of rational individuals into a coherent group preference that simultaneously satisfies the following five conditions (*Arrow's Impossibility Theorem*[430]):

---

[429] This section is oriented on standard financial textbooks.

[430] A similar theorem for simple collective decision problems has already been published by Condorcet (1765).

- *Rationality:* Each individual has a complete, reflexive, transitive collective preference order.[431]
- *Universal admissibility:* Everyone can adopt any strong or weak complete and transitive preference ordering of the alternatives.
- *Pareto optimality (or unanimity):* If everyone prefers A to B (or is indifferent between them), then the group preference must reject a preference for A over B (or indifference between them).
- *Independence of irrelevant alternatives:* If alternatives A and B stand in a particular relationship to one another in each group member's preferences, and this relationship does not change, then neither may the group preference change between A and B, even if individual preferences for other (irrelevant) alternatives change.
- *Nondictatorship:* There is no distinguishable individual whose own preferences dictate the group preference, independent of the other members.

The *arrow paradoxon* holds if there are at least three alternatives which the members of the society are free to order in any way (Arrow 1963).[432] In order to establish the basic frame for portfolio management as a partial set of decision theory, we will review the basic concepts below.

4.3.2.3 Decisions under certainty vs. decisions under risk[433]

For investors in the financial domain, there are two distinct decision frames:

- Decisions under certainty and
- Decisions under risk (uncertainty[434]).

---

[431] Additional prerequisites are monotony, continuity, independence of irrelevant alternatives and the substitution principle, see Reichling (2003), for example.

[432] Within the frame of politics, Arrow's theorem has been taken up e.g. by Sen (1997), "in order to rescue the legitimating of democracy". (…)

[433] The description of preference relations follows Bamberg and Coenenberg (2000) and can be found in various financial textbooks. Among the first researchers to explore uncertainty have been Keynes (1921) and Knight (1921).

[434] Most authors distinguish between certainty and uncertainty. Bamberg and Coenenberg (2000), however, speak of risky as opposed to uncertain situations. We will refer to their classification shown in Table 4-4 below.

The first one refers to the decision of an alternative under constraints. The environment has no influence on the decision itself. Within the sphere of finance, randomness plays a crucial role. We will neglect decision under certainty due to their unimportance in practice and refer to the latter case.

Decisions under risk are characterized by the property that each unsure state of the environment can be assigned to (subjective) probability as opposed to decisions under uncertainty that make it impossible to assign probabilities to the distinct random states. More specifically, a decision under risk means, that the ex post result of the ex ante decision is not only dependent on the ex ante choice of the individual, but on the unsure ex post realization of the random event.[435]

Bamberg and Coenenberg (1974) classified decisions according to the state of information of an investor, as shown below. We will salutary neglect decisions under uncertainty and refer to the case with security about the states (a pre-specified event tree) and risky consequences, as highlighted below.

Table 4-4: Combinations of information states of an investor (Bamberg and Coenenberg 2000, p.25)

Information related to states	**Consequences**		
	Security	**Risk**	**Uncertainty**
Security	Security	**Risk**	Uncertainty
Risk	Risk	Risk	Uncertainty
Uncertainty	Uncertainty	Uncertainty	Uncertainty

4.3.3 A solution to decision theory: The concept of expected utility[436]

The primary assumption of the theory of rational choice is that (self-interested, utility maximizing, full informed and 'rational acting') individuals ('homo oeconomici') are able to assign a utility (preference) to each alternative[437],

---

[435] e.g. the utility of a holiday is not only dependent on the attractiveness of a hotel/location, but on the weather, which is random.

[436] The decription of the expected utility concept is oriented on standard financial textbooks.

[437] Referred to as completeness.

dependent on their investment targets[438] and preferences[439]. The utility of one alternative can be compared with utilities of other alternatives and subsequently the alternatives can be ordered according to an individual's preference order as shown in Figure 4-11 below.[440]

Rational choice recognizes that an actor is often unable to choose a preferred outcome directly, but must choose between different courses of action that change the probabilities associated with alternative outcomes. It is usually assumed that rational decision makers choose their actions oriented on expected outcomes of these actions. It is mostly assumed that the preferences and probabilities of alternative outcomes are represented by expected utility functions. The overall process of portfolio selection under risk is shown below.

Figure 4-11: The process of decisions under risk

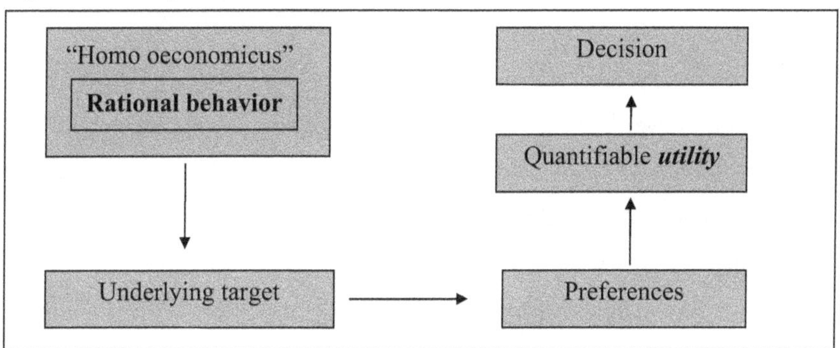

In the following, we will deal with the basic assumptions of rational choice in more formal terms.

4.3.3.1 Preference relations[441]

Let x, x' and x'' represent decision alternatives with a preference relation "$\succeq$":

---

[438] Targets are the variables used within the optimization frame, i.e. the expected return and the standard deviation.

[439] The major preference dimensions of investors are risk, return and time. See section 4.3.3.1.

[440] Transitivity according to an ordinal preference.

[441] The description of preference relations follows Rady (2003) and can be found in various standard financial textbooks, e.g. Bamberg and Coenenberg (2000).

1. Then for each pair of alternatives a relation of the following form has to exist: $x \succeq x'$ or $x' \succeq x$ or both (Completeness).
2. For arbitrary x, x' and x'' holds: $x \succeq x'$ and $x' \succeq x'' \Rightarrow x \succeq x''$ (Transitivity).

Assumption 1 and 2 are also called rationality theorems. They assume that each bundle of alternatives refers to one single indifference curve.

Additionally, it is often assumed that preference relations have to be strictly monotonous (assumption 3) and continuous (assumption 4).[442]

Preferences are assumed to be convex, i.e. for all x, x' and x'' and $0 \leq \alpha \leq 1$ holds:

$x' \succeq x$ and $x'' \succeq x \Leftrightarrow \alpha x' + (1-\alpha)x'' \succ x$.

The economic reasoning behind this is a decreasing marginal rate of substitution.[443]

Preference relations may be referred to[444]

- Return/Level[445] preferences (additional utility of marginal increase of the target value),
- Risk preference (within an incomplete decision environment).
- Time preference and
- Type preference (existence of various, partly excluding target measures),

The major issue is to assign a general assessment function to the existing opportunities comprising two (or more) preference relation dimensions. For the purpose of portfolio optimization, it is common to refer to return (level of target value) and risk preferences. If additional preferences are accounted for, the expected utility framework may be problematic (see section 4.3.2.2).

442 See Rady (2003), for example.
443 Abbreviated as MRS, see section 4.3.3.2.
444 See Reichling (2003), for example.
445 Of a target value.

4.3.3.2 Utility functions[446]

If a preference order "$\succeq$" fulfils assumption 1-4, then a continuous utility function u(x) exists, that represents this preference order[447], i.e.

$$x \succeq x' \Leftrightarrow u(x) \geq u(x')$$

Utility functions referring to convex preference relations (see above) are concave. For a consumption stream resulting from an investment it is generally assumed that the marginal utility is positive: $\partial U() / \partial C_t > 0 \quad \vee$ t. The "concave" property results from a decreasing marginal utility, i.e. the higher the consumption at time t already is, the lower the additional utility resulting from an additional consumption unit: $\partial^2 U() / \partial C_t^2 < 0 \quad \vee$ t. From a financial perspective, a concave utility function refers to a "balanced" inter-temporal consumption sequence, which is preferred against consumption in one period.

In the following, we will initially review a *one-period-model* for demonstration purposes. A one-period-model implies, that consumption is possible in t = 0 and t = 1. An eligible concave utility function is:

$$U(C_0, C_1) = \sqrt{C_0 \bullet C_1}$$

For a fixed utility level $\bar{U}(=const.)$ it is possible to define C_1 as a function of C_0. The resulting curve representing all possible consumption plans $C = (C_0, C_1)$ referred to $\bar{U}(=const.)$ is called indifference curve or iso-utility curve as shown below.

[446] The description of preference relations follows Rady (2003) and Reichling (2003) and can be found in standard financial textbooks.

[447] See Rady (2003), for example.

Figure 4-12: Indifference curves for the utility function[448]

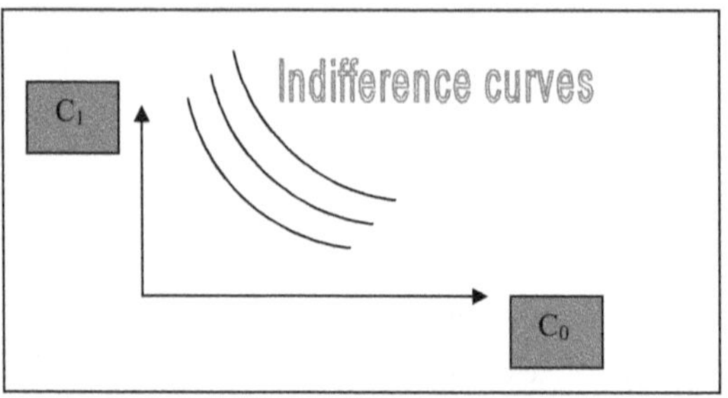

The slope of the indifference curve for a one-period-model with $C_1(C_0)$ is called marginal rate of substitution (MRS):[449]

$$C_1'(C_0) = \frac{\partial U / \partial C_0}{\partial U / \partial C_1}$$

The MRS expresses approximately how many units of C_1 may be substituted by C_0 in terms of a constant utility level $\bar{U}$. Further information about the basic properties of utility functions can be found in various (comprehensive) investment theory textbooks.

4.3.3.3 Decision under risk: The Bernoulli principle[450]

Bernoulli's assumption of an investor's target to maximize rather his expected utility than the expected value of the random event is based on the hypothesis of the expected value.[451] According to this theory a rational investor does maximize the expected value of utility $\sum_x p(x)u(x)$ and not the utility of the expected value of the random event $u(\sum p(x)x)$.

---

448 See Reichling (2003), p.7, for example.

449 In case that a continuous derivation of the indifference curve exists for all utility levels.

450 The description of preference relations follows Reichling (2003) and can be found in standard financial textbooks.

451 The famous *"St. Petersburg-Paradoxon"* has been explored by Bernoulli (1738) and can be found in standard financial textbooks.

Bernoulli's findings, a cardinal concept to utility theory, have been realized only 200 years later by Ramsey (1931), Menger (1934) and von Neumann/Morgenstern (1944).[452]

It has been found that a "rational"[453] investor behaves according to the expected value hypothesis. His/her utility function is called "von Neumann-Morgenstern" – (vNM) utility function.[454] vNM utility functions do have cardinal features.[455]

4.3.3.3.1 Pros and cons of the Bernoulli principle

The major advantage of the Bernoulli principle is that it depicts the decision in a formally correct way. The shortages of the Bernoulli principle are the following:[456]

- Derivation of the individual utility functions is difficult.
- Difficulties to set the critical probabilities.
- Information overload due to exploding information (alternatives, scenarios).
- Utility functions are time- and scenario-dependent.

4.3.3.3.2 The applicability of the Bernoulli principle in practical portfolio management

It can be concluded that the Bernoulli principle is persuasive as a model, but in realistic situations its applicability is rather difficult due to the high demand on

---

452 He already suggested a logarithmic utility function, which corresponds to a rational investor.

453 Axioms for rational behavior can be found in section 4.3.2.1.

454 The prerequisites for a vNM- preference and utility function, respectively, are completeness, transitivity, continuity and independence. See Von Neumann/Morgenstern (1947).

455 The von Neumann/Morgenstern-type utility function fulfils both the risk aversion and the positive marginal utility principle (see section 2.4.2.7.2). An example for a simple numerical instance of a decision based on a von Neumann/Morgenstern-type utility function can be found in Manz (1998).

The result of this illustrative example is a geometrical connection of all risk-return-combinations, which represent an equal utility level for a risk-averse individual, convex indifference curves (Figure 4-16). The slope of these curves equals the marginal rate of substitution (between risk and return in example C in Figure 4-16).

456 See www.unister.de – Rev. March 2004; Evaluations of the Bernouilli principle can be found in various standard financial textbooks, e.g. Bamberg and Coenenberg (2000).

information (see Bamberg and Coenenberg 2000, for example). Additional information about the Bernoulli theory can be found in Bawa (1975) and Fishburn (1977).

Higher dimensional expected utility concepts like Markowitz' (μ,σ) approach are popular alternatives to the Bernoulli concept and will be discussed in section 4.3.5f.

4.3.3.4 Risk aversion and utility functions[457]

In the following, the implication of the choice of certain types of utility functions vs. risk preferences vice versa will be discussed. After defining risk aversion in terms of expected utility and reviewing the methods for the measurement of risk aversion, distinct types of utility functions will be presented.

4.3.3.4.1 The evaluation of preferences: Risk aversion

In terms of expected utility an individual is[458]

- risk-averse, if he/she assigns a certain payment equivalent to the expected value of a random event strictly a higher value: $E(u(x)) < u(E(x)), \ \vee \mathrm{x}$
- risk neutral, if he/she is indifferent between the risky and riskless event: $E(u(x)) = u(E(x)), \ \vee \mathrm{x}$
- risk-friendly, if he/she strictly prefers the risky alternative: $E(u(x)) > u(E(x)), \ \vee \mathrm{x}$

Graphically perceived, an investor can then be assumed to be risk-averse (-neutral, -friendly), if his/her vNM- utility function is strictly concave (linear, strictly convex) as shown below.

Function A (B, C) belongs to a risk neutral (risk averse, risk friendly) investor.

457 The description of preference relations follows Manz (1998) and can be found in various standard financial textbooks.

458 See Copeland and Weston (1988) or Breuer (1999), for example.

Figure 4-13: Illustrative example for three distinct investor types (Copeland and Weston 1988, p. 85) [459]

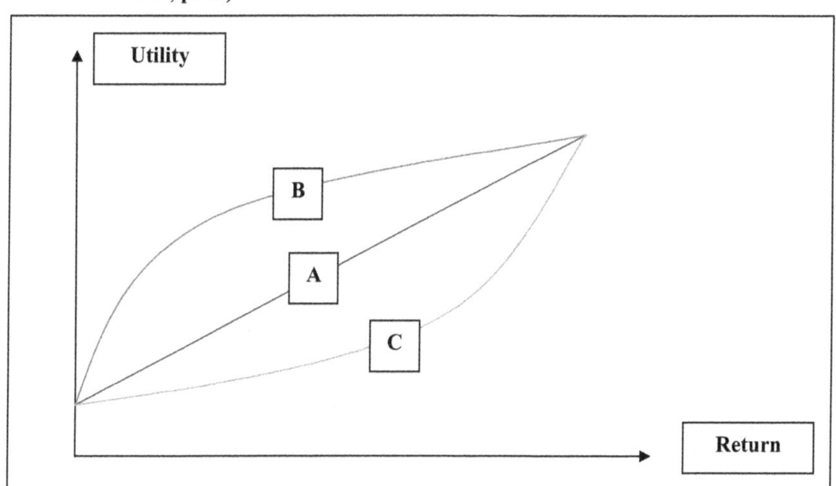

4.3.3.4.2 Measurement of risk aversion

Risk aversion in formal terms is usually handled based on two measures presented by Arrow (1961) and Pratt (1964):[460]

- The absolute risk aversion (ARA): $ARA(A) = -\frac{U''(x)}{U'(x)}$ and
- The relative risk aversion (RRA): $RRA(A) = -\frac{U''(x)}{U'(x)} \bullet A$

Further information about the measurement of risk aversion can be found in the Appendix.

4.3.3.4.3 The choice of an appropriate utility function

Principally three types of utility functions are commonly used:[461]

- *Quadratic utility functions* ($U(A) = A - bA^2$)

---

459 Similar graphics can be found in various standard financial textbooks, e.g. Reichling (2003).

460 For further reference see Elton and Gruber (1975), for example.

461 See Schlag (2003), p.29f.; A comprehensive description of utility function concepts can be found in Breuer et al. (1999), for example.

For investors seeking for an (μ,σ)-optimal portfolio, a quadratic utility function is in line with the expected utility hypothesis. However, the risk premium shows increasing absolute risk aversion with increasing income, what is rather irrational. This can be shown as follows:

$U(A) = A - bA^2, U'(A) = 1 - 2bA, U''(A) = -2b$ and

therefore $ARA = \frac{2b}{1-2bA}$, $\frac{\mathrm{dARA}}{\mathrm{dA}} > 0$ and $RRA = \frac{2bA}{1-2bA}$, $\frac{\mathrm{dRRA}}{\mathrm{dA}} > 0$.

- *Negative exponential utility function* ($U(A) = -e^{-aA}$)

  In case of exponential utility functions, a constant absolute risk aversion is assumed, i.e. an investor's willingness to invest in risky assets is independent of his/her initial wealth. This assumption does, however, imply, that an investor's relative risk aversion increases, what is rather illogical.[462] This can be shown as follows:

  $U(A) = -e^{-aA}, U'(A) = ae^{-aA}, U''(A) = -a^2e^{-aA}$ and therefore

  $ARA = a$, $\frac{\mathrm{dARA}}{\mathrm{dA}} = 0$ and $RRA = aA$, $\frac{\mathrm{dRRA}}{\mathrm{dA}} > 0$.

- *Logarithmic utility function* ($U(A) = \ln(A)$)

  To overcome the latter two utility functions' shortages, logarithmic utility functions assume constant relative risk aversion and, respectively, decreasing absolute risk aversion. This can be shown as follows:

  $U(A) = \ln(A), U'(A) = \frac{1}{A}, U''(A) = \frac{-1}{A^2}$ and therefore $ARA = \frac{1}{A}$, $\frac{\mathrm{dARA}}{\mathrm{dA}} < 0$

  and $RRA = 1$, $\frac{\mathrm{dRRA}}{\mathrm{dA}} = 0$.

The concept of logarithmic utility function has already been proposed by Bernoulli (1738) and will subsequently be evaluated for its usability for portfolio selection.

[462] It has been empirically proven that for increasing initial assets an investor is willing to invest an increasing share of his/her funds in risky assets, or - at least - an increasing absolute amount. See Arrow (1971), p. 96 or Pfennig (1998), p.130.

4.3.4 From decision theory to portfolio optimization

After a brief review of decision theory we will now gradually proceed to the techniques of portfolio optimization.

4.3.4.1 What is portfolio optimization?

Portfolio management is the process of both bying and selling assets as shown in Figure 4-14. The portfolio selection process is usually based on quantitative criteria, for example the marginal risk and return contribution of an asset. By means of advanced credit risk tools, it is possible to identify assets which are not desirable any longer, for example as a consequence of altering economic or industry conditions or the composition of the portfolio.[463]
An optimization model may be used to construct a portfolio of loans or securities from a large universe, based on their relative profitability and credit risk. Portfolio management techniques will extensively be illustrated more in section 4.3.5f.

Figure 4-14: Portfolio management: Buying and selling of assets (according to Hartmann 2002, p.45)

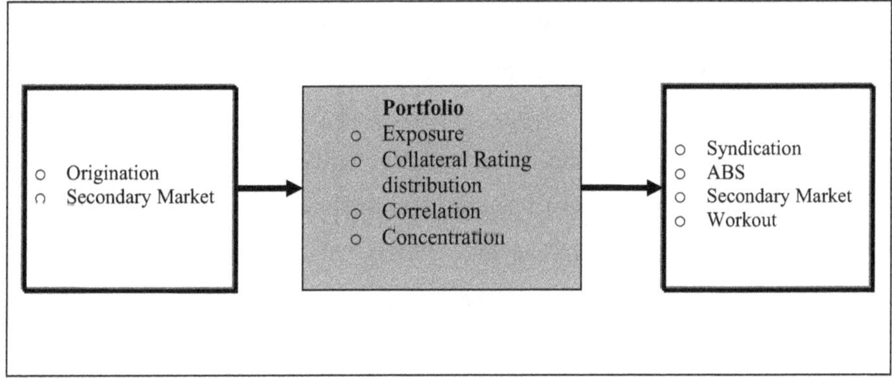

[463] An illustrative explanation about the identification of non-desirable assets can be found in JP Morgan (1997), p. 133f., for example.

4.3.4.2 The whole process of credit portfolio management[464]

While portfolio optimization refers to an advantageous buying and selling of assets it is crucial to establish a comprising credit risk management system in order to arrive at the portfolio optimization level.

The whole process to manage credit portfolios may be divided into seven distinct steps, where portfolio optimization is the last step as shown below.

Table 4-5: The whole process of portfolio management

Step	Timely perspective
Portfolio analysis	Current portfolio
Portfolio segmentation	Current portfolio
Portfolio efficiency measurement	Ex post
Portfolio assessment	Ex ante
Credit risk modeling	Ex ante
Portfolio stress testing and Backtesting	Ex ante Ex post
Portfolio optimization	Ex ante

Most of the techniques have already extensively been discussed. The remaining steps are briefly presented in order to notice that a permanent improvement of the credit risk management framework is essential to be successful.

The objective of the first sub process **portfolio analysis** is to analyze the current credit portfolio systematically in order to provide decision support to the different levels within a structured management information system (MIS).

By **segmenting the portfolio** into clusters with similar risk characteristics, management can evaluate concentrations in light of the bank's portfolio objectives and risk tolerances.[465] A broader range of risk characteristics in terms of useful segmentation criteria could be a borrower's industry, geographic area, collateral, tenor, risk rating or facility structure. We refer to risk ratings.

---

[464] Similar concepts can be found in various standard financial textbooks, e.g. Ong (1999).

[465] Hamerle (2000), for example, suggests dividing credit portfolios into bonds, commercial/wholesale, retail and derivatives.

Portfolio efficiency measures the performance of the credit portfolio against predefined targets (hurdle rates) and thereby lays the basis for systematic portfolio assessment and the portfolio strategy and planning process.[466]

The objectives of **portfolio assessment** are to determine the value and the collectability of all risk positions, to evaluate the adequacy of write-offs and write-downs initiated by the business, to estimate the potential for loss and to assess the capacity of the business to absorb any unexpected losses. The evaluation perspective is forward looking, based on an analysis of the profile of the portfolio, an assessment of the environment in which the business operates and a detailed review of a sample of individual risk positions.

The framework of **credit risk modeling** both on a stand-alone and a portfolio level has extensively been discussed in section 3.2 and 3.5.[467]

Stress testing is a form of portfolio risk analysis that evaluates how the (sub) portfolio or the business as a whole will perform under various adverse conditions. It is used to examine the inherent risk of a particular business strategy with respect to alternative strategies or forecast assumptions. **Backtesting** the prospective credit risk model heavily depends upon the availability of data. Unsolved questions with regard to backtesting (unavailable data) of credit risk models have been traced by Lopez and Saidenberg (1999).[468]

Considering a bank as a fund with the credit portfolio on one side and the obligations in form of liabilities and equity on the other side it is the objective of the funds management to maximize the value of the fund's equity (economic capital). **Active credit portfolio optimization** comprises both the determination and maintenance of capital adequacy and an optimal strategy for portfolio selection.

---

466 The efficiency analysis process consists of the following sub processes: 1.) Comparison of the risk-adjusted performance of/between (sub) portfolios from an ex post perspective. 2.) Comparison of the performance of the (sub) portfolio in comparison to a benchmark (internally or market driven)

467 In order to arrive at portfolio distribution functions to depict the credit risk result.

468 They suggest a 'Panel-dataset' approach that proclaims to use intersectoral simulations to provide a high amount of data within a short period (cross sectional dimension).

4.3.4.3 Credit portfolio management within a bank: Risks to be taken into account

As portfolio management is at the heart of a FI, it is involved in various other fields of a FI as shown below. Consequently, as Pfingsten et al. (2000) point out, there are various information risks to be taken into account. Asymmetric information may lead to moral hazards, e.g. sales could be interested in understating the risk of engagements in order to enable higher returns when selling internally positions to portfolio investment.[469] The suggested credit portfolio selection strategy therefore has to be implemented on a strategic level by closely linking the involved organizational entities (as shown below) and to thereby ensure that full advantage is captured on a bank-wide level.[470]

[469] Öhler and Unser (2001).

[470] According to Kuritzkes et al. (2000), p.43/44, it is therefore vital to strictly divide the competencies of sales and portfolio management as shown below.

Figure 4-15: Credit portfolio management embedded into a bank's organizational structure (Pfingsten and Schröck 2000, p.8)[471]

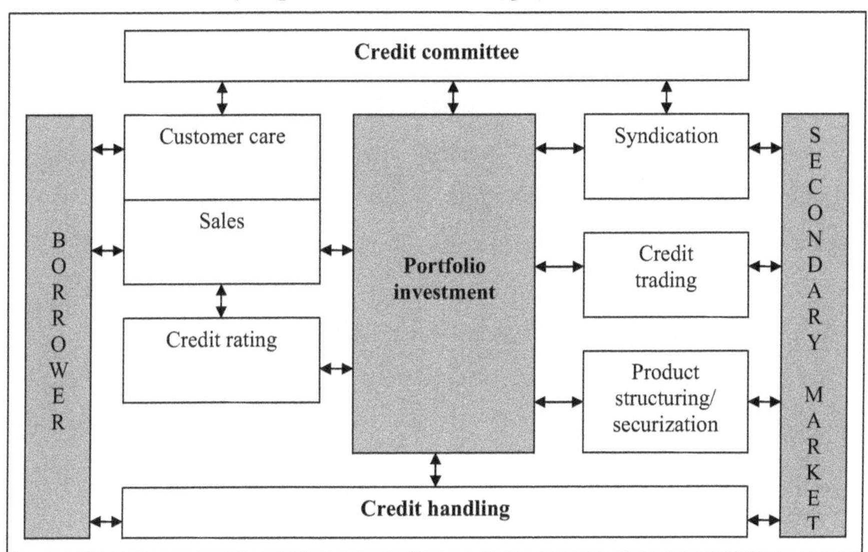

4.3.4.4 Optimization of credit vs. market portfolios

While portfolio theory has found its way to all fields of security analysis and asset management, the credit risk sphere is far behind this evolution. Two reasons can be considered as important in this context:[472]

- The sickness pressure of FIs has been to small and
- Data have been (and are still) limited.

Moreover, default risk, unlike market risk, "cannot be conveniently hedged away" (Ong 1999, p.119).[473] Nonetheless, credit risk can be reduced and managed via *diversification,* what is nothing new as portfolio theory as established by Markowitz is more than 40 years old and loan portfolios have been managed by banks for many years.[474]

[471] Pfingsten et al. (2000) adapted the original English version of Kuritzkes (1999), p.62.
[472] Manz (1998).
[473] Even credit derivatives and asset securitization programs are "merely schemes to shift as much default risk as possible, but, in the end, someone will be left holding the bag" (Ong 1999, p.119).
[474] See Morgan (1989), Morgan et al. (1993) and Ong (1999), for example.

4.3.4.5 The theory of choice: Alternative preference frames

Initially, it is important to notice that portfolio management "means different things to different people" (Caouette et al. 1998, p. 249). We will closely follow Caouette et al. (1998) in this context. While pension plan managers, for example, may see an allocation problem (how much to invest in various sectors and how to rebalance the portfolio as expectations change), they will not consider capital constraints or taxes. Insurance companies and banks, by contrast, have to consider supervisory rules with respect to capital as well as the influence of their portfolio strategy on their external rating.

The distinct perspectives of professional portfolio managers on their investment activities has been explored by Brinson et al. (1986), for example, who identified three basic components:

- Investment policy (asset mix),
- Market timing and
- Security selection.

Their results revealed that market timing and security selection influenced their portfolio returns much less than the investment policy mix. Insurance companies and banks, however, have different liability structures, for example, which must be accommodated by the portfolio strategy.

Indeed, optimal portfolio management is ultimately only a question of the individual preferences of the investor (Scheuenstuhl and Zagst 2000). Distinctive parameters for an optimal portfolio are, for example, how return preferences are formulated or how risks are observed by the investor.

4.3.4.5.1 Alternative choices

The theory of choice models the decision behavior of an individual between various alternatives at a certain stage. Copeland and Weston (1988, p.78) provide three examples for an act of choice for varying targets:

- Decision between apples and pears (A).
- An inter-temporal decision between consumption and saving (B).

- A 'timeless' decision between risk and return (C).

Figure 4-16*:* The theory of choice according to Copeland and Weston (1988, p.78)

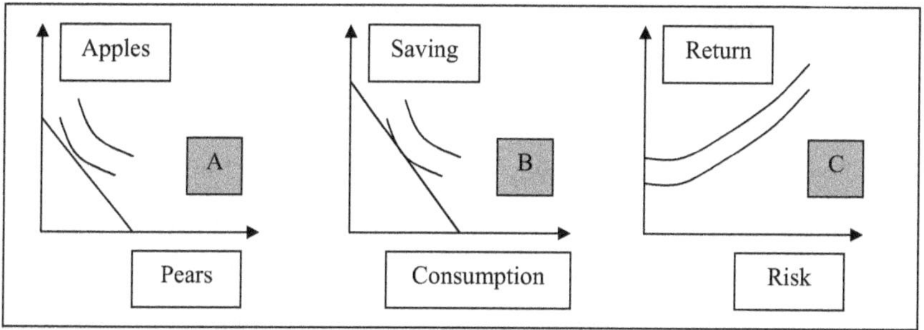

The two-dimensional Markowitz-type portfolio optimization approaches are focused on risk-return-optimization (third case), while the approach to multi-period portfolio selection presented in section 5 is focused rather on an investor's time preference of the withdrawal sequence[475] given a predefined and stationary risk-return structure of a credit portfolio.

4.3.4.5.2 The setting of portfolio optimization problems

According to Grootfeld et al. (2001, p.8) portfolio selection models are "by their very nature" *conditional-normative models*. This implies that they offer an optimal decision rule if an investor's goals, preferences and restrictions are in line with the underlying assumptions of the portfolio model (Grootfeld et al. 2001).

The basic principles of portfolio management will be explained according to Caouette et al. (1998). Portfolio optimization in general refers to "a set of tools available from operations research that expresses the relevant trade-offs and constraints as an objective mathematical function to be maximized or minimized" (Caouette et al. 1998, p. 107). In general, each optimization problem is characterized by a set of unknown **decision variables**, which are intended to be determined by means of an appropriate optimization algorithm. An optimum

[475] Given an exogenous growth path for the portfolio value with respect to the net present value.

portfolio is specified by the decision variables, which indicate the weights or the percentages of the individual assets the portfolio will include. Via the decision variables, the summation of the value added by the decision variables to the overall gain can be derived, which is known as an **objective function.** The objective function of a portfolio is made up of the returns from the individual assets multiplied by their portfolio weights. Additionally, each optimization problem entails **constraints**. An example for a constraint may be that an institution has set a lending limit for specific assets.

A general linear optimization problem has the following form:

$$\begin{aligned} &Max \quad f(x)=c'x \\ &s.t. \quad Ax = b \\ &\qquad\quad x \geq 0 \\ &\qquad\quad \sum x_i = 1 \end{aligned}$$

and can be found in every standard textbook for operations research. The decision variables, the vector x, have to be derived under the constraint of the availability of resources (Ax=b), for example. C denotes the value added by the various securities to the overall benefit.

Solution of the optimization problem

After the design of an optimization problem, computational techniques such as linear (e.g. the simplex method) and non-linear optimization techniques are used in order to determine an optimal portfolio.[476] Various computer software packages have been developed for the purpose of solving optimization problems.[477] For example, the Excel Solver may be used as practiced in section 5.[478]

---

476 See, for example, Hillier and Lieberman (1973).

477 See Caouette et al. (1998).

478 Other eligible programs are Matlab, ROMOptimizer, FinPortfolioOptimizer, etc.

4.3.5 Modern portfolio theory (MPT)

"Nothing is more soothing or more persuasive than the computer screen, with its imposing array of numbers, glowing colors, and elegantly structured graphs. As we stare at the passing show, we become so absorbed that we tend to forget that the computer only answers questions; it does not ask them." (Bernstein 1996)[479]

Before we skip into the state-of-the-art techniques of credit portfolio management, we let Cumming et al. (2001) formulate the basic target of portfolio management within a risk-return framework:

"…to asses the risk and return of different business lines and thus allow them to make more informed decisions about where to invest the scarce resources to maximize profits."

Modern Portfolio Theory (*MPT*[480]) has been introduced by Markowitz (1952), Tobin (1958) and Sharpe (1963 and 1964)[481].

It has been known already long ago that the effect of diversification related to the decision rule "don't put all your assets into the same basket" is crucial, leading to naïve diversification via limiting systems (Caouette et al. 1998).

The greatest contribution of MPT has been the foundation of a formal risk-return framework for investment risk in quantitative terms. By defining investment risk in quantitative terms, Markowitz gave investors "a mathematical approach to asset selection and portfolio management" (Rom et al. 1994).

The underlying concept for the return of financial assets is that the returns on assets – and consequently portfolio returns as well – are normally distributed. In so far, mean variance analysis is consistent with the expected utility approach.[482]

---

479 This quotation has been taken from Matten (2000), p.219.

480 See Rom et al. (1994).

481 The single index model or market model. Sharpe has pioneered factor models and laid the basis for the CAPM, which can be found in most financial textbooks.

482 The assumption of a normal distribution is only one special constraint. A detailed discussion about consistency of expected utility approaches with the Bernoulli expected utility framework and rational decisions are explained by Schneeweiss (1967), Ingersoll (1987) and Sinn (1989), for example.

Even within the non-traded credit sphere, the MPV provides an "extremely useful framework for a loan portfolio manager considering risk return trade-offs" (Saunders 1999, p. 113). Thus, by generally separating the credit- granting decision from the credit portfolio, a bank is able to generate a better risk-return trade-off and offset what has been called "the paradox of credit"[483]. The lower the correlation among loans in a portfolio is, the greater the potential for a manager to reduce a bank's risk exposure through diversification.

4.3.5.1 Portfolio models and Markowitz

"Even if you put your eggs in different baskets, as long as you are in eggs you can not escape systematic risk." – Not attributed to Harry Markowitz[484]

Markowitz (1952) laid the foundation for portfolio management and still dominates portfolio theory in various fields. Markowitz' *mean-variance approach* focuses on the individual assets' mean returns and its variances.[485] The approach enables to determine an "efficient frontier".[486] The efficient frontier is a set of portfolios with maximum return to risk ratio, where the risk is defined in terms of the standard deviation (or, equivalently, the variance) of the portfolio returns. In Markowitz' portfolio theory the differentiation properties of the standard deviation are "heavily exploited".[487] Capital optimization in Markowitz' sense is ultimately enabled by the usage of some standard software for credit risk management.

An illustrative example for the *'common view'* onto a portfolio decision with the efficient frontier is shown below.

[483] This effect has been postulated among others by KMV; see Saunders (1999), p.108.
[484] This quotation has been taken from Caouette et al. (1998), p.51.
[485] See Arvantis and Gregory (2001), for example.
[486] See Arvantis and Gregory (2001), for example.
[487] Arvantis and Gregory (2001), p.102.

Figure 4-17: The Markowitz portfolio model (according to Manz 1998, p.53)

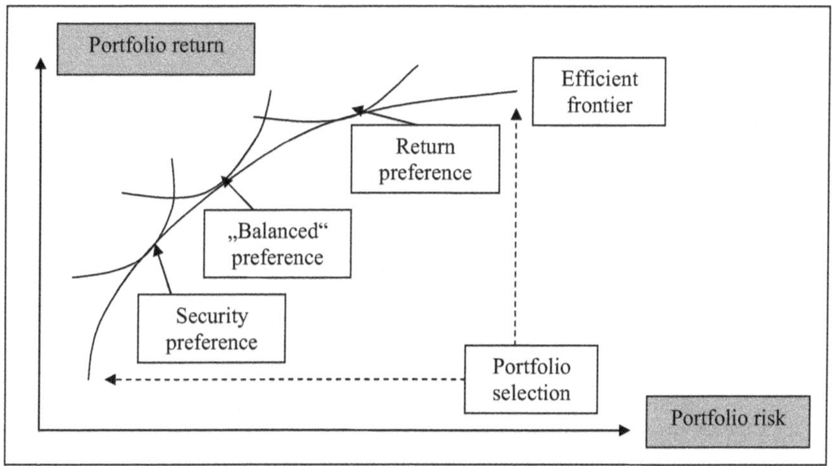

Portfolio selection should lead to a risk-return balanced portfolio on the 'efficient frontier', depending on an investor's risk preference (low, medium, high[488]).

4.3.5.2 The μ–σ criterion in formal terms[489]

The assumption of risk indifferent decision makers is not very useful in practice. It has therefore become best-practice to solve decision problems by accounting for the volatility σ_i of an event besides its expected value μ_i in order to measure the risk.

Two varieties of the application of the (μ,σ)-criterion can be distinguished:

1. All possible strategies are examined according to the μ–σ criterion and non-efficient solutions are removed from the decision (*'The efficient frontier'*, see Figure 4-17). This way of decision making has been exploited for portfolio selection. The choice of an optimal policy in formal terms is not possible.
2. A second alternative is to additionally work with utility functions. One way to incorporate a utility frame is to decrease the expected value by the

488 Depicted as „security", „balanced" and „return".

489 This section follows Reichling (2003) and can be found in various standard financial textbooks.

incorporation of penalty costs proportional to the volatility of the strategy. The selection of an optimal strategy is thereby possible.[490] A risk-averse investor will always refer to the alternative with lower risk in case of an equal expected value. The (μ,σ) decision rule is sufficiently compatible with the Bernoulli- utility concept, if a quadratic utility function is assumed.

Return and risk of single assets

Given a formal frame, the random return of a risky asset A, R_A, is not a real number in mathematical terms, but a depiction. Let Ω be the space of the possible outcomes and ℝ the space of real numbers, then $R_A : \Omega \to \mathbb{R}$. The expected value for discrete random returns R_A is $E(R_A) = \mu_A = \sum_{j=1}^{n} p(r_{A,j}) \bullet r_{A,j}$.

with the jth shaping of the random R_A, $r_{A,j}$, and the corresponding probability $p(r_{A,j})$.

The variance of a random asset is similarly defined as:

$VAR(R_A) = \sigma_A = E((R_A - \mu_A)^2) = E(R_A)^2 - \mu_A^2$.

Given the expected value and the volatility of a single (risky) asset in terms of variance, we can review the properties of these two moments for a portfolio.

A portfolio's return and risk

Given the averages of n single assets returns, the expected portfolio return is a weighted linear combination of the single assets:

$$E(R_P) = \sum_{i=1}^{n} x_i \bullet \mu_i .$$

The determination of the portfolio's volatility is not that straightforward, as it has been shown in section 3.5.1.5.2. The portfolio volatility can be derived as follows (see Saunders 1999, p.110, for example):

$$\sigma_P = UL_P = \sum_{i=1}^{n} \sum_{j=1}^{n} x_i \bullet x_j \bullet \sigma_i \bullet \sigma_j \bullet \rho_{ij}$$

490 The CAPM model refers to this approach, for example.

where the pairwise influence of all of the assets is taken into account (ρ_{ij}). This pairwise influence is what has extensively been exploited for portfolio optimization, as it leads to diversification of risk if the assets are not entirely positively or negatively correlated.

The optimization problem[491]

For an investor seeking to maximize the expected return for a given volatility of the returns the optimization problem can be formulated as follows:

$$
\begin{aligned}
&Max \sum_{i=1}^{n} \mu_i \bullet x_i \\
&s.t. \quad \sum_{i=1}^{n}\sum_{j=1}^{n} x_i \bullet x_j \bullet \sigma_i \bullet \sigma_j \bullet \rho_{ij} \leq \text{Target} \\
&\qquad \sum_{i=1}^{n} x_i = 1,\ x_i \geq 0
\end{aligned}
$$

or, if an investor is seeking for the portfolio with the lowest volatility (standard deviation) given a return target:

$$
\begin{aligned}
&Min \quad \sum_{i=1}^{n}\sum_{j=1}^{n} x_i \bullet x_j \bullet \sigma_i \bullet \sigma_j \bullet \rho_{ij} \\
&s.t. \quad \sum_{i=1}^{n} \mu_i \bullet x_i \geq \text{Target} \\
&\qquad \sum_{i=1}^{n} x_i = 1,\ x_i \geq 0
\end{aligned}
$$

The figure below shows (μ,σ)-optimized portfolios consisting of two assets, X_1 and X_2 according to Breuer et al. (1999). The portfolio combinations to the right of the portfolio with the lowest variance are called *"efficient"*, because they dominate the respective portfolios selection with an equal return variance.

The "common shape" of the efficient frontier with a portfolio's volatility on the abscissa and returns on the ordinate is shown in section 4.3.5.1.

---

[491] Similar notations can be found in standard financial textbooks. See Caouette (1998), p. 273, for example.

Figure 4-18: Portfolio selection based on the (μ–σ) – criterion (Breuer et al. 1999, p.47)

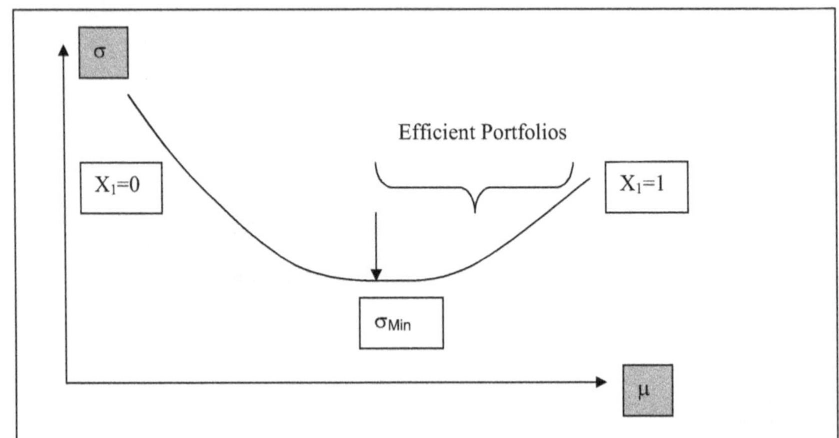

4.3.5.3 MPT meeting with criticism and solutions

To the extent that the returns of the assets are non-symmetrically distributed around their mean implying that the third (skew) and fourth (kurtosis) moments of returns are material in fully describing the distribution of asset returns, the use of simple, two moment MPT models "becomes difficult to justify" (Saunders 1999, p. 113). Although, how Saunders (1999, p.113) continues, "as the number of credit loans in a portfolio gets bigger, the distribution of returns tends to become more '*normal*'".

The limitations of the mean-variance model of Markowitz and in general for the credit risk sphere applied to fixed income credit portfolios are listed below.

Table 4-6: Limitations of the mean-variance model of Markowitz applied to fixed income (loan) credit portfolios (according to Caouette et al. 1998, p. 236 ff.)

Issue	Limitation
Correlation estimates	o The number of correlations to be calculated increases very rapidly o The variable to be used with fixed-income securities is not clear (correlation of returns/ factors explaining returns/ default probabilities/rating categories/ spreads) o Correlations are unconditional (e.g. with respect to macroeconomic shocks)
Distribution of returns	o The (μ,σ)- model is applicable if and only if security return distributions are symmetrical, what rather does no hold for credit loan portfolios[492]
Multi-period choice (holding period)	o The (μ,σ) approach is usually stated as a single-period problem
Lack of price data	o Debt securities are less traceable as equity markets
Lack of fundamental data	o Default events are rare; only reliable PDs related to external rated companies are available o Errors due to mapping of internal on external ratings (PDs) o PDs are not stationary over time

As a consequence of the limitations of the application of Markowitz' (μ,σ) approach to the domain of credit risk, alternative two-dimensional optimization concepts have been proposed. These state-of-the-art concepts for two-dimensional risk-return optimization will extensively be discussed in section 4.3.6ff.

4.3.5.4 Alternative concepts to Markowitz' MPT

Although the downside risk frame has been established by Roy (1952) in the same year as the Markowitz concept it has wrongly been fully explored only

[492] This has been specified in a stiking way by Caouette et al. (1998, p. 237): "When you make a loan, you get none of the upside and all of the downside. That is, you can lose all or most of your investment, but your upside is limited to the promised yield." Therefore, "in the region of loan loss, probability density is higher than that implied by a normal distribution curve. This is known as the *"fat tail"* problem;

within the last 10 to 20 years. The *Safety-First approach* of Roy (1952)[493] and the *semi-variance approaches*[494] proposed by Markowitz (1959, 1970, 1991) are the most famous portfolio approaches to capture downside risks. With the advent of the Value-at-Risk concept, *post-modern portfolio theory (PMPT)* has been born (see section 4.3.6). In parallel, the concept of stochastic dominance laid the theoretical basis for a loss-oriented portfolio theory.[495]

---

[493] There are basically three fundamental safety-first-criteria, which mostly differ by the definition of the shortfall probability (see Breuer et al. 1999, for example):

- Roy's criterion (Roy 1952): implies, that investors consider a minimum yield as given and try to minimize the risk of falling short of reaching this target.
- Kataoka's criterion (Kataoka 1953): implies that an investor seeks for a maximum yield under the constraint of a limited probability of falling short.
- Telser's criterion (Telser 1955): According to Telser (1955) both the target yield and the upper threshold of falling short are given. This criterion incorporates the expected yield, and thereby overcomes a major shortage of the latter two criteria. The target is to select among the feasible portfolios (which do not exceed the shortfall probability threshold) the portfolio with the highest expected yield.

[494] "Semi" implies that only the volatility beyond the mean is counted.

[495] Trend-setting approaches within the field of risk analysis have been provided by Hogan and Warren (1974), Bawa (1975, 1976, 1978), Bawa and Lindenberg (1977) and Nantell and Price (1977). Risk analysis enables the possibility to evaluate alternatives via risk profiles. Besides taking into account decisive constraints, risk analysis captures the characteristics of the first and second class stochastic dominance method.

An overview on main cornerstones of the concept of stochastic dominance and a list of selected references can be found on www.few.eur.nl/few/people/gtpost/stochastic_dominance.htm (Rev. June 2005.), in Breuer et al. (1999) and in Bamberg and Coenenberg (2000), for example. In the following, we will provide a braod-brush overview on the concept of SD oriented on these sources.

In general, the concept of stochastic dominance can be regarded as a systematic way to analyze economic behaviour under uncertainty. Major references in this context from a methodlogical viewpoint are Hadar and Russell (1969) Hanoch and Levy (1969), Rothschild and Stiglitz (1970) and Whitmore (1970). A more applied context of SD has been provided by Levy (1992,1998), for example.

An *advantage* of SD is its nonparametric approach, which underlies general preference assumptions rather than full parametric specifications of the investor's preferences as in the case of other approaches. Additionally, SD is consistent with many economic theories of choice under uncertainty, particularly with expected utility theory.

The advantages of SD, however, go along with its *limitations*. First, SD theory is relatively inflexible with respect to modelling investment possibilities (e.g. transaction costs, etc.) compared to other approaches. Second, SD requires a full empirical distribution function, what may cause sampling errors, especially in case of small samples. Third, the application of SD to empirical data is based on the prerequisite of a finite number of choice alternatives with respect to the computation of the empirical distribution

The following table summarizes the three distinct rules for decision making under risk.

Table 4-7: Distinctive decision rules under risk (according to Bamberg and Coenenberg 2000)

Investor is ...			
....Risk indifferent	...Risk sensitive		
Expected Value concept[496]	**Bernoulli Principle**	**Higher dimensional Expected value concept (e.g. μ–σ/ Safety-First)**	**Risk Analysis (e.g. stochastic dominance)**
Focus on μ	Utility Framework	Focus on μ	Focus on Risk Profiles
Suboptimal for most investors, who are risk sensitive	Exact, but significant applicability problems	Suboptimal, but comfortable application	High expenditures required; for difficult problems no solution

The bi-dimensional expected value concept (e.g. the μ–σ frame) as a partial set of the higher dimensional expected value concept is favored by most investors for portfolio selection on behalf of its easy application.

4.3.6 Post-modern portfolio theory (PMPT): Concepts beyond Markowitz

The downside risk theory benefits from a growing attractiveness and portfolio models based on this concept have even been called *'post-modern portfolio theory' (PMPT)*.[497] PMPT has been an answer to the "unsatisfactory aspects of MPT" (Rom et al. 1994, p.11), namely taking into account that credit risk losses are described by a high likelihood of small profits together with a small

functions, which limits the possible degree of portfolio diversification of the resulting optimal portfolio.

496 The *expected value concept* fully neglects risk considerations i.e. the decision maker is indifferent to risk and refers to the expected value of an investment solely: $\mu_i = \sum_i p_i \bullet R_i$, where p_i is the probability for a certain event and R_i is the corresponding return.

497 See Grootveld and Hallerbach (2001). The expression PMPT has been introduced by Rom and Ferguson (1994).

probability of large losses. In case of non-symmetric return distributions with heavy tails, downside risk measures ("partial domain view") can substitute the "full domain view" of Markowitz-type optimization (Grootveld and Hallerbach 2001, p.4/5). Nevertheless, the usage of downside risk measures has already been proposed by Markowitz.[498]

Hence, MPT becomes "nothing more than a special (symmetrical) case of the PMPT formulation" (Rom et al. 1994, p.11).

4.3.6.1 Classification of alternative financial credit risk measures

There are various alternative measures for the derivation of financial risks. Theiler (2002a) classified these risk measures according to different statistical features that determine the risk measure's usefulness for the corresponding risk type according to the loss function's distributional shape.

According to Theiler (2002a), risk measures may generally be distinguished according to

- Centralized moments are focusing on the whole range of a loss/return-distribution,
- Downside risk measures do only measure the negative deviation from a target value or percentile and
- The criterion of stochastic dominance is based on the whole range of the loss/return- distribution.

While centralized moments do not correspond to the economic interpretation of risk measures defining the negative deviation of a target, the latter two risk frames seem promising (Theiler 2002a). We will concentrate on the downside risk measure concept, which is a more intuitive concept as the criterion of

[498] Namely, the concept of the semi-variance, see Rubinstein (2002), p.1044, for example. VaR - type probabilistic analyzes of potential portfolio losses date back more than a century. Edgeworth (1888), for example, studied bank solvency by analyzing potential bank losses;

stochastic dominance.[499] Further information about the concept of stochastic dominance can be found in Breuer et al. (1999), for example.

Figure 4-19: Alternative financial risk measures (According to Theiler 2002a, p.76)

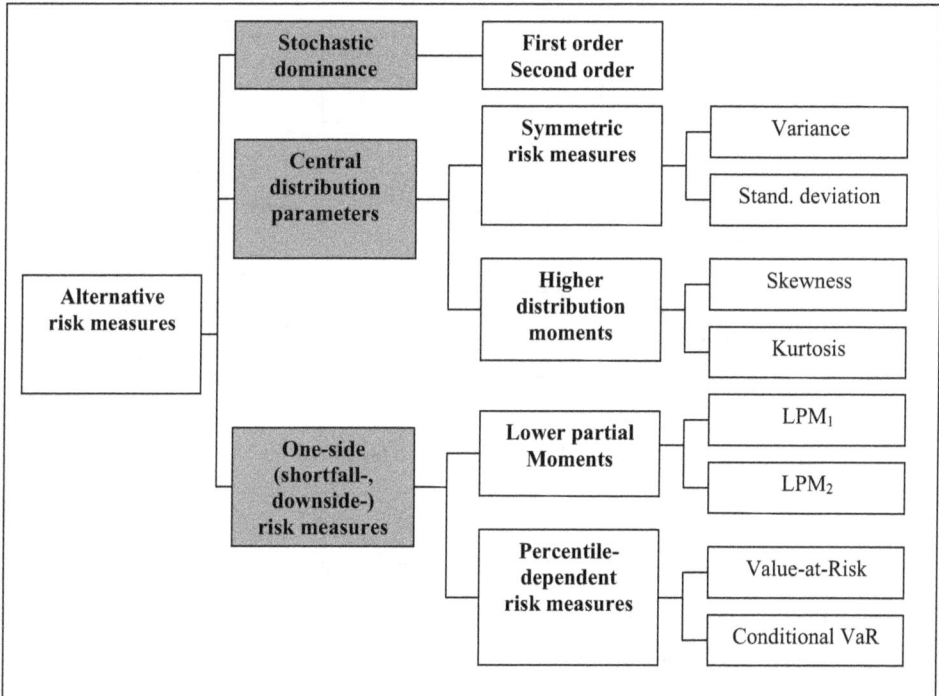

Alternative risk measures

Stochastic dominance
First order Second order

Central distribution parameters
Symmetric risk measures
Variance
Stand. deviation
Higher distribution moments
Skewness
Kurtosis

One-side (shortfall-, downside-) risk measures
Lower partial Moments
LPM_1
LPM_2
Percentile-dependent risk measures
Value-at-Risk
Conditional VaR

4.3.6.2 The coherence of risk measures

One major prerequisite for portfolio optimization is to underlie a coherent risk measure. Otherwise, one can expect to "get some strange results from the optimization procedure" (Arvanitis and Gregory 2001, p.99). The concept of *coherent risk measures* has been developed by Artzner et al. (1999) and it explained in the Appendix. Theiler (2002a) provides an overview of a discussion of risk measures with respect to their coherence property.

[499] Stochastic dominance in formal terms is defined as $E\,u(X_1) > E\,u(X_1)\ \vee u \in U_1$ where X_1 and X_2 are random variables and U_1 is a specific class of utility functions.

Figure 4-20: Alternative risk measures and their coherence (Theiler 2002b)

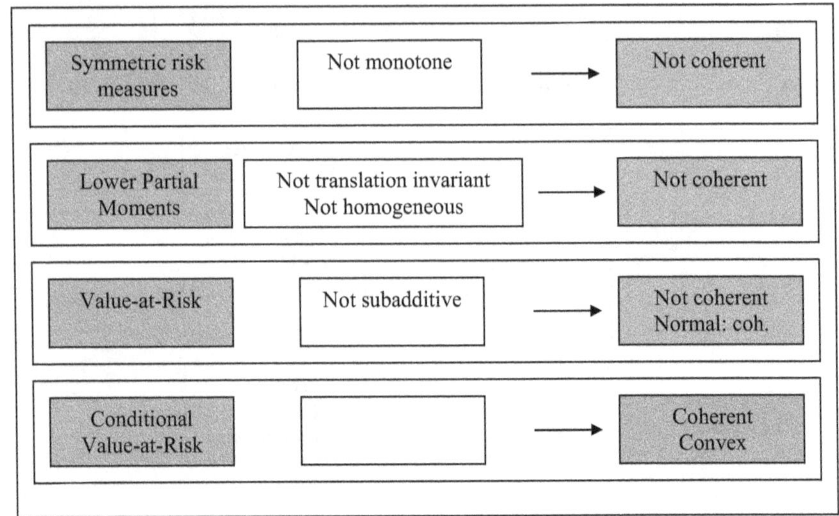

It can clearly be observed that only the conditional Value-at-Risk is a coherent risk measure.[500]

4.3.7 State-of-the-art credit portfolio optimization for single periods

In the following, the state-of-the-art concepts for credit portfolio optimization mostly based on percentile dependent downside risk measures will be presented following Theiler (2002a, p.104f.).

4.3.7.1 Variance as a risk measure

An attempt towards credit portfolio optimization derived from the variance-covariance approach can be found in Hamerle et al. (1998). It is, however, problematic to use symmetric risk measures on asymmetrically distributed credit portfolios.

4.3.7.2 The Value-at-Risk as a risk measure

An approach for portfolio optimization related to the VaR approach has been formulated by Grootveld and Hallerbach (2001). They investigated three

[500] Further information about the coherence of risk measures is summarized in the Appendix.

preference functionals (Von Neumann-Morgenstern expected utility function, Lancaster-type of multi-attribute preference functional, and lexicographic preferences) and found, that only a lexicographic preference structure can justify the role of VaR as the single risk variable.

Moreover, they indicate that portfolio optimization based on VaR does not necessarily lead to a unique solution, and choose a two-step procedure by first performing portfolio optimization without a VaR constraint. The efficient frontier of the set of all (μ, VaR) optimal portfolios will be subsequently constrained by the preferred VaR - restriction. This approach circumvents the shortage of direct optimization on the basis of the VaR.

Gaivoronski and Pflug (1998) indicate that the application of a constraint for the VaR may result in a non-convex set of feasible solutions. They reduce the optimization problem to a sequence of linear optimization problems by creating a convex set of feasible solutions for the VaR constraint and perform a linear optimization on this set. They show that the optimal solution converges towards the (μ, VaR) optimal portfolio.

Burmester et al. (1999) apply a Lagrange-method based on the variance-covariance-approach for the VaR.

An approach for the (μ, VaR) - optimization based on normally distributed portfolio returns can be found in Huisman et al. (1999). They use extended Sharpe-Ratios[501] based on VaR in the denominator for the optimization. A similar approach was performed by Gramlich et al. (1999), who worked out efficiency lines for normally distributed portfolio returns.

Alexander and Baptista (2000) found an approximation for the expected utility maximization applying the (μ, VaR) approach, but do not illustrate the shortages of the application of the VaR approach for non-normally distributed asset returns in the portfolio optimization.

[501] The Sharpe Ratio is defined as the spread over the riskless rate relative to a portfolio's risk.

Moreover, credit portfolio decision on the basis of VaR as a risk variable have been addressed in more or less detail by Andersen and Sornette (1999), Basak and Shapiro (2001), Gouriéroux et al. (2000), Huisman et al. (1999), Klüppelberg and Korn (1999), Lucas and Klaassen (1998), Puelz (1999), Tasche (1999) and Kehrbaum and Zagst (1998).

4.3.7.3 Credit portfolio optimization based on LPM

Within the expected utility framework, Bawa (1975) and Fishburn (1977) introduced a general definition of downside risk in the form of lower partial moments (LPM).[502]

Portfolio optimization based on the LPM methodology has been suggested by Albrecht (2001), for example. However, as also Albrecht (2001) points out, LPMs as decision variables and especially the question of their formal usefulness in terms of a coherence property is unclear. Theiler (2002a) affirms this theory and claims, that LPMs violate two prerequisites of coherent risk measures, what is shown in Figure 4-20.

4.3.7.4 Credit portfolio optimization based on the PD

Portfolio optimization anchored in the *probability of default* has been presented by Scheuenstuhl and Zagst (1996, 2000). Several assumptions and modifications are necessary to transfer the optimization problem into an integer programming task.

4.3.7.5 The Conditional Value-at-Risk (CVaR) as an optimization measure

Portfolio optimization founded on the Conditional VaR has been introduced by Uryasev and Rockafeller (1999).[503] The advantage of this portfolio maximization approach is to separate risk modeling and risk controlling.

Theiler (2002a) performed risk-return optimization for banks based on the proposal of Uryasev and Rockafeller (1999) coming out with a framework for

---

502 See Harlow & Rao (1989) and Harlow (1991) for further reference. More recently, Schmidt-von-Rhein (1996, 2000) used LPMs for portfolio optimization.

503 For further reference see also Rockafeller and Uruyasev (2000, 2002).

risk-adjusted bank controlling. The advantage of this method is that the application of the expected shortfall as a risk measure is possible on the whole range of bank activities, because it is independent of the underlying distribution. The optimization approach is in line with the expected utility optimization of a risk-averse investor (Bertsimas et al. 2000). Further insight of the optimization based on the CVaR is given below in section 4.3.8.1.

4.3.7.6 Risk-adjusted performance measures (RAPM) as optimization measures

Credit portfolio optimization based on risk-adjusted performance measures has been performed by Caouette et al. (1998). Using RAPM- measures like the RORAC, RAROC or RARORAC has further been proposed by Saunders (1999) Arvanitis and Gregory (2001), for example.

4.3.8 Single-period credit portfolio optimization: Deeper insights

In the following, the state-of-the-art concept for credit portfolio optimization will be outlined in a more detailed way.

4.3.8.1 Theoretical frame for the optimization based on the CVaR by Theiler (2002a)

This concept to optimize single period credit portfolios has been suggested by Uryasev and Rockafeller (1999), who postulated the following stepwise approach to handle the risk-return optimization approach. Step 2 allows solving the optimization problem in one step as a LP via the application of the simplex method.

Step	Task
1	Formulation of the risk-return - optimization problem based on the CVaR subject to certain restrictions (e.g. regulatory constraint, volume)
2	Simplification of the CVaR restriction applying auxiliary function
3	Derivation of the solution to the optimization problem o Approximation of Step 2. via a linear optimization problem o Prerequisite: scenario simulation

The formal insights to this approach are explained below.

4.3.8.1.1 The CVaR- optimization frame in more formal terms

Uryasev and Rockafeller (1999) has formulated the frame for credit portfolio selection based on the CVaR criterion as

$$
\begin{aligned}
& Max \sum_{i=1}^{n} \mu_i \bullet x_i \\
& s.t. \quad \mathrm{CVaR}_{\beta}(x) = \frac{1}{1-\beta} \int_{f(x,y)>VaR_{\beta}(x)} f(x,y)p(y)dy \leq \omega \\
& \quad \mathrm{x} \in \mathrm{X}
\end{aligned}
$$

where β refers to the desired confidence level, $f(x,y)$ to the random loss subject to the portfolio composition x and the corresponding loss composition y, weighted with a certain probability p, and ω is the upper limit of the portfolio risk.

As non-parametric methods do often substitute non-available analytical distributions, the optimization problem can be reformulated as[504]

$$
\begin{aligned}
& Max \sum_{i=1}^{n} \mu_i \bullet x_i \\
& s.t. \quad \tilde{\mathrm{F}}(x,\alpha) = \alpha + \frac{1}{J \bullet 1-\beta} \sum_{j=1}^{J} (f(x,y_j)-\alpha)^{+} \leq \omega \\
& \quad \mathrm{x} \in \mathrm{X} \\
& \quad \alpha \in \Re
\end{aligned}
$$

where $\tilde{F}_{\beta}(x,\alpha)$ is an auxiliary function, α is an arbitrary parameter and J is the scope of a sample. Loss is considered only when exceeding the confidence level β, indicated by the '+'. $\tilde{F}_{\beta}(x,\alpha)$ has been shown to be convex in α (see Uryasev and Rockafeller 1999). Moreover, α is the VaR_{β} in the optimum and a minimization of $\tilde{F}_{\beta}(x,\alpha)$ according to α delivers $CVaR_{\beta}$.

The optimization problem can subsequently be transformed into a linear optimization problem. The three- step procedure has been summarized above.

[504] See Theiler (2002a), p.121.

4.3.8.1.2 CVaR optimization applied within FI

Theiler (2002a/b) formulated the optimization problem based on Uryasev and Rockafeller (1999) for practical purposes by including capital constraints as follows:

Max RAPM
s.t. CVaR ≤ EC
Regulatory Risk ≤ Regulatory Capital
Capital ≤ Available Capital

The advantages and disadvantages of the approach are summarized below according to Theiler (2002b).

Advantages	**Disadvantages**
o Objective approach to portfolio optimization o Delivers a risk-return optimal bank-wide portfolio o The internal and regulatory risk constraint can be captured o Is based on the CVaR	o Data availability for the generation of scenarios my be difficult o Data warehouse interfaces may not exist

Efficient capital allocation is ensured and diversification is fully captured. The solvability of the risk-return optimization problem is fulfilled, because the coherent CVaR ensures convexity (see Tasche 1999). The convexity feature implies that optimization upon a convex set result in a concave and increasing efficiency line, i.e. a unique optimal solution for each risk-return-combination exists.

The following measures can be calculated for the optimal portfolio x* (Theiler 2002b).

Level	Measure
Single position	o Expected return o Risk contribution o RORAC
Portfolio	o Expected return o CVaR o RORAC

The optimization model postulated by Theiler (2002a) is founded on assigning the risk contributions of each position via the Euler principle subsequently after the optimal portfolio has been found, what has been explained in section 4.2.3.2.

4.3.8.2 Conclusion for one-period credit portfolio optimization

We can recapitulate that VaR approaches within the credit portfolio risk sphere have been proved to be inadequate despite their wide-spread usage as the percentile-based VaR is not a coherent risk measure. In practice, this means that there are "multiple solutions to an optimization problem, and these are likely to be quite different" (Arvanitis and Gregory 2001, p.102). Recently, the CVaR has been found as a coherent and useful state-of-the-art method. Due to the fact that the CVaR[505] is a convex function[506] under quite general conditions, efficient optimization algorithms can be used.[507] More specifically, a portfolio's CVaR can be minimized by using the familiar mathematical technique of linear programming.[508] Further information can be found in Andersson et al. (2001) or Rockafellar and Uryasev (2000).

4.3.9 The optimization of capital allocation

Capital allocation may be "very similar to a portfolio management problem" (Baud et al. 2000, p.1). Besides the basic principles for capital allocation as formulated by Patrick et al. (1999, see section 4.2.3.1), Theiler (2002a,

505 The Conditional Value-at-Risk. See Rockafellar and Uryasev (2002).
506 See Rockafeller (1970) and Shor (1985).
507 See Arvantis and Gregory (2001), for example.
508 See Arvantis and Gregory (2001), for example.

p.101/102) adds further properties related to asset (capital) allocation as a portfolio optimization problem.

Capital allocation should

- Be efficient.
- Ensure a risk-return optimal portfolio structure.

4.3.9.1 The capital allocation problem

Baud et al. (2000, p.7) distinguish two distinct approaches for capital management:

- *Top-down* or
- *Bottom-up.*

The top-down approach foresees first allocating capital to diverse business segments first, and afterward choosing the top securities within each business segment (Baud et al. 2000). In the latter method, the best securities are directly selected (Baud et al. 2000). Within the framework built in section 5, a top-down approach is chosen. The question is thereby how to allocate capital.

As stated by a Federal Reserve Banks Task Force (1998)[509] the banks "utilize internal economic capital allocations for two broad purposes: measuring risk-adjusted profitability, and portfolio risk management." Accordingly, the *bottom-up* approach is applicable in the former case while the *top-down* approach is tailored for portfolio management (Baud et al. 2000). According to Baud et al. (2000), a *top-down* internal allocation model can be understood as a portfolio problem where the portfolio is built up by of the bank's business lines, for example risk segments, as presented in section 5.

4.3.9.2 The solution

A solution to the capital allocation problem can be revealed by applying a Lagrange multiplier framework, with multipliers representing marginal prices.

[509] Federal Reserve System Task Force on Internal Credit Risk Models (1998).

Further information including a graphical representation of the optimization space can be found in Baud et al. (2000).

4.3.9.3 Distinct capital functions for optimization targets

Burmester et al. (1999) point out two major functions of capital:

- **Capital as investment capital:** Capital is required for a financial institution to perform its lending business, as banks are obliged to partly refinance credit by capital.
- **Capital as risk capital:** Capital cushions losses occurring from insolvencies. Thereby, the supervisory frame has to be fulfilled (see section 4.1.1.3).

They conclude that capital is therefore rare for the bank in two regards, so that two optimization problems can be performed:

- The maximization of the risky return on investments (RAPM) dependent on the availability of investments.
- The maximization of the return (risk premium) for risk bearing under the constraint of the available risk capital.

As the risk aspect of business plays an increasingly important role (shareholder's and management's short-term orientation), the first approach will be exercised in section 5.

The capital allocation problem can then be formulated as follows:

- How shall the available risk capital be distributed to generate a maximum RAPM subject to the given risk capital?

4.3.10 Technical support for credit optimization models: Securitization and credit derivatives[510]

4.3.10.1 Introduction

Modern credit risk techniques (credit derivatives, securitization) make loan portfolios more liquid. Still, before risk shifting techniques may be applied to non-liquid portfolios, a portfolio has to be chosen at first. Given their importance in today's credit business, modern credit risk techniques will be presented, although they do not play a role for the application of the portfolio approach in section 5.

As a consequence of capital arbitrage[511] caused by Basel I and the ongoing demand for diversification of portfolios, credit derivatives and asset securitization play a major role in today's credit business. Distinct from portfolio optimization, this kind of active portfolio optimization supports portfolio optimization on the one hand, and allows risk shifting on the other hand with the major target of diversification.

Under the current regulatory approach, a financial institution can decrease its regulatory capital without decreasing the inherent credit risk of its business.[512] This is why the Basel Committee seeks allowing internal models for the derivation of the necessary regulatory capital.[513] Credit derivatives were the stars under the derivatives[514]. The volume of the sector rocketed by *800% within the last five years* (Handelsblatt 2003). As a consequence of their complex structure, derivatives may cause higher risks in extraordinary situations as they can compensate for (Basel 2003).

---

510 The description of securitization and credit derivatives is oriented on Schierenbeck (2003b), Öhler and Unser (2001), Bessis (2001) and Handelsblatt (2003). See also various standard financial textbooks.

511 The divergence of regulatory and economic capital. See sections 2.3.1ff.

512 Jones (1999).

513 Still, the Basel Committtee on Banking Supervision assumes that the credit portfolio models are not yet sophisticated enough to be used for supervision (Basel 1999). A major problem is the lack of empirical data. See Mingo (2000), for example.

514 Handelsblatt (2003).

Several techniques exist to sell credit risk at the financial markets for obligors representing a significant proportion of risk. These include the following (according to Schierenbeck 2003b, p.218f.):

- **Collateralization:** Once it comes to a default event, collateral has the effect of reducing the severity of the credit loss.
- **Asset securitization:** Asset securitization means to package assets into a bond, which is then sold at the secondary markets.
- **Credit derivatives:** Credit derivatives are tools to transfer credit risk between obligors, while the client relationships remain unchanged.

The usage of distinct products for credit risk transfer is summarized below, decomposed to the corresponding products.

Table 4-8: Transfer of credit risk (according to Schierenbeck 2003b, p.218)

	Mobilization	**Usage of Credit Derivatives**
Single Transaction	Selling Syndication	Credit Default Products Credit Spread Products Total Return Products Credit Linked Notes
Portfolio	Direct Portfolio Selling Asset Backed Securities (ABS)	Basket Credit Swaps Index Credit Derivatives Synthetic Securitization

4.3.10.2 The concept of securitization (Asset Backed Securities, ABS)

Securitization is a technique to transfer on-balance sheet assets into off- balance assets via the capital markets.[515] The investors are compensated with cash flow generated by the pool of up to 150 securitized assets per transaction sold.[516] The credit losses arising from the securities are compensated by the cash flow of these assets. A limited credit risk often remains to the risk-seller (e.g. 2% of the exposure).[517]

---

515 Bessis (2001).

516 Bessis (2001).

517 See Niethen (2001), for example.

Securitization is a consequence of existing arbitrage opportunities between the banking book and the financial markets. The common rationale behind securitization is to sell non-liquid credit via secondary markets in order to save capital.[518] There are various types of assets that may be securitized, from credit cards to loans or leasing receivables, in the structuring of the notes, by size and seniority level.

Structures for offloading credit risk in the market are collateralized debt obligations (CDOs), collateralized bond obligations (CBOs) and collateralized loan obligations (CLOs).[519] The distinction among them is the nature of the securitized assets, i.e. whether they are tradable or not.

Clearly, the non-recourse selling of assets allows saving economic capital. Nevertheless, securitizations would be not interesting if they would not improve profitability. By consequence, the overall advantageness of a transaction has to be evaluated according to the following criteria, for example (Bessis 2001):

- The portion of capital savings;
- The differential cost of funding on-balance sheet through the market;
- The consequence on the return on capital;
- The capital gains or losses from the transactions;
- The related operating costs.

Further information about securitization can be found in Bessis (2001), for example.

4.3.10.3 Credit derivatives

Credit derivatives are financial instruments, which allow making bonds, loans and other credit obligations tradable.[520] They arose in 1992 in the US. By means of credit derivatives, lenders can minimize their credit risk for the case of insolvencies or accruals.

---

518 See Ong (1999), p. 23f.

519 See Schierenbeck (2003b), p.218f., for example.

520 A similar definition can be found in Ong (1999), for example.

The most common credit derivative products are credit default swaps (CDS). They stand for 45% of the credit derivatives (Handelsblatt 2003). It is common that CDS are applied according to the rules of the International Swap and Derivatives Association (ISDA), but other agreements are applicable as well (Handelsblatt 2003).

The biggest players for credit derivatives in Germany are commercial banks (50%).[521] Bank customers are usually not informed about the fact that the credit risk related to their contract is shifted outside the bank to a third person.

Besides the function of credit derivatives to enable active portfolio management and portfolio optimization, they will increasingly establish similar credit risk-return – balanced conditions worldwide and decrease arbitrage[522].

A generic overview on credit risk products is given below according to Merz (2001).

Figure 4-21: Credit derivatives: Overview according to Merz (2001)

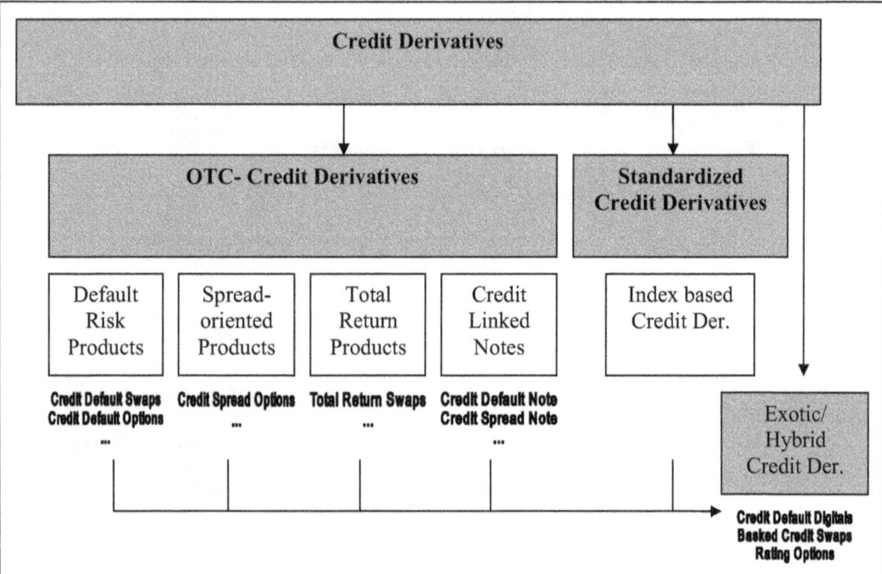

[521] Handelsblatt (2003). Other actors on the scene are investment banks, industrial enterprises, insurances and hedge funds.

[522] Öhler and Unser (2001), p. 370-371.

According to Merz (2001), credit derivatives can be characterized according to four groups. *Default risk products* are focused on the default event (DM), while *spread-oriented products* do additionally take rating migrations as potential default events into account (MTM).[523] *Total return products* do account for the overall return of an underlying, including also interest rate risk, for example. *Credit linked notes* are explained below. *Indexes* refer to the performance of a basket of borrowers. OTC (over-the-counter) markets allow direct transactions between the involved parties.

The table below links credit derivative products to be applied to insure different risks.

Table 4-9: Insurance of risks via credit derivatives (Schierenbeck 2003b, p.227)

	Credit Default Product	Credit Spread Product	Total Return Product	Credit Linked Notes
Default Risk	Secured	American Style Option	Secured	Credit Default Linked Note
Spread Risk		European Style Option	Secured	Credit Spread Linked Note
Market Risk			Secured	Total Return Linked Note
Counterparty Risk				Secured

The sellers of credit derivatives are mostly investment funds (Handelsblatt 2003). This has a good reason: the premium is normally above the risk premiums for the corresponding bonds. Additionally, fund managers have the opportunity to invest in non-traded firms.

4.3.10.3.1 Credit default swaps (CDS)

Credit default swaps are the most wide-spread type of credit derivatives (see Handelsblatt 2003, for example). The deal between creditor and the second party

[523] Default mode model respectively mark-to-market models have been explained in section 3.2.1.3.

(the risk taker) is that the lenders compensate the risk taker for the inherent risk of the trade by regular or one non-recurring payment. In case of a default event, the risk taker suffers the loss. Other in-convenient events to be subject to the contract may be non-paid interest, restructuring, provisions and write-offs.

4.3.10.3.2 Credit linked notes (CLN)

The idea behind credit linked notes is to combine bonds with CDS. A purchaser of a CLN (the risk taker) may define, for example, to repay only 70% of the nominal outstanding of an obligation in case of a credit event (Handelsblatt 2003).

4.3.10.3.3 Trends for credit derivatives

Most banks control credit risk within an integrated credit book, i.e. credit risk is centrally managed independent of the form of credit risk (credit loans, bonds, and derivates) (Handelsblatt 2003). The leveling rule for credit spreads is more and more directed by credit defaults swaps. Even the spreads of the classical firm loans approach the CDS spreads (Handelsblatt 2003).

4.3.11 From one period to multiperiod portfolio management

In imperfect capital markets, Fisher's separation theorem (Fisher 1906) does not hold valid. Consequently, risk, return and time[524] targets are dependent on the preferences of investors (see Hellwig 1999, for example).

Within a multi-period context, investors have to decide how many shares of which investment to hold at each point in time in order to maximize his/her expected utility of a portfolio's withdrawal sequence and/or terminal wealth according to their chosen preferences.[525] Most investors are focused on the maximization of a portfolio's final value.

For multi-period portfolio selection purposes, Markowitz' type models are often supposed to be handled "by running the model repeatedly, that is, the solution is

[524] Point in time of the actual and potential withdrawal and reinvestment.

[525] See Merton (1969/1971) or Samuelsom (1969).

implemented in period t, and when period t+1 is reached, the model is run again with new inputs" (Caouette et al. 1998, p. 238).

As multi-period investments are usually represented by their (net) present value, such an iterative ("myopic") procedure may be suboptimal.[526] More generally, myopic portfolio strategies are only valid if the following conditions hold true (Mossin 1968):

- The returns are intertemporally independent[527],
- There are no transaction costs and
- The investor may not withdraw or add funds during the planning horizon, i.e. the funds may not be reinvested.

As these assumptions are relatively restricted, myopic decision making is not feasible for practical purposes.

Multi-period credit portfolio selection based on the Bernoulli-principle has been performed by Elton/Gruber (1975/1995) or Ingersoll (1987), for example.

Besides utility theory, multi-stage programming techniques have been applied to optimize a multi-period portfolio. A recent research paper has been published by Boos et al. (2004), for example.

Besides, approaches to multi-period portfolio selection have been oriented on the growth pattern of a portfolio. This allows generating maximum growth portfolios[528], for example. Moreover, growth maximization is in line with utility maximization.[529]

If investors are willing to partly withdraw the generated returns, more general growth targets are required. Incentives for withdrawals may be bonus payments for employees, the accumulation of additional reserves for a strategic project and

---

526 Myopic decision making underlies that the optimal portfolio strategy at time t (x_t) depends only on the current portfolio (x_{t-1}) and the expectations of the market development in the following period (t+1). See Mossin (1968), for example.

527 With logarithmic utility functions, myopicity also holds for the depedent case. See Mossin (1968) and Hakansson (1971).

528 See Roll (1973), for example.

529 Naslund (1962) has been among the first authors to deal with multi-period portfolio investment.

dividend payments to a company's shareholders. The incorporation of withdrawals in a multi-period optimization context causes substantial difficulties. An approach to enable withdrawals termed as growth-oiented portfolio management has been proposed by Hellwig (1987). In section 5, the eligibility of this technique for credit portfolio decision making will be examined. An overview on eligible credit portfolio management techniques for practical purposes is given below.[530]

Figure 4-22: Eligible credit portfolio management frames (for practical purposes)

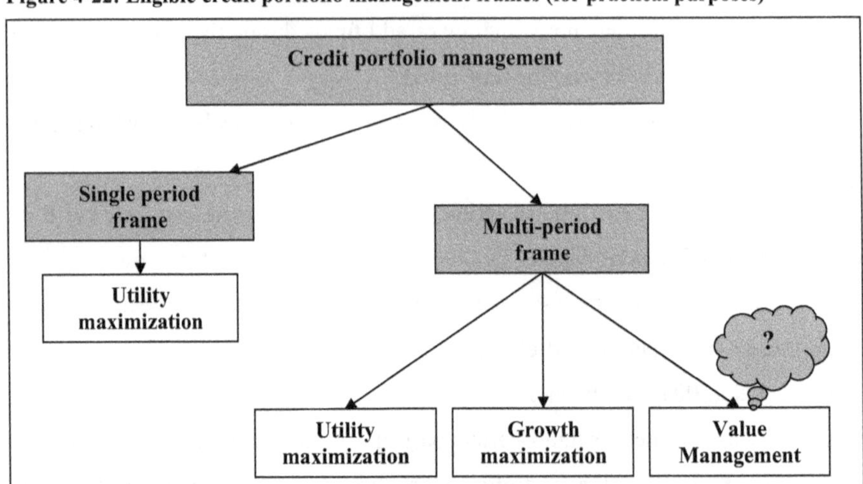

4.3.11.1 Evaluation of multi-period decisions: Static vs. dynamic evaluation methods[531]

Independent of the shape of a multi-period portfolio decision model, an evaluation method for multi-period investments has to be in place in order to enable reasonable choice. Two generic evaluation methods can be distinguished, static and dynamic methods.

Static methods for the assessment of investment opportunities comprise three methodologies[532]:

[530] The multi-attribute approach is neglected, given its difficulties for practical purposes.

[531] This section follows Reichling (2003). Further information can be found in standard finance textbooks.

- Cost comparison,
- Profit comparison,
- Profitability assessment.

As all of the static methods do not account for the timely structure of payments, they are not eligible within multi-period contexts.

In a multi-period contexts, two methodologies have been found to be appropriate[533]:

- The net present value (NPV) method (comprising the annuity method) and
- The internal interest rate method.

The first method, the NPV method, is generally used since the internal interest rate method shows logical inconsistencies.[534] The NPV method assigns time-related values to cash flow streams, e.g. for an investment j:

$$NPV_j = -I_0 + \sum_{j=1}^{T} CF_j \bullet (1+i)^{-t}$$

where I_0 is the initial investment, the CF_t's are the time-dependent cash flows[535] and i represents the underlying interest rate.

The decision rule for an investment is subsequently:[536]

- If NPV > 0: Investment is profitable.
- If NPV = 0: Investment is neutral with respect to return.
- If NPV < 0: Investment is not advantageous.

The application of the NPV plays a crucial role for all multi-period investment frames (e.g. credit portfolio selection) and will be the core building block for portfolio selection in section 5.

---

532 See Reichling (2003).

533 See Reichling (2003), for example.

534 See Reichling (2003), for example.

535 Expenses are assigned a negative sign.

536 Where the NPV represents the PV of the cash flows resulting from an investment K minus the PV of the investment K itself.

4.3.11.2 Multi-period portfolio management: Scenario-based approaches

Within a multi-period context the size of multi-period stochastic outcomes of the credit risk result is exploding. It is therefore common to refer to a set of scenarios (e.g. optimistic, pessimistic and likely) constructed from an event tree. Every scenario is thereby considered to "encompass a set of internally consistent assumptions about the state of the economy and returns earned" (Caouette et al. 1998, p. 294). Subsequently, an optimal portfolio can be determined by assigning an outcome probability to each scenario.[537]

Portfolio management based on scenario approaches for market risk has been performed by Markowitz and Perold (1981)[538] and Bennet (1984), for example. A scenario-based approach for credit portfolio management will be presented in section 5.

4.3.11.3 Measuring multi-period outcomes depicted by event trees

Besides the query of finding an appropriate credit risk measure for optimization purposes as extensively discussed above, the appropriateness of return measurement may be subject to discussion as well.

The most common way to depict the average outcome of lending is to refer to the arithmetic average return (or performance) which is the weighted average of the expected returns (r_i) of the investments (i) in a portfolio and their occurrence probabilities (p_i):

$$E=\sum_{i=1}^{n} p_i \cdot r_i$$

For multi-period horizons Latané (1959) suggested substituting the arithmetic average by the geometric average of the return:

$$E=\sum_{i=1}^{n} r_i^{p_i}$$

---

537 See Caouette et al. (1998).

538 Who suggested using a scenario approach to optimize a portfolio in order to overcome the difficulties related to the stability of correlation matrixes.

While the concept of the arithmetic average may be adequate for single periods, Latené (1959) proved that under the assumption of reinvestments of the in-period returns, the **maximization of the final value is in line with the maximization of the geometric average**, i.e. the portfolio with the highest geometric return leads ceteris paribus to the highest value for a long-term horizon.

Hakansson (1971) proved that the application of the geometric average criterion is superior to the arithmetic average at least for a planning horizon of at least 6 periods.

Although Latané's idea is very plausible, it has not been as successful as the (μ,σ) - approach favored by Markowitz (1952, 1959) and Tobin (1958), for example.

Schuhmacher (1998), for example, did show that (μ,σ)- efficient portfolios may lead into ruin in the long run.

5 Multi-period credit portfolio management with arbitrary growth targets

„Not only is there but one way of doing things rightly, there is but one way of seeing them, and that is seeing the whole of them." John Rushkin (1819-1900), The Two Paths, 1885[539]

5.1 Motivation for an alternative approach for credit portfolio management

In section 4, state-of-the-art concepts for credit portfolio management and optimization have been presented. Given specific portfolio problems in the non-traded segment, however, these concepts may not be appropriate. The target of this section is to define the technical and managerial motivation that asks for an alternative solution (section 5.1), to present and propose a conceptual solution to the specific portfolio problem (section 5.2 and 5.3) and to apply the developed concept based on a simplified example (section 5.4).

A comparison with other available concepts is addressed (section 5.4.3.4) and advantages and disadvantages of the approach are discussed (section 5.4.4f.). Finally, areas for further research are proposed (section 5.4.6) and conclusions are drawn (section 6).

An overview of the stepwise procedure is graphically illustrated below.

[539] See www.brainyquote.com/quotes/quotes/j/johnruskin139098.html, for example. Rev. March 2005.

Figure 5-1: The overall procedure for a multi-period credit portfolio management framework

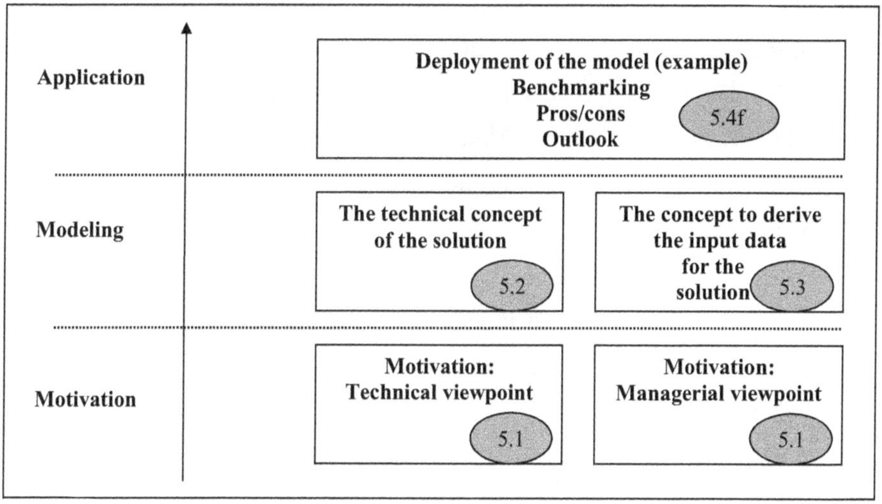

	Application	Modeling	Motivation
	Deployment of the model (example) Benchmarking Pros/cons Outlook (5.4f)	The technical concept of the solution (5.2)	Motivation: Technical viewpoint (5.1)
		The concept to derive the input data for the solution (5.3)	Motivation: Managerial viewpoint (5.1)

5.1.1 The portfolio problem to be solved

5.1.1.1 The target credit portfolio to be managed

In the domain of credit, the majority of the credit market still refers to the non-traded segment, especially in Europe and particularly in Germany.[540] The non-traded credit portfolio volume of the leading German private bank, Deutsche Bank, for example, has roughly been 145 billion in 2003 (Deutsche Bank 2003), what is a considerable amount.

Given a non-traded credit portfolio (e.g. a SME or retail portfolio within a commercial bank[541] or a captive leasing and finance company[542]), which is assumed to be managed as a credit profit center over a multi-period horizon, an appropriate methodology is searched for.

[540] In Germany, credits to non-banks had a volume of 3 billion Euros in 2004; See www.destatis.de, for example. Rev. June 2004.

[541] e.g. Deutsche Bank.

[542] e.g. DaimlerChrysler.

Following the "management by objectives" technique for profit centers (see section 2.4.2), senior management assigns risk, return and growth (i.e. market share) targets to the credit profit center.

Besides, as a FI's business has to be secured by capital as imposed by worldwide banking regulation (Basel I/II, see section 2.3), the capital portion to be used for lending purposes has to be defined by senior management for the credit profit center.[543]

It is assumed that the decentralized credit profit center has to deliver cash flows (resulting from the portfolio investments) to the overall company during the planning horizon, i.e. the generated profit center result does not entirely remain within the profit center.

The target portfolio to be managed is assumed to be

- of a substantial size (e.g. roughly 500,000 entities[544]),
- homogeneous (comparable exposure and maturity, default correlations are equally distributed over the portfolio and generally low) and
- segmented into risk classes (e.g. 8-12 according to a rating scheme).

The main cornerstones of the target credit portfolio are summarized below.

---

[543] If a FI should possess 10 billion units of capital, for example, 5 billion might be used for credit risk, 2 billion for market risk and 3 million for operative risk. The capital portion to be used for traded and non-traded credit risk has to be defined by senior management.

[544] As the credits are multi-period investments, they start and terminate in different years. A portfolio comprising of three-year credits will therefore be related to roughly 167,000 credits terminating in one year, which may be subject to credit decision.

Table 5-1: The target portfolio to be managed

Feature	Specific shape of the considered portfolio
Type of credit portfolio	Non-traded credit (e.g. SME, retail, etc.)
Target organizational entity to be managed	Profit center
Target horizon	Multi-period (2-5 years)
Composition of the portfolio	o Ca. 500,000 credit entities o Homogenous (exposure, maturity, correlations) o Segmented according to rating classes (e.g. 8-12)

For demonstration purposes, a rather small sample credit portfolio[545] will be used for the application of the portfolio selection approach in section 5.4f. A comparison between the target and simulated portfolio will be given in section 5.3.2.

5.1.1.2 The management target

The general portfolio management problem to be solved is to base a portfolio decision on a proper multi-period credit portfolio model, embedded into a (net) present value maximization framework[546] and a technical concept that represents an investor's portfolio targets in a preferably convenient way.

From a managerial viewpoint, the portfolio model should

- Be a "real" multi-period model.
- Be appropriate for the management of non-traded credit portfolios.
- Enable to depict numerous profit center targets.
- Ensure that the chosen portfolio strategy maximizes the PV of the portfolio.
- Enable other portfolio growth (in terms of (net) PV) targets than final value maximization only.
- Depict the preferences of various interest groups of a corporation.

545 See section 5.3.2.

546 Controlling methods for multi-period horizons have been discussed in section 4.3.11.1.

5.1.1.3 The question of an appropriate credit portfolio management process (framework)

Credit portfolio decision making is supposed to be embedded into an integrated credit portfolio management process (an appropriate framework), which consists of a closed loop of four steps as shown below in Figure 5-2. In the first step, credits are priced according to their rating segment.[547] Subsequently, the credit risk result for a profit center's rating segments can be forecasted and depicted in terms of a payoff matrix. Based on the information given, a credit portfolio decision, i.e. to define the optimal rating segment weights is enabled. The resulting outcome of the portfolio decision may be evaluated ex post.

As shown in Figure 5-2, both active and passive methods for credit risk management are essential to fulfill the requirements of the overall credit portfolio management process. Passive credit portfolio management methods (which have been presented in section 3) are thereby the basis for active methods.

The overall modeling process will be explained in further details in section 5.3f.

Figure 5-2: The credit portfolio management process (framework)

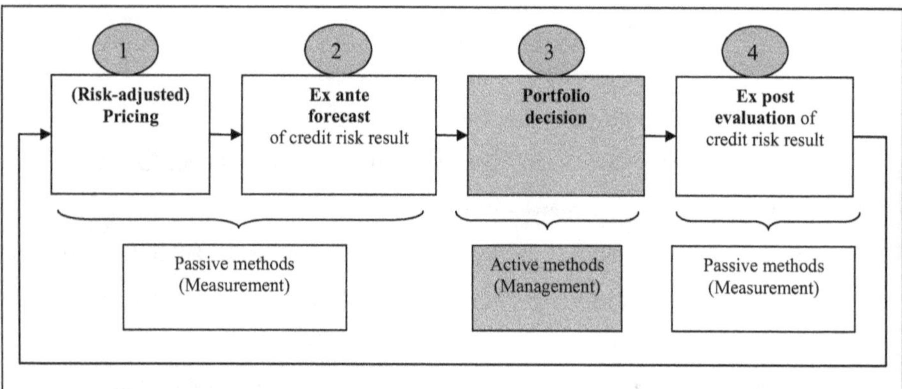

[547] It is assumed that pricing is risk-adjusted (according to the inherent risk of an obligor).

5.1.2 The choice of the appropriate technical methodology

In the following, the question of finding an appropriate methodology to solve the portfolio decision problem (step 3) will be discussed.

Figure 5-3: Choice of an appropriate technical solution for credit decision

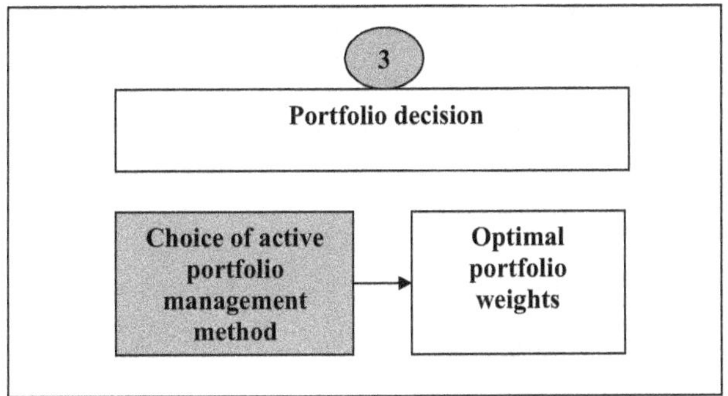

Within the last 10 to 15 years, numerous attempts for active credit portfolio management have been proposed, however, mainly for the liquid credit market, which is similar to the equity market, as the planning horizon is relatively short (e.g. one year) and the number of assets to be chosen is (very) low in contrast to the traditional (non-traded) credit domain.

The common approach to portfolio management is to refer to utility-based credit portfolio optimization in order to arrive at a risk-return optimised portfolio in terms of diversification. State-of-the-art methods for single-period credit portfolio optimization based on utility theory have been presented in section 4.3. The risk measure used for credit portfolio optimization purposes in Markowitz' sense has been replaced by tail-related risk measures within the last two decades in order to capture non-symmetric loss and profit distributions.[548] Moreover,

[548] Markowitz-type optimization models have proven their advantageousness in the domain of market risk, where the target portfolio (in terms of investments to be included into the portfolio) is mostly relatively small (10-20) and inhomogeneous with respect to the correlation structure compared to the domain of credit, particularly in the non-traded field. Diversification in Markowitz' sense comprises both exploiting the correlation structure of a portfolio and including "enough" assets into the portfolio, so that the volatility (i.e. risk) of the outcome is minimized for a pre-defined return target.

optimization based on simulated (non-parametric) data has been performed besides analytical approaches (see Theiler 2004, for example).

In the on-traded domain of credit, correlations between the investment alternatives (obligors or subportfolios) play a less crucial role for optimization in contrast to the domain of equity, as they are rarely negative[549] and are generally relatively low, particularly for SME and even more for retail portfolios.[550] As credit loans are multi-period investments, the portfolio model has to be focussed on multi-period horizons.

In section 4.3.11, a set of alternative methodological concepts for multi-period horizons has been presented. In the following, a broad discussion on the application of utility theory for multi-period credit portfolio selection will be given, followed by a motivation for the usage of alternative concepts.

5.1.2.1 From single-period to multiperiod portfolio selection

It has been shown by Coenenberg (1997) that generally all interest groups of a company are interested in the long term conservation of the economical substance of the firm. Accordingly, a company has to seek for preferably high yields in order to be competitive. For the compensation of a company's shareholders' investments, however, withdrawals are usually required in a multi-period context (e.g. dividend payments).

As indicated in section 4.3, there are indeed reasons why multi-period decision problems accounting for three and more preferences (exceeding the two-dimensional risk-return optimization frame) have been neglected for a long time. The reasons for this will subsequently be rediscussed.

---

549 Aspects of diversification and systematic vs. non-systematic risk in credit portfolios have been addressed in Figure 3-8 in section 3.5.1.2.1.

550 Empirically observed correlations in credit portfolios are summarized in section 3.5.1.2.1.4.2.

5.1.2.2 Implications for multi-period portfolio management based on the utility frame

With a shift to intertemporal planning, there are theoretical burdens for the application of utility theory.

A general point of criticism against utility theory is that the assumption of an investor to be a rational decision maker (a "homo oeconomicus"), and thus seeking for maximum utility is often violated (e.g. Allais and Hagen 1979, Kahnemann et al. 1982).[551] Moreover, it is generally very difficult to find a multi-period utility function that is in line with all interest groups involved in a decision. Furthermore, utility functions can not be aggregated for more than two portfolio selection preferences (Arrow's impossibility theorem or "Arrow Paradoxon", Arrow 1961)[552] and furthermore utility theory is critical because an investor's utility depends on the underlying investment alternatives and the investor him-/herself (Sen 1997).[553]

Still, it has to be noticed that besides all its shortages, utility theory provides a strong methodology to capture diversification via Markowitz-type portfolio optimization (see Korn 2000, for example). The question is, whether there are

551 For the concept of expected utility, it has empirically been proven that systematic behavior is often in contrast to this concept e.g. the framing effect, the Allais-paradoxon and the Ellsberg-paradoxon.

552 Arrow showed that there are no transformation rules, so that m>2 individual preference functions can be transformed into a coherent group preference (a social welfare function) without the violation of one of the five underlying constraints according to Arrow (1961, see section 4.3.2.2).

553 Recently, several theoretical modelling attempts have been directed at the potential influence of non-outcome information on portfolio choice (see Brandts and Charness 2000, for example). According to Sen (1997), who discusses the influence of the act of choice on investors' behaviour, only *chooser dependence* or *menu dependence* have to be distinguished as relevant factors. While chooser dependences would refer to differences in the characteristics of decision makers, menu dependence is linked to the possible influence of predetermined opportunities (or social costs). Sen (1997) assumes that the way, how the type of market imbalance influences the behaviour of decision makers should be classified as menu dependence. Brandts and Charness (2000, p.6) claim that Sen's classification is a rather broad-brush classification, which may be useful, but "may not easily cover all ways in which non-outcome information may affect behavior." They provide a further discussion on other relevant theroretical approaches in this field.

appropriate alternative concepts for intertemporal portfolio selection, especially for practical purposes.

5.1.2.3 Utility maximization vs. growth maximization

Given the difficulties of utility theory in a multi-period context, alternative concepts have been perspected for. Baviera et al. (1998, p.473), for example, proposed to substitute utility maximization by growth maximization, since "the rate of growth is an almost sure thing in the long run". Growth maximization in a multi-period context has a long history and is in line with utility maximization (e.g. Baviera et al. 1998)[554] as the growth maximization criterion refers to a logarithmic utility function (in wealth) which displays decreasing absolute risk aversion (Hakansson 1971).[555]

5.1.2.4 Portfolio selection based on arbitrary growth rates: Hellwig's model

In order to account for more general, arbitrary growth targets for portfolio selection purposes besides growth maximization[556], Hellwig (1987, p. 122) proposed the principle of **growth-oriented portfolio selection (GOPS).** Instead of finding an efficient portfolio by maximizing the expected utility (portfolio optimization) a solution to (growth-oriented) portfolio selection is determined by specifying requirements that a sequence of inter-temporal portfolio values should satisfy.

The principle of arbitrary growth rates is, however, no longer in line with utility theory[557], but is instead closely related to growth optimization; however, the background is rather different (Korn 2000).[558]

---

554 "The growth-optimum portfolio maximizes the probability of exceeding a given wealth level within a fixed time"; Breimann (1961).

555 Theoretical concepts to capture risk aversion have been discussed in section 4.3.3.4.

556 And thereby to enable withdrawals.

557 Utility maximization and value management are, in principle, "incompatible", as in contrast to utility theory "the solution to the portfolio problem (for GOPS) depends on the set of feasible consumption sequences" (Hellwig 2002a, p. 137), i.e. no utility function may exist that leads to the desired growth sequence required by an investor if the set of feasible consumption sequences changes. For an example see Hellwig et al. (2000), p.11.

While the approach of arbitrary growth rates has been generalized by many authors (e.g. Hellwig (1987, 1996a/b, 1998, 2002a), Hellwig et al. (2000), Korn (1997, 1998, 2000), Korn et al. (1999) and Speckbacher (1998)), it was Hellwig (2004, p. 2124f.) who did show that "based on a standard multi-period model a portfolio exists that satisfies a priori given growth objectives" under "economic meaningful conditions", which "guarantee the existence of a portfolio satisfying given growth requirements".[559]

Growth-oriented portfolio management has conceptually been applied to many economic areas including portfolio selection in discrete-time (see, e.g. Hellwig 1993, Wiesemann 1995) and in continuous-time models (see Korn 1997, 1998). The purpose of this work is to apply growth-oriented portfolio selection to the field of credit. The GOPS model is a deterministic model with respect to the risk-return structure of a credit portfolio.[560]

The approach will deliver a multi-period credit portfolio strategy that maximizes the (net) present value of the withdrawal sequence and is in line with an investor's growth preference (see section 5.2.3).

5.1.2.5 Conclusion for the choice of an appropriate model

From a practical viewpoint, the question of the usability of Hellwig's GOPS model may be put down to earth: **What is the benefit for an investor applying the model?**

Consider a credit portfolio manager who is responsible for a credit profit center. He/she is committed a certain volume of capital assigned to his/her credit profit center within a corporation in order to **manage new credit business.**

558 In a discrete-time setting one can consult Korn and Schäl (1999) for a survey of these relations.

559 The technical concept of GOPS and the economic conditions underlying portfolio decision will be explained in section 5.2.

560 For the considered, well-diversified target credit portfolio given, it is thereby assumed that risk-return optimization can be neglected, as the portfolio is roughly on the efficient frontier, if certain constraints are fulfilled (see section 5.3.4.5.5). Given the size of the target credit portfolio, optimization would be at all relatively difficult.

He/she has an obligation towards the shareholders on the one hand to generate annual payment surpluses in order to fulfill the shareholder's desired growth rate on their investment (in form of withdrawals and portfolio growth) and towards the company to generate maximum profit on the other hand. Other interests are imposed by the risk management to embark on a strategy of the lowest risk for given growth targets and by the regulatory supervision to fulfill a minimum capital level.

Within a multi-period context, the incentive or duty to withdraw the return on their credit investments during the planning horizon is of special interest for profit center managers to fulfill the interest of these various groups.

The dilemma for the credit portfolio manager is now, that it is very difficult to determine a proper multi-period utility function that represents multi-dimensional preferences of investors.

He/she will therefore search for alternative concepts. Multiperiod credit portfolio selection based on a given growth pattern as proposed by Hellwig (1987, 2002a, 2004) circumvents the utility framework and enables intertemporal decision making.

It is hereby possible to represent the common short-, medium- and long-term growth targets of various interest groups directly or indirectly involved in the portfolio decision and to enable modeling withdrawals with respect to the development of the portfolio value. [561]

As the target credit portfolios considered within this work are very large with numerous obligors and may be regarded as well-diversified, it is assumed that considering the risk-return structure of such a credit portfolio to be deterministic is valid.

Yet, in order to ensure that diversification aspects are captured when applying the portfolio selection model, upper and lower bounds for the investment

[561] The portfolio selection program allows non-symmetric decision trees with targets for each scenario according to an investor's preferences.

opportunities may be defined in order to arrive at a well-shaped portfolio decision.

The table below summarizes the major differences between traditional Markowitz-type portfolio optimization models and growth-oriented credit portfolio selection (GOPS).

Table 5-2: Comparison of Markowitz-type portfolio optimization vs. GOPS

Modeling target	**State-of-the-art methods for credit risk**	**GOPS**
Preference target of portfolio model	Usually risk-return optimization of the final portfolio value	Time preferences, arbitrary growth targets
Multi-period modeling	Usually not foreseen (single period models), Multi-period models face shortages	Intertemporal portfolio model by definition
Handling of discount factors	Exogenously defined	Endogenously handled ("Opportunity costs")
Transaction costs	Do not have to be modeled, as credits provide regular cash flows which may be reinvested	

5.1.2.6 The principle of growth-oriented portfolio selection (GOPS)

The aim of this section is to apply portfolio selection according to Hellwig (2002a, 2004) to the field of credit risk and thereby provide a framework for the management of non-liquid multi-period credit portfolios. The principle of growth-oriented portfolio selection (GOPS) is graphically illustrated below. The growth-oriented portfolio strategy provided by the solution of an optimization problem (see section 5.2.3) foresees to withdraw the differential growth generated by the portfolio exceeding the target growth rate (indicated by "1", what may refer to a pleasant scenario in the figure below). The growth rate refers to the PV of the portfolio. If the growth targets are chosen too high, subsequent payments may be necessary, as shown below (indicated by "2", what may refer to an unpleasant scenario). It is thereby assumed that the growth target of an investor is always exactly fulfilled. The intertemporal "costs" of the subsequent payments are derived via a generalized NPV concept to be explained in section 5.4.2.3.

Figure 5-4: The principle of growth-oriented portfolio management

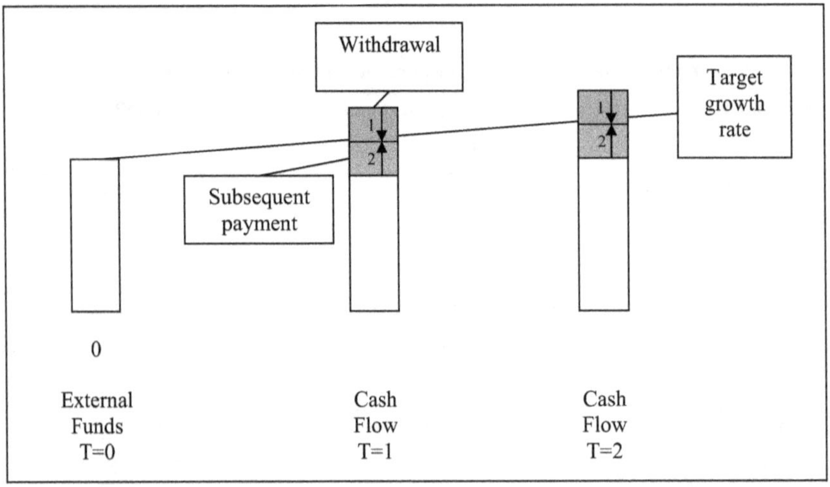

Selection of a growth function (distribution profiles) instead of utility functions

While utility functions are the main and most difficult building block for utility theory, growth functions have to be defined in case of GOPS (see section 5.2.3.2) in order to represent the time preferences of an investor. These growth functions determine, whether a withdrawal sequence refers to the outcome of the preceding ('ex post') or the succeeding ('ex ante') period, termed as the notion of the portfolio selection problem in the following (see section 5.2.3.2 for a more formal discussion).

5.1.3 A specific concept for the GOPS model applied to credit risk

5.1.3.1 Procedure underlying the credit portfolio selection model

In section 5.1.2, the choice of an appropriate active portfolio model for the decision problem formulated in section 5.1.1 has been discussed.

The next question is how to apply the GOPS model within the domain of non-traded credit risk in order to arrive at optimized portfolio weights for the specific preferences of an investor as shown below.

Figure 5-5: Choice of the appropriate model for credit decision: The GOPS model

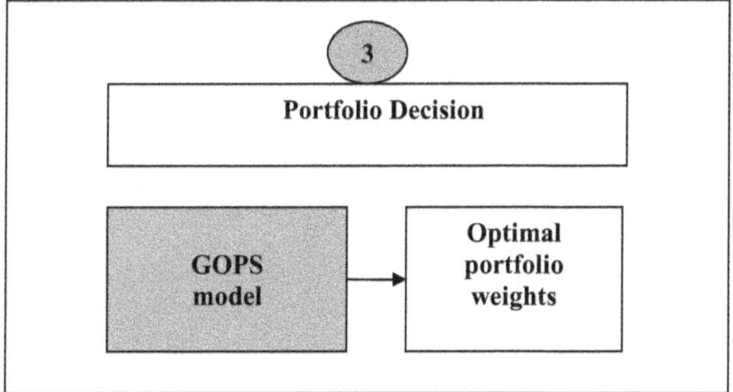

The overall decision process of the GOPS model can be divided into three distinct steps:

- **Generation of the required input data** in the required format.
- **Application of the optimization**[562] **algorithm.**
- **Interpretation and analysis of the derived output**.

as shown in Figure 5-6 below.

The input parameters entering the model are a multi-period decision tree, externally given capital, a stationary payoff matrix (for the included investment opportunities and their upper and lower bounds), an investor's pre-defined growth targets with respect to the NPV of the portfolio and the model notion (ex post or ex ante). Further insights into the model's input data are given in section 5.2.2.

The mostly non-linear, non-convex optimization problem[563] has been formulated by Hellwig (2002a, p. 136) and will be presented in further details in section 5.2.3.5.[564]

[562] The initial value management problem (GOPS) is transformed into a corresponding optimization problem as explained in section 5.2.

[563] Depending on the specific portfolio problem given. Further information can be found in Hellwig (2002a).

The final output of the portfolio selection model is a multi-period portfolio strategy (a sequence of portfolio decisions for each path in the event tree), endogenously derived discount vectors related to the portfolio strategy (for each path in the event tree) and a withdrawal sequence (for each path in the event tree) that is in line with the preferences of an investor.[565]

Figure 5-6: The overall procedure of the GOPS model

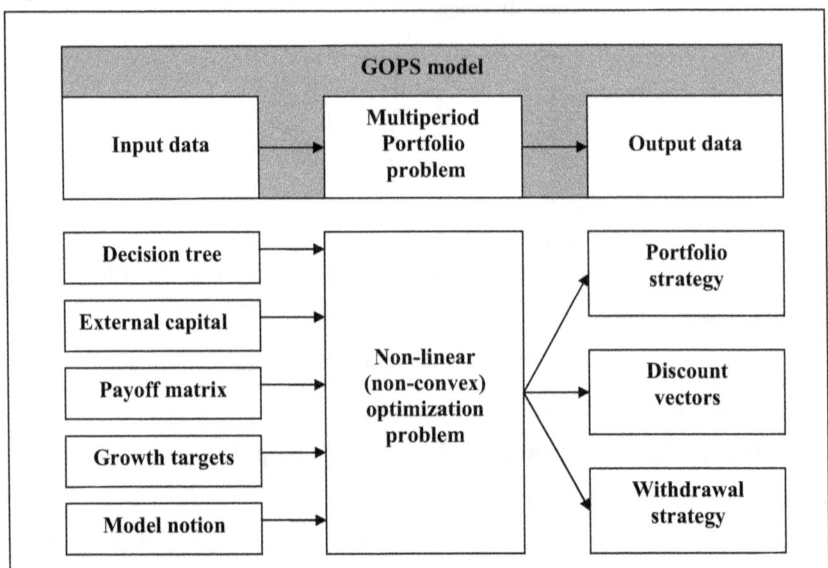

5.1.3.2 Specification of the GOPS model applied to credit risk

Given the overall procedure of the GOPS model, the question is how to apply the model to the domain of credit risk.

From a decision theoretical viewpoint, the GOPS model is a multi-period decision model under uncertainty with a finite planning horizon (see section 5.2.2).

[564] An advantage of Hellwig's approach is that the portfolio problem foresees a two-stage procedure: In the first step, inefficient solutions are excluded, and subsequently a portfolio that is in line with an investor's growth preferences is selected (see section 5.2.3.1).

[565] It has been proven by Hellwig (2002a, p. 12ff.) that a portfolio exists that fulfills the growth targets set by an investor if they are lower than the return generated by a single-period riskless investment, which is always available as an alternative investment opportunity.

The major input data shown in Figure 5-6 related to credit risk can more precisely be understood as follows:

- **Decision tree:** Representation of the conditional averages of percentile intervals of the density function of the credit risk result (see Figure 5-21 in section 5.3.4).
- **External capital:** The capital of the bank strategically foreseen for the credit profit center for business purposes related to all nodes in the event tree.[566]
- **Payoff matrix:** The deterministic payoff for the investment opportunities included into decision making.
    - Investment opportunities: Risk segments according to rating classes (see section 5.1.3.3.1).
    - Lower and upper bounds: Thresholds for the investment opportunities (see section 5.2.2.3.2 and 5.4.1.3).
- **Growth targets**: A credit portfolio's growth targets (with respect to NPV) defined by senior managers according to strategic considerations.
- **Model notion**: The time preferences of senior credit management[567].

In the following, the decision problem is reformulated in terms of the GOPS model and both investment opportunities and business determinants are more thoroughly specified for the decision problem.

Other major input and output data of the model will be explained in section 5.2 and 5.3f., respectively. Examples for the application of the model to credit risk are given in section 5.4.

---

566 In contrast to common approaches, not the exposure but the capital cash flow is focused on.

567 Withdrawals may be based on the performance of the investment in the previous (ex post) or the following period (ex ante) (see section 5.2.2.5).

5.1.3.3 Reformulation of the credit portfolio decision problem related to the GOPS model

The major question to be solved is a **decision about the investment of the scarce capital**, which enables lending. Portfolio selection will therefore be understood as capital selection.[568] Given a pre-defined decision tree, a profit center's assigned capital portion, growth targets and the model notion of the GOPS model, the target of the GOPS model is to provide an

- ***Efficient, inter-temporal portfolio program for each point in time and scenario in the event tree for the profit center manager, given the specific investment opportunities and their payoffs.***

The specification of the investment opportunities will be given below.

5.1.3.3.1 The investment opportunities: Risk segments consisting of single borrowers

As the target credit portfolio will comprise thousands of borrowers, the number of investment opportunities would be very high if every single borrower is considered. Portfolio selection related to single borrowers would therefore hardly be practicable and difficult to implement via a decision tree[569] for such a large credit portfolio. For general credit risk management purposes, it is common to classify potential borrowers (credit applicants) initially and actual

---

[568] The role and the key tasks of capital management have been derived according to Matten (2000) in section 4.

[569] Given the default probabilities for single creditors that determine the probabilities for the default and non-default scenarios of a binary decision tree (see Figure 5-25), multi-period decision modeling between single credits of different riskiness is hardly possible as the default probabilities of the obligors differ from each other and default states are absorbing states (see section 5.4.2).
Furthermore, moving beyond binary decision trees is not reasonable for a default mode model.
Thirdly, strategic business decisions based on single assets are naturally not satisfactory as loan portfolios of commercial banks consist of thousands of credits. Investors focus on risk segments (rating) as investment opportunities. Portfolio segments are thus identified for portfolio selection purposes.

borrowers in regular time intervals according to preferably homogeneous risk-return segments (referred to as rating or scoring classes).[570]

For convenience, we will therefore refer to risk segments as investment opportunities and thereby assume that each risk segment consists of a high number of equal borrowers with the same (average) credit risk characteristics, pricing and average performance.

Besides, the riskless investment opportunity (e.g. riskless state securities) will be considered for the decision problem.

The target credit portfolio (as indicated in section 5.1.1.1) is supposed to comprise 8-12 risk segments (rating classes). For a simulated portfolio example[571], we refer to Standard & Poor's[7] major seven rating classes and symbols, as there are sufficient public empirical data available. **The portfolio decision is then to assign the available capital in each node of the event tree to the distinct rating segments.**

Figure 5-7: Portfolio decision in every node of the pre-defined event tree: Rating (risk) segments as investment alternatives[572]

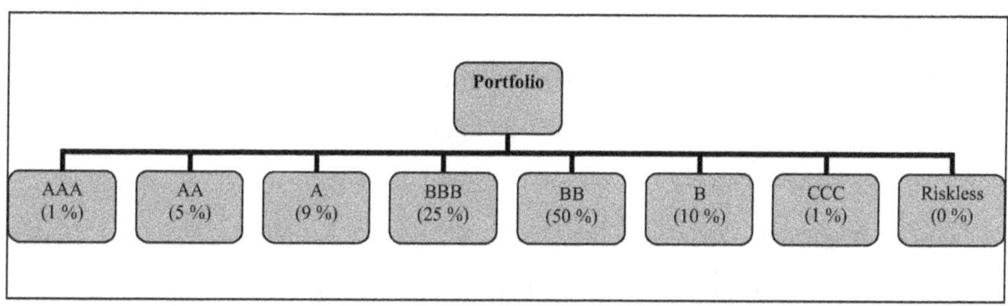

From an overall credit portfolio management process' perspective (see Figure 5-2), portfolio decision decomposes into two distinct steps.

According to the optimal subportfolio (risk segment's) portions provided by GOPS model the credit decision on a single borrower's level (as explained in section 3.4) remains, what will be explained below.

570 The major aspects of rating have been explained in section 3.3.4.1.1. Other segmentation criteria could be considered as well.

571 For a comparison of the target and simulated portfolio see section 5.3.2.

572 With arbitrary portfolio portions of a typical middle-market portfolio in %.

Figure 5-8: The portfolio problem: A two-fold problem

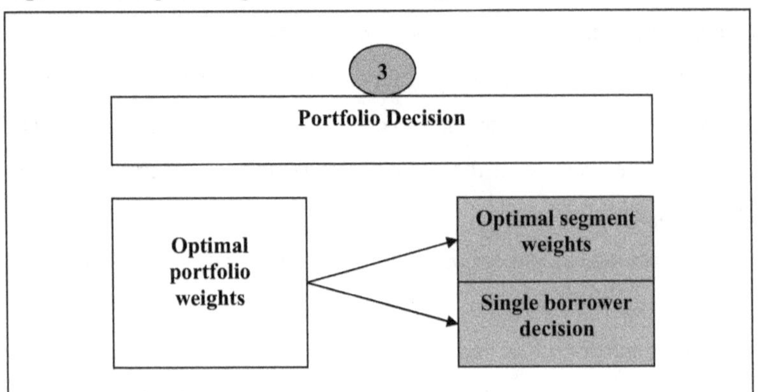

5.1.3.3.2 The portfolio decision for single borrowers

Given the optimal portfolio weights for each point in time of the planning horizon and the actual scenario in the decision tree, the credit applicants (single borrowers) are included into the portfolio accordingly until the risk segment's capital volume has been reached. Additional credit applicants will be refused.

Alternatively, credit decision may be more sophisticated. A FI may try to lend to the borrowers with the lowest risk within each risk segment. According to ex post knowledge, the total application volume per segment may be forecasted and the best x % of the borrowers of each rating segment accepted.

There is basically arbitrary space to extend the methodology to select single borrowers based on optimal segment weights, what will be neglected at this point, as this decision is related to each FI's specific credit business policy.

5.1.3.4 Business determinants of the decision problem

Portfolio management has its authorization only on a strategic level as pointed out in section 2.4 and thus has to be carefully understood and applied.

5.1.3.4.1 A typical non-traded (middle-market) credit portfolio

In order to illustrate the practical impact of portfolio operations for strategic management purposes it is crucial to have a common understanding of the typical structure of credit portfolios according to credit rating classes.

A typical middle-market banking portfolio in Germany according to S&P's rating classes is shown in Figure 5-9.

Figure 5-9: A typical middle-market credit portfolio (Taistra 2001)

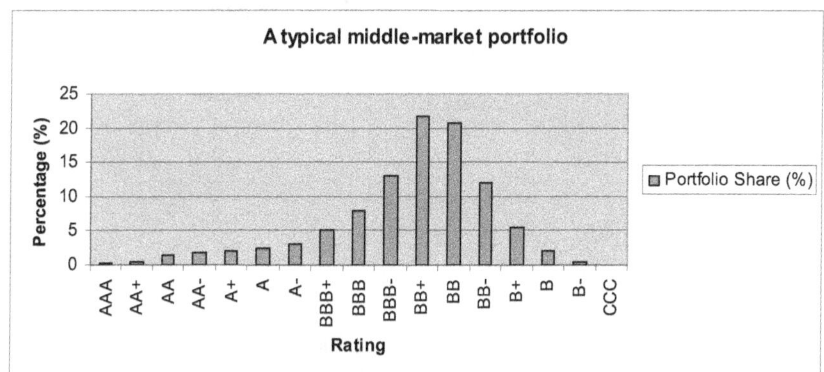

5.1.3.4.2 Business determinants for multi-period credit portfolio selection

In order to deploy the GOPS model to the field of credit, the *business determinants* have to be defined.

As discussed in section 3.5, there are several distinct methods for **quantitative analysis of credit portfolio's risk-return structures**. Given **shareholder targets for the usage of a corporation's capital** (see section 4.1.1), capital portions according to the emerging **regulatory framework of Basel II** (see section 2.3 and 3.5.2.4) and lower and upper bounds for the investment alternatives, active portfolio management techniques can be applied.

Credit portfolio management solutions focus on the reallocation of the current portfolio and on the **management of new business**. Only the latter target will be addressed within this work, as reallocation of business is related to transaction costs (e.g. for the application of credit derivatives and ABS products). The determinants for a solution to multi-period portfolio management are summarized in Figure 5-10 below.

Figure 5-10: Business determinants for multi-period credit portfolio selection in terms of capital management (according to Baud 2000, p.8)

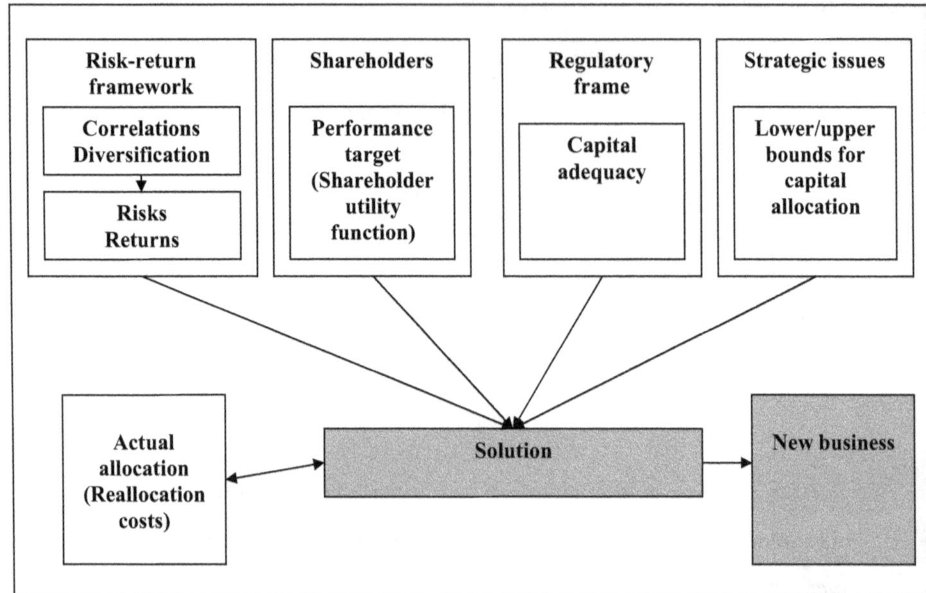

Further information can be found in Baud et al. (2000), for example.

5.2 The technical concept of the GOPS model

5.2.1 General assumptions for the design of the credit management framework underlying the GOPS model

As opposed to theoretical concepts, "simplification is often needed for practical solutions."[573] We will try to follow this principle in the following sections.

The following general assumptions have been made related to credit portfolio management when applying the GOPS model:

- We will generally refer to **non-traded credit portfolios** that are supposed to be intertemporally managed as a profit center within a commercial bank[574] or a captive leasing and finance company.[575]

---

573 See Ott (2001), p.188, for example.
574 e.g. Deutsche Bank.
575 e.g. DaimlerChrysler Bank.

- The portfolio decision is based on risk-based interest rates and ex ante performance measurement (see section 4.2.2) according to the upcoming Basel II framework with respect to the capital portions[576].
- The credit portfolio is assumed to be sufficiently large to be labeled as a well-diversified portfolio, i.e. the risk-return structure for each investment opportunity is independent of the portfolio composition. The risk-return (depicted as performance) structure (and thereby the diversification) of the subportfolios within the portfolio is represented via the coherent Euler principle explained in section 4.2.3. Additionally, the number of simulations to generate the payoffs for the investment opportunities is assumed to be sufficiently high to provide stable results for the scenarios especially in the tail region.
- Portfolio management is understood as capital management.[577]
- The total capital to be available for a profit center has strategically been defined by a FI's senior management (i.e. is exogenously given).
- The investment opportunities are risk segments. All entities within the risk segments are supposed to be equal with respect to credit risk (PD, LGD), return (pricing) and capital portion. Besides, all credit entities are assumed to have the same exposure, maturity and correlation between each other.
- All debt related payments are assumed to occur at the end of the period when they become due. In case of default, the creditor will receive a recovery at the end of the current period without any further payments afterwards.
- Portfolio decision focuses on new credit business only.[578]
- The portfolio planning horizon is equal to the term of the credits.
- Referring to a profit center allows taking subsequent payments into account.

---

576 It is thereby assumed that the credit portfolio has a very high granularity and is geographically unbiased.

577 Modeling the cash flow as a performance cash flow according to the capital portion used allows neglecting a capital budget constraint in the value management problem, what would influence the feasibility of the solution.

578 It is assumed that each year 1/(Maturity of the credits), e.g. roughly 1/3 of the capital has to be reinvested as a consequence of the termination of obligations.

The major assumptions with respect to credit risk modeling framework are summarized in Table 5-3 below oriented on Figure 3-7.

Table 5-3: Major assumptions for the design of the credit risk management framework

Modeling component	Treatment	Reference
EaD	Pre-defined, fixed	3.3.3.2, 5.3.4.1
Rating	S&P's rating classes	3.3.1, 3.3.4.1.1, 5.1.3.3.1
PD	Oriented on empirical data, fixed over planning horizon (through-the-cycle PD)[579]	3.3.4.2, 5.3.4.2f.
LGD	Oriented on empirical data, fixed over planning horizon (through-the-cycle LGD)	3.3.5.2, 5.3.4.2
Correlations	Unique asset correlations oriented on empirical data between all obligors	3.5.1.2.1.5, 5.3.4.3f.
Diversification	Well-diversified portfolio is assumed, additionally ensured by lower and upper bounds; Depiction via Euler principle	3.5.1.2.3.1, 5.3.4.2f., 5.3.4.5.5
Technical concept of credit risk modeling	Default model (asset value); Monte Carlo simulation for the payoffs; Analytical approach for economic capital	3.5.1.4.4, 3.5.2.4, 5.3.4.2, 5.3.4.3f.,
Risk capital	Oriented on the one-factor-model (for corporate borrowers, confidence level of 99.9%, effective maturity of 2.5 years, hurdle rate of 16 %, including capital cushion for EL)	3.5.1.5.6.3, 3.5.2.4, 5.3.3.1, 5.3.4.2
Risk-adjusted pricing	Simple cost + profit approach	5.3.3.1
Risk-adjusted	Multi-period recursive RORAC-concept	4.2.2.1, 4.2.3.2,

[579] The random multi-period default events of lending are supposed to follow a stochastic process (similar to a random walk for stock prices) for the risk segments, based on two assumptions:

- If not stated otherwise, the losses (or returns/performances) do have the same distributions for all years (stationary losses/returns).
- It is supposed that the random return distribution of a year t is independent of the return(s) of the previous year(s) history (known as Markov property).

performance measurement	based on the Euler principle (Performance contribution principle)	5.3.4

In the following, formal and practical aspects for the application of growth-oriented portfolio selection will be given.

5.2.2 The technical concept of the portfolio problem and input parameters

Subsequently, the **growth oriented portfolio selection (GOPS)** problem is presented in technical terms by closely following Hellwig (2002a, 2004) oriented on the overall procedure of portfolio selection according to Figure 5-6. The underlying targets of the investment problem have been summarized in section 5.1. The output of the portfolio selection model is a multi-period portfolio strategy, a withdrawal sequence and endogenous discount vectors based on various input parameters.[580]

The portfolio modeling frame is a time-discrete multiperiod decision model under uncertainty[581] with a finite planning horizon, see e.g. Huang and Litzenberger (1998), Duffie (1992) and Magill and Quinizii (1996), for example.

5.2.2.1 The decision tree

The information structure of the risk resulting from the randomness of lending is represented by an event tree (an arbitrary event tree is shown in Figure 5-11 below) spanning T periods. There are n+1 (here: 6+1 = 7) nodes s_i (indexed as $s_0,\ldots,s_n$) in the event tree, where n denotes the number of possible states. The possible states at each point in time (t=0,…,T) are mutually exclusive, i.e. only one state will occur. It is assumed that a unique path exists between node 0 (which is assumed to be known with certainty) and each node s_i.

The cumulative node probability can then be denoted as π_s[582] and the conditional

[580] Related to an exogenously defined decision tree, external funds (here: capital), a payoff matrix, growth targets and the model type.

[581] Or, more precisely, risk. For reference, see section 2.4 or Bamberg and Coenenberg (2000).

[582] Resulting to π_1=0.1; π_2=0.9; π_3=0.01; π_4= π_5 =0.09; π_6=0.81 for the nodes in the event tree below given e.g. prob (good) = 0.9 and prob (bad) = 0.1.

node probability dependent on the predeceasing node (s^-) as $\pi(s/s^-)$[583]. In the exemplified binary event tree as shown below each node is followed by a "good" or "bad" scenario that occurs with probability (good) or probability (bad).

Figure 5-11: Exemplified decision tree (according to Hellwig 2004, p. 2122)

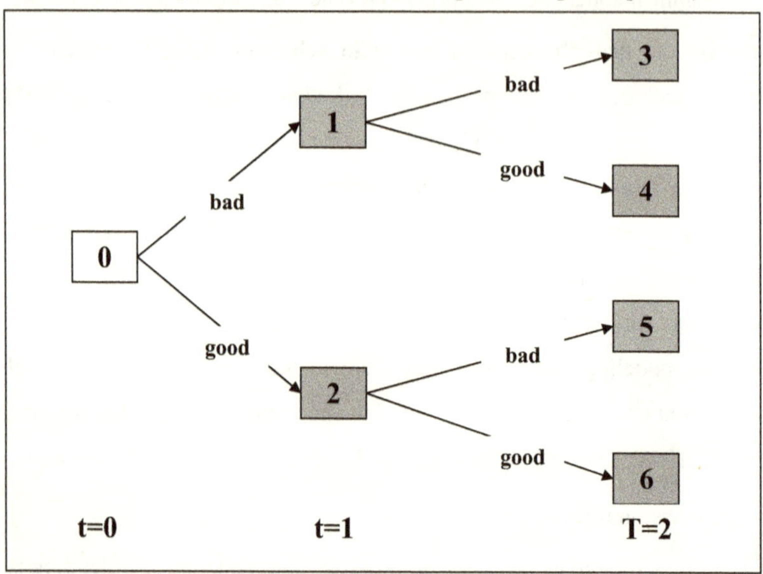

5.2.2.2 External capital

The investor (e.g. a credit risk profit center manager) is assumed to be endowed with an externally given capital vector $b_s = (b_0,\dots,b_n)^T \geq 0$ (with $b_0 > 0$) to perform lending activities. In our exemplified calculations in section 5.4, we refer to an initial capital of 100 currency units in node 0 and 0 currency units in all other nodes.

583 The conditional node probabilities in Figure 5-11 could be 10% for the good and 90% for the bad scenario.

5.2.2.3 The payoff matrix

Each credit investment opportunity is related to an outlay and the resulting multi-periodical repayment stream.[584] The payoffs for each opportunity can be brought together in the payoff matrix $A \in \mathbb{R}^{(n+1) \bullet m}$. The derivation of the payoff matrix entries will be explained in section 5.3. It is assumed that the entries refer to a well-diversified portfolio structure and are therefore constant and independent of the portfolio composition. This can be justified by applying lower and upper bounds, to be explained in section 5.4.1.3ff.

Every column vector of the payoff matrix A represents the expected capital cash flow vector of a specific opportunity while every row vector shows the cash flow in a specific node resulting from choosing the specifically given opportunities.

An example for a payoff matrix is given below. For the sample example as introduced in section 5.3.2, there is the single period riskless investment opportunity besides seven credit risk segments (AAA to CCC, see section 5.1.3.3.1). Underlying an event tree as shown in Figure 5-11 (with prob(bad)=0.1 and prob(good)=0.9), an investor investing in risk segment B, for example, would be faced to an outlay in node 0 ("-1"), followed by repayments of 0.48722 units in node 1 and 0.43937 units in node 3. Node 3 refers to the worst case, with bad scenarios both in period 1 and 2. In the best case, leading to node 6, the investor would be repaid 0.71391 units in period 1 (node 2) and 0.60944 units in period 2 (node 6). The repaid cash flows have to be appropriately discounted in order to evaluate their advantageousness, what will be an endogenous task of the GOPS model. The repayment sequences heavily depend on the default process of the borrowers in the subportfolio.

[584] Or vice versa for financing opportunities that have been neglected within this work.

Table 5-4: An example of a payoff matrix

Node	Riskless	AAA	AA	A	BBB	BB	**B**	CCC
0	-1	-1	-1	-1	-1	-1	**-1**	-1
1	1.035	0.6724	0.6670	0.6529	0.6287	0.5848	**0.4872**	0.4898
2	1.035	0.6732	0.6740	0.6760	0.6794	0.6867	**0.7139**	0.7380
3		0.6072	0.6041	0.5958	0.5808	0.5458	**0.4394**	0.3751
4		0.6076	0.6078	0.6081	0.6079	0.6016	**0.5622**	0.5071
5		0.6072	0.6043	0.5967	0.5835	0.5559	**0.4763**	0.4385
6		0.6076	0.6080	0.6090	0.6107	0.6127	**0.6094**	0.5928

The payoff matrix comprises the set of the investment opportunities to be chosen and the upper and lower bounds to restrict the incorporation of the investment opportunities by specific thresholds as desired by the investor. Both elements are explained subsequently.

5.2.2.3.1 Investment opportunities

In every node s $(s \notin S_T)$[585] the credit portfolio manager has the opportunity to invest in (exemplarily seven) credit risk segments (see section 5.1.3.3.1)[586] and the riskless investment opportunity[587], resulting in m (here: (7+1)n) total investment opportunities over the planning horizon.[588]

5.2.2.3.2 Upper and lower bounds for the investment opportunities

The chosen portfolio selection strategy $x \in X := \{x \mid x_i^l \leq x_i \leq x_i^k, i = 1,...,m\}$ may be bounded by means of lower $x_i^l < \infty$ and upper bounds $x_i^k < \infty$ for each investment opportunity dependent on the specific node. Setting bounds can be justified both from a strategic perspective (as described in section 3.4.4.1), a regulatory perspective and/or an optimization viewpoint.

The Basel Committee on Banking Supervision (2001a) suggested that when designing an internal rating system, no rating class for itself should comprise more than 30% of a portfolio's exposure, which could be considered as an upper

585 Where S_T denotes states at the end of the planning horizon.

586 Referring to the rating classes of Standard & Poor's, see section 3.3.4.1.1.

587 Among the opportunities is the opportunity to invest in every node s $(s \in S)$ for one period at the riskless rate r > 0 (e.g. at the bond market).

588 Hellwig (2004) provides the opportunity of a changing set of investment (and financing) opportunities dependent on the actual node.

bound from a regulatory viewpoint, for example.[589] Lower bounds might be oriented on the current portfolio, a bank's appetite for market share or the availability of borrowers in the market, for example 5 or 10%. Setting both upper and lower bounds in order to account for diversification aspects may be oriented on the portfolio composition recommended by an optimization model (see section 5.4.3.4.2) besides qualitative (strategic or regulatory) aspects.

5.2.2.4 Growth targets and withdrawals

$C = \{c \in \mathbb{R}^{n+1} \mid c = Ax + b, for \text{ some } x \in X\}$ represents the set of all feasible or realizable withdrawal (or consumption) sequences, associated with every feasible portfolio strategy $x \in X$.[590] The withdrawal (or consumption) sequence $c = (c_1, ..., c_n)^T$ specifies the amount c_s withdrawn in node s (for example, c_2 denotes the amount of funds withdrawn in node 2). The withdrawals related to each node s, c_s, can be interpreted as a budget constraint (as $Ax + b = c$).

In order to account for the final value remaining at the end of the finite planning horizon, T, Hellwig (2004) distinguishes between *actual* and *potential* withdrawal. The actual amount withdrawn in node s is the real amount withdrawn and the potential withdrawal is the portfolio value remaining at the end of the planning horizon.

Every rational investor will only consider **efficient withdrawal sequences** $\bar{c} \in C$, which do, additionally, correspond to the investor's growth pattern, what will be subject to section 5.2.3.

---

589 In the second consultative paper (April 2001), the Basel Committee proposed to limit the exposure assigned to one single risk grade: "There should also be meaningful distribution of exposure across grades with no excessive concentrations in any particular grade. Specifically, the Committee is proposing that no more than 30% of the gross exposures should fall in any single borrower grade." See Basel (2001a), p.49. Meanwhile, this proposal has been removed from the Basel framework as it is somehow arbitrary.

590 See Hellwig (2004, p.2121).

5.2.2.5 The notion of the model: ex post and ex ante

In order to represent the time preferences of an investor with respect to the withdrawal sequence, Hellwig (2002a) distinguishes between two notions: *ex post* and *ex ante*.

The ex post (ex ante) notion leads to a consumption sequence where the decision about consumption at time t depends upon the return of the preceding (succeeding) period. An illustrative example can be found in Hellwig (2002a, p.135):[591] An investor who wants to preserve the value of his initial funds (100 units) which may be invested at 10% will withdraw 0 units in t=0 and will be endowed with 110 units in t=1. In order to preserve his initial value, he/she will withdraw 10 units in t=1 to still possess 100 units.[592]

As the external funds are exogenously given and assumed to be used within a credit profit center the application of the ex ante notion is not foreseen within this work, as an ex ante solution would propose to invest less than the capital available in period t if the growth target in t+1 can be still fulfilled (and to withdraw the residual amount of the available and the invested funds already in t).

5.2.3 Application of the GOPS model: Technical description

A solution for portfolio selection related to an "economic meaningful" context[593] (termed as *growth-oriented portfolio value management*) can be found by operationalizing the portfolio problem by means of two requirements representing generally accepted conditions that a withdrawal sequence should satisfy (Hellwig 2002b).

---

591 See www.iop.org/EJ/abstract/1469-7688/2/2/304/ for reference. Rev. July 2004.

592 Further information about the background of the two criteria can be found in Hellwig (2002a, 2004).

593 See Hellwig (2004), p. 2120.

5.2.3.1 Formulation of the general problem to be solved

The first requirement is to restrict the set of considered solutions by an intertemporal efficiency criterion[594] (**efficiency or present value maximization criterion**) and then to choose from the feasible solutions those matching an a priori specified intertemporal value process (**growth criterion**).

From a formal viewpoint, an intertemporally efficient withdrawal sequence $\overline{c} \in C$ and simultaneously a portfolio strategy $\overline{x} \in X$ supporting $\overline{c}$ ($A\overline{x}+b=\overline{c}$) besides a vector of prices $\overline{p}$ has to be found, so that the two criteria are met, what will be further specified in the following.[595]

5.2.3.1.1 The efficiency criterion (C1)

The present value maximizing consumption sequence $\overline{c}$ is a solution to the parametric linear optimization problem

$$\begin{array}{|ll|}\hline \max & V_0(\overline{p}) := \overline{p}^T c \\ s.t. & c=Ax+b \\ & l_i \le x_i \le k_i,\ i=1,\ldots,m \\ \hline \end{array}$$

where the endogenous initial value of a multi-period portfolio, $V_0(\overline{p})$, can be understood as the sum of future cash flows generated by the portfolio $\overline{c}$ discounted by appropriate prices[596] $\overline{p}^T$ or - equivalently - as the initial economic value of the consumption plan $\overline{c}$.

The vector of state prices $\overline{p}$ can be interpreted as opportunity costs[597] and heavily depends upon the portfolio composition $\overline{x}^*$ that is simultaneously chosen.

---

594 Pareto-efficient withdrawal sequences represent situations where withdrawals in one state cannot be increased without reducing withdrawals in another state according to Pareto (1897).

595 According to Hellwig (2002a), p.134.

596 A state price represents the product of the node-dependent discount factor q (s) and the cumulative node probability π(s).

597 An increase of p_s, s $\in \{1,\ldots,n\}$ leads to an increase of c_s, since consumption (and consequently the return of the portfolio) in state s has a stronger weighting in the objective function $V_0(p) = p^T c$. Therefore, as Hellwig (1996b) points out, " p_s can be interpreted as a measure of the impact of a sufficiently small change of c_s on the maximal present value."

The first constraint ensures that the withdrawal sequence corresponds to the sum of exogenous funds (b) and the value generated by the portfolio itself (Ax). The m investment (and financing) opportunities are limited by upper (k_i) and lower bounds (l_i).

5.2.3.1.2 Growth (C2)

Additionally, the economic value of $\overline{c}$ has to satisfy the required inter-temporal withdrawal distribution structure $\overline{c} = g(\overline{p}) \bullet V_0(\overline{p})$ where g reflects the desired inter-temporal growth pattern of value.

5.2.3.2 The intertemporal distribution function g

5.2.3.2.1 Price vector (p) and discount vector (q)

When we consider the initial value of one consumption unit in node s, p_s/p_0, then V_0 is the initial portfolio value of $\overline{c}$ with respect to the price vector p.

p_s/p_0 can be decomposed into the cumulative probability of node s , π_s and a discount factor $q_s = q_s(\overline{c})$:[598]

$$\frac{p_s}{p_0} = \pi_s q_s \text{ (s=0,...,n).}$$

5.2.3.2.2 Desired growth rate (α)

Let α_s be the desired growth rate of the portfolio if node s is realized at the end of period t. Then the sequence of portfolio values that satisfies the demanded portfolio value development is $V_{s(t)} = (1+\alpha_s)V_{s(t-1)}$.

The growth rate can be interpreted as an opportunity to adjust the time pattern of withdrawals, as a portfolio's generated cash flows may always be paid out to the investor or reinvested in the portfolio.

5.2.3.2.3 The cumulated growth rate (w)

The accumulated path-dependent growth from the starting node s=0 to state s is then defined as

598 P_0 is usually set to one.

$w_0 := 1,$

$w_s := \prod_{\tau=1}^{t}(1+\alpha_{s(\tau)}),$ t=1,...,T

what allows to express the value of the portfolio in state s as $V_s = w_s V_0$.

5.2.3.2.4 The intertemporal distribution function (g) for the ex post case

Specifying the growth function g is similar to defining the (multi-period) utility function in case of utility maximization. Hellwig (2002a) distinguishes between two notions: *ex post* and *ex ante*. We will refer to the ex post notion only (see section 5.2.2.5). In case of the ex post notion, the intertemporal distribution function g can be specified as follows (see Hellwig 2002a, p.135):

$g_0(q) = 0,$

$g_s(q) = ((q_{t-1}/q_t) - (1+\alpha_t)) \bullet w_{t-1}$

$\quad = (r_t - \alpha_t) \bullet w_{t-1}$ (t=1,...,T-1)

$g_T(q) = ((q_{T-1}/q_T) \bullet w_{T-1} = (1+r_T)) \bullet w_{T-1}$

where r_t is the marginal return in period t.

5.2.3.3 Solution of the portfolio problem

According to Hellwig (2002a, p.134) a growth (or value)-oriented solution has been found, if a portfolio $(\bar{c}, \bar{x}, \bar{q})$ fulfils the two criteria C1 and C2 (see section 5.2.3.1) with respect to the intertemporal distribution function g and the following condition holds:

$V_0(\bar{p}) = \bar{p}^T \bar{c} = \bar{p}^T g(\bar{p}) V_0$

what implies that $\bar{p}^T g(\bar{p}) = 1$ is a necessary condition for the choice of the intertemporal distribution function g. Otherwise, an optimal solution would not satisfy C1 and C2 simultaneously. Further insights can be found in Hellwig (2002a, p. 134).

5.2.3.3.1 Implications of the efficiency criterion for the choice of the portfolio composition

The question is what implication the present value method has as a decision criterion for the considered portfolio problem, namely the choice of investment and financing alternatives. A solution can be found in Hellwig (2001): $V_0(p)$ is the initial portfolio value with respect to the price vector $\overline{p}$ and can be rewritten in terms of its supportive strategy $\overline{x}$ as

$$V_0(p) = \sum_{s=0}^{n} \overline{p}_s \sum_{i=1}^{m} a_{si}\overline{x}_i + \sum_{s=0}^{n} \overline{p}_s b_s = \sum_{i=1}^{m} \overline{x}_i \sum_{s=0}^{n} a_{si}\overline{p}_s + \sum_{s=0}^{n} \overline{p}_s b_s$$

Hence, the initial value of the portfolio equals the present value of the exogenously given node dependent income plus the sum of the NPVs of the available opportunities. An optimal solution $\overline{x}$ to the optimization problem of finding an efficient portfolio ($\max\{\mathrm{p}^{\mathrm{T}}c \mid c \in C\}$) by maximizing the NPV of withdrawals has to satisfy

$$\overline{x}_i = l_i,\ \text{if}\ \overline{\mathrm{v}}_{\mathrm{i}} := \sum_{s=0}^{n} a_{si}\overline{p}_s < 0$$

$$l_i \le \overline{x}_i \le k_i,\ \text{if}\ \overline{\mathrm{v}}_{\mathrm{i}} := \sum_{s=0}^{n} a_{si}\overline{p}_s = 0$$

$$\overline{x}_i = k_i,\ \text{if}\ \overline{\mathrm{v}}_{\mathrm{i}} := \sum_{s=0}^{n} a_{si}\overline{p}_s > 0$$

where $\overline{v}_i$ is the NPV of opportunity i, i=1,…,m and $\mathrm{l_i}$ ($\mathrm{k_i}$) denotes the corresponding lower (upper) bound. Hence, a NPV of zero can be seen as a benchmark that any investment and financing strategy must pass with respect to the price vector $\overline{p}$ in order to enter an efficient portfolio strategy generated by $\overline{p}$.

5.2.3.4 Summary

It can be summarized that a **growth-oriented solution can be determined by simultaneously solving two closely interrelated problems:**[599]

599 See Benteler (2003), p. 27, according to Hellwig (2002a and 2002b).

- Taking prices p as fixed, a consumption sequence maximizing the initial portfolio value under feasible constraints has to be found, what leads to intertemporally efficient consumption bundles.
- Prices p have to be found such that a corresponding efficient consumption plan exactly coincides with the consumption generated by the intertemporal distribution requirements.

5.2.3.5 Reformulation of the problem for computational solution

The solution of this twofold problem has been simplified by Hellwig (2002a, p.133), who showed that rather than solving a fixed-point problem which has been shown to be inefficient for larger problems (see e.g. Kuhn 1986, p. 215 or Bachem et al. 1996, p. 223) the solution can be more conveniently found by solving a non-linear optimization problem comprising at the same time C1 and C2 (termed as p2 by Hellwig (2002a, p.136)):

$$
\begin{array}{lll}
p2 := \min & g_0(z)(z'b+v'k)-b_0-\sum_{i=1}^{n} a_{0i}x_i & \\
\text{s.t.} & -\sum_{i=1}^{n} a_{si}x_i + g_s(z)(z'b+v'k) \le b_s & (s=1,\ldots,N) \\
 & -\sum_{s=0}^{N} a_{si}z_s + v_i \ge 0 & (i=1,\ldots,n) \\
 & z_0 = 1, z_s \ge 0 & (s=1,\ldots,N) \\
 & x_i \le k_i & (i=1,\ldots,n) \\
 & v_{i,}x_i \ge 0 & (i=1,\ldots,n)
\end{array}
$$

The optimization problem may become linear in some special cases (Hellwig 2002b, p.136/137).

Ensuring a risk-return-balanced portfolio strategy asks for diversification and therefore the application of upper and lower bounds for the opportunities as discussed in section 5.2.2.3.2. The existence of a solution to the portfolio selection problem under reasonable conditions has been proven by Hellwig (2002a, p. 12ff.).

When including a lower bound for the opportunities, the value management problem has the following form: [600]

$$
\begin{array}{lll}
p2 := \min & g_0(z)(z'b + v'k - w'l) - b_0 - \sum_{i=1}^{n} a_{0i} x_i & \\
s.t. & -\sum_{i=1}^{n} a_{si} x_i + g_s(z)(z'b + v'k - w'l) \leq b_s & (s = 1,...,N) \\
 & -\sum_{s=0}^{N} a_{si} z_s + v_i - l_i \geq 0 & (i = 1,...,n) \\
 & z_0 = 1, z_s \geq 0 & (s = 1,...,N) \\
 & l_i \leq x_i \leq k_i & (i = 1,...,n) \\
 & v_i, w_i, x_i \geq 0 & (i = 1,...,n)
\end{array}
$$

We will refer to the latter optimization problem when applying the GOPS model in section 5.4.[601]

5.2.3.6 Excursus: Growth maximization (of the portfolio value)

Given the maximum growth vector $g_s = r_s$ (see section 5.2.3.2.4), the maximum growth rate in t=T can be derived. In order to find the optimal solution, the following optimization problem may be solved according to Hellwig (1998)[602]:

$$
\begin{array}{ll}
\text{Max} & \sum_{s \in S_T} \pi_s \bullet \ln c_s \\
\text{s.t.} & c \in C \\
 & c \geq 0
\end{array}
$$

The set of feasible withdrawals C consists of $c_s = 0 \vee s$ in non-terminal nodes and $c_s = Ax + b_s \vee s$ in terminal nodes. The existence of a feasible solution has been proven by Hellwig (2001).[603]

600 We thank Prof. Dr. Klaus Hellwig for providing this solution.

601 In case of additional preferences (especially non-negative withdrawals and pre-defined withdrawals), Selinka (2005) has proven the existence of a growth-oriented solution.

602 See also Hellwig (2002b).

603 It has to be mentioned, however, that the growth optimization problem as formulated by Hellwig (1998) does not foresee a constraint to capture diversification in terms of risk-return optimization. The application of a logarithmic growth function has already been justified by Latané (1959), who did show that the geometric average is a better choice for multi-period portfolio selection as the arithmetic average, as the latter criterion may lead into ruin. Further information can be found in Breuer et al. (1999), for example.

5.2.4 The output of the portfolio selection model

5.2.4.1 The portfolio selection strategy

The selected portfolio strategy $\bar{x} = (x_1, \ldots, x_m)$ denotes the activity level chosen by the credit portfolio manager. For the multi-period portfolio selection strategy $\bar{x} \in X$[604] and payoff matrix A, a capital cash flow vector[605] (see section 5.3.4) $A\bar{x}$ is generated.

$A\bar{x}$ includes all the credit input parameters (risk parameters, pricing, capital) necessary to determine the desired portfolio selection strategy, subject to section 5.3ff.

5.2.4.2 The withdrawal sequence

An efficient withdrawal sequence $\bar{c}$ in line with the selected portfolio strategy $\bar{x} = (x_1, \ldots, x_m)$ will be delivered simultaneously with the portfolio strategy itself (see section 5.4.3.2).

5.2.4.3 The discount vectors

The node-dependent discount factors $\bar{q}(s)$ are derived simultaneously with the optimal portfolio weights and can be understood as the marginal portfolio return ("opportunity costs") in period t for the specific path between two nodes in the event tree. The discount factors can be represented by state prices which are the product of the discount vector and the cumulative node probability $\pi(s)$ (see section 5.4.3.2).

[604] Where X denotes the set of feasible portfolio selection strategies.

[605] Cash flows refer to capital cash flow in terms of repayment of capital and interest on capital (RORAC) as opposed to the general view on exposure-related cash flows.

5.3 Development of a concept for credit risk modeling in order to apply the GOPS model

5.3.1 Introduction

In the following, we will gradually derive a concept to apply the GOPS model to the field of credit risk. The major assumptions with respect to the design of the credit management framework and formal properties of the GOPS model have been explained in section 5.2.

The basis for the portfolio decision is the forecasted risk result of a credit profit center within a financial institution, which can be decomposed into three result components (the market result, the credit risk result and the productivity result) as it has been explained in section 2.4.4.2.[606] We will refer to the credit risk result which represents the credit losses.[607]

Recalling Figure 5-2 for the sequence of the overall (iterative) proceeding the target is to provide a concept for portfolio selection based on risk-based pricing (step 1) and the ex ante forecast of the credit risk result in terms of a payoff matrix (step 2). Subsequently, the portfolio model will be applied in section 5.4 (step 3). The former two steps will be adressed as follows.

[606] The market result refers to treasury, the credit risk result to the stochastic default process of the credit portfolio and the productivity result to the ability of a bank to handle its fixed costs for providing lending activities.

[607] The credit risk result of a portfolio investment can be measured in terms of loss, profit/loss or performance distributions. For decision purposes, the credit risk result is depicted in form of a payoff matrix.

Figure 5-12: The credit portfolio management process: a concept to apply the GOPS model

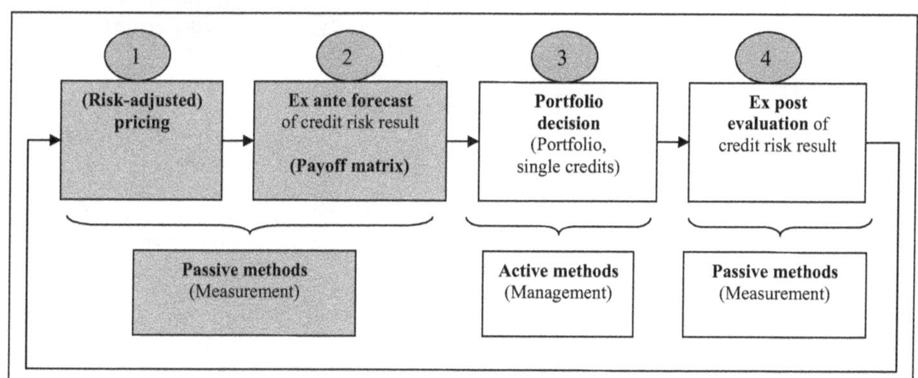

5.3.2 Input data for the deployment of the GOPS model: Simulated portfolio and target portfolio

For the purpose of a better understanding of the credit risk modeling concept for the application of the GOPS model, a simulated sample credit portfolio will be used.

The simulated portfolio is much smaller than the target portfolio that is supposed to be managed. It has to be critically mentioned that decision making based on the simulated portfolio is not considered to be valid for practical purposes, but is used for demonstration purpose only, as the diversification constraint is not fulfilled for the investment alternatives with the lowest default probabilities, especially the AAA and the AA segment (see section 5.4). A comparison of the simulated and the target portfolio to be managed is given below.

Table 5-5: Simulated portfolio vs. target portfolio

Portfolio features	Simulated portfolio	Target portfolio
Type of credit portfolio	Non-traded credit (e.g. SME, retail)	Non-traded credit (e.g. SME, retail)
Target horizon	2 periods	Multi-period
Number of credit entities	700 (100 per segment)	> 150,000 credits/year (arbitrary distribution among segments)
Number of investment opportunities	7 credit segments (AAA to CCC) + 1 riskless segment	8 to 12 credit segments + 1 riskless segment
Homogeneity	Exposure, maturity, correlations	Exposure, maturity, correlations
Credit term/Decision tree	2 periods/2 scenarios per period (binary decision tree with 7 nodes)[608]	Arbitrary (3-5 periods)/arbitrary number of scenarios per period and nodes[609]

5.3.3 Risk-based credit pricing

In the following, a simple comprehensive method how to price credits of different rating segments will be presented which will be used in terms of the application of the GOPS model.

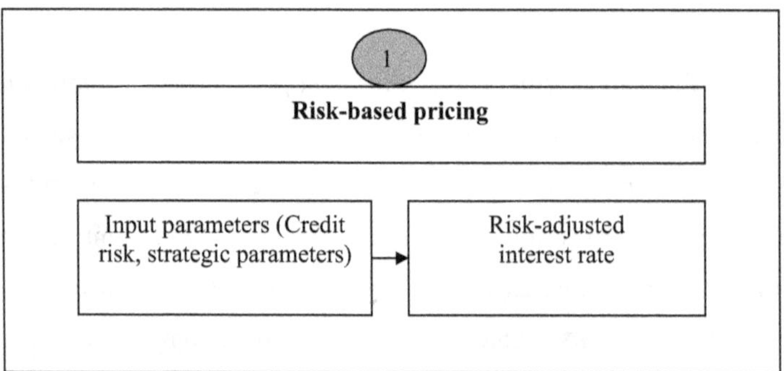

5.3.3.1 Credit pricing: an illustrative example

In order to adequately price credit risk, several basic credit risk parameters have to be taken into account. Based on the level of sophistication more or less parameters will be considered. The basic credit risk parameters to be considered for the following example are shown in Figure 5-13 below.

---

[608] As shown in Figure 5-11.

[609] A limiting factor for the derivation of the solution is the exploding number of nodes (see Table 5-30).

Figure 5-13: Credit risk input data for pricing purposes

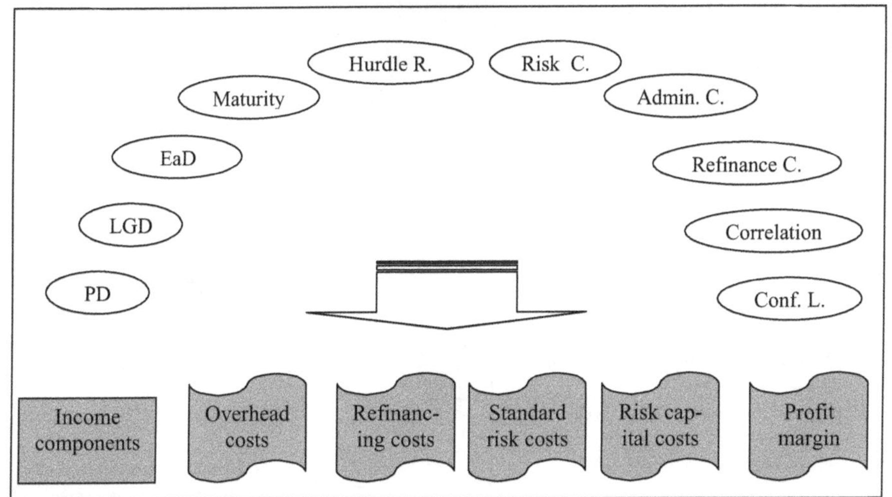

Each basic risk parameter influences at least one of the five aggregated pricing components that are usually considered for credit pricing and performance measurement (see section 4.2.1.2):

- **Overhead costs (FC),**
- **Refinancing costs (RFC),**
- **Standard risk costs (SRC),**
- **Risk capital costs (Target return on capital) and**
- **Profit margin,**

where the last two components do refer to the invested capital portion of a bank. For the illustration of the overall pricing process based on a straightforward simplified pricing method a B–rated borrower will be used. The calculation of the risk capital portion is based on the para. 272 - formula of the revised Basel II framework (Basel 2004, section 3.5.2.4.2) including cushion for EL. The main characteristics of a single B borrower, a PD of 0.06245 and a recovery rate of 0.35 are shown in Table 5-6 together with other input parameters.

Table 5-6: Pricing scheme for a loan: Credit risk input parameters

Credit risk input parameters	Value	Description
Risk grade	B	S&P's notation
Average PD (decimal)	0.06245	Annual Probability of Default
LGD (decimal) (=1-Recovery rate)	0.65 (=1-0.35)	Loss Given Default in case of bankruptcy
EAD	1[610]	Exposure at Default
Confidence level (decimal)	0.999	Defined as (1-α), representing the prudence level of the credit risk policy
Maturity (in years)	2.5[611]	The effective maturity as explained in section 3.3.6, assumption
Hurdle rate (ROC, decimal)	0.16	Interest rate on risk capital portion according to strategic considerations
Administrative and other operating costs (FC, decimal)	0.005	Fixed, assumption
Refinancing interest rate (RIR, decimal)	0.045	IBOR/Swap-rate + 50 bps, assumption
Profit margin (decimal)	0.0136825	Additional return for risk-taking according to strategic considerations
Borrower type[612]	0	Corporate = 0, Retail =1

For a comprehensive understanding, the next table denotes the MS Excel formulas to calculate the derived credit risk measures in order to estimate the risk capital portion (see Table 5-8).

Table 5-7: Calculation scheme: MS Excel formulas for the derived credit risk measures

Derived measures	Formulas
Asset correlation (corporate)	0.12*(1-EXP(-50*PD))/(1-EXP(-50))+0.24*(1-(1-EXP(-50*PD))/(1-EXP(-50))
Maturity adjustment b (corporate)	0.08451-0.05898*LOG$_{10}$(PD))^2
Risk capital (RC)	LGD*NORMVERT((1-AssetCorrelation)^(-0,5)*NORMINV(PD;0;1)+(Corr./(1- Corr.))^0,5*NORMINV(Conf.Level;0;1);0;1;TRUE)*(1-1.5*b)^(-1)*(1+(Maturity-2.5)*Maturity)

For a B- rated borrower, the following values can be calculated.

610 Th exposre has been set to one as the exposures of the creditors are assumed to be of a comparable size.

611 For simplification purpose as the Basel II corporate formula is calibrated to 2.5 years (Basel 2004, para 272).

612 The Basel II formulas have been calibrated for retail and corporate borrowers, see section 3.5.2.4.2. We refer to the formula for large corporates according to Basel (2004), para. 272.

Table 5-8: Pricing-scheme for a loan: Derived credit risk measures

Derived measures	Value	Description
Asset correlation (decimal)	0.1253	Asset correlation, calibrated by BCBS dependent on the PD
Maturity adjustment (decimal)	0.0242	Calibrated by BCBS dependent on the PD
Risk capital portion (RC, decimal)	0.2150	Capital requirement according to Basel II as a portion of the exposure

Given the risk capital portion, the five aggregated pricing components can be found as shown below (Table 5-9).

Table 5-9: Calculation scheme: Income components

Income parameters	No.	Formulas
Expected loss (SRC)	1	PD • LGD • EAD
Risk capital costs	2	RC • ROC
Refinancing costs (RFC)	3	(1-RC) • RIR
Overhead costs (FC)	4	0.005
Profit margin	5	Pre-defined per risk segment (see Table 5-6)
Interest rate due		1+2+3+4+5

For the B-rated borrower, the pricing components finally add up to an annual interest rate due of 12.9% according to Table 5-10.

Table 5-10: Pricing-scheme for a loan: Income components

Income parameters	Value	Description
Refinancing costs (RFC)	0.035325	Charge for the exposure that is not covered by capital and has to be refinanced
Overhead costs (FC)	0.005	Fixed percentage for overhead costs
Expected Loss (SRC)	0.0405925	Charge for the ex ante expected credit risk losses
Risk capital costs	0.0344	Capital charge related to the hurdle rate of the bank for the risk capital per unit of exposure
Profit margin	0.0136825	Additionally charged premium
Total annual interest rate due	0.129	

5.3.3.2 Further insights into pricing

In order to clarify the derivation of the pricing components more comprehensively, we will summarize the main steps to arrive at the nominal annual interest rate of 12.9% as shown in Table 5-10.

From a controlling perspective, the five pricing components can be decomposed and understood as four major components (referring to capital costs and profit margin as one component) as shown below in Figure 5-14.[613]

As the overhead costs and refinancing expenses of a credit are just fixed traversing expenses for a bank, they may be denoted as 'costs'. The other two pricing components, the capital charge[614] and the standard risk costs can be considered as potential profit components. They are, however, '*potential profit*', as they will cushion the credit losses that occur.

Overhead costs refer to administrative costs and other operating costs and have been assumed to be 0.5% per year. The refinancing costs and the capital charge are directly linked to the portion of capital (see section 3.5.1.5.6.3.1). The capital portion for the B-segment can be observed in Table 5-8 (21.5%). This means that 21.5% of the nominal credit exposure is financed by a bank's capital and 78.5% is refinanced. The refinancing interest rate of the bank is assumed to be 4.5%.[615] Hence, the refinancing costs to be charged to the borrower are $0.785 \bullet 0.045 = 0.035325$. A bank's target return on capital (called "hurdle rate") may be 16%. Consequently, the capital costs are $0.215 \bullet 0.16 = 0.0344$. Additionally, it is assumed that the bank charges the customer a profit margin for its risk-bearing activity of 0.0136825.[616] The capital charge in total adds up to $0.0480825\ (=0.0344+0.0136825)$. The standard risk costs (EL) refer to the average loss per borrower and equal $0.06245 \bullet 0.65 = 0.0405925\ (=PD_B \bullet LGD_B)$ in this example. An illustrative overview is given below.

---

[613] The profit margin may then be understood as an additional return on capital.

[614] Capital charge comprises capital costs and the profit margin (see Figure 5-13, for example).

[615] Which might be 0.5% above the IBOR-rate in the capital markets. A bank's refinancing rate depends on its external rating and aspects of asset-liability management. A spread of 0.5% would roughly refer to a rating of BBB.

[616] The value is arbitrary and depends on strategic considerations. In this case, it is convenient that the final interest rate to be paid thereby yields to 12.9%.

Figure 5-14: Pricing components of a credit (in %)

Traversing costs		Potential profit	
Overhead costs (Costs)	Refinancing costs (Costs)	Standard Risk Costs (Variable profit)	Capital charge (Variable profit)
0.5 %	3.5325 %	4.05925 %	4.808 %

The decomposition of the performance measurement of the B-rated credit from an ex ante perspective is summarized below in an illustrative way (as explained in section 4.2.1.4.1) assuming average losses equal to the ex ante expected standard risk costs.

Table 5-11: Performance measurement for a B - rated credit based on the exemplified example (rounded in %)

Level	Item	Interest (%)
	Lending rate	12.9
	- Refinancing costs (RFC)	3.53
Profit Contribution Level I	**= Condition contribution margin**	**9.37**
	- Standard Risk Costs (SRC)	4.06
Profit Contribution Level II	**= Risk-adjusted margin**	**5.31**
	- Overhead costs (FC)	0.5
Profit Contribution Level III	**= Net return**	**4.81**
	- Risk capital costs (16%)	3.44
Profit Contribution Level IV[617]	**= Profit margin**	**1.37**

617 The profit contribution level IV refers to the Economic Value Added, a popular concept for risk controlling introduced by Stewart (1991). EVA™ is a trademark of Stern Stewart & Company. It is applied in corporations like Siemens, Telekom, Metro, AT&T, Coca Cola, for example, for risk controlling purposes. Evaluations of the EVA™ concept can be found in Macharzing (1995), for example. The main *advantage* is EVA™'s usability in practice, comprising simple understanding and friendliness for implementation. It can be well communicated as it is based on external accounting. The information about the value added of a certain strategy as well as for performance measurement is another asset of EVA™.

The consideration of the return of a bank may be oriented on profit contribution level III or IV, depending on the specific controlling target perceived at. In this representation the principle of traversing costs and potential profit becomes obvious.

5.3.4 The derivation of the payoff matrix: Procedure

The generation of the payoff matrix can be decomposed into three distinct steps (see Figure 5-15), which will be explained in the following sections.

Figure 5-15: Procedure to derive the payoff matrix

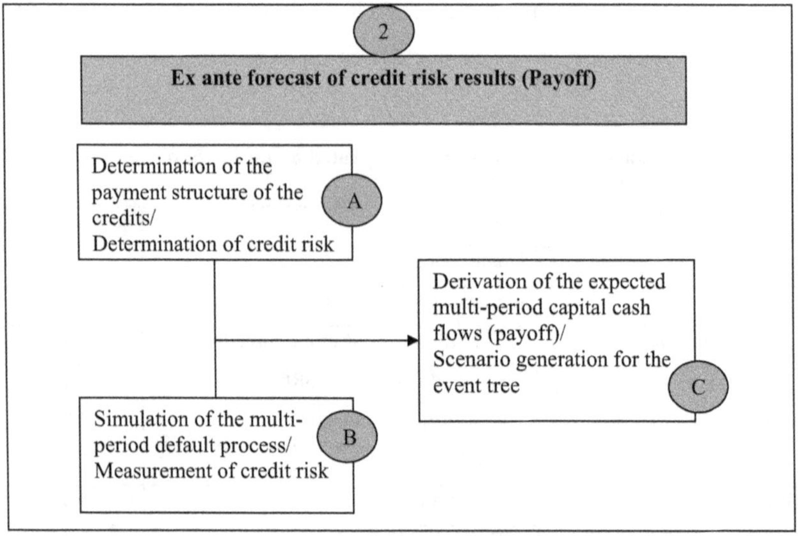

2

Ex ante forecast of credit risk results (Payoff)

Determination of the payment structure of the credits/ Determination of credit risk (A)

Simulation of the multi-period default process/ Measurement of credit risk (B)

Derivation of the expected multi-period capital cash flows (payoff)/ Scenario generation for the event tree (C)

5.3.4.1 Determination of credit payment structure and measurement of credit risk (step 2.A)

It is generally assumed that the multi-period payment structure of all credits in the portfolio is fixed and unique.[618] We refer to annuity installments, i.e. a more or less linear repayment pattern over time (see section 3.1.4). Cash flows

Shortages of the EVA™ concept comprise methodical inconsistencies of the input parameters as well as the measure being a one-period measure and thus inconsistent with the NPV method. Further information about shortages can be found in Schmidbauer (1999), p. 371f.

618 Dependent on the interest rate due.

(interest and repayments) are assumed to be annual and occur at the end of each period.

Moreover, we assume that each borrower has only one single transaction with a bank (a 'master contract'). The referred time horizon for the derivation of credit risk parameters is generally one year.

The measurement of credit risk comprises three dimensions according to section 3.5.1.4:

- **The definition of credit risk** (see below),
- **The technical concept** (see section 5.3.4.2) and
- **The measurement of default interdependencies between obligors** (see section 5.3.4.2).

With respect to the **credit risk definition**, we will refer to a **default mode model (DM)**[619], what is common for non-traded credit portfolios (caused by the lack of transition matrices, mapping problems, etc.). We will refer to the BCBS's default definition (section 3.3.2).

It is assumed that solvent borrowers will deliver all payments that are due over the multi-period horizon at the point in time that has been pre-defined.

Insolvent borrowers, however, will pay only until the point in time of insolvency. In the period of default the contract is terminated with the payment of the recovery.[620]

From a FI's perspective, the payment structure of a two-year B-segment credit might look as follows.

[619] As explained in section 3.2.1.3, i.e. only default and non-default is taken into account.
[620] Which results from reselling the product to be financed or guarantees, e.g. a vehicle.

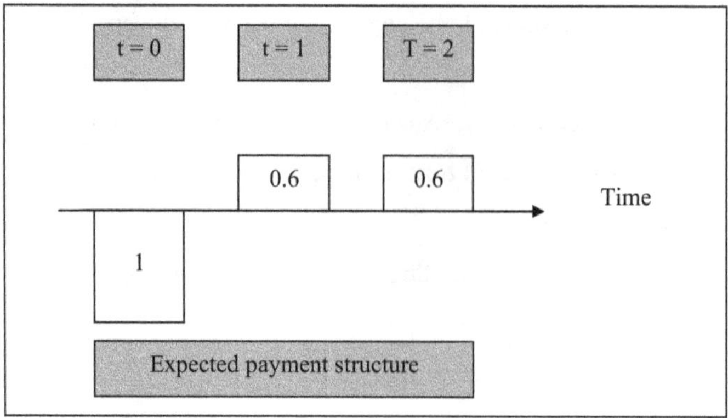

Formally, the cash flow structure (related to the exposure) from the viewpoint of a bank may be written as an investment:

$$R_{CF} = (-E_0; i_1(E_0) + R_1, i_2(E_1) + R_2),$$

where E_0 denotes the original amount financed (e.g. of an automotive), while i_t and R_t, respectively, represent the interest and repayment cash flows due in period t. It is assumed that the interest due in period t is a fraction of the remaining credit exposure at the beginning of the respective period (E_{t-1}).

The interest rate has to account for the general interest level (IBOR/swap rate), which fluctuates over time. For demonstration purposes, we assume a **constant IBOR rate over the multi-year lending period.**

A more detailed representation of the concrete payment structure for two-year credits of each of the seven rating segments given an initial amount financed of 100, an annual interest rate of 12.9% and equal installments (annuity[621]) is shown below. The credit risk parameters and pricing components for all seven rating segments are listed in Table 5-13 and Table 5-14.

[621] Annuity means that the amount due is the same for each year of the credit term, but the portion of interest payment and repayment changes over time. The interest payment of a certain year refers to the remaining outstanding credit exposures at the beginning of the corresponding year.

Table 5-12: The (exposure related) repayment structure for two year credits

No		AAA	AA	A	BBB	BB	B	CCC
1	**Annual Interest Rate**	0.0514	0.0519	0.0524	0.0566	0.0727	0.1290	0.2708
2	**Annuity**[622]	0.5389	0.5393	0.5396	0.5429	0.5552	0.5987	0.7111
3	**Exposure (t=0)**	1.0000	1.0000	1.0000	1.0000	1.0000	1.0000	1.0000
4	**Exposure (t=1)**	0.5125	0.5127	0.5128	0.5138	0.5175	0.5303	0.5596
5	**Exposure (t=2)**	0.0000	0.0000	0.0000	0.0000	0.0000	0.0000	0.0000
6	**Interest (t=1)**	0.0514	0.0519	0.0524	0.0566	0.0727	0.1290	0.2708
7	**Interest (t=2)**	0.0264	0.0266	0.0269	0.0291	0.0376	0.0684	0.1515
8	**Repayment (t=1)**	0.4875	0.4873	0.4872	0.4862	0.4825	0.4697	0.4404
9	**Repayment (t=2)**	0.5125	0.5127	0.5128	0.5138	0.5175	0.5303	0.5596

The first row indicates the annual interest rate to be paid for borrowers of the corresponding rating segment on the remaining exposure at the beginning of the perceived period. The annuity (in the second row) denotes the total payment that is due per year, including both interest payments (row 6 and 7) and repayment (row 8 and 9). The remaining exposure at the beginning of the corresponding period (e.g. $E(t=0)$ is the exposure at the beginning of period 1) is shown in row 3 to 5.

The regular repayment structure (for a solvent borrower) is illustrated below for a B credit. In the first year, a relatively high portion of interest (0.129) is due and the repayment portion (0.4697) is rather low. Interest and repayment add up to the annuity (0.5987).

In the second period, the interest payment is significantly reduced as the remaining exposure is roughly 53% $(=1-0.4697)$ of the initial exposure and the interest to be paid is oriented the on remaining exposure

622 The annuity is calculated as $\frac{(1+i_r)^t-1}{(1+i_r)^t \bullet i_r}$, where i denotes the annual interest rate, t the period and r the considered rating segment.

$(=0.129 \bullet 0.5303 = 0.0684)$. The repayment portion, by contrast, is clearly higher as in the first period and exactly equals the remaining exposure (0.5303).

Figure 5-16: Regular repayment structure of a B credit

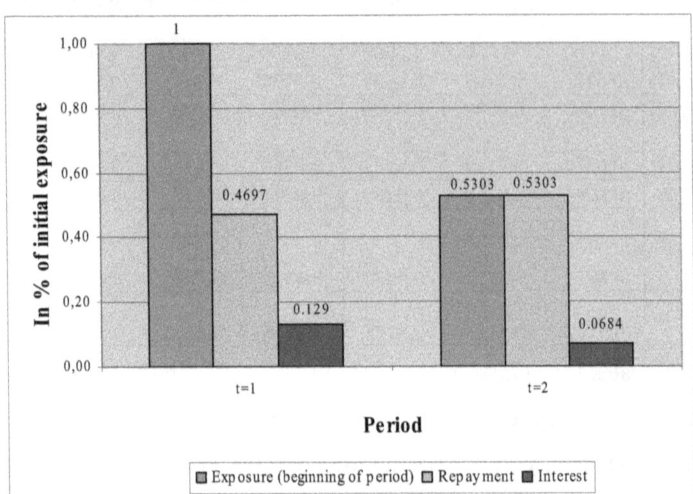

5.3.4.2 A concept to model the multi-period default process (step 2.B.1)

Moving to the portfolio level, the major question from a bank's perspective is now, how many borrowers will become insolvent and at what point in time, because insolvency is related only to partial repayment of the credit (i.e. full repayment until the preceding period of default and a recovery in the period of default).

Recalling formal aspects of credit risk portfolio modeling as presented in section 3.5, we will built a simple framework stepwise.

From a scientific viewpoint, there are two major **technical concepts** for the ex ante depiction of the stochastic default process of credit portfolios:

- Analytical modeling or
- Simulation.

It becomes common to combine the advantages of both concepts. Nevertheless, the latter concept (especially Monte Carlo simulation[623]) becomes more and more popular as a consequence of the opportunities resulting from the technological revolution of the IT. We will therefore refer to **Monte Carlo simulation**.[624]

For the deployment of the simulation, the following information is required:

- The credit risk parameters of each borrower according to his/her rating segment,
- The number of borrowers per rating class and
- The dependency structure between the single borrowers in the portfolio (correlations).

For convenience, we assume that all borrowers within the same risk segment do have the same credit risk parameters. The required number of borrowers per rating segment will be dealt with in section 5.3.4.5.5.

Modeling the dependency structure between the single borrowers of a portfolio (**default interdependencies between obligors)** may be handled using empirically derived default correlations or by means of asset correlations as explained in section 3.5.1.4. We refer to a fixed empirical-oriented asset correlation of 20% between all borrowers in the portfolio[625] for the simulation of the portfolio's default process. This is higher as an asset correlation of 10% (1%) that has been suggested by Blache and Bluhm (2001) for SME (well-diversified retail) credit portfolios based on empirical data (see section 3.5.1.2.1.4.2), but conservative from a risk management perspective as the probability of extreme events increases with higher correlations.

---

623 The concept of Monte Carlo simulation has been explained in section 3.5.1.4.3.2. In contrast to ordinary simulation, Monte Carlo simulation means that a random event is simulated numerous times.

624 Simulations allow ex ante forecasts of the random loss events and their distributions and compensate for the scarcity of data for the calibration of analytical approaches.

625 An asset correlation of 20% corresponds roughly to a default correlation of 1%.

In the simulated portfolio that serves for demonstration purposes (according to section 5.3.2) seven rating segments according to Standard & Poor's have been foreseen (AAA, AA, A, BBB, BB, B, CCC). The simulated portfolio comprises 700 borrowers with 100 borrowers of each rating segment.

The credit risk input data used for simulation purposes are shown below. Both the empirical PD and the LGD shown in section 3.3 have been adjusted for inconsistencies. The required risk rating capital for each credit is oriented on the analytical one-factor-model as foreseen by Basel (QIS 3) with convenient modifications as documented in Table 5-13, especially for the low-risk segments. Thereby, the initial cap on regulatory capital reduction foreseen by BCBS is taken into account and techniqually more stable payoffs are guaranteed (as the capital portion is in the denominator).

Table 5-13: Applied vs. empirical credit risk data for the S&P's rating classes (According to Caouette et al. 1998, p. 247)

Rating	PD used (vs. empirical) (in %)	Recovery rate[626] used (vs. empirical) (in %)	Capital portion used (vs. Basel II IRB[627]) (in %)
AAA	0.005 (no default)	85 (78)	1 (0.06)
AA	0.03 (0.02)	80 (77)	1.3 (0.32)
A	0.075 (0.01)	70 (57)	2.25 (0.93)
BBB	0.305 (0.15)	60 (53)	4 (3.17)
BB	1.385 (1.22)	45 (42)	10 (9.49)
B	6.245 (6.32)	35 (35)	21.5 (21.49)
CCC	15 (-)	20 (20)	42 (42.29)

The basis for the derivation of the payoff matrix is a risk-adjusted annual interest rate due for borrowers of each rating segment.

Similarly to a B-creditor (see section 5.3.3.1), credits of all seven S&P's rating segments may now be decomposed into their pricing components as displayed in

626 The recovery rates have been adapted for consistency reason for demonstration purpose.

627 According to the Basel II formula in section 3.5.2.4 for a corporate borrower including EL cushion.

Table 5-14 below based on the input data listed in Table 5-13. Besides the specific PD, LGD and risk capital the other pricing input data have been the same as for the B-segment shown in Table 5-6.

Table 5-14: Pricing components used to apply the GOPS model: Overview

Rating	Interest rate due/ Year	Refinancing costs + overhead (0.5%)	SRC (EL)	Capital costs	Profit margin
AAA	0.051415	0.04955	0.0000075	0.0016	0.0002575
AA	0.0519	0.049415	0.00006	0.00208	0.000345
A	0.05343	0.0489875	0.000225	0.0036	0.0006175
BBB	0.05701	0.0482	0.00122	0.0064	0.00119
BB	0.07265	0.0455	0.0076175	0.016	0.0035325
B	0.129	0.040325	0.0405925	0.0344	0.0136825
CCC	0.27025	0.0311	0.12	0.0672	0.05195

5.3.4.3 Modeling the multi-period default process: Simulation (step 2.B.2)

The simulation of the default process will be based on a firm value model. In line with the assumptions for listed firms, the asset value may be interpreted as the borrower's creditworthiness also in case of illiquid borrowers. As the asset value is, however not observable nor are the equity prices available, we will refer to a broad-brush concept that serves the modeling purpose. For this purpose, we simulate the borrowers' creditworthiness in each period t by means of uniform random drawings in the interval [0;1], which account for the dependency structure of the credit portfolio.[628]

As a consequence of the choice of the random drawings' interval, the resulting uniformly distributed variable may conveniently be compared with the default probability of each borrower.

Thus, if the uniformly distributed random variable $x_{i,t}$ of borrower i in period t falls below his/her default threshold $pd_{i,t}$ (as shown in Table 5-13), the borrower will be classified as insolvent:

[628] What is technically realized by a Cholesky - decomposition with Excel's 'Corand'-functionality, see section 3.5.1.2.1.6.

$$d_{i,t} = \begin{cases} 0, \text{ if } x_{i,t} \geq pd_{i,t}, & \text{No default} \\ 1, \text{ if } x_{i,t} < pd_{i,t}, & \text{Default} \end{cases}$$

In a multi-period context, this can graphically be understood as follows.

Figure 5-17: Multi-period default process of a single borrower

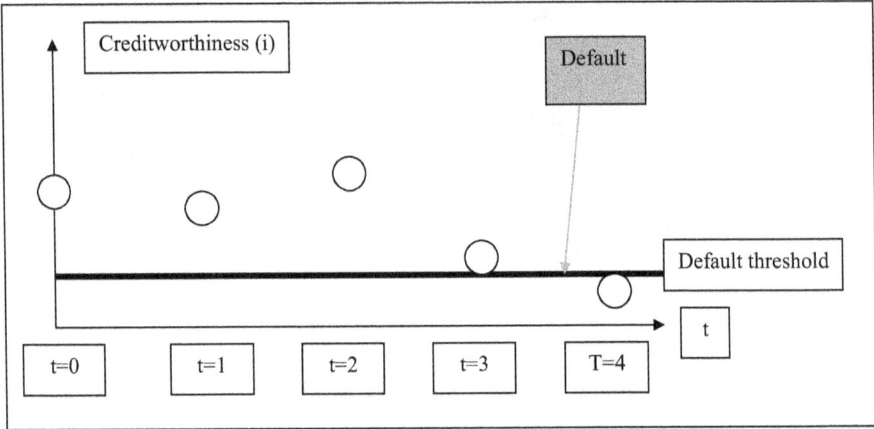

The creditworthiness may be measured discretely (here: annually) by drawing a random variable for each year (modeled e.g. as a random walk), for example.[629] In the arbitrary example, the borrower would thereby default in the fourth year.

In the current example, it has been assumed that the default threshold remains constant over time, what is usually not realistic as a consequence of macro-economic developments and the mean-reversion effect (see section 3.3.4).

Simplification of modeling for risk segments

Modeling the multi-period default process as explained above is very complex due to the size of the target portfolio to be managed.

As the investment alternatives for the portfolio problem have been assumed to be rating segments (see section 5.1.3.3.1) what substantially reduces the focus on the developments of the individual borrowers, default process modeling for

629 More sophisticated approaches are eligible and should be taken into account dependent on the considered portfolio.

the rating segments will be based on annual segment default rates, which are recursively linked to each other year by year.

It will thereby be assumed that it is sufficient to simulate the portfolio default structure in one period, to derive the number of defaults per risk segment and then to depict the default process over time as a cumulative default rate or survival probability, respectively (assuming that the segment default rates are independent over time).

The idea behind this assumption is that it is arbitrary which specific borrower becomes insolvent and that the initial distribution of creditworthiness of the single borrowers per rating segment remains the same over time, i.e. up - and downturns do neutralize each other.

Certainly, other modeling techniques are possible dependent on the specific credit portfolio composition. For example, for the very best and worst rating segments, the mean reversion effect[630] plays an important role for multi-period horizons. The mean reversion effect may conveniently be included into the concept by altering the default thresholds for each rating segment over time. While the threshold would approximately remain the same for the rating segments in the "middle" over time (in the simulated portfolio e.g. the BB segment) the thresholds would increase (decrease) for the very best (worst) rating segments. However, modeling the mean reversion effect accordingly has not been performed for the exemplified example.

Simulation based on a sample portfolio

Let us assume that the first 10 random drawings of totally 700 per simulation (representing the creditworthiness of the 700 borrowers in the simulated portfolio) correspond to borrowers of the B-segment.

Consequently, random drawing 1 corresponds to borrower 1 and so on. The result of the first one of 20,000 simulations for random drawing 1 to 10 is shown

[630] The mean reversion effect has been explained in section 3.3.4.

below. An asset correlation of 20% between the random drawings has been incorporated with Excel's Corand functionality.

Table 5-15: Random drawings 1 to 10 from the first of the 20,000 simulations

No.	**1**	**2**	**3**	**4**	**5**	**6**	**7**	**8**	**9**	**10**	**...**
Random Draw-ings	0.3436	0.4618	**0.0279**	0.4585	0.2273	0.5023	0.4170	0.7393	0.1825	0.5205	...

The default probability (PD) of the B-segment is assumed to be 6.245%, as shown in Table 5-13. Consequently, borrower 3 is highlighted, because his/her creditworthiness (random 3, $x_{i,t} = 0.02796$) is worse than his/her default threshold of $pd_{i,t} = 0.06245$.

More formally, the number of insolvencies per rating segment r in a specific period t equals:

$$D_{r,t} = \sum_{i=1, i \in r}^{n_{r,t}} d_{i,t}$$

With the overall number of borrowers per rating segment $n_{r,t}$ in period t the default rate of the rating segment r in period t yields to:

$$PD_{r,t} = \frac{D_{r,t}}{n_{r,t}}$$

Dependent on the change of the credit risk parameters over time (e.g. the default threshold due to macroeconomic reasons and/or the mean reversion effect) also the average number of insolvencies per rating segment will change and can be uptaken in the recursive concept. In the following, however, a constant default rate per rating segment will be underlied.

The cumulative default rate per rating segment over time is the residual of the cumulative survival probability $SP_{r,t}$:

$$SP_r(t) = \prod_{i=1}^{t} (1 - PD_{r,t})$$

and is illustrated in the table below based on an arbitrary example with a $PD_{r,t}$ of 10%.

Table 5-16: Development of the portion of solvent borrowers per rating segment over time

Point in time	**Solvent borrowers/ rating segment**	$PD_{r,t}$	Insolvencies	$SP_{r,t}$
0	100			
1	90	0.1	10	0.9
2	81	0.1	9	0.81

In the example considered, only 81% of the borrowers remain solvent after period 2. The property of remaining solvent can conveniently be saved by means of the survival probability. The survival probability represented as a discrete Markov chain is shown below.

Figure 5-18: Graphical representation of the survival probability

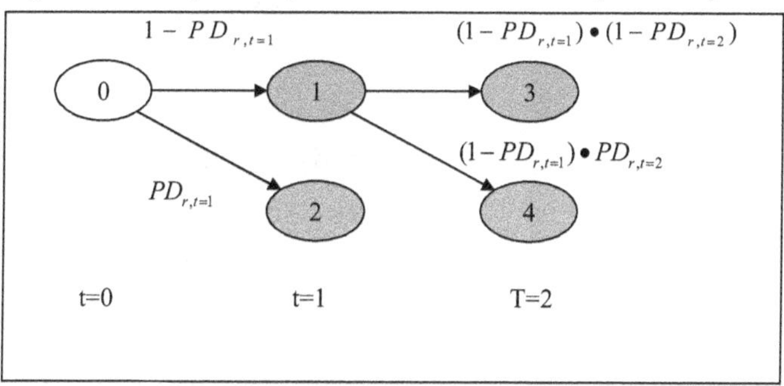

Node 1 and 3 represent nodes for the invested subportfolio portion remaining solvent as opposed to node 2 and 4, which represent absorbing default nodes. In the example as given in Table 5-16, the survival probability in node 1 $(1-PD_{r,t=1})$ would be 90%, and the survival probability in t=2 $((1-PD_{r,t=1})\bullet(1-PD_{r,t=2}))$ would be 81%. Similarly, the default rate in the first year $(PD_{r,t=1})$ would equal 10% and 9% in the second year $((1-PD_{r,t=1})\bullet PD_{r,t=2})$.

5.3.4.4 Summary: Storage of the overall information required (Step A and B, Figure 5-15)

It can be recorded that the overall information required about the default process for each rating segment can be stored by means of only two components: the survival probability and the remaining exposure. Information about these two components enables to derive the density function of a portfolio's performance distribution, what is required to apply the GOPS model.

5.3.4.5 Underlying portfolio model and design of the scenarios for the event tree (step 2.C)

Multi-period portfolio management under risk (here: GOPS) is usually modeled via event trees to depict the uncertain states of the environment discretely as scenarios (see Figure 5-11).

In the following, a binary decision tree (i.e. each node in the event tree has two successors) with 7 nodes as shown in Figure 5-11 will be considered to represent the risk result[631] of a two-period credit portfolio investment.

Figure 5-19: Overview for the construction of the scenarios: Step 2.C

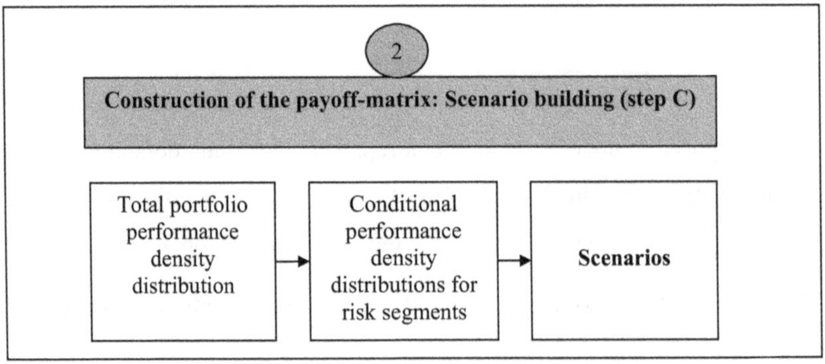

2

Construction of the payoff-matrix: Scenario building (step C)

Total portfolio performance density distribution → Conditional performance density distributions for risk segments → **Scenarios**

Every investor will focus on the development of the overall portfolio value. The development of the credit risk result of each rating segment (subportfolio) therefore depends as a conditional density function on the development of the total portfolio value.

[631] The credit risk result represents a portfolio's performance.

In order to make the credit risk results of the subportfolios comparable, they are standardized with the corresponding risk capital required as shown in Table 5-13.

Subsequently, the density function for the *gross*[632] *portfolio RORAC for single periods* can be determined (see Table 5-19).

5.3.4.5.1 Determination of net return and RORAC

In the following, the determination of the rating segment's (r) RORACs for single periods (t) will be explained.

Dependent on the pricing of credits according to their risks, a "net return" of the interest paid after subtracting traversing costs (operative costs (FC_t), refinancing costs ($RFC_{r,t}$)) and the losses due to insolvent borrowers in the segment (no interest payment and loss on the remaining exposure ($LGD_{r,t}$)) remains:[633]

$$\text{NetReturn}_{r,t} = (1 - PD_{r,t}) \bullet i_t - PD_{r,t} \bullet LGD_{r,t} - (FC_t + RFC_{r,t})$$

The net return of each rating segment r standardized with the corresponding risk capital portion required (RC_r[634], see Table 5-13) is called return on risk-adjusted capital (RORAC) in the technical jargon:

$$RORAC_{r,t} = \frac{\text{NetReturn}_{r,t}}{RC_r}$$

The concept of net return and RORAC for each subportfolio can be understood as follows:[635] It is assumed that B-rated borrowera annually pay 12.9% interest on the remaining exposure (see Table 5-14). For an IBOR-rate of 4% it is assumed that a bank refinances its exposure at 4.5% (RIR_{Bank}).[636]

---

632 Defined as (property in t+1)/(property in t).

633 This representation of the net return is independent of time-related payments.

634 It has been assumed that the required risk capital (RC) is constant over time.

635 Further information can be found in section 4.2.2.

636 Aspects of Asset-Liability management will be neglected.

Under the assumption that 10% of the B-rated borrowers will become insolvent, a net return of 1.08% would remain for the bank at the end of the year.

In contrast to the calculation of the profit contribution for a single borrower (see Table 5-11), the occurred losses comprise both the exposure lost due to default (here: $PD_{r,t} \bullet LGD_{r,t} = 0.1 \bullet 0.65$) and the non-paid interest for the defaulted borrowers (here: $PD_{r,t} \bullet i_{r,t} = 0.1 \bullet 0.129$). Standardized with the capital portion needed for the B-segment this random case corresponds to a return on risk-adjusted capital (RORAC) of roughly 5% (=1.08/21.5).

Table 5-17: Determination of net return and RORAC for a subportfolio: An illustrative example

Component	Determination	Interest (%)
Interest due (B-borrower)	Assumption	12.9
- Refinancing costs (RFC): $(1 - RC_r) \bullet RIR_{Bank}$	(1-0.215) • 4.5% [637]	3.53
Profit Contribution Level I		9.37
- Occured losses: $PD_{r,t} \bullet (i_{r,t} + LGD_{r,t})$	$0.1 \bullet (0.129{+}0.65)$ [638]	7.79
Profit Contribution Level II		1.58
- Fixed costs (FC)	Assumption	0.5
= **Profit Contribution Level III (Net return[639])**		**1.08**
= **RORAC: (Net return/RC)**	1.08/21.5	**5.03**

For the average default rate of the B-segment ($PD_{r,t} = 0.06245$, see Table 5-13), a net return of 4.0026% would remain what equals a RORAC of 18.62% (= 4.0026/21.5).

5.3.4.5.2 Determination of the conditional RORAC of the rating segments

Based on the technical concept and credit risk parameters as explained in section 5.3.4.1 to 5.3.4.3 20,000 simulations of the single period default process have been performed for the sample portfolio (see section 5.3.2) and the simulations

637 It has been assumed that the refinance interest rate is due annually.

638 For B-rated borrowers, it has been assumed that 65% of the remaining exposure is lost in case of a default event.

639 According to the profit contribution level III in Table 5-11.

have been ordered according to the total portfolio's gross performance[640] as shown in Table 5-19 below.

The concept of the gross portfolio performance ($grRORAC_p$) circumvents multi-period repayment aspects by assuming that a credit is fully paid back after one period.[641] Multi-period modeling of the repayment stream will be handled recursively. A typical gross annual performance distribution for a credit portfolio is graphically shown below.

Figure 5-20: The typical shape of the gross performance distribution for a credit portfolio

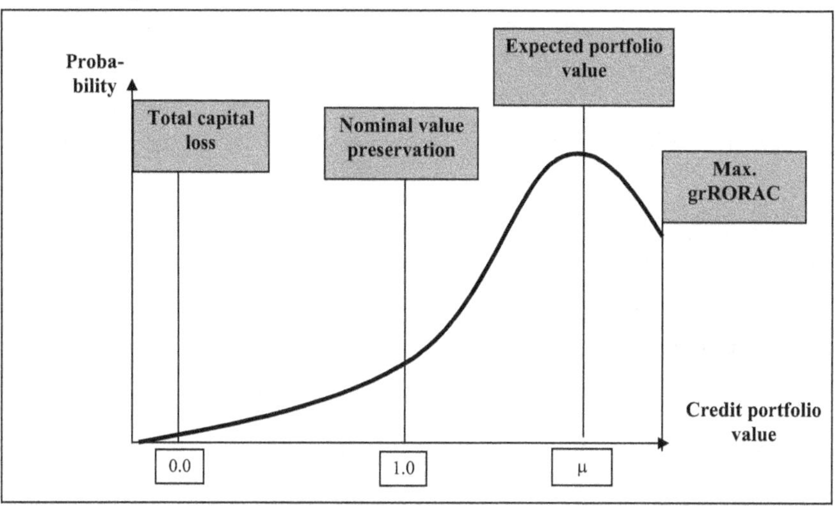

It can clearly be observed that the achievable gross RORAC is limited to the right - the ideal case when all borrowers in the credit portfolio repay their obligations as it has been foreseen. A crucial question is how to determine a portfolio's gross RORAC.

---

640 Denoted as $1+RORAC_p$.

641 A credit i is thereby assumed as an investment of capital (-1), with repayment of the capital portion together with the interest rate on this capital $(-1;1+RORAC_i)$.

In our illustrative example, the gross portfolio RORAC ($grRORAC_p$) is calculated as the arithmetic average of the gross RORACs of the rating segments ($grRORAC_r$):

$$grRORAC_p = \frac{1}{7} \bullet \sum_{r=1}^{7} grRORAC_r, \text{ where } r = \{1,...7\} = \{AAA,...,CCC\}.$$

For simplification purposes, the criterion for the calculation of the $grRORAC_p$ has been the number of borrowers per rating segment. Alternatively, the $grRORAC_p$ could be derived as the gross RORACs of the rating segments ($grRORAC_r$) weighted according to their corresponding capital portion within the portfolio (α_r):

$$grRORAC_p = \sum_{r=1}^{7} \alpha_r \bullet grRORAC_r, \text{ where } r = \{1,...7\} = \{AAA,...,CCC\}$$

A large simulation will deliver a well-diversified conditional distribution for each rating segment. In order to guarantee the stability of the conditional default rates per segment from an overall portfolio perspective, the average gross rating segment RORACs should not vary too much from each other.

For illustrative purposes, the rating segment's gross RORACs ($grRORAC_r$) dependent on the number of defaults per risk segment (consisting of 100 borrowers) are listed in Table 5-19 in order to fully understand the impact of the following examinations. The highest $grRORAC_r$ without any defaults varies significantly with the ratings as simulations (and realized random events) without any defaults for the CCC segment are very unlikely in contrast to the AAA segment, where defaults occur rather seldom and cause a high volatility of the performance. On average, however, the risk segments promise to generate a comparable $grRORAC_r$, as shown in Table 5-19. Negative values for a segment's $grRORAC_r$ represent a scenario, where more than the invested capital portion is lost, i.e. a 0% return on the invested capital and, on top, more than a full loss of the capital portion as a component of the total exposure. The implication of this context can be reviewed in section 3.5.1.5.6.3.

Table 5-18: Borrower defaults per rating segment and gross performance

PD(Segment)	AAA	AA	A	BBB	BB	B	CCC
0	1.1865	1.1912	1.1974	1.2203	1.2715	1.4124	1.5694
0.01	0.9851	0.9974	1.0404	1.1060	1.2092	1.3762	1.5439
0.02	0.7837	0.8036	0.8833	0.9917	1.1470	1.3400	1.5184
0.03	0.5823	0.6098	0.7262	0.8775	1.0847	1.3037	1.4930
0.04	0.3808	0.4161	0.5691	0.7632	1.0224	1.2675	1.4675
0.05	0.1794	0.2223	0.4120	0.6490	0.9602	1.2313	1.4420
0.06	-0.0220	0.0285	0.2550	0.5347	0.8979	1.1950	1.4165
0.07	-0.2234	-0.1652	0.0979	0.4205	0.8356	1.1588	1.3910
0.08	-0.4248	-0.3590	-0.0592	0.3062	0.7734	1.1226	1.3655
0.09	-0.6262	-0.5528	-0.2163	0.1920	0.7111	1.0863	1.3401
0.1	-0.8277	-0.7465	-0.3734	0.0777	0.6489	1.0501	1.3146

In the worst of the 20,000 simulations with respect to the gross portfolio RORAC labeled as “simulation No. 1”, roughly 10.8% of the invested portfolio capital will be lost, i.e. 0.8922 (=1/7•(1.1865+...+0.3717) units of every original capital unit remains after the period.

In the 9th simulation, more than the capital portion used for the CCC-subportfolio segment would be lost (-0.1124).[642] This results from the losses corresponding to a PD of 66% for the CCC segment exceeding the initially invested capital portion as a part of the exposure and reflecting the task of the capital to cushion losses in a very clear way.

In case of the AAA-segment, only in simulation 8 one of the 100 AAA-borrowers defaults (0.9851), while in the AA-segment one borrower defaults in simulation No. 16 (0.9974) and two in simulation 4 (0.8036). Besides, none of the 100 AAA and AA borrowers, respectively, default in the worst 20 simulations. It hereby becomes obvious that clustering only a few simulations without any defaults in these segments will not provide stable results for portfolio selection purposes. Extrapolation may be an alternative besides carrying out numerous simulations.

642 The same happens for the B-segment in the 20th worst simulation.

The corresponding default rates for the 20 simulations related to each rating segment (conditional segment PD, $PD_{r,t}$) are provided in Table 5-20.

Table 5-19: Determination of the gross performance of the portfolio and the subportfolios

Simulation No.	AAA	AA	A	BBB	BB	B	CCC	Portfolio performance
1	1.1865	1.1912	1.1974	0.9917	1.2715	0.0356	0.3717	0.8922
2	1.1865	1.1912	1.1974	0.6490	1.2092	0.6878	0.2443	0.9093
3	1.1865	1.1912	1.1974	1.2203	0.0262	0.9414	0.6520	0.9164
4	1.1865	0.8036	1.1974	0.8775	0.5243	1.0501	0.8304	0.9243
5	1.1865	1.1912	1.1974	0.9917	1.2092	0.0718	0.6520	0.9286
6	1.1865	1.1912	1.1974	1.2203	1.0847	0.5066	0.1679	0.9364
7	1.1865	1.1912	1.1974	1.2203	0.3375	0.5791	0.8814	0.9419
8	0.9851	1.1912	0.8833	1.1060	0.8979	0.7240	0.8304	0.9454
9	1.1865	1.1912	1.1974	0.9917	1.2092	0.9777	-0.1124	0.9488
10	1.1865	1.1912	1.0404	0.1920	1.2715	0.7965	1.0088	0.9553
11	1.1865	1.1912	1.1974	0.9917	1.0847	0.6516	0.3972	0.9572
12	1.1865	1.1912	1.1974	1.1060	1.0847	0.5791	0.3717	0.9595
13	1.1865	1.1912	0.7262	1.2203	1.2092	1.0501	0.1424	0.9608
14	1.1865	1.1912	1.1974	0.8775	0.6489	0.7965	0.8559	0.9648
15	1.1865	1.1912	1.1974	0.9917	0.2130	1.0863	0.9069	0.9676
16	1.1865	0.9974	1.1974	1.2203	0.4621	0.8690	0.8559	0.9698
17	1.1865	1.1912	0.5691	0.7632	1.0847	1.3762	0.6266	0.9711
18	1.1865	1.1912	1.1974	1.2203	0.4621	0.6153	0.9578	0.9758
19	1.1865	1.1912	1.1974	1.2203	0.9602	0.8327	0.2443	0.9761
20	1.1865	1.1912	1.1974	1.2203	1.0224	-0.0006	1.0343	0.9788
...	...	...	...	...	...	...	...	...
Avg 1-20	1.1764	1.1621	1.1189	1.0146	0.8637	0.7113	0.5960	0.9490
Avg 21-20000	1.1856	1.1858	1.1861	1.1866	1.1872	1.1895	1.1918	1.1875
Avg	1.1856	1.1858	1.1861	1.1864	1.1869	1.1890	1.1912	1.1873

Based on the results of Monte Carlo simulation, arbitrary "groups" of simulations may be clustered to a scenario enabling to derive the data for arbitrary event trees as desired by an investor.[643]

Given the worst 20 of the 20,000 simulations in the latter example, they can be grouped to a very tail-related scenario, namely the worst 0.1% outcomes to be

[643] If an investor wants to group the worst 0.1% of the simulations for a tail scenario in an event tree, he/she has to ensure that the number of simulations is sufficiently high to provide stable results, e.g. 100,000 what would yield to 100 simulations for the 0.1% - tail scenario.

expected according to the total portfolio value (=20/20,000 simulations). In case of a binary decision tree as shown below, the best 19980 simulations (the best 99.9%) would then built up the other scenario.

Figure 5-21: The decision tree to group the simulations

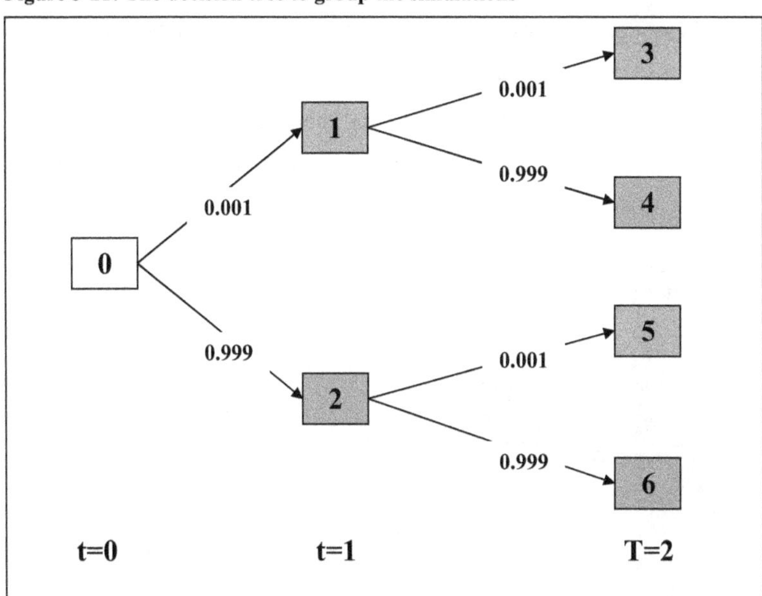

When comparing the average conditional gross RORACs of the rating segments for the worst 20 simulations labeled as “Avg. 1-20” in Table 5-19, it can be observed that there is a consistent order between the rating segments: The rating segment that is the least risky, AAA, performs best (1.1764) and the CCC-segment is the riskiest investment with 0.5963. For the best 99.9% of the simulations (labeled as “Avg. 21-20000”), the situation is adverse: the riskiest segment (CCC) provides the highest average conditional gross RORAC (1.1913) and the AAA-segment is supposed to deliver the lowest average conditional gross perrformance (1.1856).

Based on this procedure, diversification aspects can conveniently be modeled according to the Euler principle as described in section 4.2.3 and the assumption of a well-diversified portfolio is properly depicted as shown in Figure 5-22.[644] The conditional gross performance of a subportfolio within the overall portfolio is presented below (see Figure 5-22), where the y-axis indicates the expected gross RORAC for the entire portfolio and the B-subportfolio and the x-axis shows the cumulative percentile of the total portfolio RORAC distribution (which ranks the gross expected subportfolio RORACs of the B-segment according to the overall portfolio's gross RORAC).

Figure 5-22: The conditional gross performance of a subportfolio vs. the gross portfolio performance

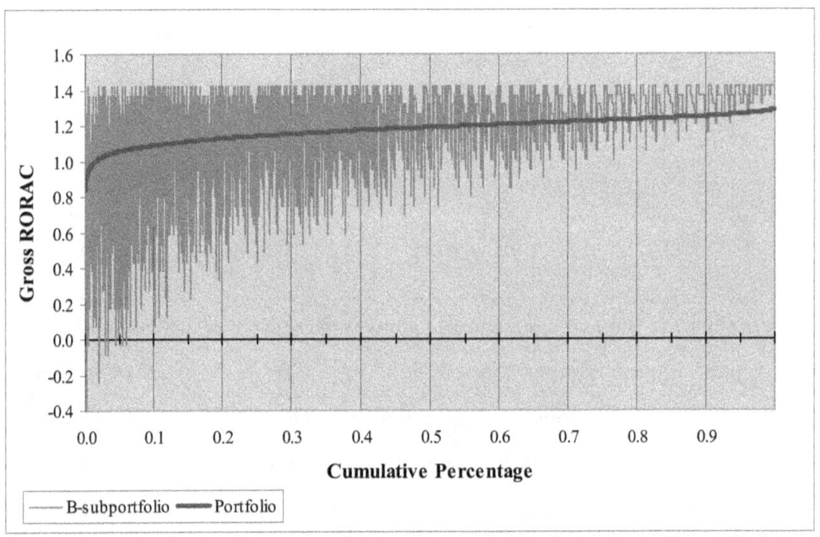

The credit risk input parameters, credit pricing and capital requirements may be altered for each year and are thereby adapted to the specific expectations of the credit portfolio manager.[645]

644 For stress testing purposes, an investor could assume that all risk segments underperform at the same time, for example.

645 E.g. according to macroeconomic effects, the mean reversion effect, etc..

5.3.4.5.3 From conditional segment RORAC to conditional default rate

While the conditional gross segment RORAC has been valuable for the construction of the scenarios, the conditional number of defaults per segment is used in order to bring the multi-period payment structure (in terms of the survival probability) and the default process recursively together. The corresponding conditional segment default rates, $PD_{r,t}$, are shown below.

Table 5-20: Determination of the performance of the portfolio and the subportfolios: conditional PD

Simulation No.	AAA	AA	A	BBB	BB	B	CCC
1	0	0	0	0.02	0	0.38	0.47
2	0	0	0	0.05	0.01	0.2	0.52
3	0	0	0	0	0.2	0.13	0.36
4	0	0.02	0	0.03	0.12	0.1	0.29
5	0	0	0	0.02	0.01	0.37	0.36
6	0	0	0	0	0.03	0.25	0.55
7	0	0	0	0	0.15	0.23	0.27
8	0.01	0	0.02	0.01	0.06	0.19	0.29
9	0	0	0	0.02	0.01	0.12	0.66
10	0	0	0.01	0.09	0	0.17	0.22
11	0	0	0	0.02	0.03	0.21	0.46
12	0	0	0	0.01	0.03	0.23	0.47
13	0	0	0.03	0	0.01	0.1	0.56
14	0	0	0	0.03	0.1	0.17	0.28
15	0	0	0	0.02	0.17	0.09	0.26
16	0	0.01	0	0	0.13	0.15	0.28
17	0	0	0.04	0.04	0.03	0.01	0.37
18	0	0	0	0	0.13	0.22	0.24
19	0	0	0	0	0.05	0.16	0.52
20	0	0	0	0	0.04	0.39	0.21
…	…	…	…	…	…	…	…
Avg 1-20	0.0005	0.0015	0.005	0.018	0.0655	0.1935	0.382
Avg 21-20000	0.000044	0.00028	0.00073	0.0029	0.0135	0.0615	0.1483

Given the event tree as shown in Figure 5-21 the conditional segment PDs in period 1 ($PD_r(t=1)$) would be as shown in Table 5-20.

Table 5-21: The conditional rating segment default rates

	AAA	AA	A	BBB	BB	B	CCC
Bad (0.001)	0.0005	0.0015	0.005	0.018	0.0655	0.1935	0.382
Good (0.999)	0.000044	0.00028	0.00073	0.0029	0.0135	0.0615	0.1483

For the application of the GOPS model the conditional PD for the tail-related scenarios has been extrapolated in order to generate more stable results (see Table 5-33) and is therefore different from the actual conditional segment PDs.

5.3.4.5.4 Survival probabilities

Given the conditional default probabilities of the risk segments ($PD_{r,t=1}$) as shown above in Table 5-21, the survival probability of the rating segments can be calculated as illustrated in Table 5-16:

$$SP_r(t) = \prod_{i=1}^{t}(1 - PD_{r,t})$$

Assuming, for example, that the conditional rating segment default probabilities $PD_{r,t}$ remain the same for the second period the following values can be derived.

Table 5-22: Survival probabilities

Node\r	AAA	AA	A	BBB	BB	B	CCC
1	0.9995	0.9985	0.9950	0.9820	0.9345	0.8065	0.6180
2	0.9996	0.9997	0.9993	0.9971	0.9865	0.9385	0.8517
3	0.9990	0.9970	0.9900	0.9643	0.8733	0.6504	0.3819
4	0.9995	0.9982	0.9943	0.9792	0.9219	0.7569	0.5264
5	0.9995	0.9982	0.9943	0.9792	0.9219	0.7569	0.5264
6	0.9999	0.9994	0.9985	0.9942	0.9732	0.8808	0.7254

5.3.4.5.5 Minimum number of borrowers per risk segment

Bröker (2000) analytically analyzed the minimum number of borrowers that are required to consider a credit portfolio as well-diversified.

Accordingly, homogeneous credit portfolios of **correlated obligors** might be regarded as well - diversified, if they consist at least of N_{min} borrowers (Bröker 2000, p.80):

$$N_{\min} = \frac{(1-\rho)(1-p_i)}{p_i - \rho(1-p_i)} \text{ if } \rho < \frac{p_i}{(1-p_i)}$$

where p_i is the default probability of a homogeneous portfolio and ρ is the default correlation within the portfolio. For uncorrelated borrowers, the formula is $N_{\min} = \frac{1}{p_i} - 1$. For a default correlation of 0.00002, N_{min} is as follows.

Table 5-23: The minimum number of borrowers per risk segment

Risk segment	PD (%)	N_{min} uncorr.	N_{min} corr.
AAA	0.005	19999	33329.9
AA	0.03	3332.3	3570.2
A	0.075	1332.3	1368.8
BBB	0.305	326.9	329.0
BB	1.385	71.2	71.3
B	6.245	15.0	15.0
CCC	15	5.66	5.7

Although the considered default correlation is close to 0, the minimum number of borrowers is significantly higher than in the uncorrelated case, especially for the AAA segment. If the constraint $\rho < \frac{p_i}{(1-p_i)}$ is not fulfilled (what arises especially for the low-risk rating segments), the minimum number of required borrowers cannot be derived by means of this formula.

5.3.5 Joining payment structure and survival probability to determine the payoffs

Given the average conditional segment PDs for arbitrary event trees, which may be determined for each year according to the specific considerations of the credit portfolio manager (especially market constraints for pricing), the pre-defined multi-period payment structure for all credits and the conditional survival probability can be brought together.

For demonstration purposes, it is assumed that all credits refer to a two-year term and have a repayment structure as shown in Table 5-12 in section 5.3.4.1. Instead of the exposure-related repayment structure, the capital-related repayment structure (capital cash flow) is used. It is thereby assumed that the repaid exposure contains the same portion of capital and refinanced exposure as the initial exposure in order to ensure that the total capital portion of the credit risk profit center is concervative. The repayment sequence of the exposure has been excluded from modeling aspects, as it does not influence the capital cash flow structure.[646]

The regular[647] repayment structure of the capital portion for each rating segment is $R_{EK,r,t} = (-C_{r,t=0}; i_{E,r,t=1} + R_{C,r,t=1}, i_{E,r,t=2} + R_{C,r,t=2})$ what is just analogous to the exposure-related repayment cash flow derived in section 5.3.4.1. R stands for the repaid capital (C) and i for the interest rate on capital (RORAC) dependent on the remaining exposure E and the cumulative losses occurred till period t.

Additionally, it will be assumed that the average conditional segment default probabilities remain the same over the two year planning horizon.

For the net return introduced in section 5.3.4.5.1 ($\text{NetReturn}_{r,t} = (1 - PD_{r,s(t)}) \bullet (i_{r,s(t)}) - PD_{r,s(t)} \bullet LGD_{r,s(t)}) - (FC_{s(t)} + RFC_{r,s(t)}))$[648] the capital payoffs corresponding to rating segment r in non-terminal (t<T) and terminal nodes s (t=T), respectively, can be derived as follows:[649]

$$\text{Payoff}_{r,t(s)} = \begin{cases} (\text{SP}_{r,s(t-1)} \bullet \text{E}_{r,s(t-1)} \bullet (\text{NetReturn}_{r,s(t)}))/\text{RC}_{r,s(t=0)} + \text{SP}_{r,s(t)} \bullet \text{R}_{C,r,s(t)} + \text{SP}_{r,s(t-1)} \text{PD}_{r,s(t)} \bullet \text{C}_{r,s(t-1)} & \text{for } t<T \\ (\text{SP}_{r,s(t-1)} \bullet \text{E}_{r,s(t-1)} \bullet (\text{NetReturn}_{r,s(t)}))/\text{RC}_{r,s(t=0)} + \text{SP}_{r,s(t-1)} \bullet \text{C}_{r,s(t-1)} & \text{for } t=T \end{cases}$$

$C_{r,s(t-1)}$ $(E_{r,s(t-1)})$[650] denotes the remaining capital exposure (remaning nominal credit exposure) at the beginning of the period t (denoted as t-1)[651] as a fraction of the initial capital portion (exposure portion) lent to the borrower (see Table

[646] A brief discussion of this issue can be found in section 5.4.1.4.

[647] For solvent borrowers.

[648] For the losses it has been assumed that they correspond to the remaining exposure at the beginning of the period. In case of underyear payments it could have also been assumed that the losses equal the average outstanding exposure during the year, $0.5(C_{s(t-1)} + C_{s(t)})$.

[649] s(t) denotes the considered node at time t, and s(t-1) the preceding node in t-1.

[650] $C_{r,s(t-1)}$ and $E_{r,s(t-1)}$ are equal as they denote the fraction of the remaining capital and exposure relative to the initial capital exposure, but $E_{r,s(t-1)}$ is used to derive the performance as net returns refer to interest on exposure.

[651] Similar to the exposure in Table 5-12.

5-12 in section 5.3.4.1)[652], $RC_{s(t=0)}$ represents the risk capital portion of the overall exposure according to Table 5-13, and $R_{C,r,s(t)}$ the regularly repaid capital in period t.

The modeling approach foresees that all losses occured will be included in the net returns (in terms of the LGD), whereby a consequent separation of interest payments on capital and capital repayment is enabled.

For all non-terminal nodes the first term $(SP_{r,s(t-1)} \bullet E_{r,s(t-1)} \bullet (NetReturn_{r,s(t)}))/RC_{r,s(t=0)}$ indicates the interest on the originally invested capital RC (labeled as $i_{E,r,t}$ in the regular capital cash flow structure above). The net returns are standardized by the originally invested capital because the capital paid back to the bank is reinvested (see below) and generates separate returns.

The following two terms $(SP_{r,s(t)} \bullet R_{C,r,s(t)} + SP_{r,s(t-1)} PD_{r,s(t)} \bullet C_{r,s(t-1)})$ indicate the repayment of the capital portion in period t. While the repaid capital in period t in case of solvent borrowers equals a regular capital repayment (with a probability of $SP_{r,s(t)}$), the whole remaining outstanding capital will be repaid in period t in case of insolvent borrowers, what occurs with a probability of $SP_{r,s(t-1)} PD_{r,s(t)}$. The idea behind this modeling is that the losses occurred in case of a default event (the LGDs) have been cushioned by the interest payments in the net return term.

Modeling in the last period is analogous, with the difference that all borrowers repay the remaining capital exposure.

It is important to notice that the corresponding payoff matrix contains nominal (independent of PV considerations) capital cash flows. The discount vectors are determined endogenously within the GOPS model, what will be explained subsequently.

652 The exposures have been standardized with the initial exposure.

5.3.5.1 The resulting payoff matrix

The survival probabilities for a specific event tree (with probabilities of 0.001 for the bad and 0.999 for the good case) have been presented in section 5.3.4.5.4.

The derivation of the payoffs for the B-segment based on the formulas provided in section 5.3.5 is shown below.

Table 5-24 shows the formulas for the payoffs of the B-segment.

Table 5-24: Generation of the payoff matrix-entries: Formulas

Node	Formulas
1	$(SP_{r,s(t-1)} \bullet E_{r,s(t-1)} \bullet (NetReturn_{r,s(t)}))/RC_{r,s(t=0)} + SP_{r,s(t)} \bullet R_{C,r,s(t)} + SP_{r,s(t-1)} PD_{r,s(t)} \bullet C_{r,s(t-1)}$
2	$(SP_{r,s(t-1)} \bullet E_{r,s(t-1)} \bullet (NetReturn_{r,s(t)}))/RC_{r,s(t=0)} + SP_{r,s(t)} \bullet R_{C,r,s(t)} + SP_{r,s(t-1)} PD_{r,s(t)} \bullet C_{r,s(t-1)}$
3	$(SP_{r,s(t-1)} \bullet E_{r,s(t-1)} \bullet (NetReturn_{r,s(t)}))/RC_{r,s(t=0)} + SP_{r,s(t-1)} \bullet C_{r,s(t-1)}$
4	$(SP_{r,s(t-1)} \bullet E_{r,s(t-1)} \bullet (NetReturn_{r,s(t)}))/RC_{r,s(t=0)} + SP_{r,s(t-1)} \bullet C_{r,s(t-1)}$
5	$(SP_{r,s(t-1)} \bullet E_{r,s(t-1)} \bullet (NetReturn_{r,s(t)}))/RC_{r,s(t=0)} + SP_{r,s(t-1)} \bullet C_{r,s(t-1)}$
6	$(SP_{r,s(t-1)} \bullet E_{r,s(t-1)} \bullet (NetReturn_{r,s(t)}))/RC_{r,s(t=0)} + SP_{r,s(t-1)} \bullet C_{r,s(t-1)}$

The resulting values according to the formulas denoted in Table 5-24 are as follows.

Table 5-25: Generation of the payoff matrix-entries (rounded values)

Node	Values
1	= 1*1*(0.8065*0.129-0.1935*0.65-(0.035325+0.005))/0.215+0.8065*0.4697+1*0.1935*1 = 0.2837
2	= 1*1*(0.9385*0.129-0.0615*0.65-0.0403)/0.215+0.9385*0.4697+1*0.0615*1 = 0.6920
3	= 0.8065*0.5303*(0.8065*0.129-0.1935*0.65-0.0403)/0.215+0.8065*0.5303 = 0.3043
4	= 0.8065*0.5303*(0.9385*0.129-0.0615*0.65-0.0403)/0.215+0.8065*0.5303 = 0.5088
5	= 0.9385*0.5303*(0.8065*0.129-0.1935*0.65-0.0403)/0.215+0.9385*0.5303 = 0.3541
6	= 0.9385*0.5303*(0.9385*0.129-0.0615*0.65-0.0403)/0.215+0.9385*0.5303 = 0.5921

The input data for the derivation of the payoffs are based on the following references:

- Survival probability (SP): Table 5-22.
- Exposure: Table 5-12.
- Credit risk input data: Table 5-13.
- Pricing: Table 5-14.

5.3.5.2 The payoff matrix to be used for model deployment

The capital payoff matrix for the decision tree as given in Figure 5-21 (with node probabilities of 0.1 (and 0.9) for "bad" ("good") nodes in the event tree) is shown below and will serve as an illustrative example for the deployment of the model. It has thereby been assumed that the input data are more stable as the payoffs shown in Table 5-25 above, as the bad scenario comprises 2000 simulations instead of 20.

The conditional segment PDs have subsequently been used for the simulation as shown below.

Table 5-26: The conditional rating segment default rates

	AAA	AA	A	BBB	BB	B	CCC
Bad (0.1)	0.00008	0.00062	0.00210	0.00714	0.02965	0.12769	0.26094
Good (0.9)	0.00004	0.00024	0.00057	0.00249	0.01179	0.05439	0.13604

Thereby, the corresponding payoff matrix yields to the payoffs as follows.

Table 5-27: The payoff matrix (according to the decision tree shown in Figure 5-11)

Node	Riskless	AAA	AA	A	BBB	BB	B	CCC
0	-1	-1	-1	-1	-1	-1	-1	-1
1	1.035	0.6724	0.6670	0.6529	0.6287	0.5848	0.4872	0.4898
2	1.035	0.6732	0.6740	0.6760	0.6794	0.6867	0.7139	0.7380
3		0.6072	0.6041	0.5958	0.5808	0.5458	0.4394	0.3751
4		0.6076	0.6078	0.6081	0.6079	0.6016	0.5622	0.5071
5		0.6072	0.6043	0.5967	0.5835	0.5559	0.4763	0.4385
6		0.6076	0.6080	0.6090	0.6107	0.6127	0.6094	0.5928

It can clearly be observed that there are some "inconsistencies" in the payoff-matrix: the payoff for the very best segments is higher in the second period as for the worse rating segments, as their segment default rates are lower (see section 5.3.4.5.4). It thereby becomes clear, what crucial impact PV considerations do have for credit portfolios and the determination of their level even more importantly, as for low discount factors the better rating segments may be more advantageous in contrast to a usage of higher discount rates, what is related to a further improvement of the weaker risk segments with an earlier occurrence of payoffs.

5.3.5.3 Reinvestment of the repaid capital

It is assumed that the capital repaid before the planning horizon may be reinvested. In the figure below, reinvestment is illustrated for node 1. The decision tree probabilities correspond to 10% for node 3 and 90% for node 4. The cash flows arising after the planning horizon (T=3) are assumed to be discounted at the riskless rate (here: 4%).[653] Furtermore, no distinction according to scenarios is made after the planning horizon any more, but instead the average default rate per segment (here: represented by node 7 and 8) is taken to derive the payoffs as shown in Figure 5-23.

Figure 5-23: Reinvestment of the repaid capital

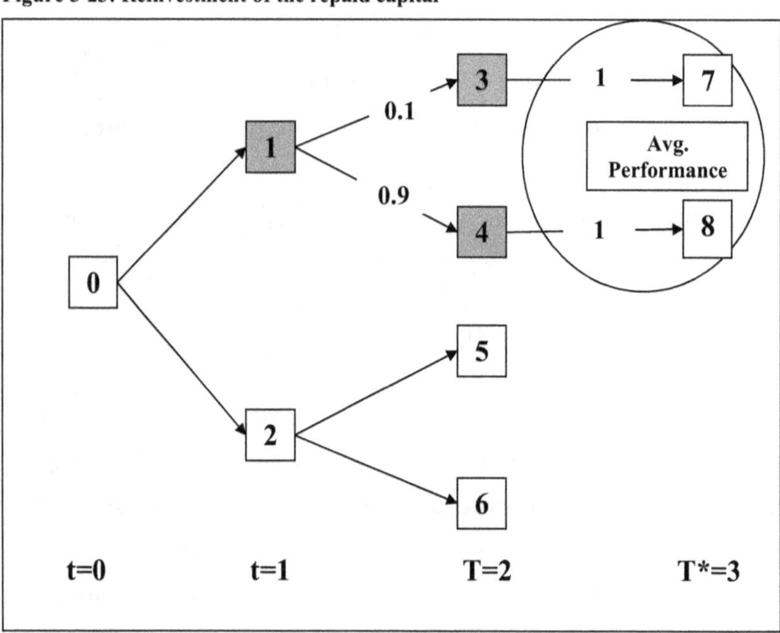

The preliminary payoff matrix for an investment in node 1 is shown Table 5-28, virtually including node 7 and 8. The payoff corresponding to node 7 for the B segment equals 0.1•0.43937+0.9•0.56221=0.549926 (see Table 5-27, B-

[653] This may be seen as arbitrary, but corresponds to other portfolio approaches for the whole observation period. An alternative rate may be the hurdle rate on capital (e.g. 16%).

segment, node 3 and 4), for example, without PV considerations after the planning horizon.

Table 5-28: Preliminary payoff- matrix for investments in node 1 with payoff after the planning horizon (rounded values)

Node	Riskless	AAA	AA	A	BBB	BB	B	CCC
0								
1	-1	-1	-1	-1	-1	-1	-1	-1
2								
3	1.035	0.6724	0.6670	0.6529	0.6287	0.5848	0.4872	0.4898
4	1.035	0.6732	0.6740	0.6760	0.6793	0.6867	0.7139	0.7379
5								
6								
7		0.6075	0.6074	0.6068	0.6052	0.5960	0.5499	0.4939
8		0.6076	0.6077	0.6078	0.6080	0.6070	0.5961	0.5774

Similarly, the other entries are calculated according to the following formulas including PV considerations after the planning horizon:

$$Payoff_{r,t(s)}=\begin{cases}\text{see above for } t<T\\ \text{see above for } t=T\\ ((SP_{r,s(T)}\bullet\overline{PD_r}^{t-T-1}\bullet E_{r,s(t-1)}\bullet(NetReturn_{r,s(t)}))/RC_{r,s(t=0)}+SP_{r,s(T)}\bullet\overline{PD_r}^{t-T}\bullet R_{C,r,s(t)}+SP_{r,s(T)}\bullet\overline{PD_r}^{t-T-1}\bullet C_{r,s(t-1)})/(1+i_{Riskless})^{t-T} & \text{for } t>T,\ t<T^*\\ ((SP_{r,s(T)}\bullet\overline{PD_r}^{t-T-1}\bullet E_{r,s(t-1)}\bullet(NetReturn_{r,s(t)}))/RC_{r,s(t=0)}+SP_{r,s(T))}\bullet\overline{PD_r}^{t-T-1}\bullet C_{r,s(t-1)})/(1+i_{Riskless})^{t-T} & \text{for } t>T,\ t=T^*\end{cases}$$

The payoffs are thereby discounted to the final planning period T at the riskless interest rate and the survival probability is adjusted after the planning horizon, referring to the average PD to be expected for each rating segment $\overline{PD_r}$[654], thereby distinguishing similarly to the concept before between nodes related to periods before the termination of the credits $t<T^*$ and the termination period $t=T^*$. The payoff in the final period of the planning horizon T is then the payoff in the terminal node and the sum of the discounted cash flows after the planning horizon.

For the current example, the resulting payoff matrix for node 1 is shown below. The virtual payoffs arising after the planning horizon have thereby to be discounted at the riskless rate of 4%. For segment B and node 3, for example,

[654] It has been assumed that the $\overline{PD_r}$ remains constant over time, what may easily be altered.

the payoff yields to 0.487221+0.549926/1.04=1.015996. The rounded value would be 1.0160, as shown below.

An analogous payoff matrix would hold in node 2, as the decision tree has been assumed to be symmetric.

Table 5-29: Final payoff- matrix for investments in node 1 (rounded values)

Node	Riskless	AAA	AA	A	BBB	BB	B	CCC
0								
1	-1	-1	-1	-1	-1	-1	-1	-1
2								
3	1.035	1.2566	1.2510	1.2364	1.2106	1.1579	1.0160	0.9647
4	1.035	1.2574	1.2583	1.2604	1.2640	1.2703	1.2871	1.2931
5								
6								

The values are again consistent with respect to riskiness, i.e. in the unpleasant scenario (node 3) the less riskiest investment (AAA) is related to the highest payoff (1.2566 in contrast to 0.9646 for the CCC segment) vice versa in node 4 (1.2574 for the AAA segment vs. 1.2931 for the CCC segment).

5.4 Application of the GOPS model

5.4.1 Introduction and settings

5.4.1.1 General assumptions

General assumptions with respect to the design of the credit management framework and the application of the GOPS model have been summarized in section 5.2.1. Additional crucial considerations have to be made for the size of the decision tree to be used, with respect to upper and lower bounds for the investment opportunities and modeling via capital cash flows and will be discussed below.

5.4.1.2 Decision tree principle

Business risk is captured via discrete outcomes, scenarios. One of the key issues linked to decision trees is the question which size of a decision tree is feasible and realizable.

Regarding realistic credit portfolio planning it is reasonable to refer to a time horizon of 2 to 5 years. The planning horizon should be adapted to the term structure of the credits, as payments after the planning horizon are related to a certain degree of arbitrariness with respect to the discount vectors (see section 5.3.5.3).

The size of the decision tree with respect to the **number of nodes in the final period (t=T)** is shown below.

Table 5-30: Decision tree structure: Number of nodes in the final period t

Decision tree structure				
No. of scenarios	**Nodes (t=2)**	**Nodes (t=3)**	**Nodes (t=4)**	**Nodes (t=5)**
2	2^2=4	2^3=8	16	32
3	9	27	81	243
4	16	64	216	864
5	25	125	625	3.125
6	36	216	1296	7776
8	64	512	4096	32768
10	100	1000	10000	100000

The exploding number of nodes from t=3 on will be a concern with respect to the decision. The total number of nodes is significantly higher.

5.4.1.3 Lower and upper bounds for the risk segments

As it has been outlined in section 5.2.2.3.2 and 5.3.4.5 it is very important to ensure that the underlying credit portfolio is well-diversified, as the payoff matrix is assumed to be stationary, i.e. the risk-return structure of the portfolio is independent of the chosen portfolio composition. For large loan portfolios within universal banks this condition can be assumed to be approximately fulfilled.

With respect to the conditional segment PD ($PD_{r,s(t)}$), setting upper (to guarantee diversification in other segments) and lower bounds (diversification within the considered segment) guarantees that the $PD_{r,s(t)}$ of each rating segment is stable, as graphically illustrated below: For additional borrowers included or excluded into a rating segment the $PD_{r,s(t)}$ remains the same.

Figure 5-24: Diversified portfolio ensured by lower and upper bounds for the risk segments

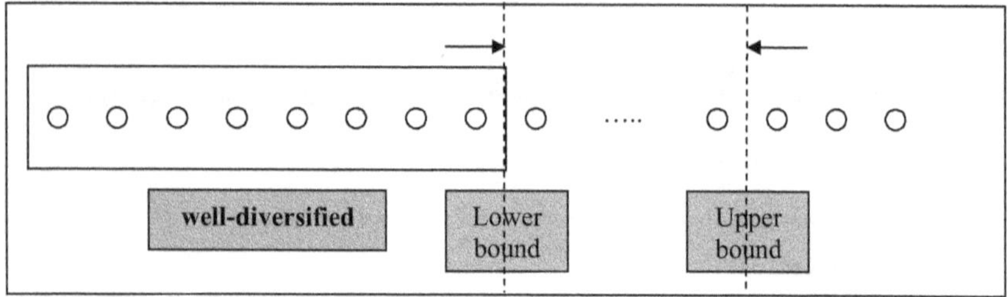

However, the final strategy should always be backtested (see section 5.4.5).

5.4.1.4 Why portfolio selection based on capital?

There are three main reasons to model the payoff relatively to the invested capital portion (denoted as *performance cash flow*).

- First, diversification aspects may conveniently be modeled according to the Euler principle (see section 4.2.3) as risk segments are comparable (see Table 5-19).
- Second, the performance cash flow distinguishes comfortably between interest payments and losses on the one hand and repayments without any influence on the net return on the other hand (see section 5.3.5). This distinction corresponds to the function of capital as a cushion against losses.
- Third, there is no need for an additional constraint in the GOPS model (see section 5.2.3.3), which would have an influence on the property of the solution and is difficult to implement.[655]

The second advantage comes along with the shortage that *the repaid exposure is not considered in the model.* As the repayment structures of the credit risk segments with respect to the exposure are relatively similar (see Table 5-12) and

655 e.g. the convexity of the optimization problem would have to be ensured in order to arrive at a growth-oriented solution, i.e. a feasible solution of the GOPS model.

repaid capital and thereby exposure is supposed to be reinvested, this shortage is assumed to have little influence on the final decision.

5.4.2 The general decision problem based on the net present value (NPV) criterion: An illustrative example

In order to understand the full impact of the multiperiod decision frame according to Hellwig (2002a), we will initially deal with illustrative examples for single borrowers and single periods.

5.4.2.1 The decision problem for a single credit

A simple decision problem subject to credit risk can be defined, for example, as a choice between:

- **A risky credit loan and**
- **An investment** opportunity **at the riskless rate** (e.g. a state loan).

Consider a binary decision tree as shown below. An investor has to initially decide in node 0 between two possible investments. In t=1 the investor may be faced to two distinct scenarios with respect to his/her investment decision in t=0, represented by node 1 and 2. Node 1 may refer to the default state (and therefore the node probability equals the default probability of the loan) of the risky loan, while node 2 represents the non-default state.

Figure 5-25: Binary decision tree for a simple portfolio

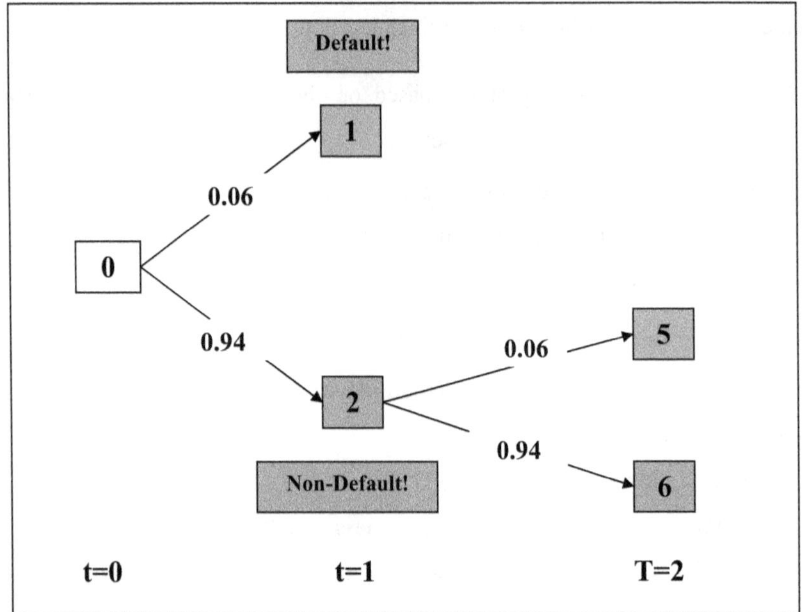

The decision tree is non-symmetrical, as node 1 represents an absorbing state for the loan. In so far, portfolio decision modeling based on single credit loans is not appropriate. Moreover, the choice of the node probabilities is complicated if not impossible when various credit risk segments with distinct PDs are compared besides shortages with the required property of portfolio diversification.

As extensively explained in section 5.3, we will focus on ROC-type[656] ratios in order to evaluate investments under risk, i.e. to measure the profitability of an investment relative to the used capital portion and thereby capturing the stationary risk-return properties of the risky opportunities. For a single credit the concept of performance measurement (RORAC) may be confusing, in contrast to the specific portfolio problem given for subportfolios as investment opportunities (see section 5.4.1.4). For clarification purposes, however, we will deal with a single-period example.

[656] Return on Capital;

Assume that the annual interest rate for the risky loan is $i_{loan} = 10\%$ and its default probability is 0.06 (e.g. a 'B'- rated loan). Hence, the probability for node 1 has been set to 0.06 and for node 2 to 0.94 (=1-0.06). The riskless interest rate may be $i_{riskless} = 4\ \%$. For an interest rate of 10%, the annual net return for a non-defaulting B-rated loan would be 6.3% calculated with the procedure as shown in Table 5-11.[657] An insolvent borrower is assumed not to pay the interest rate due and additionally a part of the exposure is lost. In an unpleasant state of insolvency, the investor would be faced to a recovery rate of 0.35.

Consequently, the gross RORAC for the default state would yield to $1+((-0.65-0.037)/0.2)=-2.435$[658] (=1+net return/capital).

Similarly, the gross RORAC for the non-default state (node 2) would be$1+((0.1-0.037)/0.2)=1.315$. A ratio of -2.435 means that the invested capital has been fully wasted, and, additionally 243.5% of the capital originally invested has to be externally added to cushion the occurred losses. Figure 5-26 below graphically shows the reduced decision tree for one period comparing the outcomes of the two investments.

657 The interest to be paid has been assumed to be 10%. Subtracting the traversing costs comprising fix costs (FC, 0.5 %) and refinancing costs (RFC with a capital ratio of 20% and a refinance rate of 4%, = 3.2%), 6.3% interest remains as a net return.

658 The net return is the loss of exposure (0.35-1) plus the traversing costs due (0.037) are thereby lost.

Figure 5-26: Gross performance of a single risky credit subject to a binary default event and the riskless investment opportunity

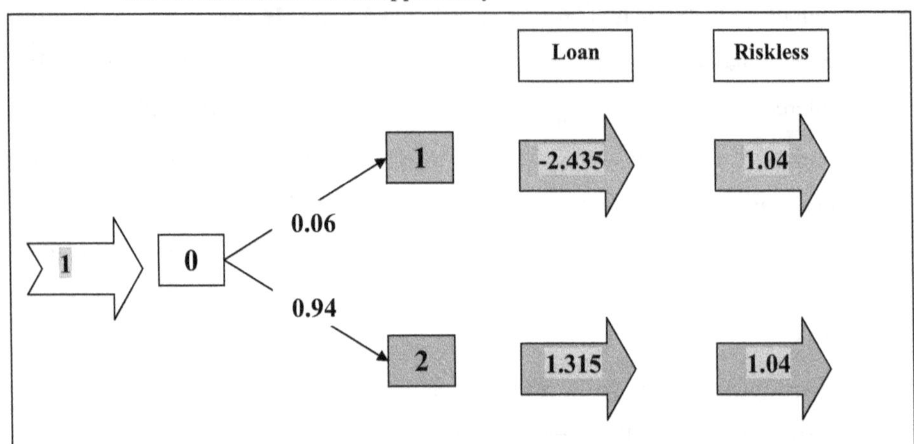

5.4.2.2 A decision based on the average performance criterion

An investor may concentrate on the average expected gross performance as explained in section 4.3.5.4. The average gross performance (RORAC) of the B-rated credit in period 1 would be:

$$\text{Average grRORAC}_{\text{loan}} = \sum_{\text{Node(i)}=1}^{2} \text{Prob}_i \bullet \text{grRORAC}_i = 0.94 \bullet 1.315 + 0.06 \bullet (-2.435) = 1.09$$

The (arithmetic) average gross performance is therefore much higher than the gross performance of 1.04 of a corresponding riskless contract which cannot default, but for the cost of a relatively high risk and particularly the risk that more capital than invested will be lost. The final decision of an investor will therefore depend on his/her utility function (see section 4.3f.).

5.4.2.3 A decision based on a generalized NPV method: Example 1

The net present value (NPV) method is a common decision criterion for multi-period portfolio selection. In the following, an example for the deployment of the NPV criterion for portfolio selection according to Hellwig (1993, p.91) is given. Hellwig (1993) suggests a **generalized NPV method**, which is based on the random portfolio yield as an opportunity rate. It is thereby assumed that the underlying discount rate is higher for a favorable scenario than in an inconvenient case. This principle plays a major role for the deployment of the GOPS model.

Consider a two-point decision first. An investor will underlie the investment's gross performance rate (dependent on the scenario, e.g. default/non-default-state) as a minimum target for alternative investment opportunities, because otherwise they don't need to be considered for arbitrage reasons.

In the latter example, the investor evaluates the relative advantage of the riskless investment opportunity against the risky B-credit: he/she will calculate with a discount factor of 1/1.315 and 1/(-2.435) in the non-default and default state, respectively.

For the riskless investment opportunity based on a gross performance of 1.04 he/she finds the generalized net present values of the riskless alternative

$$NPV_{Riskless} = -1 + 0{,}06 \bullet \frac{1{,}04}{-2.435} + 0{,}94 \bullet \frac{1{,}04}{1{,}315} = -0.282$$

to be negative, while the generalized NPV of the loan,

$$PV_{B\_Credit} = -1 + 0{,}06 \bullet \frac{-2.435}{1.04} + 0{,}94 \bullet \frac{1{,}315}{1.04} = 0.048$$

is positive and therefore comparatively advantageous.

Similarly to the average gross performance criterion, the investor would prefer a B-credit against the riskless investment alternative when relying on the generalized NPV criterion.

5.4.2.4 A decision based on a generalized NPV method: Example 2

For investment alternatives with average gross performances that are more competitive against each other as in the latter example, an investor has to find out the portion of the two (or more) investment opportunities so that the generalized NPV for both (all) alternatives is 0.[659] Credits of different riskiness,

[659] So that no 'hidden' portfolio value remains.

priced according to their risk-return structure may be relatively advantageous, for example.

Initially, we will still consider a portfolio consisting of both one risky and one riskless investment opportunity as shown in the table below.

Table 5-31: Illustrative example: NPV criterion and relative advantageous investment opportunities

Investment	Non default state (good)	Default state (bad)	Generalized NPV (i)
Riskless asset	1.05	1.05	0.0017
Credit loan	1.06	0.5	0.0042
Probability of state (good/bad)	0.99	0.01	

While the gross performance of the riskless asset is 1.05 in both the good and the bad scenario for the riskless asset, a loan may have a gross performance of 1.06 in case of solvency (with a probability of 99%) and 0.5 in the bankruptcy case (PD = 1%). The gross performance values are arbitrary and close to the nominal cash flow.

For both investment alternatives, the generalized net present value as shown in the last column of Table 5-31 is positive, so the investor has to include both opportunities by dividing up his/her capital between the two alternative investment opportunities.

After a finite number of attempts, the optimal solution is found: 16% of the capital will be invested in the riskless investment and 84% into the loan (see Table 5-32). It can be observed very clearly that both generalized net capital values increase/decrease towards zero when approaching the ideal weights. A negative generalized net present values may be interpreted as a sign to decrease the weight of an alternative, while positive net present values indicate that there is an additional value "hidden" in the alternative when increasing its weight. **This principle is applied in the GOPS model to account for diversification in terms of NPV.**

Table 5-32: Searching for the ideal portfolio composition according to the NPV criterion

Weight (loan)	Weight (riskless)	Gen. NPV (loan)	Gen. NPV(riskless)
0.3	0.7	0.0123	-0.0055
0.5	0.5	0.0059	-0.0059
0.84	0.16	0	0
0.9	0.1	-0.0016	0.0141

The outcome of the optimal portfolio decision is as follows: In the bad case (default event of the loan), the investor will be faced to a total gross performance of $0.16\bullet 1.05+0.84\bullet 0.5=0.588$. On the other hand, in 99% of the cases, he/she possesses 1.0584 capital units after one year from each capital unit invested, almost one percent more than with the riskless investment alternative solely.

In the following, the developed portfolio concept for risk segments is applied and discussed.

5.4.3 The application of the GOPS model

This section presents numerical examples of the GOPS model applied to credit portfolios. We will generally refer to two-period examples for illustrative purposes. An extension of the modeling for 3 to 5 periods is straightforward, but imposes some limitations for computation in terms of the exploding size of the decision tree (see Table 5-30) dependent on the setting of the example.[660]

Besides the opportunity to invest in the seven credit risk segments the opportunity to invest at the riskless interest rate for a single period for an interest rate of 3.5% has been taken into consideration. It has generally been assumed that the planning horizon is divided into years, with payments occurring at the end of each year.

5.4.3.1 Technical solution: Credit portfolio optimization tool (CPOT)

The GOPS problem as described in section 5.2.3.5 has been implemented in C++ supported by calls of Lingo 8.0, a commercial optimization software for

[660] Related to singularities of the price vectors. See Table 5-38 and Table 5-39.

non-linear problems. The credit risk input data used have been explained in section 5.3. The following figure shows the start screen of the tool.

Figure 5-27: The credit portfolio optimization tool: Start screen

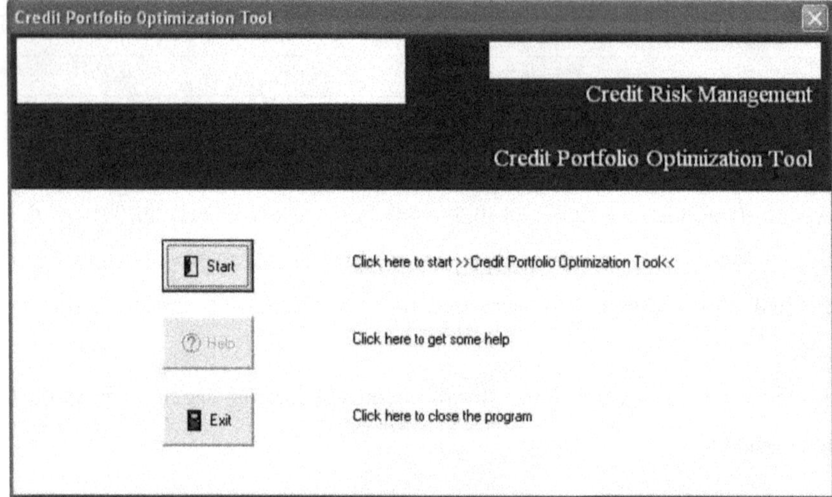

The sequence of the menus in the tool has been chosen according to the overall procedure of the GOPS model displayed in Figure 5-6.

A convenient methodology to generate the graphical representation of arbitrary decision trees for calculation purposes has been implemented via a *tree builder*. Through this menu, the external capital and the growth targets may additionally be set.

Figure 5-28: The generation of the decision tree

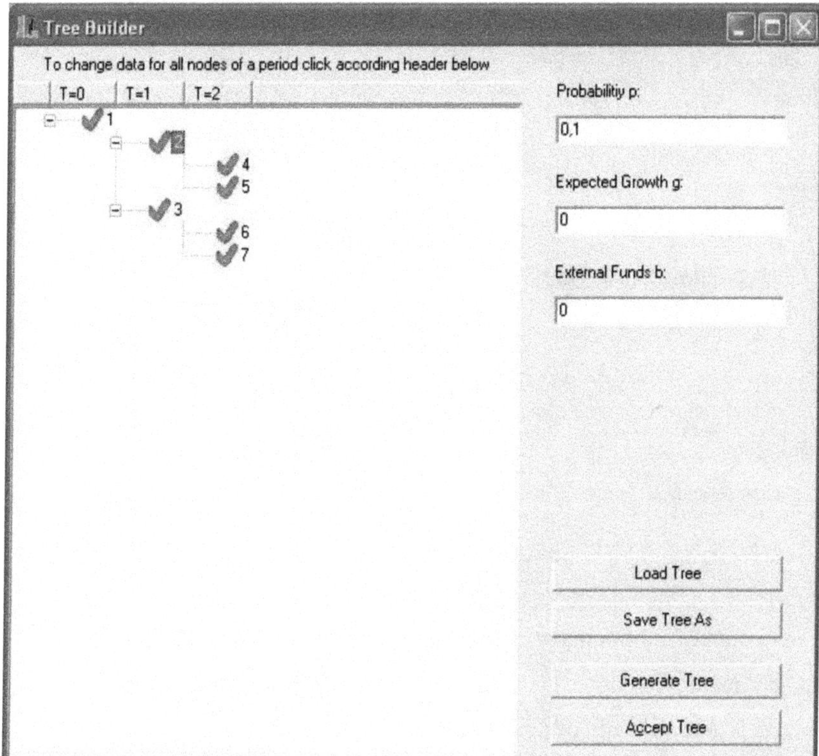

Through an additional menu, the *preferences* of the investments can be chosen. On the first tab, the credit risk related business preferences are chosen (hurdle rate, operating costs, etc. according to Table 5-6) and on the second tab the investment opportunities, their related credit risk input parameters and the upper and lower bounds may be selected and modified.

Figure 5-29: Choice of the investment preferences

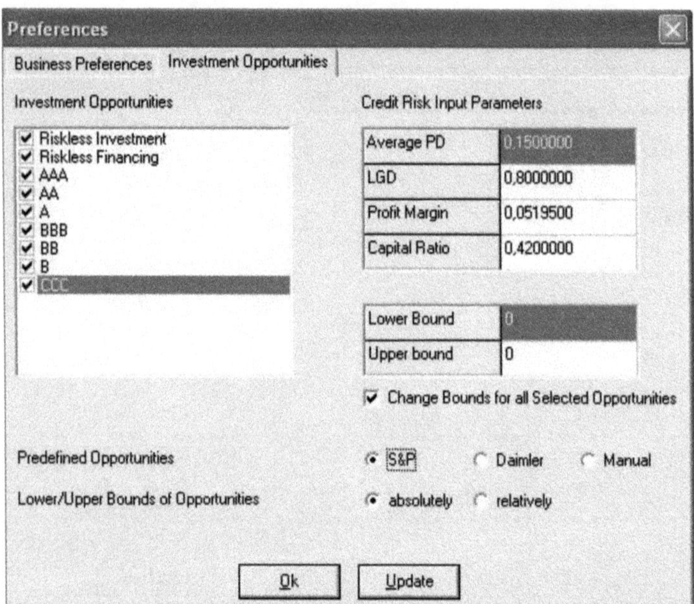

Based on the information with respect to the decision tree (including the growth targets and the external capital) and the credit risk related preferences, the *payoff matrix* is automatically generated and displayed.

Figure 5-30: Generation of the payoff matrix

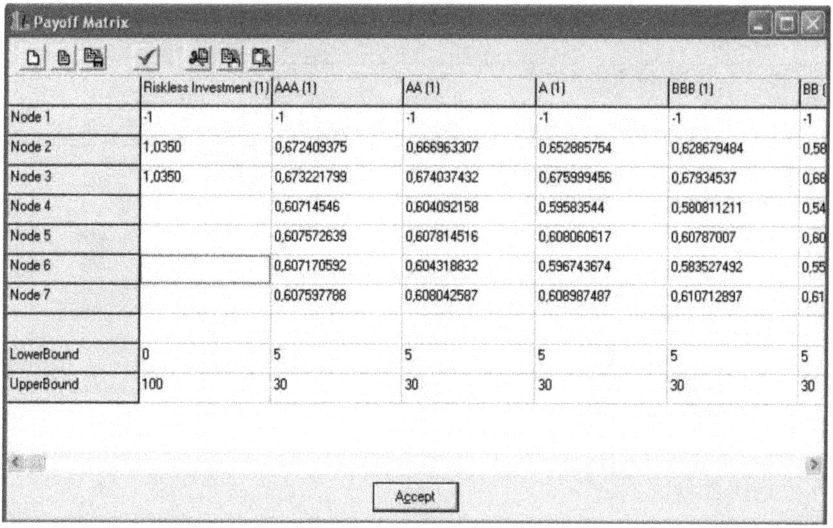

Payoff Matrix

	Riskless Investment (1)	AAA (1)	AA (1)	A (1)	BBB (1)	BB (
Node 1	-1	-1	-1	-1	-1	-1
Node 2	1,0350	0,672409375	0,666963307	0,652885754	0,628679484	0,58
Node 3	1,0350	0,673221799	0,674037432	0,675999456	0,67934537	0,68
Node 4		0,60714546	0,604092158	0,59583544	0,580811211	0,54
Node 5		0,607572639	0,607814516	0,608060617	0,60787007	0,60
Node 6		0,607170592	0,604318832	0,596743674	0,583527492	0,55
Node 7		0,607597788	0,608042587	0,608987487	0,610712897	0,61
LowerBound	0	5	5	5	5	5
UpperBound	100	30	30	30	30	30

Accept

After choosing the model notion (here: ex post) and setting the upper and lower bounds for the investment opportunities, the *output* screen provides the growth-oriented ("optimal") portfolio selection strategy as shown below. In the left column, the available capital ('available funds') related to the corresponding point in time is displayed. The second column shows the suggested withdrawal sequence and the following columns refer to the proposed investment strategies related to the corresponding node and thereby point in time, indicated by (InvestmentAlternative(node)), e.g. A(1).

Scrolling to the right provides the proposed strategies for all investment opportunities, and the corresponding discount and price vectors for all nodes in the event tree. The PV of the portfolio with respect to the endogenous discount vectors is displayed in the left corner on the bottom ("100,0807992").

Figure 5-31: The credit portfolio optimization tool: The working and output screen

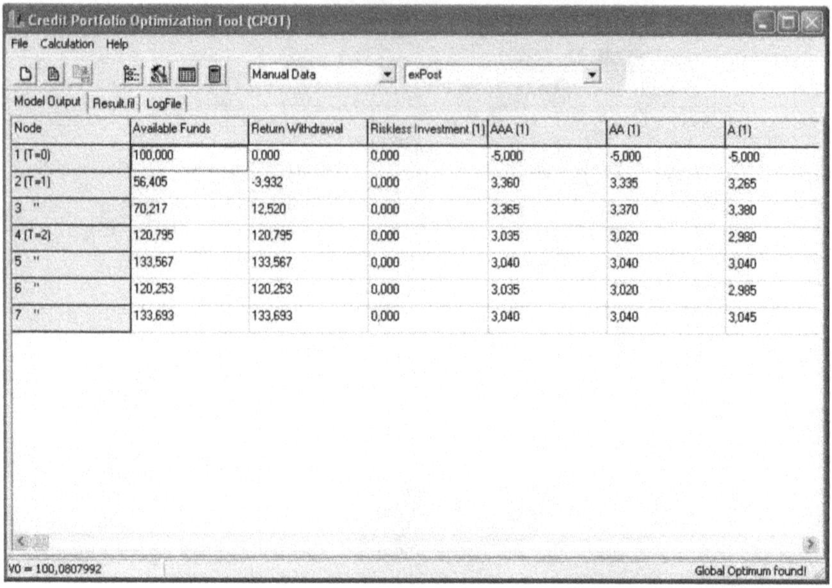

Credit Portfolio Optimization Tool (CPOT)

File Calculation Help

Manual Data | exPost

Model Output | Result.fil | LogFile

Node	Available Funds	Return Withdrawal	Riskless Investment (1)	AAA (1)	AA (1)	A (1)
1 (T=0)	100,000	0,000	0,000	-5,000	-5,000	-5,000
2 (T=1)	56,405	-3,932	0,000	3,360	3,335	3,265
3 "	70,217	12,520	0,000	3,365	3,370	3,380
4 (T=2)	120,795	120,795	0,000	3,035	3,020	2,980
5 "	133,567	133,567	0,000	3,040	3,040	3,040
6 "	120,253	120,253	0,000	3,035	3,020	2,985
7 "	133,693	133,693	0,000	3,040	3,040	3,045

V0 = 100,0807992 Global Optimum found!

5.4.3.2 Decision tree: The influence of the node probabilities on the decision

The exemplified decision tree as shown in Figure 5-11 will be used for illustrative purposes to examine the influence of the choice of the scenarios for portfolio selection.

Eleven scenarios will be considered. Example 1 ('No.1'), for example, refers to a binary decision tree with a probability of 0.001 for the bad scenario (i.e. the worst 20 of 20000 simulations) and 0.999 for the good one (i.e. the best 19980 of 20000 simulations).

Table 5-33: Decision tree and scenario choice

No.	1	2	3	4	5	6	7	8
Pr(Worst)	0.001	0.005	0.01	0.02	0.05	0.1	0.15	0.2
Pr(Best)	0.999	0.995	0.99	0.98	0.95	0.9	0.85	0.8

No.	9	10	11
Pr(Worst)	0.25	0.33	0.5
Pr(Best)	0.75	0.67	0.5

„PrWorst": Probability for the bad scenario; „PrBest": Probability for the good scenario

The input parameters for the GOPS problem have been externally given capital of 100 units in node 0, a growth targets of 5% in each non-terminal node (with respect to the NPV of the portfolio value), nominal upper and lower bounds for the investment opportunities of 5 and 30 for the capital to be assigned to the credit risk segments[661] and unlimited bounds for the riskless investment opportunity in every node as shown below. The credit risk parameters have been chosen as shown in Table 5-13.

Table 5-34: The input parameters for the application of the GOPS model

Input parameter	Values
Decision tree	Various examples as shown in Table 5-33
External capital	100 units in node 0
Payoff matrix	• Derived as explained in section 5.3.5 • 8 investment opportunities in all nodes (the riskless investment + 7 credit rating segments) • Lower/upper bounds of 5/30 for the credit risk segments and 0/100 for the riskless opportunity for investments in each node
Growth targets	5% in each non-terminal node
Model notion	Ex post

The result of portfolio selection based on the node probabilities and scenarios as indicated in Table 5-33 is shown in Table 5-35 below. The '-5' for the AAA segment in "No.1" indicates, for example, that 5 units of capital should be invested in the AAA-segment, what corresponds to a credit exposure of 500[662] units.

661 Other bounds reflecting the availability of capital in different nodes may be more appropriate.

662 Based on the risk capital ratio for each risk segment as shown in Table 5-13 and the optimal investment strategy proposed by the model, e.g. $1/0.01 \bullet 5 = 500$ ($1/RC \bullet 5$ units) for the AAA segment.

Table 5-35: Results for the suggested portfolio selection strategy in node 0

Decision Tree No.	Funds	Risk-less	AAA	AA	A	BBB	BB	B	CCC
1	100	0	-5	-5	-5	-5	-20	-30	-30
2	100	0	-5	-5	-5	-20	-5	-30	-30
3	100	0	-5	-5	-5	-5	-20	-30	-30
4	100	0	-5	-5	-5	-20	-5	-30	-30
5	100	0	-5	-6.696	-5	-5	-18.304	-30	-30
6	100	0	-5	-5	-5	-14.201	-30	-10.799	-30
7	100	0	-5	-5	-6.823	-30	-5	-18.177	-30
8	100	0	-5	-5	-5	-20	-30	-5	-30
9	100	0	-5	-30	-10.803	-5	-5	-14.197	-30
10	100	0	-5	-5	-12.945	-30	-5	-12.055	-30
11	100	0	-5	-5	-30	-12.358	-5	-12.642	-30

The resulting portfolio selection strategy for node 1 and 2 is shown in Table 5-36 and Table 5-37, respectively. As there has been an initial decision in node 0 (period 1), the backflow from this investment is shown together with the amount to be withdrawn in each node. The backflows and withdrawals add up to the amount available. A negative sign with respect to the withdrawals indicates that subsequent payments are required to fulfill the growth target set by an investor. All entries do represent nominal (time-independent) values. The discount and price vector, respectively, are shown in Table 5-38 and Table 5-39 below.

Table 5-36: Suggested portfolio strategy in node 1

No.	Back-flow	With-drawal	Avail-able	Risk-less	AAA	AA	A	BBB	BB	B	CCC
1	32.92	-40.972	73.892	0	-5	-5	-5	-5	-5	-30	-18.892
2	41.474	-23.389	64.863	0	-5	-5	-5	-5	-5	-9.863	-30
3	44.285	-18.671	62.956	0	-5	-5	-5	-5	-7.956	-5	-30
4	48.095	-14.258	62.353	0	-5	-5	-5	-5	-5	-30	-7.353
5	51.08	-5.624	56.704	0	-5	-5	-5	-26.703	-5	-5	-5
6	56.401	-3.939	60.34	0	-5	-5	-5	-30	-5.34	-5	-5
7	58.177	-1.952	60.129	0	-5	-5	-5	-30	-5.129	-5	-5
8	60.005	0.426	59.579	0	-5	-5	-5	-5	-29.579	-5	-5
9	61.368	1.789	59.579	0	-5	-5	-5	-5	-29.579	-5	-5
10	62.316	3.02	59.296	0	-5	-5	-5	-29.296	-5	-5	-5
11	64.427	5.59	58.837	0	-5	-5	-5	-28.837	-5	-5	-5

The available capital to be invested in node 2 is generally lower as in node 1, as there are no subsequent payments (withdrawal < 0) necessary to fulfill the arbitrary growth target of the investor of 5%.[663] As the payoff matrix for investments in node 2 has been analogous to node 1, the decision is analogous as well.

Table 5-37: Suggested portfolio strategy in node 2

No.	Back-flow	With-drawal	Avail-able	Risk-less	AAA	AA	A	BBB	BB	B	CCC
1	69.198	10.851	58.347	0	-5	-5	-5	-5	-5	-5	-28.346
2	69.26	10.927	58.333	0	-5	-5	-5	-5	-5	-5	-28.333
3	69.365	11.089	58.276	0	-5	-5	-5	-5	-5	-5	-28.276
4	69.535	11.374	58.161	0	-5	-5	-5	-5	-5	-28.161	-5
5	70.07	17.043	53.027	0	-5	-5	-5	-23.027	-5	-5	-5
6	70.217	12.521	57.696	0	-5	-5	-5	-27.697	-5	-5	-5
7	70.798	13.164	57.634	0	-5	-5	-5	-27.634	-5	-5	-5
8	70.91	13.499	57.411	0	-5	-5	-5	-5	-27.411	-5	-5
9	71.288	13.889	57.399	0	-5	-5	-5	-5	-27.399	-5	-5
10	72.058	14.824	57.234	0	-5	-5	-5	-27.234	-5	-5	-5
11	73.183	16.238	56.945	0	-5	-5	-5	-26.945	-5	-5	-5

The corresponding discount factor vectors and price vectors as outlined in section 5.2.3.2.1 are shown below. These core building blocks of the GOPS model are based and derived according to the **concept of the generalized NPV** as explained in section 5.4.2.3f.

Both for the first and second example, the decision trees with conditional node probabilities of 0.001 (0.005) and 0.999 (0.995), a singularity has occurred in node 3 both for the discount vector and the price vector, so that the entry has left empty in this cases ("NA"). As these nodes are in the final period of the planning horizon, the optimal decision has still been found. For longer horizons, however, no solution can be found any more with the current software.

It can be observed that the discount factors significantly differ from each other. In unfavorable nodes, the discount factors based on the generalized NPV concept[664] exceed one, what indicates that an investor would estimate the value of one currency unit of invested capital higher than in the period before.

[663] It may be interesting for an investor to choose lower growth rates in unpleasant scenarios.
[664] As explained in section 5.4.2.

Generally, payoffs in unpleasant nodes (e.g. node 4) are estimated higher than in more pleasant cases (e.g. in node 6).

Table 5-38: The discount factor vectors for the regarded examples

Node\No.	1	2	3	4	5	6	7	8	9	10	11
0	1	1	1	1	1	1	1	1	1	1	1
1	1.56	1.225	1.158	1.102	1.06	0.989	0.97	0.949	0.936	0.926	0.904
2	0.863	0.863	0.862	0.859	0.855	0.851	0.846	0.844	0.841	0.835	0.825
3	NA	NA	1.189	1.091	0.957	0.861	0.833	0.81	0.791	0.771	0.742
4	1.143	0.959	0.917	0.871	0.836	0.778	0.761	0.74	0.729	0.718	0.696
5	1.032	0.924	0.891	0.851	0.779	0.743	0.729	0.722	0.713	0.697	0.678
6	0.685	0.684	0.682	0.679	0.674	0.669	0.663	0.658	0.654	0.646	0.633

The price vectors, which represent the state prices of the investments (the discount factors multiplied with the cumulative node probabilities) are shown below. The price vector for node 1 has been set to one by convention.

Table 5-39: The price vectors for the regarded examples

Node\No.	1	2	3	4	5	6	7	8	9	10	11
0	1	1	1	1	1	1	1	1	1	1	1
1	0.002	0.006	0.012	0.022	0.053	0.099	0.146	0.19	0.234	0.308	0.452
2	0.862	0.858	0.853	0.842	0.812	0.766	0.719	0.675	0.631	0.557	0.412
3	NA	NA	0.000[665]	0.000[666]	0.002	0.009	0.019	0.032	0.049	0.086	0.185
4	0.001	0.005	0.009	0.017	0.04	0.07	0.097	0.118	0.137	0.159	0.174
5	0.001	0.005	0.009	0.017	0.037	0.067	0.093	0.116	0.134	0.155	0.169
6	0.683	0.677	0.668	0.652	0.608	0.542	0.479	0.421	0.368	0.288	0.158

In Figure 5-32, the overall result for case 6, an event tree with conditional node probabilities of 10% and 90%, respectively, is shown.

[665] Lower than $5*10^{-4}$.
[666] Lower than $5*10^{-4}$.

Figure 5-32: The overall result for case 6: Nominal capital cash flows

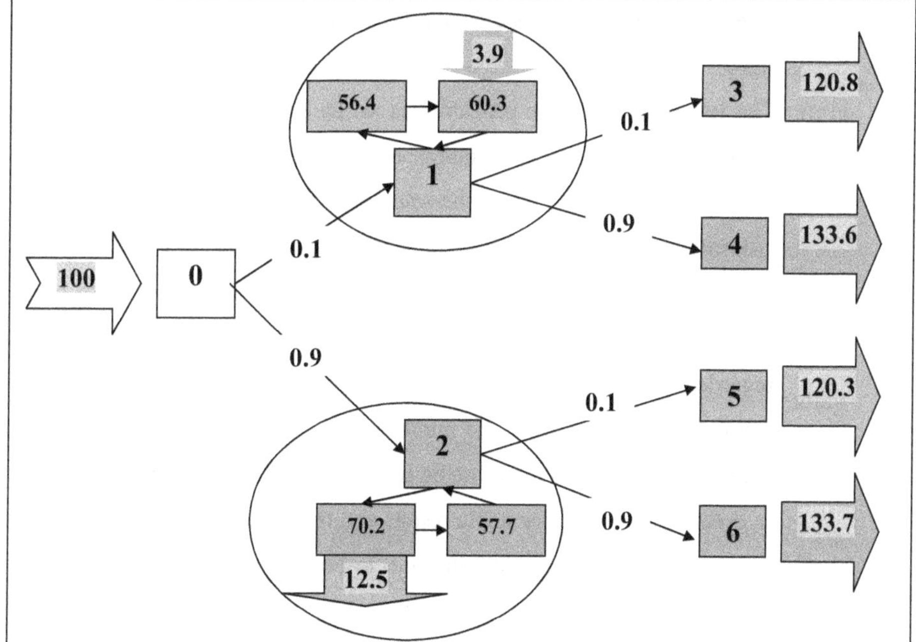

In node 0, 100 units are invested, resulting in a backflow of 56.4 (70.2) in node 1 (2). To this backflow, 3.9 units have to be added as a subsequent payment in node 1. In node 2, the situation is more pleasant, as 12.5 units may be withdrawn to still reach to target portfolio growth rate of 5%. Consequently, 60.3 (57.7) units are reinvested in node 1 (2) leading to the final portfolio value in node 3 to 6 as shown below. The indicated numbers refer to nominal (time-independent) values again. For the GOPS model's inherent representation, they would have to be multiplied with the corresponding discount factors and price vectors, respectively.

The following conclusions can be drawn from the calculated examples:

For consistency reasons, credit pricing has been chosen so that increasing risk leads to an increasing PV compared to other risk segments, i.e. the PV of the CCC segment is the highest.

Table 5-40: Payoff matrix in node 0 for example 6

Node	Riskless	AAA	AA	A	BBB	BB	B	CCC
0	-1	-1	-1	-1	-1	-1	-1	-1
1	1.0350	0.6724	0.6670	0.6529	0.6287	0.5848	0.4872	0.4898
2	1.0350	0.6732	0.6740	0.6760	0.6793	0.6867	0.7139	0.7379
3		0.6071	0.6041	0.5958	0.5808	0.5458	0.4394	0.3751
4		0.6076	0.6078	0.6081	0.6079	0.6016	0.5622	0.5071
5		0.6072	0.6043	0.5967	0.5835	0.5558	0.4763	0.4385
6		0.6076	0.6080	0.6090	0.6107	0.6127	0.6094	0.5928
PV (Avg)	0.9952	1.2090	1.2092	1.2096	1.2102	1.2107	1.2115	1.2118

Subsequently, the annual interest rate for the CCC segment (actually: 0.27025) will be decreased step by step ceteris paribus. Thereby, the PV corresponding to the backflow of the CCC segment as well as the segment's portfolio portion is supposed to decrease. For the original initial pricing, all A*-risk segments have optimal portfolio portions of 5%, the BBB-segment of 14.201%, the B-segment 10.799% and the BB as well the CCC-segment 30% (see case 6 in Table 5-35).

Decision Tree No.	**Funds**	**Risk-less**	**AAA**	**AA**	**A**	**BBB**	**BB**	**B**	**CCC**
6	100	0	-5	-5	-5	-14.201	-30	-10.799	-30

The original annual interest rate for the CCC segment of 0.27025 is gradually decreased by 2.5 bps (= 0.025%) as shown below. With the fifth decrease of the interest rate for the CCC segment, the optimal portfolio portion "jumps" to 12.535. The PV calculated based on the riskless interest rate has meanwhile already decreased below all the other risk segments. It thus seems that the high payoff to be expected for the CCC segment for the pleasant scenario is weighted very high, what can be regarded to be reasonable as the unpleasant scenario occurs only with a probability of 10%. Decreasing the interest rate by another 2.5 bps, the optimal portfolio portion decreases to the lower bound of 5%.

Table 5-41: Pricing and portfolio portion for the CCC segment in node 0

Component\No.	Original	1	2	3	4	5	6
Interest rate due (CCC)	0.27025	0.27	0.26975	0.2695	0.26925	0.269	0.26875
Present value (Avg.)	1.2118	1.2111	1.2104	1.2097	1.2089	1.2083	1.2075
Optimal portfolio portion (%)	30	30	30	30	30	12.535	5

The portfolio strategies for the six CCC-credit interest rates (example "Original" and No. 1 to 6) are shown below.

Table 5-42: Optimal portfolio strategy for altering credit pricing of the CCC segment in node 0

Pricing Example No.	Risk-less	AAA	AA	A	BBB	BB	B	CCC
0	0	-5	-5	-5	-14.201	-30	-10.799	-30
1	0	-5	-5	-5	-14.25	-30	-10.75	-30
2	0	-5	-5	-5	-14.149	-30	-10.851	-30
3	0	-5	-5	-5	-14.249	-30	-10.751	-30
4	0	-5	-5	-5	-14.267	-30	-10.733	-30
5	0	-5	-5	-5	-12.465	-30	-30	-12.535
6	0	-5	-5	-5	-20	-30	-30	-5

For pricing example 1 to 4, the portfolio weights remain approximately the same, with a tendency of a marginal shifting from the B to the BBB risk segment. For example 5, the portfolio portion of the CCC "jumps down" to 12.535, while the B segment becomes advantageous (30). The BBB and the CCC segment are relatively advantageous against each other for this pricing level. For a further decreased interest rate for the CCC segment in example 6, the BBB segment becomes superior to the CCC segment as well.

It has again been shown that the diversification property according to the generalized NPV criterion tends to "jumping" portfolio weights for gradually adapted interest rates.

5.4.3.4 Comparison with Markowitz-type approaches

5.4.3.4.1 Derivation of benchmark data

We will recall event tree example 6 (see section 5.4.3.2, conditional decision tree probabilities 0.1/0.9) and neglect the riskless investment opportunity and the low-risk segments AAA and AA. The upper bound for the investment opportunities has been set to 40 and the lower bound to 5 leaving all the input parameters unchanged. The investment decision in node 0 according to the portfolio sequence suggested by the GOPS model (based on a target growth rate of 5%) will serve as a benchmark for Markowitz-type optimization and is shown below.

Table 5-43: Optimal investment in node 0 according to the GOPS model

Node	Funds	A	BBB	BB	B	CCC
0	**-100**	-10	-5	-40	-5	-40
1	**55.11**	6.53	3.145	23.4	2.435	19.6
2	**70.725**	6.76	3.395	27.48	3.57	29.52
3	**47.9**	5.96	2.905	21.84	2.195	15
4	**56.29**	6.08	3.04	24.08	2.81	20.28
5	**51.03**	5.97	2.92	22.24	2.38	17.52
6	**60.43**	6.09	3.055	24.52	3.045	23.72

In the following, we will compare this extract result with (traditional) Markowitz-type portfolio optimization.

The present values of the cash flows following the GOPS investment strategy in node 0 according to Table 5-43 weighted with the cumulative node probabilities and exogenous discount factors are shown below. As Markowitz-type portfolio optimization requires exogenous discount factors, **the two alternative portfolio models may only be compared when the cash flows of a valid GOPS investment strategy are discounted at a pre-defined discount rate.** For this purpose, a discount rate equal to the hurdle rate for the economic capital of 16% has been used, resulting in discount factors of 1.16^{-1} for cash flows occurring in period 1 and 1.16^{-2} for cash flows occuring in period 2. The resulting PV of the portfolio value generated by the GOPS investment strategy of approximately

103.539 currency units will be used as the target discounted final performance value for Markowitz-type approaches as illustrated below.

Table 5-44: PV of the optimal GOPS investment strategy discounted with the hurdle rate

Node	Cum. prob-ability	Discount factor	A	BBB	BB	B	CCC	PV (A to CCC) per Node
0	1	1						
1	0.1	0.8621	6.53	3.145	23.4	2.435	19.6	4.751
2	0.9	0.8621	6.76	3.395	27.48	3.57	29.52	54.875
3	0.01	0.7432	5.96	2.905	21.84	2.195	15	0.356
4	0.09	0.7432	6.08	3.04	24.08	2.81	20.28	3.765
5	0.09	0.7432	5.97	2.92	22.24	2.38	17.52	3.413
6	0.81	0.7432	6.09	3.055	24.52	3.045	23.72	36.378
Total PV								**103.539**

5.4.3.4.2 Comparison with other approaches: Results according to Markowitz-type optimization

Given a PV portfolio performance target of 103.539 (based on an investment of 100 units), a two-period default process of the sample portfolio according to section 5.3 has been simulated, yielding a complete PV performance distribution[670] for each risk segment with the corresponding mean PV of the portfolio performance, its standard deviation, Value-at-Risk and Conditional Value-at-Risk (the latter two measures both for a confidence level of 99%) as shown below. The PV performance distribution is based on 5000 simulations.[671] With respect to the default process of the single credits, it has been assumed that they are inter-temporally independent in line with the assumptions made in section 5.3. Within a period, an asset correlation of 20% between all 500 obligors[672] in the portfolio has been assumed. As Markowitz-type portfolio optimization does not foresee withdrawals during the planning horizon, the

---

[670] Based on a discount rate of 16% as applied to the cash flows resulting from the GOPS model.

[671] A higher number of simulations may be used in order to narrow the confidence level of the statistical outcome according to an investor's preferences.

[672] 100 obligors per risk segment. This figure is arbitrary, but in line with the assumption in the previous chapters.

target of this exercise is to maximize the PV of performance, or, analogously, to minimize the risk for a given performance. For convenience, the PV of the performance has been standardized to one currency unit for the following analysis.

Table 5-45: Input data for Markowitz-type optimization based on a simulated credit portfolio

	A	BBB	BB	B	CCC
Avg Perf. PV	1.0325	1.0335	1.0339	1.0354	1.0384
StD	0.0681	0.0780	0.1115	0.1728	0.2015
VaR	0.2700	0.2731	0.3810	0.5628	0.5771
CVaR	0.4050	0.4106	0.5307	0.6823	0.7104

The portfolio optimization target can be formulated as follows, thereby minimizing the risk measure for the PV performance target:[673]

$$\begin{aligned} &\mathit{Min}\ \text{Risk - measure (Variance/VaR/CVaR)} \\ &\text{s.t.}\ \ \text{Perf. (PV)} \geq 1.03539 \\ &\qquad x_i \in [0.05; 0.4] \end{aligned}$$

The optimization has been carried out directly on the outcome of the simulations.[674] In Table 5-46, the target risk measure that has been minimized is highlighted together with both other risk measures and the optimal portfolio strategy. These values are derived from the simulated portfolio when the optimal portfolio weights are used. The results are - in general - similar to the outcomes of the GOPS model, with a more “balanced” strategy. The risk segments are thereby treated as one asset, as their risk-return characteristics are assumed to remain the same when the portfolio weights are altered. This treatment may only be justified if the risk segments are well-diversified. For a large credit portfolio, this requirement can be assumed to be fulfilled.[675]

673 See section 4.3.5.2 for a formal representation of the portfolio problem.

674 Thanks to Jürgen Bohrmann for providing the solution of portfolio optimization.

675 For the sample portfolio with 500 assets, the requirement of diversification may not be fulfilled. This portfolio serves rather as an illustrative example.

Table 5-46: Optimal portfolio portions according to Markowitz-type portfolio optimization

Perf. (PV)	StD	VaR	CVaR	A	BBB	BB	B	CCC
1.03539	**0.0832**	0.2339	0.2847	**0.05**	0.2266	0.237	0.1834	0.303
1.03539	0.0839	**0.2314**	0.2835	0.1217	0.1416	0.2292	0.1935	0.3140
1.03539	0.0835	0.2359	**0.2826**	0.0813	0.1957	0.2152	0.2056	0.3022

For the growth-oriented portfolio strategy according to the GOPS model, the risk parameters (StD, VaR and CVaR) are determined accordingly based on the simulated portfolio.

PV				Portfolio				
Perf.	StD	VaR	CVaR	A	BBB	BB	B	CCC
1.03539	0.0944	0.2777	0.3475	0.05	0.40	0.10	0.05	0.40

The efficient frontiers for the Markowitz-type optimization models without upper and lower bounds for the investment opportunities are shown below.[676]

The risk-minimal Markowitz-type portfolios are indicated using a vertical (green) circle. For the GOPS model, no efficient frontier can be derived, as the optimal strategy refers to the PV optimal portfolio with a fixed risk-return structure. The horizontal circles represent the GOPS portfolio's risk measures.

---

[676] From the MVP (Minimum Variance Portfolio), MVaRP (Min. Value-at-Risk P.) and MCVaR (Min. Cond. Value-at-Risk P.) to the right, highlighted with vertical circles.

Figure 5-33: The efficient frontier for Markowitz-type portfolio optimization vs. growth-oriented portfolio

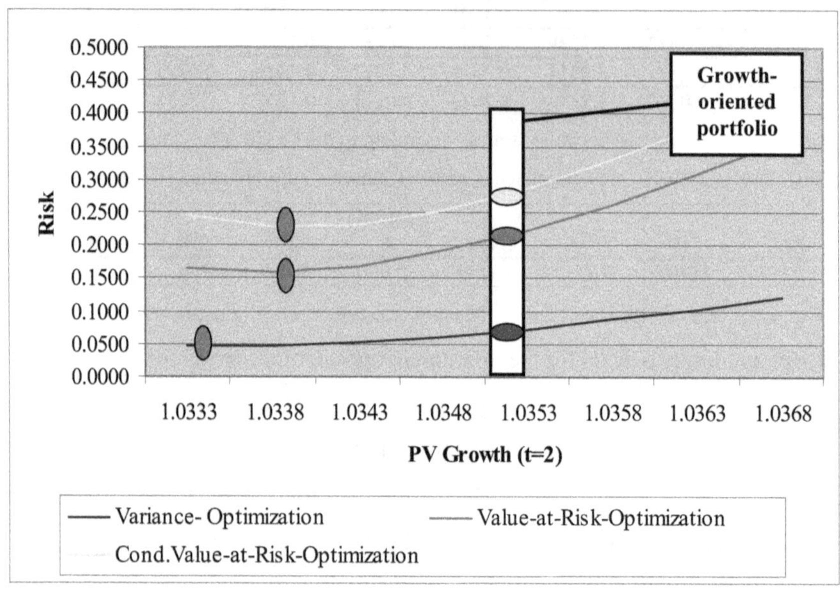

Due to relatively arbitray assumptions made to enable the comparison of the two model types (exogenous discount rate for the payoffs of the GOPS model, no considerations of withdrawals), an interpretation has to be done very carefully. In fact, the growth-oriented portfolio strategy according to the GOPS model does only provide valuable support based on its specific PV context to enable pre-defined growth targets. In so far, the two models are hardly comparable as their targets differ from each other.

5.4.3.4.3 Critical appraisal, evaluation and further considerations

Modeling credit risk is complex. The more aspects are used for modeling purpose, the higher become the inherent risks hidden in the model itself besides the quality risk of the input data, which are the basic source of modeling. It has been shown that credit portfolio management techniques rely on a variety of ex ante estimated input data both on a single borrower's level and on the portfolio level (often derived from ex post data). Collecting the input data, which are subsequently stored in a Data Warehouse, for example, may be related to errors both resulting from the data quality itself and the estimation methods used to provide derived measures, for example (e.g. the PD estimation methods). A sound credit risk measurement framework (as shown in Figure 2-2 up to level 3) is a fundamental prerequisite for the application of credit portfolio management techniques as presented in section 4 and 5.

A permanent improvement of the quality of the input data will improve the output of the decision model and has to be the first priority of a FI before relying on the results provided by active portfolio management tools.[677]

Yet, it has not been intended to assess the quality of the input data and thereby to give advice to a FI when the credit risk measurement framework is solid enough to apply active credit management techniques (like the GOPS model). By contrast, senior credit management should decide about the specific situation of the corresponding FI.

In terms of the comparison of the state-of-the-art portfolio optimization techniques and the GOPS model it can be summarized that Markowitz-type optimization and the GOPS model brought together in an optimization problem show similar general results, i.e. the same risk segments seem to be preferred. Treating risk segments as one asset requires that they are well-diversified, which may not always be fulfilled, especially for smaller credit portfolios. Additionally, other assumptions had to be made to compare the two distinct portfolio approaches, which are weakening the results. For a large homogeneous illiquid credit portfolio with an equal portfolio correlation structure among the borrowers the assumption of being well-diversified is usually fulfilled, so the disadvantage (or model risk) of moving away from the efficient frontier in terms of risk-return diversification can be regarded as relatively low. In this case, Markowitz-type portfolio optimization provides only a moderate additional

[677] See Löffler (2003), for example, for an analysis on the impact of estimation errors on credit portfolio risk and Deutsche Bundesbank (2003) for validation methodolodies for rating models.

benefit and PV considerations play the major role for the portfolio choice. For illiquid credit loans supposed to be held to maturity, the output of Markowitz-type portfolio optimization may be even misleading, as PV considerations are based on exogenous discount factors which are somehow arbitrary.

Generally perceived, the target of traditional portfolio optimization approaches and the GOPS model is entirely different, as the GOPS model is based on endogenous discount vectors assuming a risk-return optimized portfolio by the nature of the target portfolio while Markowitz-type portfolio approaches are directed at risk-return optimization. Once more, it has to be concluded that the two approaches are - in principle - not comparable.

5.4.4 Pros and cons of the approach

Given multi-period, timely shifted payoffs for different rating segments and illiquid credit portfolios asks for a sophisticated PV methodology to provide a credit decision. In the specific case, portfolio management with GOPS seems very promising, especially when the planning horizon is extended to 4 or 5 years, for example, so that PV considerations are even more important.

In Table 5-47 below, advantages and disadvantages of the GOPS approach that have been documented while discussing the model within this chapter are summarized.

Table 5-47: Pros and cons of the GOPS model

Pros	Cons
Credit portfolio selection is based on an intertemporal model	High effort required to make input data available
Endogenous handling of discount factors	Approach is relatively difficult for senior management
Diversification according to NPV (Generalized NPV criterion)	Accurateness of the input and output of multi-period models is lower than for single period approaches (i.e. interest rate level prediction)
Most credit loan portfolios are adequate candidates for the application of the model	The present value of the principal is not considered, as it does not affect net income[678]
The model may be combined with a Markowitz-type model leading to a two-fold solution of the portfolio problem (first setting thresholds for the investment opportunities, then choose the appropriate GOPS portfolio thereof)	Arbitrary discount vectors are used after the planning horizon

5.4.5 Solution for the framework of credit portfolio selection

Based on the findings in section 5.4.3.4.2 a two (or three) - stage optimization frame for credit portfolios seems to be appropriate in order to ensure that the solution is valid.

In the first step, a portfolio is optimized according to a state-of-the art credit portfolio optimization method (e.g. Theiler 2004, see section 4.3.8.1[679]) and upper and lower bounds for the investment opportunities for the GOPS model are chosen. Alternatively, the upper and lower bounds may be defined strategically, for example, if the portfolio is too large for optimization purposes.

In the second stage, credit portfolio selection according to Hellwig (2002a/2004) provides an appropriate multi-period portfolio strategy.

Finally, the diversification structure of the portfolio provided by the portfolio selection model may be backtested.[680]

678 See section 5.4.1.4.

679 Or section 5.4.3.4.

680 For example via Monte Carlo simulation.

Table 5-48: A three-stage credit portfolio optimization frame

Step	Task
1	Set upper and lower bounds for the investment opportunities, e.g. by referring to a risk-return oriented portfolio structure derived based on optimization or to strategically motivated bounds
2	Application of the GOPS model
3	Evaluation of the diversification strategy

5.4.6 Future extensions

The proposed framework is promising. Extensions with respect to the application of the model are necessary, if an investor seeks for portfolio growth rates exceeeding at least a certain rate, for example.[681]

Another preference of an investor may be to include a "hedging" constraint, i.e. to ensure that subsequent payments become impossible (Selinka 2005). It has to be noticed, however, that thereby the number of feasible portfolio strategies is significantly reduced.[682] Instead of referring to growth rates as a decision criterion, an investor may be interested in removing a certain, pre-defined withdrawal sequence from the portfolio, what is a similar task to the considered portfolio problem.[683]

Focusing on exposure-related cash flows allows a more straightforward (common) view on the output data. However, additional constraints for the capital used for lending purposes are thereby necessary which influence the solution of the GOPS model and have to be mathematically proven.

From a technical viewpoint, the current software has to be improved, if large event trees are seeked to be handled properly.

[681] Hellwig (1997b) discussed a portfolio value process where the intertemporal value path is attained "at least", instead of an exact matching of the desired and the efficient growth path.

[682] Further information can be found in Selinka (2005).

[683] Further information can be found in Selinka (2005).

6 Conclusion

The ultimate aim of this work has been to provide a framework to proactively manage traditional credit portfolios. The deployment of the GOPS model to the field of credit risk enables to approach credit portfolio management from an entirely new perspective and is supposed to be an appropriate methodology for the portfolio problem imposed.

As credit loans are illiquid multi-period investments supposed to be held to maturity, a multi-period model to manage such portfolios is required. Most of the state-of-the-art credit portfolio models currently used in practice are, however, directed at single periods and lack of an integrated intertemporal view on the portfolio problem. An investor may then optimize the portfolio recursively for single-period horizons or refer to arbitrary discount factors, for example, what is, however, not a sophisticated way of handling the problem.

Using growth-oriented portfolio selection (GOPS) to actively manage credit portfolios allows generating discount factors endogenously based on a coherent technique called the generalized NPV method. Thereby the discount vectors represent opportunity costs of the investment opportunities included in the portfolio. If a non-included investment would offer a yield exceeding the opportunity costs of the current portfolio a preferably high portion of this investment would be included into the portfolio, until the investment's relative contribution for the portfolio value is zero or its upper bound in terms of the portfolio weight has been reached. Similar to the diversification constraint to find risk-return optimal portfolios the generalized NPV method enables diversification with respect to the portfolio's PV. It has been found that the criterion is very sensitive to changes of the input parameters, which therefore have to be determined preferably accurately.

Given the additional preference of an investor within a multi-period horizon to move away from the target of growth maximization and thereby to withdraw the generated growth exceeding a pre-defined growth target optimally with respect to the portfolio's present value, the GOPS model is an appropriate choice. A major advantage of decision making based on growth targets is that utility theory, which has significant burdens within a multi-period context, may be circumvented. A financial institution using the GOPS model, which is committed to various interest groups, will thereby orient its business policy on a sequence of common growth targets of these interest groups over the planning horizon. Given the growth sequence for the decision tree, the portfolio principle of the GOPS is then to generate a PV maximizing withdrawal sequence in line with the desired growth sequence. The withdrawal sequence comprises withdrawals during the planning horizon and the final portfolio value in the terminal node as potential withdrawals dependent on the specific path in the decision tree. In each non-terminal node, the growth generated by a portfolio is compared with the target growth rate and thereby leads to withdrawals (if the generated growth exceeds the target growth) or subsequent payments (if the generated growth is less than the target growth).

Given large illiquid credit portfolios it is hardly feasible to model portfolio decision based on every single obligor. As it is common within the sphere of credit risk to assign internal risk grades (based on rating and scoring models) to each obligor it is convenient to use homogeneous subportfolios (rating segments) as investment opportunities.[684]

As the credit risk result of a profit center within a corporation (the result dependent on the stochastic default process) should be oriented on the shareholder value concept, it is likely to be measured relative to the capital portion invested, subsumed as risk-adjusted performance measurement. The specific performance measure to be used is return on risk-adjusted capital

[684] Additionally, portfolio management based on single obligors would hardly be possible based on the decision tree principle.

(RORAC). Thereby, the credit risk result becomes comparable with the other business lines of the bank.

Given a decision variable that incorporates the ex-ante risk and return to be expected for credits of each rating segment based on a pre-defined interest rate due, the portfolio selection problem is to optimize the capital allocation of a credit profit center (in terms of maximizing the present value of the capital withdrawal sequence) by optimally assigning the strategically defined capital of a credit profit center to the eligible risk segments.

It has to be carefully noticed that the underlying payoff matrix has been assumed to be stationary, i.e. independent of the portfolio composition. The GOPS model in the current shape applied to credit portfolios is thereby only an appropriate choice for large portfolios which may be regarded as well-diversified. Especially for (SME and/or retail) loan portfolios of universal banks or captive leasing and finance companies this constraint seems to be fulfilled as they are of a substantial size and usually more or less homogeneous (with respect to exposure, maturity and correlation). In this case, applying a Markowitz-type portfolio optimization model will rather have a subordinated additional benefit. By contrast, portfolio selection based on the GOPS model will provide an intertemporally efficient portfolio strategy while moving marginally away from the efficient frontier from the perspective of risk-return optimization.

Especially for smaller credit portfolios, however, it has to be ensured that the selected portfolio strategy is in line with the risk-return preferences of an investor. Therefore, a two- (or three-) stage approach (as suggested in section 5.4.5) has been suggested. First, an investor will apply a portfolio optimization model to find risk-return optimal portfolio portions or refers to strategic upper and lower bounds. Growth-oriented portfolio selection will then deliver an appropriate strategy in line with the time preferences of an investor. The portfolio's resulting risk-return structure may subsequently be backtested.

Additionally, it has to be taken into account that the result of GOPS depends on the available opportunities in contrast to traditional Markowitz-type optimization. Hence, a portfolio decision on a subordinated company level, i.e. a profit center, may change if other business lines are included into the decision process, i.e. the GOPS model. As it has been assumed that the capital portion assigned to each profit center of a FI will be pre-determined and that each profit center will concentrate on its specific business only, portfolio decision is regarded to be valid. As a result of the opportunity to (re)invest the available funds during the whole planning horizon, cash flows will arise after the planning horizon.

Active portfolio management techniques are based on numerous input parameters that have to be thoroughly chosen. Only a credit risk measurement framework that provides sound and backtested data (provided by a management information system, e.g. a data warehouse) for active portfolio management purposes will lead to promising portfolio strategies. Given data or even modeling failures (when estimating the input data) will yield to a misleading credit strategy of a FI and causes high risks.

In general, every tool used for strategic purposes will only be as strong as its developer's concept. Therefore, a solution suggested by a model should not be blindly followed, but may serve as an orientation.

Increasing complexity of an already very sophisticated portfolio methodology as the GOPS model will be related to confusion or even failures. In terms of the credit risk measurement framework used for input data derivation it has therefore been the main goal to refer to a solution that is as simple as possible, with the least assumptions for the relatively difficult problem imposed, in Einstein's words summarized as:

"The grand aim of all sciences is to cover the greatest number of empirical facts by logical deduction from the smallest number of hypotheses or axioms."[685]

[685] This quotation has been taken from Caouette et al. (1998), p.102.

7 Bibliography

Acharya, V. V., Bharath, S. T. and A. Srinivasan, 2003, Understanding the Recovery Rates of Defaulted Securities, Working Paper available at http://papers.ssrn.com/sol3/papers.cfm?abstract_id=442901.

Albrecht, P., 2001, Portfolioselektion mit Shortfallmaßen; *Mannheimer Manuskripte zu Risikotheorie, Portfolio Management und Versicherungswirtschaft No. 133*, Mannheim, September.

Alexander, G. J. and A. M. Baptista, 2000, Economic implications of using a mean-VaR model for portfolio selection: A comparison with mean-variance analysis, *Working Paper, University of Minnesota, Carlson Scholl of Management, Department of Finance*, May.

Allais, M. and O. Hagen, 1979, *Expected utility hypothesis and the Allais paradox*, Reidel Publishing Company.

Allen, L., and A. Saunders, 2003, A survey of cyclical effects in credit risk measurement models, BIS Working Papers No. 126, http://www.bis.org/publ/work126.pdf, January.

Altman, E. I., 1968, Financial ratios, Discriminant analysis and the prediction of corporate bankruptcy. *Journal of Finance 23(4)*, pp. 589-611.

Altman, E. I, 2002, Managing credit risk: The challenge for the new millennium, *Finance Conference, Taipei*, May 25.

Altman, E.I., R. Haldeman, and P. Narayanan, 1977, ZETA Analysis: A New model to identify bankruptcy risk of corporations, *Journal of Banking and Finance*, pp. 29-55.

Altman, E. I., and V. Kishore, 1996, Almost everything you wanted to know about recoveries on defaulted bonds, *Financial Analysts Journal 52*, pp. 57-64.

Altman, E. I. and P. Narayanan, 1997, An international survey of business failure classification models, *Financial markets, institutions & instruments* 6(2), pp. 1-57, May.

Altman, E. I, A. Resti and A. Sironi, 2001, Analyzing and explaining default recovery rates. *Report submitted to the International Swaps and Derivatives Association,* www.isda.org/c_and_a/pdf/Analyzing_Recovery_rates_010702.pdf, Rev. April 2004. December.

Altman, E. I, A. Resti and A. Sironi, 2005, Recovery Risk: The next challenge in credit risk management, Risk Books, June.

Altman, E. I. and A. Saunders, 1998, Credit risk management: Developments over the last 20 years, *Journal of Banking and Finance 21*, pp. 1721-1742.

Altman, E. I. and A. Saunders, 2001, An analysis and critique of the BIS proposal on capital adequacy and ratings. *Journal of Banking and Finance 25 (1)*, pp. 25-46.

Amemiya, T., 1981, Qualitative response models: A survey. *Journal of Economic Literature 19*, pp. 1483-1536.

Andersen, J. V., and D. Sornette, 1999, Have your cake and eat it too: increasing returns while lowering large risks!; *Working Paper, University of California, Los Angeles*. January.

Andersson, F., and S. Uryasev, 1999, Credit risk optimization with conditional value-at-risk criterion. *Research Report 99-9*. ISE Dept., University of Florida, August.

Andersson, F., H. Mausser, D. Rosen, and S. Uryasev, 2001, Credit risk optimization with conditional value-at-risk criterion, *Mathematical Programming Series B89*, pp. 273-91.

Araten, M., Jacobs, M. Jr., and P. Varshney, 2004, Measuring LGD on commercial Loans: An 18-Year internal Study, The RMA Journal 4, pp. 96-103.

Arrow, K. J., 1961, *Social choice and individual values*, New York, John Wiley & Sons.

Arrow, K. J., 1963, *Social choice and individual values*, 2nd ed., New Haven/London.

Arrow, K. J., 1971, *Essays in the theory of risk-bearing*, Amsterdam.

Arvanitis, A., J. K. Gregory, and R. Martin, 1998, A credit risk toolbox, *Risk 11(12)*, pp. 50-60, 1998.

Arvanitis, A., and J. K. Gregory, 2001, *Credit: The complete guide to pricing, hedging and risk management*, London.

Artzner, P., and F. Delbaen, 1992, Credit risk and prepayment option. in: *Astin Bulletin 22*, pp. 82-96.

Artzner, P., F. Delbaen, J.-M. Eber, and D. Heath, 1999, Coherent measures of risk, *Mathematical Finance 9/3*, pp. 203-228.

Asarnow, E., and D. Edwards, 1995, Measuring loss and defaulted bank loans, A 24-year-Study, *Journal of Commercial Lending 77*, p. 11-23.

Aziz, A., D. Emanuel, and G. Lawson, 1988, Bankruptcy prediction: An investigation of cash flow based models. *Journal of Management Studies 25*, pp. 35-51.

Aziz, A., and G. Lawson, 1989, Cash flow reporting and financial distress models: Testing of hypothesis. *Financial Management 18 (1)*, pp. 55-63.

Bachem, A., W. Hochstättler, B. Steckemetz, and A. Vollmer, 1996, Computational experience with general equilibrium problems, *Comput. Optim. Appl. 6*, pp. 213-25.

Back, B., T. Laitinen, and K. Sere, 1994, Neural networks and bankruptcy prediction. *Paper presented at the 17th Annual Congress of the European Accounting Association, Venice, Italy*, April, p. 116 ff.

Back, B., T. Laitinen, K. Sere, and M. van Wezel, 1996, Choosing bankruptcy predictors using discriminant analysis, logit analysis, and genetic algorithms, Turku Center for Computer Science, *Technical Report No. 40,* September.

Bamberg, G., and A. G. Coenenberg, 1974, *Betriebswirtschaftliche Entscheidungslehre*, 1st ed., München.

Bamberg, G., and A. G. Coenenberg, 2000, *Betriebswirtschaftliche Entscheidungslehre*, 10th ed., München.

Bankers Trust New York Corporation, 1995, *RAROC and risk management: Quantifying the risk of business*, New York, Bankers Trust New York Corporation.

Bartram, S. M., 2000, Corporate risk management as a lever for shareholder value creation, *Financial Markets, Institutions & Instruments 9(5)*, pp. 279-324.

Basak, S., and A. Shapiro, 2001, *A model of credit risk, optimal policies and asset prices*, September.

Basel Committee on Banking Supervision, 1988, *International convergence of capital measurement and capital standards*, July.

Basel Committee on Banking Supervision, 1999, *Credit risk modeling: Current practices and applications – Executive summary*, Basel Committee on Banking Supervision, April.

Basel Committee on Banking Supervision, 2000, *Range of practice in banks' Internal Ratings Systems, A discussion paper by the Basel Committee on Banking Supervision*, January.

Basel Committee on Banking Supervision, 2001a, *The New Basel Capital Accord, Consultative Document,* Basel.

Basel Committee on Banking Supervision, 2001b, *The internal ratings-based approach*, Consultative Document, January.

Basel Committee on Banking Supervision, 2002, *Quantitative Impact Study 3*, Technical Guidance, October.

Basel Committee on Banking Supervision, 2003, *Third consultative paper*, April.

Basel Committee on Banking Supervision, 2004, *International convergence of capital measurement and capital standards: A revised framework*, June 26.

Baud, N., A. Frachot, P. Igigable, P. Martineu, and T. Roncalli, 2000, *An analysis framework for bank capital allocation*, Groupe de Recherche Opérationelle, Crédit Lyonnais, February.

Baviera, R., M. Pasquini, M. Serva and A. Vulpiani, 1998, Optimal strategies for prudent investors, *International Journal of Theoretical and Applied Finance 1*, pp. 483-486.

Bawa, V., 1975, Optimal rules for ordering uncertain prospects. *Journal of Financial Economics 2*, pp. 95-121.

Bawa, V., 1976, Admissible portfolios for all individuals. *Journal of Finance 31*, pp. 1169-1183.

Bawa, V., 1978, Safety first, stochastic dominance, and optimal portfolio choice. *Journal of Financial and Quantitative Analysis 13*, pp. 255-271.

Bawa, V. and E. Lindenberg, 1977, Capital market equilibrium in a mean-lower partial moment framework. *Journal of Financial Economics 5*, pp. 189-200.

Beaver, W., 1966, Financial ratios as predictors of failure. *Journal of Accounting Research*, Supplement on Empirical Research in Accounting, pp. 71-111.

Bennet, P., 1984, Applying portfolio theory to global bank lending. *Journal of Banking and Finance 8*, pp. 153-169.

Benteler, C., 2003, The determination of intertemporal growth-oriented portfolio value management strategies, *PhD thesis, University of Ulm.*

Bernoulli, D., 1738, *Versuch einer neuen Theorie der Wertbestimmung von Glücksfällen.*

Bernstein, P. L., 1996, *Against the Gods: The remarkable story of risk*, John Wiley & Sons.

Bertsimas, D., G. Lauprete, and A. Samarov, 2000, Shortfall as a risk measure: Properties, optimization and applications, *Working Paper, Sloan School of Management and Operations Research, Massachusetts Institute of Technology, Cambridge, MA*, October.

Bessis, J., 2001, *Risk management in banking*, 2nd edition, John Wiley & Sons.

Bierman, H., and J. Hass, 1975, An analytical model of bond risk differentials. *Journal of Financial and Quantitative Analysis 10*, pp. 757-773.

Bitz, M., 2000, *Finanzdienstleistungen*, Oldenbourg Verlag, München et al.

Blache, R., and C. Bluhm, 2001, Die Steuerung von Kreditrisiken mit Hilfe der RAROC- Methodik, in: *Rolfes/Schierenbeck, Ausfallrisiken: Quantifizierung, Bepreisung und Steuerung*, Frankfurt, pp. 207-260.

Black, F. and M. Scholes, 1973, The pricing of options and corporate liabilities, *Journal of Political Economy 81*, pp. 637-59.

Bluhm, C., L. Overbeck, and C. Wagner, 2003, *An introduction to credit risk modeling*, Chapman & Hall.

Board of Governors of the Federal Reserve System, 1999, Assessing capital adequacy in relation to risk at large banking organizations and others with complex risk profiles, *Supervisory Letter SR99-18*, July 1.

Boos, D., Schmid, O., and J. Koller, 2004, Dynamic Asset Allocation with Regime Shifts, *Working Paper Series in Finance. Paper No. 7, University of St. Gallen*, April.

Boyadjian, H. J. and J. F. Warren, 1987, *Risks: Reading corporate signals*, John Wiley & Sons, New York.

Brandts, J., and G. Charness, 2000, *Do market conditions affect preferences? Evidence from experimental markets with excess supply and excess* *demand*, www.econ.upf.es/docs/papers/downloads/491.pdf. Rev. June 2005.

Breimann, L., 1961, Optimal gambling systems for favorable games. *4th Berkeley Symposium on Mathematical Statistics and Probability. University of California Press, Berkley,* CA.

Breuer, W., M. Gürtler, and F. Schuhmacher, 1999, *Portfoliomanagement: Theoretische Grundlagen und praktische Anwendungen*, Wiesbaden.

Brinson, G. P., L. R. Hood, and G. L. Beebower, 1986, Determinants of portfolio performance, *Financial Analysts Journal 51 (1)*, May/June, pp. 40-48.

Bröker, F., 2000, *Quantifizierung von Kreditportfoliorisiken*, Eine Untersuchung zu Modellalternativen und Anwendungsfeldern, Frankfurt.

Bröker, F., Lehrbass, F., 2001, Kreditportfoliomodelle in der Praxis, in: *Rolfes/Schierenbeck, Handbuch Bank-Controlling, 2nd ed.*, Basel et al., pp.773-788.

Bühler, W., 1998, *Risikocontrolling in Industrieunternehmen*, Buchbeitrag in Controlling und Rechnungslegung für Unternehmen im internationalen Wandel.

Burmester, C., C. Hille, and H.-P. Deutsch, 1999, Risikoadjustierte Kapitalallokation, in: *Eller, R., Gruber, W., Reif, M., Handbuch, Bankenaufsicht und Interne Risikosteuerungsmodelle*, Stuttgart 1999, pp. 389-418.

Büschgen, H., 1998, *Bankbetriebslehre: Bankgeschäfte und Bankmanagement*, 5th ed., Wiesbaden.

Caouette, J. B., E. I. Altman, and V. Narayanan, 1998, *Managing credit risk: The next great financial challenge*, New York.

Carey, M., 1998, Credit risk in private debt portfolios, *Journal of Finance 53 (4)*, pp. 1363-87.

Carey, M., 2002, Dimensions of credit risk and their relationship to economic capital requirements, in: *Mishkin, F., 2002, Prudential Supervision: What works and what doesn't*, Chicago.

Carling, K., Jacobson, T., Lindé, J., and K. Roszbach, 2002, Capital charges under Basel II: Corporate Credit Risk Modelling and the Macro Economy, *Sveriges Riksbank Working Paper Series, No. 142*, September.

Carty, L. V., and D. Lieberman, 1996, *Defaulted bank loan recoveries*, Moody's Investor Services, Global Credit Research, November.

Casey, C., and N. Bartczak, 1985, Using operating cash flow to predict financial distress: Some extensions. *Journal of Accounting Research 23 (1)*, pp. 384-401.

Casserley, D., 1991, *Facing up to the risks*, Harper Business.

Coenenberg, A. G., 1997, *Jahresabschluss und Jahresabschlussanalyse,* 16th ed., Landsberg/Lech.

Coles, S., 2001, An Introduction to Statistical Modeling of Extreme Values, Springer Verlag, December.

Condorcet, M. J. de, 1765, *Essai sur le calcul intégral.*

Copeland, T., and J. Weston, 1988, *Financial theory and corporate policy*, 3rd ed., New York, Addison-Wesley.

Credit Suisse Financial Products, 1997, *CreditRisk+ – A credit risk management framework;* www.csfb.com/creditrisk/. Rev. May 2005.

Crosbie, P. , 1999, *Modeling default risk*, KMV corporation.

Crouhy, M., D. Galai, and R. Mark, 2000, A comparative analysis of current credit risk models, *Journal of Banking and Finance 24*, pp. 59-117.

Cumming, C. M. and B. J. Hirtle, 2001, The challenges of risk management in diversified financial companies, *FRBNY Economic Policy Review*, pp. 1-17.

Das, S. (ed.), 1998, *Credit derivatives: Trading and management of credit and default risk*, John Wiley, Singapore.

Deakin, E., 1972, A Discriminant Analysis of predictors of business failure, *Journal of Accounting Research, Spring*, pp. 167-179, 1972.

Denault, M., 1999, Coherent allocation of risk capital, in: *Journal of Risk 4(1)*, Fall.

De Roover, R., 1963, *The rise and decline of the Medici bank, 1397-1497*. Cambridge, MA.

Derviz, A., and N. Kadlčáková, 2001, Methodological Problems of quantitative credit risk modeling in the Czech Economy, *Working Paper No. 39*, http://defaultrisk.com/pp_model_29.htm. Rev. March 2004.

Deutsche Bank, 2003, *Geschäftsbericht (Annual report)*.

Deutsche Bank, 2004, *Geschäftsbericht (Annual report)*.

Deutsche Bundesbank, 2003, Approaches to the validation of internal rating systems, *Monthly report*, September.

Dev, S., 1974, Ratio analysis and the prediction of company failure; in: *Ebits, Credits, Finance and Profits, ed. H. C. Edy and B. S. Yamey*, Sweet and Maxwell, London, pp. 61-74.

Dimitras, A. I., R. Slowinski, R. Susmaga, and C. Zopounidis, 1999, Business failure prediction using rough sets. *European Journal of Operational Research 114*, pp. 263-280.

Douglas, W. D., A. E. Kocagil, and R. M. Stein, 2004, *Moody's KMV EDF™ RiskCalc™ V3.1 Model*, April.

Dresel, T., 2002, *Allokation von Risikokapital in Banken*, Uhlenbruch Verlag, Bad Soden/Ts.

Duffee, G., 1999, Estimation of price of default risk. *Review of Financial Studies 12(1)*, Spring, pp., 197-226.

Duffie, D., 1992, *Dynamic asset pricing theory*, Princeton University Press.

Duffie, D., and N. Gârleanu, 1999, Risk and valuation of collateralized debt obligations, *Working paper, Graduate School of Business, Stanford University.*

Duffie, D., and M. Huang, 1995, Swap rates and credit quality: Supplementary results, *Working Paper, Stanford University*, August.

Duffie, D., and D. Lando, 1999, Term structures of credit spreads with incomplete accounting information, *Working Paper*, August.

Duffie, D., M. Schroder, and C. Skiadas, 1996, Recursive valuation of defaultable securities and the timing of resolution of uncertainty. *The annals of Applied Probability* 6(4). pp. 1075-1090.

Duffie, D., and K. Singleton, 1997, An econometric model of the term structure of interest-rate swap yields. *Journal of Finance 52(4)*, September, pp. 1287-1321.

Duffie, D., and K. Singleton, 1998, Simulating correlated defaults, *Working paper, Graduate School of Business, Stanford University.*

Duffie, D., and K. Singleton, 1999, Modeling term structure of defaultable bonds, *Review of Financial Studies 12*, pp. 687-720.

Dumas, B., 1978, The theory of the trading firms revisited. *Journal of Finance 33(3)*, pp. 1019-30.

Dunemann, O., 2001, Kreditportfoliomodelle, in: *Rolfes/Schierenbeck, Ausfallrisiken: Quantifizierung, Bepreisung und Steuerung,* Frankfurt, pp.185-206.

Edgeworth, F. Y., 1888, The mathematical theory of banking. *Journal of the Royal Statistical Society 51(1)*, March, pp. 113-127.

Elton, E. J., and M. J. Gruber, 1975, *Finance as a dynamic process*, Prentice-Hall, Englewood Cliffs, New Jersey.

Elton, E. J., Gruber, M. J., 1995, *Modern Portfolio Theory and Investment Analysis*, 5th ed., John Wiley & Sons, New York et al.

Embrechts, P., C. Klüppelberg, and T. Mikosch, 1997, *Modeling extremal events for insurance and finance*, Berlin, Springer Verlag.

Embrechts, P., S. Resnick, and G. Samorodnitsky, 1998, Living on the edge, *Risk*, January, p. 96-100.

Fama, E., and K. R. French, 1993, Common risk factors in the returns on stocks and bonds, *Journal of Financial Economics 33*, pp. 3-56.

Federal Reserve System Task Force on Internal Credit Risk Models, 1998, *Credit risk models at major U.S. banking institutions: Current state of the art and implications for assessment on capital adequacy*, Executive Summary, May.

Finger, C. C., 1998, *Sticks and stones*, http://riskmetrics.com/research/working, Rev. January 2004. October.

Finger, C. C., 1999a, *Conditional approaches for CreditMetrics' portfolio distributions*, CreditMetrics Monitor, April.

Finger, C. C., 1999b, *Towards a better estimation of wrong-way credit exposure,* http://riskmetrics.com/research/working. Rev. December 2003. September.

Fisher, I., 1906, *The nature of capital and income*, Macmillan, New York NY.

Fishburn, P. C., 1977, Mean-risk analysis with risk associated with below-target returns. *American Economic Review 67*, pp. 116-126.

Fitzpatrick, 1932, A comparison of ratios of successful industrial enterprises with those of failed firms, *Certified Public Accountant*, pp. 598-605, 656-662, 727-731.

Flesaker, B., L. Houghston, L. Schreiber, and L. Sprung, 1994, Taking all the credit, in: *Risk* 7(9), September, pp. 105-108.

Franks, J., de Servigny, A. and S. Davydenko, 2004, A comparative analysis of the recovery process and recovery rates for private companies in the U.K., France and Germany, S&P's Risk Solutions Report, http://www3.imperial.ac.uk/pls/portallive/docs/1/568016.pdf, May.

Frees, E. W. and E. A. Valdez, 1997, Understanding relationships using copulas. *Paper presented at the 32nd Actuarial Research Conference, held August 6-8, at the University of Calgary*, Alberta, Canada.

Frey, R., and A. J. McNeil, 2001, *Modeling dependent defaults*, Draft, March.

Frey, R., A. J. McNeil, and M. Nyfeler, 2001, Copulas and credit models, *Risk 14,* pp.111-114.

Frydman, H., E. I. Altman, and D. L. Kao, 1985, Introducing recursive partitioning for financial classification. *Journal of Finance 1*, pp. 269-291.

Frye, J., 2000a, Collateral damage; *Risk 13(4)*, April.

Frye, J., 2000b, Depressing recoveries; *Risk 13(11)*, November.

Fu, Y. et al., 2004, Moody's Revisits Its Assumptions Regarding Corporate Default (and Asset) Correlations for CDOs, Moody's rating methodology, 30 November.

Gabler, 1988, *Wirtschafts-Lexikon in 6 Bd.*, 12th ed., Wiesbaden.

Gaivoronski, A., and G. Pflug, 1998, Finding optimal portfolios with constraints on Value-at-Risk, Department of Industrial Economics and Technology Management, Norwegian University of Science and Technology, Trondheim, Norway; *Working Paper, Department of Statistics, University of Vienna, Vienna.*

Galai, D. (ed.), 1999, *Risk management and regulation in banking*, Proceeding of the Int. Conference on Risk Management and Regulation in Banking (1997), Kluwer Academic Publishers, Boston.

Gay, G. D., and J. Nam, 1998, The underinvestment problem and corporate derivatives use. *Financial Management 27(4)*, pp. 53-69.

Goldfarb, R., 2004, Setting risk tolerance levels. Enterprise Risk Management Symposium April 26-27, 2004, Session CS 2B, Chicago, IL, Ernst & Young, www.casact.org/ coneduc/erm/2004/handouts/goldfarb2b.pdf. Rev. May 2004.

Gordy, M. B., 2000a, A comparative anatomy of credit risk models. *Journal of Banking and Finance 24*, January.

Gordy, M. B., 2000b, A risk-factor model foundation for ratings-based bank capital rules, *Mimeo, Board of Governors of the Federal Reserve System, Washington D.C.*

Gouriéroux, C., J. P. Laurent, and O. Scaillet, 2000, Sensitivity analysis of Value-at-Risk, *Université catholique de Louvain, Institut de Recherches Economiques et Sociales (IRES)*, revised Jan.

Graham, J. R., and D. A. Rogers, 2002, Do firms hedge in response to tax incentives. *Journal of Finance 54(6)*, pp. 2241-2262.

Gramlich, D., T. B. Peylo, and M. Staaden, 1999, Effiziente Portfeuilles im μ/VaR-Raum; *Die Bank 6/1999*, pp. 422-425.

Greene, H. W., 1993, *Economic Analysis*, Prentice -Hall, Englewood Cliffs, N.J.

Gregory, A. B., B. Russell, and G. V. Henderson, 1991, A brief review of catastrophy theory and a test in a corporate failure context. *Financial Review 26 (2)*, pp. 127-155.

Grinold, R. C., and R. N. Kahn, 1999, *Active portfolio management*, McGraw-Hill, New York.

Grootveld, H., and W. Hallerbach, 2001, Upgrading value-at-risk from diagnostic metric to decision variable: A wise thing to do?, *Erasmus University Rotterdam and Tinbergen Institute Graduate School of Economics*, 2nd Version March 2, 2001, London.

Grossman, S., and J. Stiglitz, 1980, On the impossibility of informationally effienct markets. *The American economic review*, pp. 6-8 and 29, June.

Grunert, J., and M. Weber, 2005, Recovery Rates of Bank Loans: Empirical Evidence for Germany, Working Paper, http://www.defaultrisk.com/pp_recov_68.htm, March.

Gupton, G. M., C. C. Finger, and M. Bhatia, 1997, *CreditMetrics - Technical Document*, Morgan Guaranty Trust Co.

Hadar, J., and W. R. Russell, 1969, Rules for ordering uncertain prospects, *American Economic Review 59*, pp.25-34.

Hakansson, N., 1971, Capital growth and the mean-variance approach to portfolio selection, *Journal of Finance and Quantitative Analysis VI*, pp. 517-557.

Hale, R., 1983, *Credit Analysis: A complete guide*, John Wiley & Sons, New York.

Hallerbach, W. G., 2001, Capital allocation, portfolio enhancement and performance measurement: A unified approach, *Working Paper for EUOR WGFM 2001, Harlem/NL and QMF&BS 2001, Sydney/AUS*, November.

Hallerbach, W. G., and J. Spronk, 1997, A multi-dimensional framework for portfolio management, in: *M.H. Karwan, J. Spronk & J. Wallenius (eds), Essays in Decision Making, A Volume in Honour of Stanley Zionts*, Springer-Verlag, Berlin, pp. 275-293.

Hamerle, A., 2000, Statistische Methoden im Kreditgeschäft der Banken, in: *Johanning, L. Rudolph, B., Handbuch Risikomanagement*, pp. 459-490.

Hamerle, A., M. Knapp, B. Ott, and G. Schacht, 1998, Aktives Kreditportfolio-Management (AKM) - ein neuer Ansatz zur Prognose und Sensitivitätsanalyse von Branchenrisiken, *Die Bank*, pp. 428-430, July.

Hamerle, A., T. Liebig, and D. Rösch, 2002, Credit risk factor modeling and the Basel II IRB approach, *mimeo, Deutsche Bundesbank*, 2002.

Handelsblatt, 2003, Mit Kreditderivaten können Risiken übertragen werden: Die Bank für internationalen Zahlungsausgleich zeigt Gefahren auf, September 5.

Hanoch, G., and H. Levy, 1969, The efficiency analysis of choices involving risk, *Review of Economic Studies 36*, pp. 335-346.

Harlow, W. V., 1991, Asset allocation in a downside risk framework. *Financial Analysts Journal*, Sept-Oct, pp. 28-40.

Hartmann, W., 2002, Aktuelle Trends im Kreditrisikomanagement der Banken. *Presentation held at the conference of the association "Credit Management e.V." on the topic „Credit Management without limits"*, 16 April.

Hartmann-Wendels, T., A. Pfingsten, and M. Weber, 1999, *Bankbetriebslehre*, Springer Verlag, Berlin.

Heim, U., and C. Balica, 2001, Zentrale Aspekte des Risikomodellierung, in: *Rolfes/Schierenbeck, Ausfallrisiken: Quantifizierung, Bepreisung und Steuerung*, Frankfurt, pp. 207-260.

Hellwig, K., 1987, *Bewertung von Ressourcen*, Physica Verlag Heidelberg.

Hellwig, K., 1993, Renditeorientierte Portfolioplanung, *Zeitschrift für Betriebswirtschaft 63*, pp. 89-98.

Hellwig, K., 1996a, Portfolio selection under the condition of value preservation, *Review of Quantitative Finance and Accounting 7*, pp. 299-305.

Hellwig, K., 1996b, Intertemporal choice reexamined, *Jahrbücher für Nationalökonomie und Statistik 216/2*, pp. 153-163.

Hellwig, K., 1997a, Was leistet die Kapitalwertmethode?, *Die Betriebswirtschaft 57*, pp. 31-37.

Hellwig, K., 1997b, Sustaining value, *Working Paper, University of Ulm.*

Hellwig, K., 1998, Creating value, *International Review of Economics and Finance 7*, pp. 141-147.

Hellwig, K., 1999, Der ökonomische Gewinn bei unvollkommenem Kapitalmarkt, in: *Betriebswirtschaftliche Forschung und Praxis*, Heft 4/1999, Berlin.

Hellwig, K., 2001, Wachstumsorientierte Wertpapieranalyse, *Zeitschrift für Betriebswirtschaft 71/3*, pp. 271-279.

Hellwig, K., 2002a, Value management ; *Quantitative Finance 2*, pp. 133-138.

Hellwig, K., 2002b, Growth and utility maximization: *European Investment Review 1*, pp. 51-56.

Hellwig, K., 2004, Portfolio selection subject to growth objectives, *Journal of Economic Dynamics and Control 28*, pp. 2119-2128.

Hellwig, K., G. Speckbacher, and P. Wentges, 2000, Utility maximization under capital growth constraints, *Journal of Mathematical Economics 33*, pp. 1-22.

Hickman, A. and H. U. Koyluoglu, 1998, A generalized framework for credit risk models; *Working Paper*; an abridged version appeared as "Reconcilable Differences"; *Risk* 11(10), October.

Hickman, A., and J. Wollman, 2002, An evolutionary leap into credit portfolio risk modeling, *ERisk*, New York.

Hillier, F. S., and G. J. Lieberman, 1973, *Introduction to Operations Research*, San Francisco, Holden-Day.

Hinterhuber, H. H., 1996, *Strategische Unternehmensführung, Vol. 1: Strategisches Denken*, 6th ed., Berlin/New York, 1996 *und Vol. 2: Strategisches Handeln*, 6th ed., Berlin/New York.

Hirtle, B., M. Levonian, M. Saidenberg, S. Walter, S. and D. Wright, 2001, Using credit risk models for regulatory capital: Issues and options, *Federal Reserve Bank of New York Economic Policy Review*, March.

Hogan, W., and J. Warren, 1974, Towards the development of an equilibrium capital market model based on semivariance. *Journal of Financial and Quantitative Analysis 9*, pp. 1-12.

Homer, S. and R. Sylla, 1996, *A history of interest rates*, Rutgers University Press.

Huang, C. F., and R. H. Litzenberger, 1988, *Foundations of financial economics*. North-Holland.

Hu, H. T. C., 1996, Behind the corporate hedge: Information and the limits of "Shareholder Wealth Maximization". *Journal of Applied Corporate Finance 9(3)*, pp. 39-51.

Huge, B., and D. Lando, 1999, Swap pricing with two-sided default risk in a rating-based model, *Working Paper, University of Copenhagen*, June.

Huisman, R., K. G. Koedijk, and R. A. J. Pownall, 1999, Asset allocation in a value-at-risk framework, *Erasmus University Rotterdam, Faculty of Business Administration, Financial Management, Working Paper, Rotterdam*, April.

Huschens, S., 2001, Abhängigkeitsmodellierung für Kreditausfälle, *Paper presented at* a *workshop in Bamberg*, November.

Ingersoll, J., 1987, *Theory of financial decision making*, Rowman & Littlefield Publishers, Savage.

James, C., 1996, RAROC based capital budgeting and performance evaluation: A case study of bank capital allocation, *Working Paper, Wharton School, Financial Institutions Center, 96-40.*

Jarrow, R. A., D. Lando, and S. M. Turnbull, 1997, A Markov model for the term structure of credit risk spreads. *Review of Financial Studies 10*, pp. 480-523.

Jarrow, R. A., and S. M. Turnbull, 1995, Pricing derivatives on financial securities subject to credit risk. *Journal of Finance 50(1)*, pp. 53-58, March.

Jarrow, R. A., and S. M. Turnbull, 1998, The intersection of market and credit risk, September 1998, *Working Paper presented at the conference "Credit risk modeling and regulatory implications" on September 21/22*, 1999, London.

Jensen, M. C., and W. H. Meckling, 1976, Theory of the firm: Managerial behavior, Agency costs and ownership structure. *Journal of Financial Economics* 3(4), pp. 305-360.

Johnson, T., and R. W. Melicher, 1994, Predicting corporate bankruptcy and financial distress: Information value added by multinomial logit models. *Journal of Economics and Business* 46 (4), pp. 269-286.

Jones, D., 1999, Emerging problems with the Accord: Regulatory capital arbitrage and related issues, *Journal of Banking and Finance 24*, pp. 35-58.

Jorion, P., 1997, *Value-at-Risk: the new benchmark for controlling Market Risk.* Irwin, Chicago.

Jorion, P., 2001, *Financial Risk Manager Handbook 2001-2002*, John Wiley & Sons, New York.

JP Morgan & Co. Incorp., 1997, *Credit Metrics*; www.jpmorgan.com. Rev. March 2005.

Kahnemann, D., P. Slovik, and A. Tversky, 1982, *Judgement under uncertainty: Heuristics and biasis*, Cambridge University Press.

Karacadag, C., and M. W. Taylor, 2000, The new capital adequacy framework: Institutional constraints and incentive structures, *IMF WP 93*, pp. 1-39.

Kataoka, S., 1963, A stochastic programming model, *Econometrica 31/1-2*, Jan-April, pp.181-196.

Kealhofer, S., S. Kwok, and W. Weng, 1998, *Uses and abuses of bond default rates*, March 1998, KMV Corporation, San Francisco.

Kehrbaum, J., and R. Zagst, 1998, Portfolio optimization under limited Value-at-Risk, *Risklab Research Paper No. 9802.*

Kendall, M., 1953, The analysis of economic time series, Part I: prices. *Journal of the Royal Statistics Society 96*, pp. 11-25, London.

Keynes, J. M., 1921, *A Treatise on probability*, Macmillan, London/Basingstoke.

Kiesel, R., W. Perraudin, and A. Taylor, 1999, The structure of credit risk. *Birkbeck College, Department of Economics, London, Mimeo.*

Klose, S., 1996, Asset-Management von Länderrisiken, *Baseler Bankenstudien, Hrgs.: H. Schierenbeck*, Bern/Stuttgart/Wien.

Klüppelberg, C., and R. Korn, 1999, Optimale Portfolios mit beschränktem Value-at-Risk; *Solutions 3*, pp. 23-32.

KMV Corporation, 1996, *PortfolioManager description, usage and specification, Version 4.0*, San Francisco.

Knight, F. H., 1921, *Risk, Uncertainty and Profit*. Houghton Mifflin, Boston.

Köllhofer, D., 1975, Die Bankostenrechnung, in: *Bank-Enzyklopädie (Unterrichts- und Nachschlagewerk der Bankakademie)*, Vol. 3, Wiesbaden, pp. 197-262.

Korn, R., 1997, Value preserving portfolio strategies in continuous-time models, *Mathematical Methods of Operations Research 45*.

Korn, R., 1998, Value preserving portfolio strategies and the minimal martingale measure, *Mathematical Methods of Operations Research 47*, pp. 169-179.

Korn, R., 2000, Value preserving portfolio strategies and a general framework for local approaches to optimal portfolios, *Mathematical Finance 10*, pp. 227-241.

Korn, R., and M. Schäl, 1999, On value preserving and growth optimal portfolios, *Mathematical Methods of Operations Research 50*, pp. 189-218.

KPMG, 2001, Neue Anforderung an die Eigenmittelunterlegung bankgeschäftlicher Risiken - Das zweite Basler Konsultationspapier (Basel II). *Presentation of Klaus Ott held at the chair for Business Administration, Prof. Dr. Jürgen Steiner. June.*

Krall, M., 2000, Internes Rating als Wettbewerbsvorteil – Voraussetzungen, Potentiale, Strategien, *Tagungsunterlage, Internes und Externes Rating im Kreditgeschäft in der Zukunft*, Überreuter, Wiesbaden, Mimeo.

Koyluoglu, H. U., and A. Hickman, 1998, Reconcilable differences, *Risk 11(10)*, pp.56-62, October.

Kuhn, H. W., 1986, How to compute economic equilibria by pivotal methods; *Studies in Mathematical Economics 25*, ed. S. Reiter, Mathematical Association of America.

Kupiec, P.H., 1999, Risk capital and VaR, *Journal of Derivatives*, Winter, pp. 41-52.

Kuritzkes, A., 1999, Kreditportfoliomanagement: Neues Geschäftsmodell im Firmenkundengeschäft, *Die Bank*, pp. 60-64.

Kuritzkes, A., S. Harris, and. G. Strothe, 2000, Redesign des Kreditprozesses, *Die Bank*, pp. 42-47.

Lakonishok, J., A. Shleifer, R. W. Vishny, 1994, Contrarien investment, extrapolation and risk, *Journal of Finance 49*, pp. 1541-1578.

Lando, D., 1994, Three essays on contingent claims pricing. *Ph.D. Thesis, Cornell University.*

Lando, D., 1997, *Modelling bonds and derivatives with default risk*, Mathematics of Derivative Securities, M. Demster and S. Plieska, eds. Cambridge University Press.

Lando, D., 1998, On Cox processes and credit risky securities, *Working Paper, University of Copenhagen*, 2nd edition (1st title: On Cox Processes and Credit Risky Modeling), March.

Lando, D., 1999, Some elements of rating-based credit risk modeling, *Working Paper, University of Copenhagen*, February.

Latané, H., 1959, Criteria for choice among risky ventures. *Journal of Political Economy 67*, pp. 144-155.

Leland, H., 1994, Corporate debt value, Bond covenants and optimal capital structure, *Journal of Finance 49(4)*, pp.1213-1252, September.

Lennox, C., 1999, Identifying failing companies: A re-evaluation of the logit, probit and DA approaches; *Journal of Economics and Business 51*, pp. 347-364.

Levy, H., 1992, Stochastic dominance and expected utility: Survey and analysis, *Management Science 38(4)*, pp. 555-593.

Levy, H., 1998, *Stochastic dominance*, Kluwer Academic Publishers, Norwell, MA.

Li, D. X., 1999, The valuation of basket credit derivatives, *CreditMetrics Monitor*, pp. 34-50, April.

Li, D. X., 2000, On default correlation: A copula function approach, *Journal of Fixed Income 6,* pp. 43-54.

Libby, R, 1975, Accounting ratios and the prediction of failure: some behavioral evidence, *Journal of Accounting Research*, pp. 150-161.

Lintner, J., 1965, The valuation of risky assets and the selection of risky investments in stock portfolios and capital budgets, *Review of Economics and Statistics 47*, p.13ff.

Lintner, J., 1972, Equilibrium in a Random Walk and lognormal securities market, *Discussion Paper 235, Harvard Institute of Economic Research, Harvard University*, Cambridge, MA.

Löffler, G., 2003, The Effects of Estimation Error on Measures of Portfolio Credit Risk, Journal of Banking and Finance, Vol. 27, No. 8, pp. 1427-1453, August.

Loistl, O., 1992, *Computergestütztes Wertpapiermanagement*, 4th ed., Munich, Vienna, Oldenbourg, 1992.

Lopez, J. A., and M. R. Saidenberg, 1999, *Credit risk models*, p.2 ff.

Lucas, D. J., 1995, Default correlation and credit analysis, *Journal of Fixed Income*, New York.

Lucas, A., and P. Klaassen, 1998, Extreme returns, downside risk, and optimal asset allocation. *Journal of Portfolio Management* 25 (Fall), pp. 71-79.

Macharzing, 1995, *Unternehmensführung: Das internationale Managementwissen*, 2nd ed., p. 242ff.

MacMinn, R. D., 2002, Value and risk, in: *Journal of Banking and Finance* 26(2/3), pp. 297-301.

Maddala, G.S., 1983, *Limited dependent and qualitative variables in econometrics*. Cambridge University Press, Cambridge.

Magill, M., and M. Qunizii, 1996, *Theory of incomplete markets*, MIT Press, Vol.1.

Manz, F., 1998, *Prozessorientiertes Kreditmanagement. Ein integriertes Konzept zur Risiko/Rendite- Optimierung von Einzelkredit und Portfolio*, Haupt, Bern u.a.

Markowitz, H. M., 1952, Portfolio selection, *Journal of Finance 7*, pp. 77-91.

Markowitz, H. M., 1959, *Portfolio selection: Efficient diversification of investments*, John Wiley, New York/NY.

Markowitz, H. M., 1970, *Portfolio selection: Efficient diversification of investments*, John Wiley & Sons.

Markowitz, H. M., and A. F. Perold, 1981, Portfolio analysis with scenarios and factors, *Journal of Finance 36*, pp.871-877.

Markowitz, H. M., 1991, *Portfolio selection*, Blackwell.

Mar Molinero, C., and M. Ezzamel, 1991, Multidimensional scaling applied to corporate failure. *Omega 19 (4)*, pp. 259-274.

Martin, D., 1977, Early warnings of bank failure: A logit regression approach. *Journal of Banking and Finance 1*, pp. 249-276.

Martin, B., and C. S. Cinca, 1993, Self organizing neural networks for the analysis and representation of data: some financial cases, *Neural Computing & Applications* 1(2), December, pp. 193-206, Ed. Springer Verlag.

Matten, C., 2000, *Managing bank capital*, John Wiley & Sons, New York, October.

McKinsey & Co., 2001, *Credit Portfolio View 2.0*, Technische Dokumentation, June.

McNeil, A. J., 1998, Estimating the tails of loss severity distributions using extreme value theory, *Astin Bulletin 27*, p.117-37.

Meier, C., 1999, *Credit Analyzer- Technische Dokumentation*, www.rcg.ch. Rev. May 2004.

Menger, K., 1934, Das Unsicherheitsmoment in der Wertlehre. Betrachtungen in Anschluss an das sogenannte Petersburger Spiel, *Zeitschrift für Nationalökonomie 5*, pp.459-85.

Merton, R., 1969, Lifetime portfolio selection under uncertainty: the continuous-time
case. *Review of Econom. Statistics* 51, pp. 247-257.

Merton, R., 1971, Optimum consumption and portfolio rules in a continuous time.
model. Journal of Economic Theory, 3(4), pp. 373–413.

Merton, R., 1974, On the pricing of corporate debt: The risk structure of interest rates, *Journal of Finance 29*, pp. 449-70.

Merwin, C., 1942, Financing small corporations in five manufacturing industries, 1926-36. *National Bureau of Economic Research.*

Merz, A., 2001, Kreditderivate als innovatives Instrument zur Steuerung von Kreditrisiken, in: *Kreditrisikomanagement im Bankenwesen*/ 2. Norddeutscher Bankentag, 5. Kreditwirtschaftliches Kontaktforum. Bankseminar Lüneburg. Ulf G. Baxmann (Hrsg.). 1st ed. – Frankfurt am Main, Bankakademie-Verlag, pp. 105-136.

Meyer, C., 1999, *Value-at-Risk für Kreditinstitute: Erfassung des aggregierten Marktrisikopotentials*, Wiesbaden, 1999.

Mingo, J. J., 2000, Policy implications of the Federal Reserve study of credit risk models at major U.S. banking institutions, *Journal of Banking and Finance 29*, pp. 449-470.

Modigliani, F., and M. Miller, 1958, The cost of capital, corporation finance and the theory of investment, *American Economic Review 48*, pp. 261-297, 1958.

Mossin, J., 1968, Optimal Multiperiod Portfolio Policies, Journal of Business, Vol. 41, pp. 215-229

Mossman, C. E., G. G. Bell, L. M. Swartz, and H. Turtle, 1998, An empirical comparison of bankruptcy models. *The Financial Review 33*, pp. 35-54.

Moody's Investor Services, 1997, *Rating migration and credit quality correlation, 1920-1996*, Global Credit research, www.moodyskmv.com/research/whitepaper/ 25097.pdf, Rev. April 2004. July.

Moody's Investor Services, 2000a, *Validation methodologies for default risk models*, www.moodyskmv.com/research/whitepaper/p51p56.pdf. Rev. May 2004. May.

Moody's Investor Services, 2000b, *RiskCalc™ For Private Companies: Moody's Default Model*, http://defaultrisk.com/pp_score_06.htm. Rev. Jan. 2005. Author: Eric Falkenstein, May.

Morgan, J. B., 1989, Managing a loan portfolio like an equity fund. *Bankers Magazine January/February*, p. 28-35.

Morgan, J. B., and T. L. Gollinger, 1993, Calculation of an efficient frontier for a commercial loan portfolio. *Journal of Portfolio Management* (winter).

Morisson, D. F., 1976, *Multivariate statistical methods*, 2nd ed., Bew York, NY, McGraw-Hill.

Mossin, J., 1966, Equilibrium in a capital asset market, *Econometria 34*, pp. 768-783.

Mueller, P. H., 1995, Cycles and the credit culture, *Journal of Commercial Lending*, September, pp. 41-46.

Nantell, T., and B. Price, 1979, An analytical comparison of variance and semivariance capital market theories. *Journal of Financial and Quantitative Analysis 14(2)*, pp. 221-242.

Naslund, W., 1962, A model of multi-period investment under uncertainty. *Management Science*, January, pp. 184-200.

Nelson, R., 1999, *An introduction to copulas*, Springer, New York.

Nickell, P., W. Perraudin, and S. Varotto, 1998, Stability of Rating Transitions. *Bank of England: Conference on Credit Risk Modeling and Regulatory Implications, London*, September 21-22.

Oda, N., and J. Muranga, 1997, A new framework for measuring the credit risk of a portfolio: The ExVaR Model, in: *Monetary and Econometric Studies*, pp. 27-62, www.boj.or.jp/en/ronbun/ronbun_.htm. Rev. June 2004. December.

Öhler, A., and M. Unser, 2001, *Finanzwirtschaftliches Risikomanagement*, Berlin, Heidelberg.

Öhler, A., and M. Voit, 1999, Informationsökonomische Aspekte des Bond-Ratings, *Bankarchiv 47*, pp. 968-974.

Ohlson, J. S., 1980, Financial ratios and the probabilistic prediction of bankruptcy, *Journal of Accounting Research.*

Ong, M., 1999, *Internal credit risk models: Capital allocation and performance measurement*, Risk Books, London.

Ott, B., 2001, *Interne Kreditrisikomodelle*, Uhlenbruch, Bad Soden/Ts.

Palmquist, J., S. Uryasev, and P. Krokhmal, 1999, Portfolio optimization with conditional Value-at-Risk objective and constraints, *Research Report #99-14, Center for Applied Optimization, University of Florida, Gainesville FA*, available at www.gloriamundi.org. Rev. May 2004.

Palisades Corporation, 1996, *@Risk – Advance risk analysis for spreadsheets*, Newfield, NY.

Pareto, V., 1897, *The new theories of economics*, JPE.

Patrick, G., S. Bernegger, and M. B. Ruegg, 1999, The use of risk-adjusted capital is to support business decision making, in: *Casualty Actuarial Society* (Eds.), Casualty Actuarial Forum, Spring 1999 Edition, Baltimore.

Paul, S., 2001, *Risikoorientierte Gesamtbanksteuerung*, Bern et al.

Paul, S., S. Stein, and H. J. Thieme, 2004, Deflation, Kreditklemme, Bankenkrise – Erwacht Deutschlands Finanzindustrie 2004 aus ihrem (medialen) Albtraum?. In: *ifo Schnelldienst*, 57. Jg., pp. 14-24, January.

Perridon, L., and M. Steiner, 1991, *Finanzwirtschaft der Unternehmung*, 6th ed., München, Vahlen.

Perold, A. F., 1995, The payment system and derivative instruments, in: *The global Financial System*, Boston, Harvard Business School Press.

Pfennig, M., 1998, *Optimale Steuerung des Währungsrisikos mit derivativen Instrumenten*, Wiesbaden.

Pfingsten, A., and G. Schröck, 2000, Bedeutung und Methodik von Krediteinstufungsmodellen im Bankwesen, in: *Öhler, A., Kreditrisikomanagement. Portfoliomodelle und Derivate*, Schäffer-Poeschel, Stuttgart, pp. 1-23.

Phelan, K., and C. Alexander, 1999, Different strokes. *Risk*, October.

Porter, M. E., 1998a, Competitive strategy: Techniques for analysing industries and competitors, *Free Press*, June.

Porter, M. E., 1998b, Competitive Advantage: Creating and sustaining superior performance, *Free Press*, June.

Pratt, J. W., 1964, Risk aversion in the small and in the large, *Econometrica 32*, pp. 122- 136.

Press, W. H., S. A. Teukolsky, W. T. Vetterling, and B. P. Flannery, 1992, *Numerical receipts in C*; Second Edition, Cambridge, Cambridge University Press.

Puelz, A. V., 1999, *Value-at-Risk based optimization*, www.quantnotes.com/publications/var.htm. Rev. April 2004.

Punjabi, S., 1998, Many happy returns, *Risk,* June, pp. 71-76.

Pyle, D., 1997, Bank risk management: Theory, Research program in finance, *Working paper RPF-272*, www.haas.berkeley.edu/finance/WP/rpf272.pdf. Rev. May 2004.

Rady, S., 2003, Lecture notes for micro economics, University of Munich, www.vwl.uni-muenchen.de/ls_rady/lehre/mikro/mikro_1.pdf. Rev. May 2004.

Ramser, J., and L. Foster, 1931, A demonstration of ratio analysis. *Bulletin No. 40, Urbana, Ill. University of Illinois, Bureau of Business Research.*

Rappaport, A., 1986, *Shareholder value - The new standard for business performance*, New York.

Rau-Bredow, H., 2002, Kreditrisikomodelle und Diversifikation, *Zeitschrift für Bankrecht und Bankwirtschaft, 14. Jg., 2002/*1, pp. 9-16.

Reichling, P., 2003, Investition und Finanzierung, *Lecture notes, University of Magdeburg.*

Rockafeller, R. T., 1970, Convex analysis, *Princeton Mathematics* 28.

Rockafeller, R. T., and S. Uryasev, 2000, Optimization of conditional Value-at-Risk, *Journal of Risk 2(3)*, pp. 21-41.

Rockafellar, R. T., and S. Uryasev, 2002, Conditional Value-at-Risk for general loss distributions. *Journal of Banking and Finance 26(7)*, pp. 1443-1471.

Roland Berger, 2004, Strategien für deutsche Banken im Kontext des Jahres 2004, *Presentation held at the Friedrich-Alexander-Universität Erlangen-Nürnberg, T. Eichelmann, Nürnberg, 21.01.2004,* www.bankundboerse.wiso.unierlangen.de/ _Download/Bankman_Vortrag_Berger_WS0304.pdf. Rev. June 2004.

Rolfes, B., and H. Schierenbeck, 2001, *Ausfallrisiken: Quantifizierung, Bepreisung und Steuerung*, Frankfurt.

Roll, R., 1973, Evidence of the 'growth-optimum' model. *Journal of Finance 18*, pp. 551-556.

Rom, B. M., and K. W. Ferguson, 1994, Post-modern portfolio theory comes of Age, *The Journal of Investing*, Fall, pp. 11-17.

Ross, S., 1976, The arbitrage theory of capital asset; *Journal of Economic Theory 3/1976*, pp. 341-360.

Rothschild, M., and J. E. Stiglitz, 1970, Increasing risk I: A definition, *Journal of Economic Theory 2*, pp. 225-243.

Roy, A. D., 1952, Safety first and the holding of assets, *Econometrica 20/3*, July, pp. 431-449.

Rubinstein, M., 2002, Markowitz's "Portfolio selection": A fifty-year retrospective. *Journal of Finance*, June 2002, pp. 1041-1045.

Rudolph, B., 1993, Risikomanagement in Kreditinstituten-Betriebswirtschaftliche Konzepte und Lösungen, in: *Zeitschrift Interne Revision*, 28. Jg., No. 3, pp. 117-134.

SAS Institute Inc., 1999, *Logistic regression using the SAS system: Theory and applications.* SAS Institute Inc., Cary, US.

Samuelson, P., 1969, Lifetime Portfolio Selection by Dynamic Stochastic Programming, REStat.

Saunders, A., 1999, *Credit risk measurement: New approaches to Value-at-Risk and other paradigms*, John Wiley & Sons.

Scaillet, O., 2000, *Nonparametric estimation and sensitivity analysis of Expected Shortfall,* see Internet reference.

Scheuenstuhl, G., and R. Zagst, 1996, Optimal optioned portfolios with limited downside risk; in: *Albrecht, P., Aktuarielle Ansätze für Finanz-Risiken,* Vol. II, VVW Karlsruhe, pp. 1497-1517.

Scheuenstuhl, G., and R. Zagst, 2000, Portfoliosteuerung bei beschränktem Verlustrisiko, *in: Johanning/Rudolph, Handbuch Risikomanagement,* Vol. 2, Bad Soden, pp. 941-970.

Schierenbeck, H., 1983, Strategische Finanzplanung in Kreditinstituten, in: *Strategische Bankplanung, H.-J. Krümmel and B. Rudolph*, Frankfurt, pp. 224-239.

Schierenbeck, H., 1985, *Ertragsorientiertes Bankmanagement. Ein Lehrbuch zum Controlling in Kreditinstituten.*Wiesbaden XIII,464 pages.

Schierenbeck, H., 1997, *Ertragsorientiertes Risikomanagement*, Vol. 1, 5th ed., Wiesbaden.

Schierenbeck, H., 1999, *Ertragsorientiertes Risikomanagement*, Vol. 1, 6th ed., Wiesbaden.

Schierenbeck, H., 2003a, *Ertragsorientiertes Risikomanagement*, Vol. 1, 8th ed., Wiesbaden.

Schierenbeck, H., 2003b, *Ertragsorientiertes Risikomanagement*, Vol. 2, 8th ed., Wiesbaden.

Schlag, C., 2003, *Basiskurs Finanzen*, Lecture notes, www.finance.uni-frankfurt.de/index.php?men=3&case=lehre; Rev. June 2004.

Schmalenbach, E., 1947, *Pretiale Wirtschaftslenkung Vol. 1: Die optimale Geltungszahl*, Bremen- Horn.

Schmidbauer, R., 1999, Vergleich der wertorientierten Steuerungskonzepte im Hinblick auf die Anwendbarkeit im Konzern-Controlling, *FB 1999*, pp. 365-377.

Schmidt-von Rhein, A., 1996, *Die Moderne Portfoliotheorie im praktischen Wertpapiermanagement*, Bad Soden/Ts.

Schmidt-von Rhein, A., 2000, Portfoliooptimierung mit der Ausfallvarianz, in: *Klehberg/Rehkugler (Hrsg.): Handbuch Portfoliomanagement*, Bad Soden/Ts., pp. 591-625.

Schmieder, C., 2002, Validation and optimization of an empirical rating-based model, *Unpublished Master's thesis, University of Karlsruhe.*

Schneeweiss, H., 1967, *Entscheidungskriterium bei Risiko*, Springer Verlag.

Schönbucher, P. J., 2001, Factor models for portfolio credit risk, *Preprint, University of Bonn*, Germany.

Schuermann, T., 2004, What do we know about Loss Given Default, Wharton School of Pennsylvania, http://fic.wharton.upenn.edu/fic/papers/04/0401.pdf, Working Paper 04-01.

Schuhmacher, F., 1998, Portfolioselektion unter Berücksichtigung des geometrischen Mittels, *WiSt Heft 6*, June, pp. 315-318.

Schweizer, S., 2001, Portfolioorientierte Kreditrisikosteuerung, *Speech at the University GH Paderborn*, July 6.

Selinka, M., 2005, *Ein Ansatz zur wertorientierten Portfolioplanung mit nichtnegativen Konsumentnahmen.*

Sen, A., 1997, Maximization and the Act of Choice; *Econometrica*, 65(4), pp. 745-779.

Sharpe, W. F., 1963, A simplified model for portfolio analysis, in: *Management Science*, Vol. 9, p. 277-293.

Sharpe, W., 1964, Capital asset prices: A theory of market equilibrium under conditions of risk. *Journal of Finance* 19 (3), pp. 425-442.

Sharpe, W., 1994, The sharpe ratio. *Journal of Portfolio Management* (fall), pp. 49-58.

Shen, H., 2001, Cumulative losses, capital reserves, and loss limits, *Journal of Risk Finance* , Winter, pp. 6-17.

Shor, N.Z., 1985, *Minimization methods for non-differentiable functions*, Springer Verlag.

Shumway, T., 2001, Forecasting bankruptcy more accurately: A simple hazard model. *Journal of Business 74(1)*, pp. 101-124.

Simon, H., 1982, *Models of bounded rationality*, Vol.2, The MIT Press.

Sinn, H.-W., 1989, *Economic decisions under uncertainty*, Physica Verlag.

Sklar, A., 1959, Fonction de repartition a n dimension et leur marges, *Publication of the Institute for Statistics at the University of Paris 8*, pp.229-231.

Smith, C. W. jr., 1995, Corporate risk management: Theory and practice, *Journal of Derivatives 2(4)*, pp. 21-30.

Sobehart, J. R., S. C. Keenan, and R. Stein, 2000, *Benchmarking quantitative default risk models: A validation methodology*, Risk Management Services Rating Methodology, March.

Speckbacher, G., 1998, Maintaining capital intact and WARP, *Mathematical Sciences 36*, pp. 145-155.

Spremann, K., 1996, *Wirtschaft, Investition und Finanzierung* (5th ed.), München, Wien.

Spremann, K., 2002, *Finanzanalyze und Unternehmensbewertung*, München et al.

Standard & Poor's, 1999, *Ratings performance 1998*, Stability and Transition, 1999.

Standard & Poor's, 2002, *Corporate ratings criteria: "Ratings methodology"*, Standard & Poor's, June 20.

Stewart, G. B., 1991, *The quest for value*, New York.

Stiglitz, J. E., 1974, On the irrelevance of corporate financial policy. *American Economic Review 64(6)*, pp. 851-866.

Stiglitz, J., and A. Weiss, 1981, Credit rationing in markets with imperfect information, *American Economic Review*, June, pp. 393-410.

Strothe, G., 1999, Credit Risk Mitigation. Techniken der Exposure – Reduzierung, *Tagungsunterlage, Kreditrisiko und Bankenaufsicht, Deutsche Bundesbank, Frankfurt, Mimeo.*

Stroughton, N. M., and J. Zechner, 1999a, Optimal capital allocation using RAROC and EVA^{TM}, *Working Paper, University of California Irvine*, March.

Stroughton, N. M., and J. Zechner, 1999b, The dynamics of capital allocation, *Working Paper, University of California Irvine*, March.

Taistra, G., 2001, Basel II: Auswirkungen auf die Finanzierungsbedingungen von KMU, *Tagung des Zentralverbandes des deutschen Handwerks*, 26.11.2001, Berlin.

Tam, K., 1991, Neural network models and prediction of bank bankruptcy. *OMEGA 19* (5), pp. 429-445.

Tanew-Illitschev, G., 1982, Portfolio-Analyse als Instrument strategischen Bankmanagements, in: *ÖBA, 30. Lg.*, pp. 133-149.

Tasche, D., 1999, Risk contributions and performance measurement, *Working Paper, Zentrum Mathematik, TU München*, November.

Telser, L. G., 1955, Safety first and hedging, *Review of Economic Studies* 23, pp. 1- 16.

Testuri, C. E., and S. Uryasev, 2000, On the relation between expected regret and conditional Value-at-Risk, *Research Report #2000-9, Center for Applied Optimization, University of Florida, Gainesville FA*, available at www.gloriamundi.org. Rev. Feb. 2004.

Theiler, U., 2002a, *Optimierungsverfahren zur Risk-/Return- Steuerung der Gesamtbank*, Wiesbaden.

Theiler, U., 2002b, Integrierte Gesamtbanksteuerung, *Risk Training, Augsburg*, June.

Theiler, U., 2004, Risk return management approach for bank portfolios, in: *Szegö, G. (ed.), New risk measures for investment and regulation*, John Wiley & Sons, New York et al.

Tobin, J., 1958, Liquidity preference as behavior towards risk, *Review of Economic Studies* 25(2), pp. 65-86.

UBS, 2000, *Finanzbericht 1999*, Basel Zürich.

Uryasev, S., 2000, Conditional Value-at-Risk optimization algorithms and applications, *Financial Engineering News* 14, February, http://fenews.com/. Rev. Feb. 2004.

Uryasev, S., and T. Rockafeller, 1999, Optimization of conditional Value-at-Risk, Center for Applied Optimization, *University of Florida, Research Report No. 99-4*, Gainsville/FL, June.

Varian, H. R., 1993, *Intermediate microeconomics*- 3rd ed., New York, USA.

Vasicek, O.A., 1987, *Probability of loss on loan portfolio*, KMV Corporation.

Volkart, R., 1995, Shareholder Value Management, in: *Der Schweizer Treuhänder 12/95,* pp. 1064-1068, Zürich.

Von Neumann, J., and O. Morgenstern, 1947, *Theory of games and economic behavior*, Princeton University Press, Princeton.

Wang, S. S., 1998, Aggregation of correlated risk portfolios: Models & Algorithms, *CAS Committee on Theory of Risk*, Preprint.

Watt, R. C., 1985, A factor-analytic approach to bank conditions. *Journal of Banking and Finance*, pp. 253-266.

Weber, M., 1920, Conceptual exposition; In: *Economy and Society, Ed. G. Roth and C. Wittich.*

Whitmore, G. A., 1970, Third-degree stochastic dominance, *American Economic Review* 60, pp. 457-459.

Wiesemann, T., 1995, *Wertorientiertes Portfoliomanagement: Ein intertemporales Modell zur Portfoliowerterhaltung.*

Wiginton, J. C., 1980, A note of the comparison of logit and discriminant models of consumer credit behavior. *Journal of Financial and Quantitative Analysis* 15 (3), pp. 757-770.

Wilson, R. L., Sharda, R., 1995, Bankruptcy prediction using neural networks; *Decision Support Systems 11/1995*, pp. 545-557.

Wilson, T., 1997, *Credit risk modeling: A new approach*, New York, McKinsey Inc.

Wilson, T., 1998, Portfolio credit risk, in: *FRBNY Economic Policy Review*, October.

Wilson, T., 1999, Value-at-Risk, in: *Alexander, C., Risk Management and Analysis, Vol. 1: Measuring and modeling financial risk*, 1999, John Wiley & Sons, pp.61-124.

Winakor, A., and R. Smith, 1935, Changes in the financial structure of unsuccessful industrial corporations. *Bulletin No. 51, 1935. University of Illinois, Bureau of Business Research: Urbana, Illinois.*

Wong, M., and S. Song, 1997, A loan in Isolation, *AsiaRisk*, June, p. 21ff.

Wübker, G., 2003, Ertragsimpulse durch professionelles Pricing. *Die Bank 03/2003*, p.156ff.

Wübker, G., 2004, Pricing-Prozesse: Gewinnpotentiale erschließen. *Die Bank* 1/2004, pp. 7-11.

Zaik, E., J. Malter, G. Kelling, and C. James, 1996, RAROC at Bank of America: From theory to practice, *Journal of Applied Corporate Finance 9*, pp. 83-93.

Zavgren, C., 1983, The prediction of corporate failure: The State of the Art, *Journal of Accounting*, pp. 1-38.

Zimmermann, H., and B. Varnholdt, 1996, Die moderne Finance. Ein Überblick über die Entwicklung und Anwendungsgebiete, *Vortragsserie „Fit for Finance“, Zürich.*

Zopounidis, C., and M. Doumpos, 1999, A multicriteria aid methodology for sorting decision problems: The case of financial distress. *Computational Economics* 14, pp. 197-218.

Internet References (Rev. March 2005):

www.bis.org (Bank for International Settlement, Basel).

http://add-url.deutsche-bank.com/deuba/catalog.nsf/HTML/dContentCatV4_4 (Bank- und Börsenlexikon Deutsche Bank).

www.bafin.de (Bundesanstalt für Finanzdienstleistungsaufsicht).

www.bdb.de (Bundesverband Deutscher Banken).

www.creditmetrics.com (CreditMetrics).

www.creditreform.de (Creditreform).

www.csfb.com/creditrisk/ (CreditRisk+).

www.bundesbank.de (Deutsche Bundesbank).

www.stanford.edu/~duffie/working.htm (Duffie).

www.efalken.com/banking/html's/defaultcurves.htm (Empirical Default Rates).

http://europa.eu.int/comm/internal_market/en/finances/capitaladequacy/ (EU and Basel II).

www.ecb.int/ (European Central Bank).

www.bog.frb.fed.us/boarddocs/staffreports/summary.pdf (Federal Reserve Bank).

www.tu-dresden.de/wwqvs/VaR/VaR.html (Huschens).

www.investorwords.com (Investorword dictionary).

www.moodys.com (Moody's/KMV).

www.math.ku.dk/~dlando (Lando).

http://riskmetrics.com/working (RiskMetrics, e.g. Finger, Gupton).

www.ires.ucl.ac.be/CSSSP/home_pa_pers/scaillet/scaill.htm (Scaillet 2004).

http://privatewww.essex.ac.uk/~scottj/socscot7.htm; (University of Essex).

8 Glossary of Terms[686]

Asset Correlation Correlation of the returns of two risky assets.

Asset Value of a firm The present value of the expected future cash flows attributable to all the firm's lines of business.

Asset -Volatility Approach Generic expression to describe the quantification of risk capital by reference to the potential loss in value of trading positions, assets, etc. caused by movements in underlying risk factors. See also *Value-at-risk.*

Back-testing The validation of a model by feeding it historical data and comparing the model's results with the historical reality.

Bankruptcy The liquidation of a firm's assets when it is unable to meet its financial obligations; used similar to default.

Basel Accord (Basel I) Agreement reached in 1988 – and subsequently modified- between the banking regulatory authorities of the G10 countries on a minimum standard framework for assessing the capital adequacy of banks. The standard is generally adopted by all OECD countries.

Basel II (The New Basel Accord) A new Basel Accord to be worked out until the end of 2003 due to the problem of capital arbitrage resulting from Basel I. The new Accord will come active in 2006.

Business Risk The risk of incurring a loss through a strategic error in the selection of business or the approach taken to manage a particular business.

Capital Amount held or required to be held by a financial institution to underpin the risk of loss in value of exposures, businesses, etc., so as to protect the depositors and general creditors against loss (see also *Equity*).

Capital Allocation Process of assigning capital to individual transactions, portfolios, businesses, etc., as a measure of the riskiness associated with those transactions etc.; Allocation is usually a notional process such as for performance measurement purposes, and does not necessarily involve actual investment of funds.

[686] The definitions in the glossary are taken from Ong (1999), Matten (2000) and other standard financial textbooks.

Conditional Value-at-Risk (CVAR) The Conditional VaR measures the expected loss in case of a loss superior to a certain confidence level. It thus considers the tail region of a portfolio.

Confidence Interval Statistical measure of the probability of an event occurring or not occurring.

Correlation A measure of the extent to which two or more variables tend to move in the same direction at the same time.

Credit Risk Risk that losses caused by credit downgrades, defaults, etc. are greater than expected loss levels.

Credit Risk Result Stochastic result of lending from a portfolio perspective.

Default Failure of a firm to make a payment on a coupon or reimburse its debt.

Default Correlation The degree to which the default of one obligor is related to the default of another. The quantity that ties the *risk contribution* of a risky asset in the portfolio.

Default Probability See *Probability of Default.*

Diversification Putting your eggs in more than one basket as a way of reducing risk.

Earnings-at-Risk Measure of the riskiness of a business based on the volatility of its earnings; usually expressed in terms of the standard deviation (or a multiple thereof) of its annual earnings or revenues.

Earnings-Volatility Approach Generic expression to describe methods of allocating risk capital based on earnings volatility of individual businesses.

Economic Capital The amount of shareholder's investment is either at risk in a business or has already been utilized to purchase future earnings.

Economic Profit The amount of profit left over after deducing the cost of capital employed in the enterprise. Economic profit is a measure of the value generated by the enterprise for its owners.

Economic Value Added (EVA™) See *economic profit.* EVA™ is a registered trademark of Stern Steward & Co.

Enterprise-wide Risk Controlling Controlling of a financial institution (a firm) with a single risk measure in order to compare the efficiency of the profit centers.

Equity Shareholder's funds invested in an enterprise. Equity is a narrower form of capital (although the two are often used interchangeably), as the latter may include components beyond equity.

Event Risk The risk that an operational event, such a computer failure, human error or an earthquake causes a loss through business disruption, erroneous payment, etc.

Expected Default Frequency (EDF^{TM}) See *Probability of Default.*

Expected Loss The average level (mean) of loss we would expect from any given exposure or set of exposures over a given period.

Expected Shortfall see *Conditional Value-at-Risk.*

Exposure at Default The current outstanding at the time of default.

Goodwill A manifestation of the future benefits that the buyer expects to receive as a direct consequence of a takeover.

Holding Period Period over which exposures are deemed to be held in order to estimate the potential loss in value over that period (see *value-at-risk*).

Hurdle Rate Rate of the return required in a business enterprise.

Loan An agreement whereby one party provides monies to another party for a set period in return for regular payment of interest and principal.

Loan Equivalent Exposure (LEE) See *potential credit exposure.*

Loan Portfolio A collection of illiquid assets, e.g. loans, held by an institution in its banking book.

Loss Given Default (LGD) The amount of credit exposure which will be lost should a borrower go into default. Usually expressed as a percentage of the credit exposure.

Market Risk Risk that the value of open transactions could be adversely affected by movements in financial asset prices.

Mark-to-market Valuation Valuing securities on the basis of the current market values of a counterparty's obligations.

Modern Portfolio Theory The establishment of a formal risk-/return framework for investment decision-making.

Monte Carlo Simulation Technique used to determine the likely value of a contract and thereby to derive loss distributions of a portfolio.

Operational Risk The risk of financial loss owing to the failure of or disturbance to the basic operating mechanisms of markets or a financial firm. This in turn is sub-divided into *event risk* and *business risk.*

Post-Modern Portfolio Theory PMPT has been a recent answer to the unsatisfactory aspects of MPT in business.

Potential credit exposure The likely amount of a credit line outstanding at the time of default. It can be expressed either as a percentage of the notional value of the exposure, or directly as an absolute amount; alternatively know as *LEE.*

Probability of Default The probability that a borrower will default at any time over a given period (usually expressed as an annual percentage).

Recovery rate The amount of credit exposure which can be recovered should a borrower go into default expressed as a percentage.

Regulatory Capital Definition of eligible capital established by the banking regulatory authorities; this is generally split into *tier 1* (basically shareholders funds) and tier 2 (perpetual and subordinated debt meeting certain requirements, plus some other items such as general loan loss provisions).

Regulatory Capital Requirement Minimum level of regulatory capital which banks are required to hold, based on regulations established by the supervisory authority.

Regulatory Capital Arbitrage Process whereby a financial institution reduces its regulatory capital requirement with little or no corresponding reduction in its overall levels of risk.

Return on risk-adjusted Capital (RORAC) Net earnings subject to the *credit risk result*, divided by *risk capital* or *economic capital.*

Risk-adjusted Performance Measurement (RAPM) Generic term referring to techniques for measuring returns and performance by adjusting returns for the risk incurred in earning those returns.

Risk-adjusted Return on Capital (RAROC) Earnings net of expected losses, divided by *risk capital* or *economic capital.*

Risk Capital The amount needed to cover the potential diminution in the value of assets and other exposures over a given period, at a statistical confidence level. Generic term for *economic capital* (internal view) and *regulatory capital* (external view).

Risk Category Sub-division of risk class. For example, "equity position risk" is a risk category within the risk class "market risk".

Risk Class Broad type of risk, typically market risk, credit risk and business/ operational risk.[687]

Risk Contribution The incremental risk that the exposure of a single asset contributes to the portfolio's total risk.

Risk Factor Individual risks within a risk category. For example, "US equity markets" is a risk factor within the "equities" risk category; "short-term US dollar interest rates" form a risk factor within the risk category "interest rates".

Risk Result *see Credit risk result.*

Risk-Weighted Assets (RWA) Credit-Risk equivalent measurement under the Basel Accord, as the basis for capital adequacy assessment. Assets and off-balance-sheet exposures are converted by means of conversion factors into risk-weighted assets; sufficient capital has t be held to cover a minimum percentage (8%) of RWA.

Tier 1 Regulatory measure of core capital; essentially ordinary equity and disclosed reserves, plus non-cumulative, irredeemable preference shares.

Tier-1 ratio Tier-1 capital divided by the sum of *risk-weighted assets*, expressed as percentage.

Tier 2 Regulatory measure of supplementary capital, consisting mainly of general loan loss reserves, perpetual and subordinated debt meeting certain criteria, and cumulative and/or redeemable preference shares.

---

[687] As this work deals with credit risk only, risk class is used synonymously with rating class.

Tier 3 Regulatory measure of additional eligible capital, consisting of short-term subordinated debt, allowed supporting only the market risk component of regulatory capital.

Total Capital Sum of tier1, 2 and 3 capitals.

Total capital ratio Total capital divided by the sum of risk-weighted assets, expressed as a percentage.

Unexpected Loss Volatility of *expected loss*, usually measured as one standard deviation, and used in determining the amount of risk capital required to cover extra-ordinary ("unexpected") potential losses.

Value-at-Risk (VaR) Specific technique used to quantify risk capital (usually the market risk in the trading area) by reference to the sensitivity of the positions held to changes in underlying risk factors. The measure of sensitivity to given change in risk factor is the multiplied out by the potential change in that risk factor, usually over a given time horizon and at a given statistical confidence level (e.g. "99% confident that we could not lose more than $X over a ten-day period).

9 Appendix

A. A Development of insolvencies in the EU (Creditreform 2003)

Tab. 1: Insolvencies in Europe 1997 - 2002

■	Absolute						Changes in percent				
	1997	**1998**	**1999**	**2000**	**2001**	**2002**	**97/98**	**98/99**	**99/00**	**00/01**	**01/02**
Austria	6,400	7,319	8,934	9,006	8,777	9,023	14.4	22.1	0.8	- 2.5	2.8
Belgium	7,700	6,925	7,150	6,791	7,062	7,121	- 10.1	3.2	- 5.0	4.0	0.8
Denmark	1,800	1,800	1,586	1,732	2,189	2,472	0.0	- 11.9	9.2	26.4	12.9
Finland	3,611	3,136	3,080	2,908	2,793	2,904	- 13.2	- 1.8	- 5.6	- 4.0	4.0
France	61,068	55,000	41,186	37,449	34,876	38,688	- 9.9	- 25.1	- 9.1	- 6.9	10.9
Germany	33,398	33,977	33,870	41,780	49,510	82,400	1.7	- 0.3	23.4	18.5	66.4
Greece	1,300	871	694	636	591	512	- 33.0	- 20.3	- 8.4	- 7.1	- 13.4
Ireland	550	686	815	344	427	379	24.7	18.8	- 57.8	24.1	- 11.2
Italy	14,878	15,000	14,760	15,000	15,200	15,600	0.8	- 1.6	1.6	1.3	2.6
Luxembourg	425	423	545	597	750	695	- 0.5	28.8	9.5	25.6	- 7.3
Netherlands	5,547	5,031	3,920	3,726	5,832	6,358	- 9.3	- 22.1	- 4.9	56.5	9.0
Norway	3,300	3,347	3,342	3,576	3,541	4,276	1.4	- 0.1	7.0	- 1.0	20.8
Portugal	621	783	999	1,308	1,594	1,924	26.1	27.6	30.9	21.9	20.7
Spain	1,135	896	620	602	335	448	- 21.1	- 30.8	- 2.9	- 44.4	33.7
Sweden	11,000	9,200	7,261	7,301	8,012	8,387	- 16.4	- 21.1	0.6	9.7	4.7
Switzerland	9,190	8,850	8,490	8,300	8,145	8,802	- 3.7	- 4.1	- 2.2	- 1.9	8.1
UK	37,000	37,500	46,900	47,404	48,397	50,988	1.4	25.1	1.1	2.1	5.4
Total	**198,923**	**190.744**	**184,152**	**188,460**	**198,031**	**240.977**	**- 4.1**	**- 3.5**	**2.3**	**5.1**	**21.7**

A. B: The revised Basel II proposal according to the three pillars (according to Hartmann 2002, p.19)

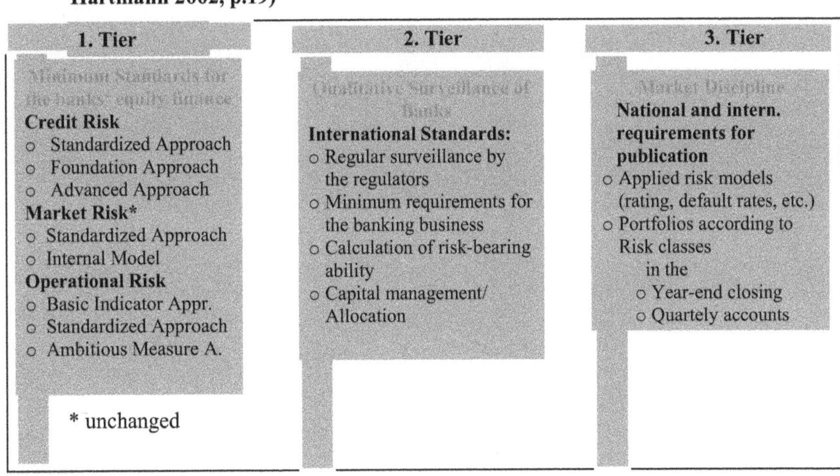

1. Tier
Minimum Standards for the banks' equity finance
Credit Risk
o Standardized Approach
o Foundation Approach
o Advanced Approach
Market Risk*
o Standardized Approach
o Internal Model
Operational Risk
o Basic Indicator Appr.
o Standardized Approach
o Ambitious Measure A.
* unchanged
2. Tier
Qualitative Surveillance of banks
International Standards:
o Regular surveillance by the regulators
o Minimum requirements for the banking business
o Calculation of risk-bearing ability
o Capital management/ Allocation
3. Tier
Market Discipline
National and intern. requirements for publication
o Applied risk models (rating, default rates, etc.)
o Portfolios according to Risk classes
in the
o Year-end closing
o Quartely accounts

A. C: Free Cash Flow as the origin of Shareholder Value (Manz 1998, p. 73)

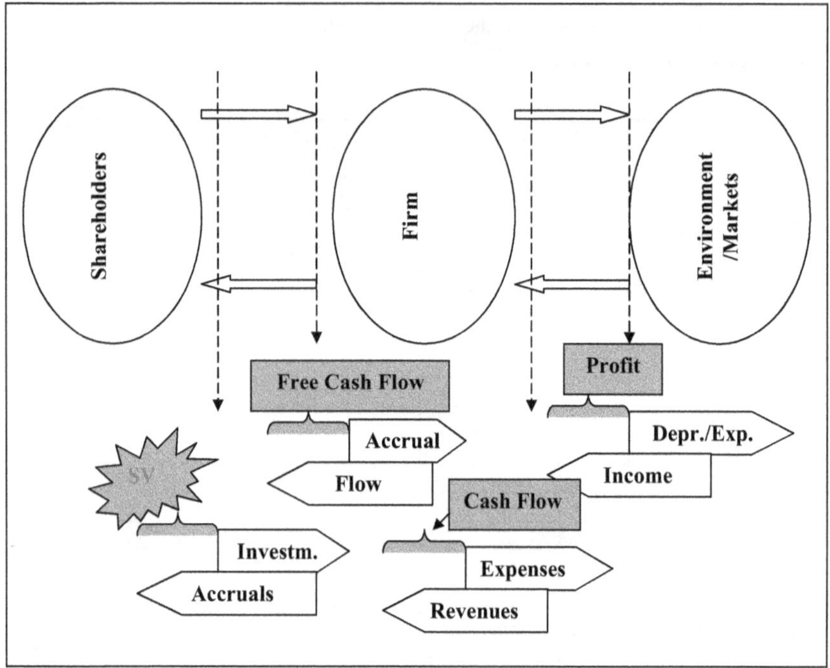

A. D: S&P's rating symbols and meanings (see www.standardandpoors.com)

Rating	Description
AAA	The obligor's capacity to meet its financial commitment on the obligation is extremely strong.
AA	An obligation rated 'AA' differs from the highest rated obligations only to a small degree. The obligor's capacity to meet its financial commitment on the obligation is very strong.
A	An obligation rated 'A' is somewhat more susceptible to the adverse effects of changes in circumstances and economic conditions than obligations in higher rated categories.
BBB	An obligation rated 'BBB' exhibits adequate protection parameters. However, adverse economic conditions or changing circumstances are more likely to lead to a weakened capacity of the obligor to meet its financial commitments on the obligation.
BB	An obligation rated 'BB' is less vulnerable to nonpayment than other speculative issues. However, it faces major ongoing uncertainties or exposure to adverse business, financial or economic conditions that could lead to the obligor's inadequate capacity to meet its financial commitment on the obligation.
B	The obligor currently has the capacity to meet its financial commitment on the obligation. Adverse business, financial or economic conditions will likely impair the obligor's capacity or willingness to meet financial commitments.
CCC	An obligation rated 'CCC' is currently vulnerable to nonpayment, and is dependent upon favorable business, financial and economic conditions for the obligor to meet its financial commitment on the obligation.

A. E: Commonly used financial ratios according to Caouette et al. (1998, p.87)

Category	Ratio
Operating Performance	EBITDA/Sales Net Income/Sales Effective Tax Rate Net Income/Net Worth Net Income/Total Assets Sales/Fixed Assets
Debt Service Coverage	EBITDA/Interest Free Cash Flow – Capital Expenditure/Interest Free Cash Flow – Capital Expenditure/Interest – Dividends/Interest
Financial Leverage	Long-term debt/Capitalization Long-term Debt/Tangible Net Worth Total liabilities/Tangible Net Worth Current Liabilities/Tangible Net Worth
Liquidity	Current Ratio Quick Ratio Inventory to net sales Inventory to Net Working Capital Current Debt to Inventory Raw Material, work in process and finished goods as percentage of total inventory
Receivables	Aging of receivables: 30, 60, 90, 90 + days Average collection period

A. F: The credit analysis process flow (Caouette et al. 1998, p.86)

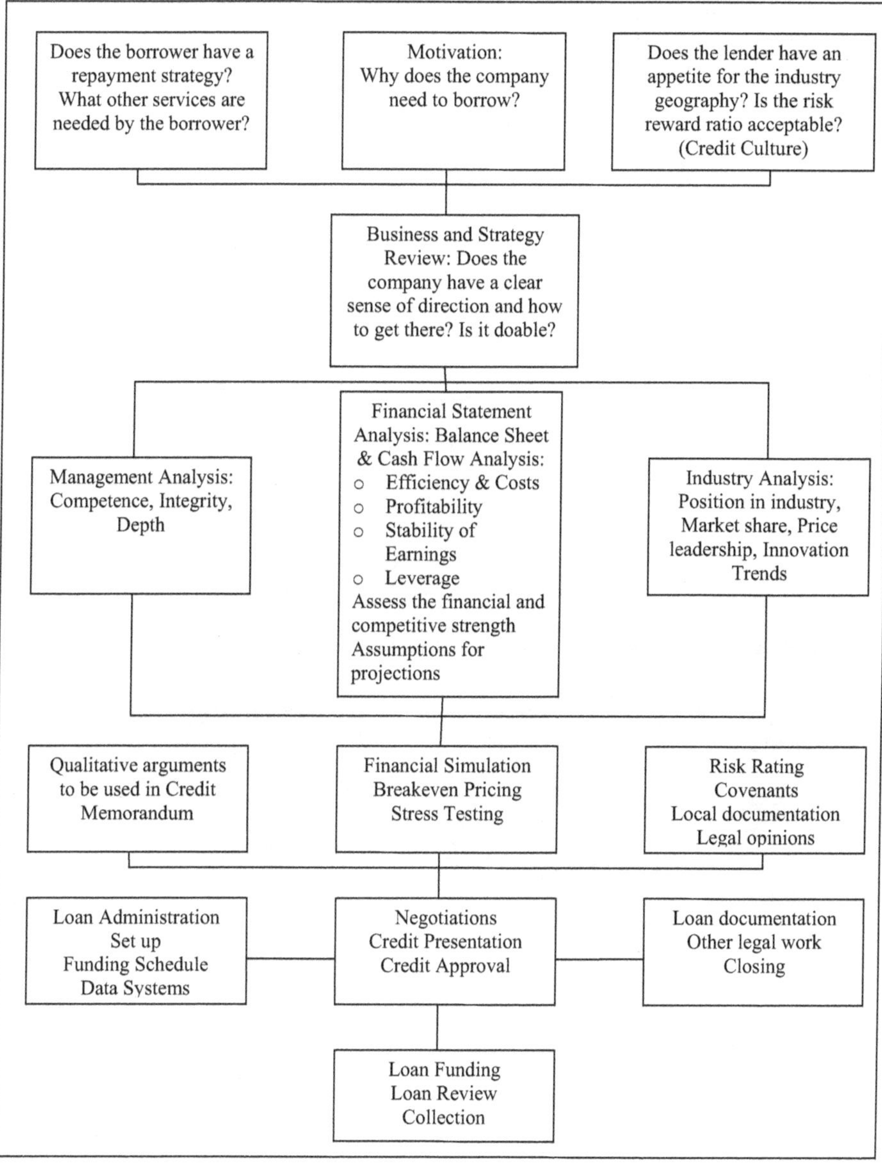
Does the borrower have a repayment strategy? What other services are needed by the borrower?
Motivation: Why does the company need to borrow?
Does the lender have an appetite for the industry geography? Is the risk reward ratio acceptable? (Credit Culture)
Business and Strategy Review: Does the company have a clear sense of direction and how to get there? Is it doable?
Management Analysis: Competence, Integrity, Depth
Financial Statement Analysis: Balance Sheet & Cash Flow Analysis:
o Efficiency & Costs
o Profitability
o Stability of Earnings
o Leverage
Assess the financial and competitive strength
Assumptions for projections
Industry Analysis: Position in industry, Market share, Price leadership, Innovation Trends
Qualitative arguments to be used in Credit Memorandum
Financial Simulation
Breakeven Pricing
Stress Testing
Risk Rating
Covenants
Local documentation
Legal opinions
Loan Administration
Set up
Funding Schedule
Data Systems
Negotiations
Credit Presentation
Credit Approval
Loan documentation
Other legal work
Closing
Loan Funding
Loan Review
Collection

A. G: Hazard rates implied by Moody 's Investors Service Default Studies (Douglas et al. 2004, p.24)

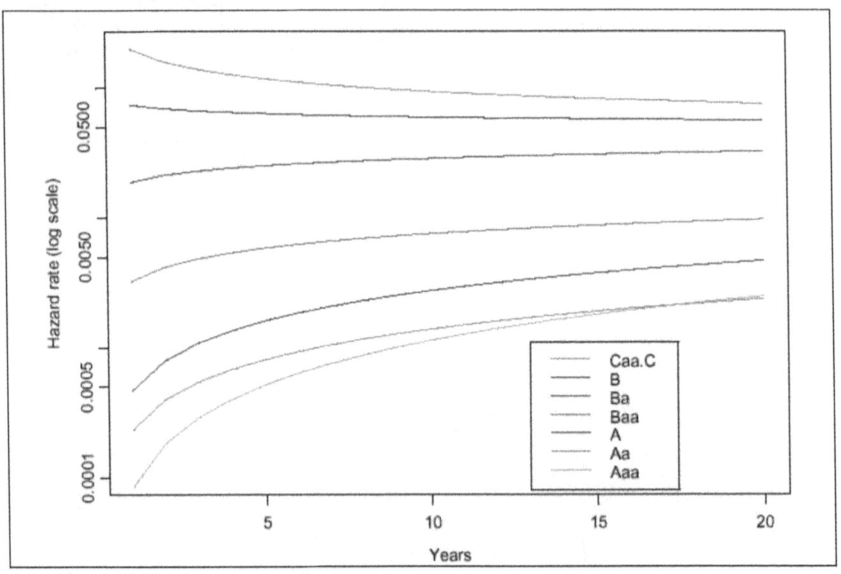

A. H: S&P Historical multi-year cumulative default probabilities in % (Goldfarb 2004, p.10)

	Year 1	Year 2	Year 3	Year 4	Year 5	Year 6	Year 7	Year 8	Year 9	Year 10
AAA	0	0	0.04	0.07	0.12	0.21	0.31	0.49	0.56	0.63
AA	0.01	0.04	0.11	0.2	0.33	0.48	0.68	0.85	1	1.18
A	0.05	0.15	0.3	0.5	0.75	1.01	1.29	1.55	1.88	2.2
BBB	0.37	1.06	1.8	2.84	3.84	4.83	5.66	6.42	7.11	8
BB	1.45	4.38	7.98	11.39	14.45	17.64	20.23	22.51	24.88	26.72
B	6.59	15.03	22.46	28.47	33.02	39.91	40.44	43.73	45.93	48.3
CCC	34.14	44.07	50.54	55.65	61.35	63.93	64.94	65.58	68.78	71.46

A. I: A model's performance measurement[688]

In order to graphically illustrate the performance of credit risk models, Cumulative Accuracy Profiles (CAP) seem to be useful as a representation of the cumulative default probability discriminated relative to the entire sample (see Moody's 2000a, for example).[689]

The procedure is as follows (Moody's 2000a). First, all obligor's are rank-ordered ex ante according to the credit risk model's internal score. Second, a credit risk model's performance is measured ex post. This can be realized by plotting the cumulative percentage of the total sample according to the ex ante score of the internal credit risk model on the x- axis and the cumulative percentage of the ex post defaulted borrowers on the y axis.

A model's performance is the better the earlier real (ex post) defaulted borrowers can be identified by forecasted creditworthiness score of the credit risk model.

An ideal model would forecast are correct rank-order the defaulted borrowers, i.e. the ex ante forecasted internal score of the credit risk model assigns a worse creditworthiness score to every defaulted borrower than for the non-defaulted borrowers. In this case, the the CAP curve would be very steep (indicated as ideal model below). As a benchmark, a random model would show a linearly increasing line, indicating that in the first x % of the population are an equal percentage x of defaulters (called random CAP below).

---

688 The description follows Moody's (2000a).

689 Alternatively, similar methodologies exists under different names (e.g. lift-curves, dubbed-curves, receiver-operator curves, power curves).

A.Figure 1: Measuring the power of a model[690]

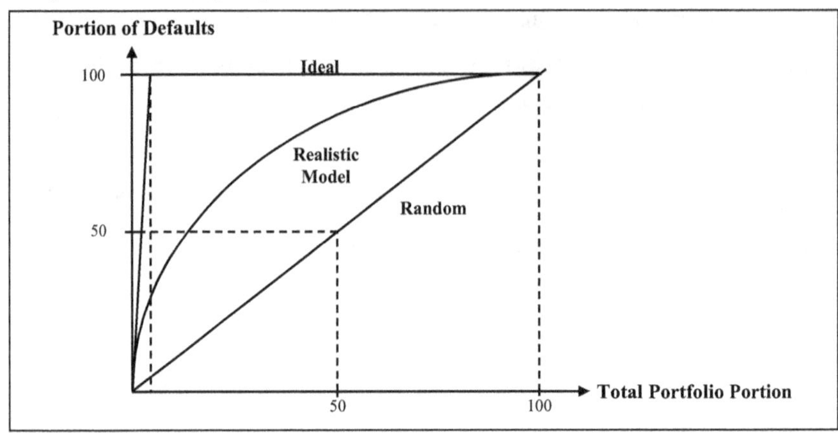

The discriminating power of a model according to its graphical CAP- curve is measured using the Gini ratio, Accuracy ratio, Somer's D, Tau-c, etc.[691]

A. J: Major influence factors on the LGD

The value of the collateral and the amount outstanding ("loan-to-value")

The type of the collateral plays a crucial role as the value of the collateral usually depends on its market value, which deteriorates over time. Tangible collateral (e.g. automotives to be financed) is usually related to higher volatilities than non-tangible collateral (e.g. real estate), for example. The relationship between the outstanding and the collateral value ("loan-to-value") during the repayment process is a key indicator for the determination of the LGD. As a principle of caution the value of the collateral is usually capped (e.g. 10% "haircut"), in order to have an additional cushion against an unforeseen decrease of the collateral value.

A possible relation between the expected collateral value and the expected outstanding of an obligation (e.g. a contract to finance a vehicle) during the

690 Similar graphics can be found in various financial articles and textbooks, e.g. Moody's (2000a).

691 SAS, for example.

lifetime of a loan is shown below. In this case, the risk is that obligors default shortly after origination.

A.Figure 2: Development of the credit exposure (outstanding) and the collateral value to maturity[692]

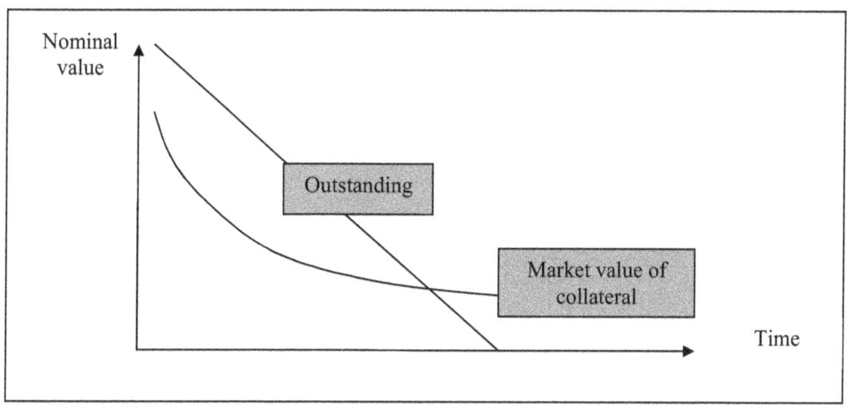

The seniority of collateral ("Pecking order")

The availability ("seniority") and type (secured/ unsecured) of the collateral for the creditors in case of a default event on the common scale is usually as follows (see Jorion 2001, p. 477, for example):

- Senior secured
- Senior unsecured
- Senior subordinated
- Subordinated
- Junior subordinated

This scale is used both by S&P's and Moody's publishing their empirical recovery data (see section 3.3.5.1.1 below).

Seniority is related to a "pecking order", i.e. the order of the creditor's claims in case of bankruptcy. In the sphere of European law (German law, for example), however, such a rather clear-defined pecking order is not foreseen and makes the judical process even worse. In practice, nevertheless, subordinated debt will be

692 Similar graphics are used by other authors.

originated by banks in rather seldom cases, for example, if guarantees are in place.

A.Table 1: Pecking order in U.S. Federal Bankruptcy Law (Jorion 2001, p. 475)

Seniority	Type of creditor
Highest (Paid first)	○ Secured creditors (up to the extent of secured collateral) ○ Priority creditors: ○ Firms that lend money during bankruptcy period ○ Providers of goods and services during bankruptcy period (e.g. employees, laywer, vendors) ○ Taxes ○ General creditors: ○ Unsecured creditors before bankruptcy ○ Shareholders
Lowest (Paid last)	

The state of the economy

The recovery rate has been shown to depend on the state of the economy: recovery rates tend to be lower when the economy is in a recession, while default rates are higher.[693] The dependence of the recovery rates and the PD and on an identical principal factor is "certainly reasonable", as empirical findings demonstrate "that recovery rates tend to decrease in times where default rates rise up sharply" (Bluhm et al. 2003, p. 86). A more comprehensive evaluation of the relationship between the PD and LGD with respect to the macroeconomic environment[694] can be found in Altman et al. (2001), Altman and Saunders (2001) and Frye (2000a/b).

---

693 See Altman et al. (2001), Altman and Saunders (2001), Frye (2000a/b) and Allen and Saunders (2003), for example.

694 Empirical evidence has also been provided by Carey (1998), as documented by Ong (1999, p.107), for example, among an increasing number of other studies.

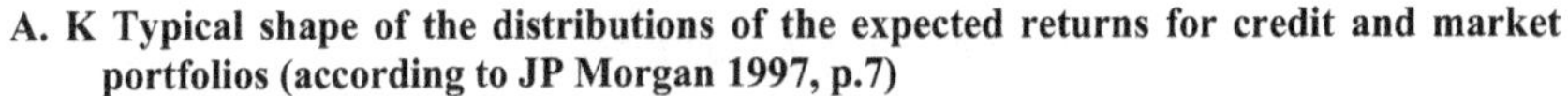

A. K Typical shape of the distributions of the expected returns for credit and market portfolios (according to JP Morgan 1997, p.7)

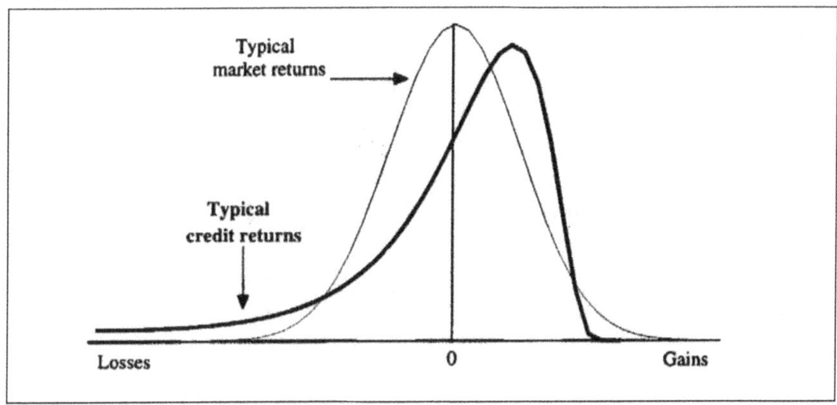

A. L: Formal concepts for the measurement of risk aversion[695]

A rather rudimentary approach would be to measure risk as the reduction of utility due to risk, i.e. $u(E(x))-E(u(x))$. As utility is, however, undefined, this approach has to be neglected.

There are basically two approaches to derive a measure of risk aversion:

1. A **security equivalent** S(x) is the riskless payment for which an individual is indifferent against the expected value of the risky event: $u(S(x))-E(u(x))$. Consequently, a **risk premium** is the expected return that an individual agrees to give up to accept the riskless payment: $p(x)=E(x)-S(x)$.
2. The concept of a security equivalent lead to the concept of assigning concave utility functions for risk-averse investors, with the property that the risk-aversion is the higher, the more concave the utility function is (see Figure 4-12). As it has been shown above, risk-aversion can be formally measured based on the second derivation of the utility function, which is negative in case of concave investors ($u''(x)<0,\ \vee x$). While utility functions are

[695] The formal concept for the measurement of risk aversion is closely following Reichling (2003) and can be found in various standard financial textbooks.

invariant against affine-linear transformations[696], their second derivation is not. Arrow (1961) and Pratt (1964) have therefore identified two measures to define an investor's (possessing the assets A) relationship to risk for a given utility function representing a standardization of the second derivation by the first derivation (Arrow/Pratt- measures):[697]

- **Absolute risk aversion (ARA)**: $ARA(A) = -\frac{U''(x)}{U'(x)}$ and
- **Relative risk aversion (RRA)**: $RRA(A) = -\frac{U''(x)}{U'(x)} \bullet A$

Given a risk-averse investor seeking for a $(0,\sigma^2)$- optimal decision the risk premium[698] can be derived to be approximately proportional to the variance divided by two, $p(x) \approx -\frac{u''(x)}{u'(x)} \bullet \frac{\sigma^2}{2}$, and is indeed approximately proportional to the Arrow/Pratt - measures for risk aversion. The risk premium may be characterized to be a probability premium as well.

In order to fully depict an investor's behavior pattern subject to absolute and relative risk aversion, an investor's given assets do play a role, and have to be taken into account. It seems to be plausible to assume that an investor's absolute risk aversion decreases with increasing initial funds: $\frac{\partial}{\partial x}\left(-\frac{U''(x)}{U'(x)}\right) = -\frac{U'(x) \bullet U'''(x) + (U''(x))^2}{(U'(x))^2} < 0$,

where $U'(x) > 0$ and $U'''(x) > 0$.[699] The table below shows the eligible behavior patterns of investors following the ARA and RRA risk aversion pattern, respectively.

---

[696] What is a formal prerequisite for utility functions.

[697] For further reference see Elton and Gruber (1975), for example.

[698] The risk premium may be characterized to be a probability premium as well, if the state probabilities do represent an investor's desire to be indifferent between riskless and risky assets.

[699] For quadratic utility function, for example, this relationship is not fulfilled.

A.Table 2: Different behavior patterns vs. ARA/RRA pattern (see Schlag 2003, p.28, for example)

	If the assets of an investor increase, the risky **nominal value** invested....	If the assets of an investor increase, the risky **share** of the investment....
Increasing ARA $\frac{dARA}{dA} > 0$	**Decreases**[700]	**Decreases**
Constant ARA $\frac{dARA}{dA} = 0$	**Remains constant**	**Decreases**
Decreasing ARA $\frac{dARA}{dA} < 0$	**Increases**	**Cannot be defined**
Increasing RRA $\frac{dRRA}{dA} > 0$	**Cannot be defined**	**Decreases**[701]
Constant RRA $\frac{dRRA}{dA} = 0$	**Increases**	**Remains constant**
Decreasing RRA $\frac{dRRA}{dA} < 0$	**Increases**	**Increases**

A. M: The coherence of risk measures

Given two random variables X and Y (representing losses), a coherent[702] risk measure ρ is a function that satisfies the following requirements (Arvanitis and Gregory 2001, p. 99):

1. Monotonicity For $X \geq Y$, $\rho(X) \geq \rho(Y)$
2. Positive homogeneity $\rho(\lambda X) = \lambda \rho(X)$, where λ is a positive real number.
3. Translation invariance $\rho(X+a) = \rho(X)$, where a is a real number.

700 For quadratic utility functions, the feature is "increasing", what is not plausible.

701 For exponential utility functions, this feature would be "increasing", what is not plausible.

702 The concept of coherent risk measures has been provided by Artzner et al. (1999).

4. Subadditivity $\rho(X+Y) \leq \rho(X)+\rho(Y)$

Arvanitis and Gregory (2001) claim that these requirements would be reasonable and intuitive for a risk measure. The most important requirement would be the **subadditivity**, ensuring that two risks together will "never create more risk than the sum of the individual risks", which is the **diversification condition** (Arvanitis and Gregory 2001, p. 99). As discussed in section 4, the coherence condition is neither fulfilled by the standard deviation nor by the well-known Value-at-Risk (see Figure 4-20), as the Value-at-Risk does not fulfill the subadditivity criterion.[703]

With respect to the usage of the VaR for optimization purposes, Arvanitis and Gregory (2001, p.100) state that while the VaR's lack of coherence may not be "such an issue" for the calculation of portfolio risk or "even of risk sensitivities", but "it may give erroneous results in portfolio optimization". The reason behind that is that the algorithm for optimization "may reduce the risk falsely – for example, by putting all the weight into a single exposure" (Arvanitis and Gregory 2001, p.100).

In order to meet all the requirements of a coherent measure of risk as outlined above, several authors (e.g. Arvanitis and Gregory 2001) suggested alternative

703 Arvanitis and Gregory (2001) suggest having a look at a simple illustrative example. One may consider two equal but independent exposures with a PD of 0.75%. By consequence, the risk of each individual exposure based on the 99th percentile is zero, as the PD of both exposures is below 1 %. However, the joint risk of the two exposures, measured in terms of the VaR at the 99 percentile, for example, is non zero, as the probability for the occurrence of at least one default is almost 1.5% . Hence, this rudimentary example shows that the VaR violates effect of diversification.
Arvanitis and Gregory (2001, p.100) additionally provide a more realistic example: "Let us denote the capital at the $(100\text{-}\alpha)^{th}$ percentile by K. Now suppose we add a large exposure to the portfolio that is greater than K but has a probability of default approximately equal to α. If the probability of default is less than α, the capital will not increase because the new large loss has a probability of occurring outside the confidence interval. Conversely, if the probability of default is greater than α,the capital will increase considerably since the default of the new exposure now represents the "worst case". In the latter case, the new exposure would have a large risk contribution, whereas in the former the risk contribution would be zero. So, for a small change in the default probability there is a huge change in the portfolio capital." Arvanitis and Gregory (2001, p.100) therefore conclude that "the VaR is not a feasible measure of risk."

risk measures that account for higher moments of the underlying distribution, which may have fat tails, for example. As the VaR is "well understood and commonly used", the search for other risk measures led towards *Conditional Value-at-Risk* (or *expected shortfall)*, a related risk measure that fulfils the coherence feature (Arvanitis and Gregory 2001, p.100).

CV

Personal Data

Name: Christian Schmieder
Date of birth: June 5, 1976
Location: Sulz am Neckar (Adm. District: Rottweil/Southern Germany)

Education

2004: Visiting Researcher at the London School of Economics and Political Sciences, London/UK, Financial Markets Group
2002-2005: PhD-program (Dr. rer. pol.) at the University of Ulm/Germany, Department of Business Administration, PhD supervisor: Prof. Dr. K. Hellwig
1997-2002: Fridericiana University of Karlsruhe/Germany, Diplom Wirtschaftsingenieur (equivalent to MSc. Industrial Engineering and Management)
1993-1996: High School (Kepler-Gymnasium) Freudenstadt (Black Forest)/Germany, Abitur
1987-1993: Junior High School ("Progymnasium") Baiersbronn (Black Forest)/Germany
1983-1987: German School Helsinki/Finland

Professional Experience

2004 - : Economist, Deutsche Bundesbank (German Central Bank), Department of Banking Supervision, Frankfurt/Germany
2002-2004: Research Assistant, DaimlerChrysler AG, Ulm/Germany, Finance Group
1997-2002: Bürkle GmbH, Freudenstadt/Germany (1997);
Kreissparkasse Freudenstadt/Germany (1998);
SAP AG, Walldorf/Germany (1998);
Arthur Andersen GmbH, Stuttgart/Germany (2000);
Deutsche Bank AG, New York/USA (2001);
Deutsche Bank AG, Munich/Germany (2002);

Others

2000: German University Champion, Cross-Country Skiing
1999-2002: Excellence scholarship by the Konrad-Adenauer-Foundation
1999: Participation at the Student's World Championships in Winter Sports ("Universiade"), Cross-country skiing, Poprad-Tatry/Slovakia; German University champion Cross-Country skiing
1996-1997: Military service in the German Army, Professional Sports Group ("Sportfördergruppe") Todtnau-Fahl (Black Forest)/Germany, Cross-Country Skiing

www.ingramcontent.com/pod-product-compliance
Lightning Source LLC
Chambersburg PA
CBHW020908210326
41598CB00018B/1814
* 9 7 8 3 8 2 8 8 8 9 8 4 2 *